Contemporary Graphic Artists

ISSN 0885-8462

Contemporary Graphic Artists

A Biographical, Bibliographical, and Critical Guide to Current Illustrators, Animators, Cartoonists, Designers, and Other Graphic Artists

Maurice Horn
Editor

Volume 1

Gale Research Company • Book Tower • Detroit, Michigan 48226

STAFF

Maurice Horn, *Editor*
Richard Calhoun, Javier Coma, Pierre Horn, Frederik Schodt,
Lawrence Watt-Evans, Dennis Wepman, *Contributors*

Linda S. Hubbard, *Production Editor*
Thomas Bachmann, Darryl Bridson,
Timothy Schuman, *Editorial Assistants*

Carol Blanchard, *Production Director*
Sandy Rock, *Internal Senior Production Assistant*
Art Chartow, *Art Director*
Roger D. Hubbard, *Layout Artist and Graphic Arts Coordinator*
Charles Hunt, *Cameraman and Keyliner*
Gabe Kirchheimer, *Keyliner*

Frederick G. Ruffner, *Publisher*
Dedria Bryfonski, *Editorial Director*
Christine Nasso, *Director, Literature Division*

Every effort has been made to trace copyright for the illustrations in this
volume, but if omissions have been made, please contact the publisher.

Copyright © 1986 by Gale Research Company

ISBN 0-8103-2189-0
ISSN 0885-8462

Computerized photocomposition by
AMTEC Information Services, Inc.
Lakewood, California

Contents

Preface

Within recent years, the work of illustrators, animators, cartoonists, designers, and other graphic artists has emerged as an important and lively development in contemporary art. Since their works influence our lives in countless ways each day, graphic artists of all types are subjects of high interest—humor cartoonists drawing for newspapers or for magazines; editorial cartoonists of the left, right, or center; theatrical and televisual animators whose creations are intended for entertainment or commerce; newspaper comic strip artists and story strip creators; comic book and magazine artists; book, magazine, or newspaper illustrators; cover and poster designers; and even artists in developing fields such as computer graphics. Unfortunately, comprehensive biographical and critical information on these popular artists, presented in an easy-to-use format and enhanced with numerous illustrations of their work, is often difficult to find. With the publication of *Contemporary Graphic Artists (CGA),* Gale Research Company has taken a step toward meeting this need.

Scope

CGA is a comprehensive new biographical, bibliographical, and critical guide that provides detailed information about the lives and accomplishments of graphic artists who have made a significant contribution to contemporary art. With more than 100 entries in each biannual volume, *CGA* includes biographies on a wide variety of graphic artists—illustrators, animators, cartoonists, designers, and other graphic artists whose work appears in books, newspapers, magazines, film, and other media.

Primary emphasis is given to modern-day American artists. *CGA* includes major, established figures whose positions in artistic history are assured, as well as new and highly promising individuals, some of whom have yet to be discovered by the public at large. Among the noteworthy artists featured in *CGA*, Volume 1, are the following:

Illustrators of books, magazines, and other publications—R.O. Blechman, Brad Holland, James McMullan, Barbara Nessim, Bob Peak, and Edward Sorel

Graphic designers—Saul Bass and Milton Glaser

Editorial cartoonists—Tom Engelhardt, Tom Toles, Don Wright, and Larry Wright

Magazine cartoonists—Joseph Farris, Sam Gross, William Hamilton, Paul Peter Porges, and Jack Ziegler

Newspaper artists—Dik Browne, Burne Hogarth, Bil Keane, and Ted Key

Comic book artists—Richard Corben, Will Eisner, Joe Kubert, and Trina Robbins

Animators, animation directors and producers—Joe Barbera, Sally Cruikshank, David Ehrlich, and Faith Hubley

To round out this survey of contemporary art, *CGA* also includes foreign artists whose work is well known in the United States, such as Italian comic artist Guido Crepax, Spanish illustrator and cartoonist Fernando Fernandez, Canadian editorial cartoonist Robert LaPalme, and Japanese comic strip artist and animator Osamu Tezuka. To add historical perspective to the series, selected *CGA* sketches record the achievements of outstanding artists of the past whose influence is widely acknowledged by contemporary practitioners. Prominent nineteenth-century artists, such as French illustrator and cartoonist Gustave Dore and American cartoonist Thomas Nast, and early twentieth-century American artists, such as cartoonist and animator Winsor McCay and comic strip artist R.F. Outcault, are examples of important historical figures included in this volume.

With its broad coverage and detailed entries, *CGA* is designed to assist a variety of users—researchers seeking specific facts, librarians fielding questions, students preparing for classes, teachers drawing up assignments, or general readers looking for information about a favorite artist. Individually, *CGA* sketches present a concise but detailed record of the achievements of a variety of graphic artists. Collectively, *CGA* entries provide a survey of comic art, cartoons, caricature, design, illustration, and animation in their historical, aesthetic, cultural, sociological, ideological, and commercial contexts. It is the editors' hope that from this and future volumes will emerge not only a record of contemporary artistic achievement but also a "bird's eye" view of our times as reflected through the artistic sensibility.

Compilation Methods

The editors make every effort to secure information directly from the artists through questionnaires, correspondence, telephone calls, and, in many cases, personal meetings. If artists of special interest to *CGA* users are deceased or fail to reply to requests for information, material is gathered from other reliable sources. Biographical dictionaries and art encyclopedias are checked, as are bibliographical sources such as *Cumulative Book Index*. Published interviews, feature stories, and reviews are examined, and often material is supplied by the artists' agents, publishers, syndicates, or studios. All sketches, whether prepared from questionnaires or through extensive research, are sent to the artists for review prior to publication.

The editors recognize that entries on particularly active artists may eventually become outdated. To insure *CGA*'s timeliness, future volumes will provide revisions of selected sketches when they require significant change.

Format

CGA entries, modeled after those in the Gale Research Company's highly regarded *Contemporary Authors* series, are written in a clear, readable style with few abbreviations and no limits set on length. So that a reader needing specific information can quickly focus on the pertinent portion of an entry, typical *CGA* listings are clearly divided into topical sections with descriptive rubrics, among them the following:

> **Entry Heading**—Cites the complete form of the listee's name, followed by birth and death dates, when available. Pseudonyms or name variations under which the artist has issued works are included within parentheses in the second line of the entry heading.

> **Personal**—Provides date and place of birth, family data, and information about the subject's education, politics, and religion. Home, office, studio, and agent addresses are noted, when available.

> **Career**—Indicates past and present career positions, with inclusive dates, as well as civic activities, military service, and professional memberships.

> **Awards, Honors**—Notes artistic awards as well as writing awards, military and civic honors, and fellowships and honorary degrees received.

> **Writings**—Lists published books, syndicated features, illustrated works, and contributions to periodicals, with pertinent bibliographic data.

> **Films**—Highlights all film work, whether as animator, director, producer, designer, or in some other capacity, along with film production data.

> **Exhibitions**—Reports both group shows and one-person shows in which the artist's work has been represented, with locations and dates.

> **Work in Progress**—Notes artistic activity in progress and other projects of all kinds, some of which may result in future publication.

> **Sidelights**—Provides a comprehensive overview of the artists' careers, achievements, and contributions to their chosen fields.

All *CGA* sketches contain sidelights, written by contributors who are knowledgeable about the artists' particular fields and often personally acquainted with the biographees. Some artists have worked closely with *CGA*'s contributors to develop sidelights. Cartoonist and illustrator Burne Hogarth and cartoonist Frank Thorne, for example, commented at length in their sidelights sections about their works and interests. By filling in the details that make for fascinating biography, sidelights add a personal dimension to the listings and provide informative and enjoyable reading.

Biographical/Critical Sources—Lists newspaper and magazine articles and books containing additional information about the artists and their work.

To allow for easy access to all of the entries in *CGA*, a cumulative index to artists will be included in *CGA*, Volume 2, and all subsequent volumes.

Illustrations

To provide a visual sampling of the artists' themes and styles, the majority of *CGA* entries are accompanied by numerous illustrations, often chosen by the listees themselves as being among their most representative work. Reflecting the diverse graphic arts covered in these pages, this volume contains a multitude of illustrations—newspaper, magazine, sports, and political cartoons; caricatures; posters; animation frames and sequences; magazine and book illustrations; comic book pages; and newspaper strips. In most cases, these illustrations and the textual material are further complemented by a photogaph or self-portrait of the artist. And some of the self-portraits are unique to *CGA*, having been drawn specially for this series. Among the never-before-published self-portraits included in this volume are those created for *CGA* by David Cuccio, Don Orehek, and Jack Ziegler. Together, the portraits and copious illustrations that enliven the text not only offer a visual guide to the careers of the artists profiled in *CGA* but also allow for hours of pleasant browsing.

Obituary Notices Make *CGA* Timely and Comprehensive

To be as timely and comprehensive as possible, *CGA* publishes brief obituary notices on recently deceased artists within the scope of the series. These notices provide dates and places of birth and death, highlight the artist's career and works, and list other sources where additional biographical information and obituaries may be found. To distinguish them from full-length sketches, obituaries are identified with the heading "Obituary Notice."

Acknowledgments

The editor would like to extend special and sincere thanks to Mr. Terry Brown of the Society of Illustrators for his help in recommending American illustrators for inclusion in this volume of *CGA*.

Suggestions Are Welcome

If readers would like to suggest people to be covered in future *CGA* volumes, they are encouraged to send these names (along with addresses, if possible) to the editor. Other suggestions and comments are also most welcome and should be addressed to: The Editor, *Contemporary Graphic Artists,* Gale Research Company, 150 E. 50th St., New York, NY 10022.

The Graphic Arts: An Overview

There are about as many definitions of the term "graphic arts" as there are art dictionaries. Their elusive and multiform qualities often require lengthy commentaries to supplement a general definition. Perhaps some of this elusiveness is best conveyed in the definition given in the second edition of George A. Stevenson's *Graphic Arts Encyclopedia* (McGraw-Hill, 1979): "Arts represented by drawing or imposing on a flat surface an image that communicates a message." It is the concept of communication—of an idea, a political slogan, the qualities of a product, or a set of data—that sets the graphic arts apart from other art forms (indeed they are sometimes referred to as "communication arts"). They are by and large a concrete art form, in which expression is closely tied to its ultimate aim.

The graphic arts well into the nineteenth century were limited to painting, etching, engraving, and drawing—the root word for the term is the Greek *graphikos,* or what is conveyed by writing. Graphic artists in earlier centuries confined themselves to illustrating books and producing prints and etchings with subjects often taken from the fine arts. Their role became one of disseminating among a large public the knowledge and iconography that were once restricted to a privileged few. Slowly the graphic arts came to assume some of the functions that so-called High Art was no longer willing or able to perform, those of documentation, narration, entertainment, and escape.

This process was further hastened by the photographic and photocomposition techniques that came into wide use in the middle of the nineteenth century: images could now be duplicated cheaply by the hundreds of thousands. The conflict between the artistic and the commercial use of the graphic arts widened. In the twentieth century, however, practitioners have combined artistic sensibility with such advanced technical knowledge that the term graphic arts has again broadened to include both the fine arts and practical applications of technology.

The Art of Illustration

Illustration well predates the invention of typography. The elaborate illuminations of medieval manuscripts are the forerunners of modern illustration, even down to their name ("illustrate" and "illuminate" both come from the Latin *lux* or light, thus emphasizing their enlightening function). Illustrations originally were used to give a pictorial representation of a scene, a piece of dialogue, or an idea expounded in the accompanying text. They could be found in books of all kinds, though the rise of the novel gave illustration new applications, as artists set out with gusto in their task as enlighteners of the author's meaning. Dickens's novels, for instance, owe much of their popularity to his

illustrators, George Cruikshank and Hablot Knight Browne ("Phiz"), as has been noted in many literary histories. The ability to act as an interpreter, explainer, and elucidator, rather than to function subserviently as mere decorator, is what sets apart the outstanding illustrator from the mere craftsman. This artistic side of the illustrator's calling is well exemplified by the towering *oeuvre* of Gustave Dore, in many ways the most famous and most inspirational of all the illustrators.

An illustration for the Bible by the father of modern illustration, Gustave Dore, 1861.

Beginning in the late eighteenth century, magazines and newspapers ("gazettes") began to compete for readership with printed books. Periodical publishers were not slow in discovering the appeal of drawings to illustrate their stories, articles, poems, and prose pieces. In the nineteenth century, therefore, a new breed of specialized illustrator was born who concentrated more on quick impressions, telling compositions, or realistically detailed minutiae than on broad exposition. Thus illustration began to move in the direction of some of the innovations brought on by cartooning. Indeed, all the great print illustrators of the nineteenth century, including Dore himself, dabbled to a certain extent in the fields of social, political, or humorous cartoons.

Up to the end of the nineteenth century, the illustrator had used the same methods as the craftsman—etching, wood and copper engraving—but these procedures were slowly being displaced by the newer and more efficient techniques of mechanical and photomechanical reproduction. In the final years of the century, technological advances made it possible to print images on flat surfaces directly from photographs, without intervention from either draftsman or engraver. This release from the time-consuming processes of reproduction by hand had the effect of encouraging a new artistic freedom among illustrators (especially those working for magazines), away from imitation toward more lyrical, personal, or romantic depictions of life. Norman Rockwell is certainly famed for this kind of interpretation of American life and American scenes, while the Wyeths, N. C. and Andrew, took illustration onto a more personal plane in which external realities and personal longings fused into what has been called "magic realism." The trend toward making illustration into an art at once recognizable and yet not simply representational is much in evidence among today's illustrators. Artists such as *Contemporary Graphic Artists,* Volume 1, listees Bob Peak, James McMullan, Brad Holland, Barbara Nessim, and others are all striving to

A computer-generated illustration by Barbara Nessim.
(© 1983, Barbara Nessim. Reprinted with permission.)

make their illustrations transcend the limitations of subject matter and editorial format. Going back to the original meaning of illustration, they enlighten their subjects with wit, insight, and clarity of expression.

The role of publicity and advertising in the development of illustration is more than subsidiary. The first advertisements aimed at a mass public had been crude and repetitive, but manufacturers and businessmen soon discovered that a successful advertisement is one that makes its association instantly. This realization was the origin of the poster, which, in a single image, could make identification with a product or service immediate and unmistakable. French lithographer Jules Cheret was among the first in the nineteenth century to grasp this simple notion, but he also understood that for the image to be appreciated and viewed with pleasure—in a word, to sell—it also must exhibit artistic qualities. He was thus not only "the father of the modern poster," as he has been called, but also the first proponent of art in advertising.

Art posters for every product imaginable—soap, automobiles, clothes, lipstick—have been and are still being produced in the thousands. While their primary function remains selling, they have also contributed to the elevation of artistic taste among the general public. This has been nowhere as evident as in the movie poster, where the product itself is also an art form. Thus the great artistic developments of the 1920s and 1930s—surrealism, cubism, expressionism—were reflected in many posters of the times. In recent years the movie poster as both a statement of content and a statement of art has been affirmed in the works of such talented innovators as Bob Peak and, especially, Saul Bass, whose posters are instantly recognizable in their ability to define the character of a film with a simple graphic sign or a few economical, effective lines.

Illustration and Graphic Design

We are now coming to the juncture of illustration and graphic design. In her *Dictionary of Graphic Arts Terms* (Van Nostrand, 1981), Patricia Barnes Mintz defines graphic design as "any type of visual communication." This is a bit sketchy: I would add that as a designer, the graphic artist must often travel away from illustration, or the art of recognizable forms, toward semiotics, or the science of signs and symbols. In this respect he must not only select and arrange all the formal elements present in a work into a single visual statement, but he must also express his conception of what is being communicated (the identity of a big corporation, the characteristics of a new product, etc.) to achieve unmistakable identification. The direction, sizes, shapes, relationships, symmetry or asymmetry, emotional content, dynamics of the different elements of design must all be factors. Good design is the seamless integration of all these factors into a distinguishable whole, irrespective of product or message. Nowhere is Marshall McLuhan's dictum that "the medium is the message" proved so true as in design. So great designers, such as Milton Glaser or Saul Bass, both of whom are listed in this volume, are able to create with equal effectiveness a corporation logo, the title for a movie, the look of a magazine, or the atmosphere of a supermarket. In design the graphic arts are able to achieve the same abstract character long present in the fine arts.

Cartoons and Cartooning

Unlike illustration, which ideally finds its counterpart in real life, any drawing that encapsulates a complete thought can be called a "cartoon." In actuality, the European artists of the eighteenth and nineteenth centuries whom we consider as the first and foremost cartoonists—William Hogarth, Thomas Rowlandson, James Gillray, Honore Daumier, Grandville—were also fine illustrators. What chiefly distinguishes the cartoon in its initial stage from straight

An early cartoon by Thomas Rowlandson, mocking the "back to nature" school in painting, 1809.

illustration are the cartoonist's intent and his use of caricature. The cartoon is a weapon of persuasion and, as such, must make its point quickly and economically; decorative flourishes and subtle details are therefore shed in favor of a sort of graphic shorthand that focuses on the main thrust of the drawing. Caricature contributes greatly to the impact of the cartoon.

The art of caricature was an almost exclusive invention of the Italians. To the brothers Annibale and Agostino Caracci at the end of the sixteenth century goes the credit for coining the word *caricature,* which derives from their *rittratini carichi,* or loaded portraits. In these drawings they satirized well-known personalities of their time as well as ordinary individuals. The universal acceptance of the print medium spread the art of caricature throughout Europe and led to the transition from caricature to cartooning. The latter technique was no longer devoted solely to cataloguing external human idiosyncrasies but sought an enlarged field of vision, a field large enough to encompass the entire political, social, and cultural scene—indeed, the human condition itself.

William Hogarth of England is the first artist to whom the term *cartoonist* can be legitimately applied, and he is widely regarded as the founding father of the art. He gave cartooning a function as well as a form: the subject of the cartoonist's pen would henceforth be the state of the world and, more specifically, society. A tradition was thus born: for a long time (and to a great extent until this day) cartooning would be an art of social protest against the failings of society and mankind, perhaps the most effective means of social protest and social comment yet devised.

For many years political cartooning (and editorial cartooning generally) was the very substance of the medium. The potency of the cartoon lay in its ability to make a point immediately and sharply, and it was therefore well suited for the political battles of the nineteenth century, when cartoonists for the most part embraced unquestioningly the causes of revolt and social protest—at least in Europe.

"Ideal Money," a political cartoon by the master of American cartooning, Thomas Nast, 1878.

Ironically, it was the American cartoonists who first injected a dose of evenhandedness and skepticism in their cartoons by attacking all comers, whether from the Left or the Right. Eventually the trend grew as American newspaper cartoonists, thanks to the spread of syndication, freed themselves to a large extent from the dicta of party or publisher.

The pattern of editorial cartooning, set in the last century by such giants as Thomas Nast, has to a remarkable degree

A political cartoon, ca. 1978, by Don Wright, winner of two Pulitzer Prizes. (© *Miami News*.)

survived into our own. In today's newspapers can be found, in almost equal parts, those artists who identify with a party or a cause (Democrat or Republican, conservative or liberal) and those who attack with the same relish every target of opportunity, from whatever field it may come. Both categories are well represented in this first volume of *Contemporary Graphic Artists,* with the likes of Tom Engelhardt and Tom Toles, Don Wright and Larry Wright, and many other talented practitioners of the form.

The humor or gag cartoon, as differentiated from the political cartoon, is a relative latecomer to the cartooning scene. Early cartoonists certainly were capable of turning out a funny drawing without being too concerned about its ultimate meaning, but humor cartoons as an accepted genre only came about in the second half of the nineteenth century, and their flowering can be ascribed to the popularization of the illustrated magazine. Magazine editors discovered that the general public craved entertainment more than it did polemics; accordingly, a new form of cartooning came into being, with an aim mainly or solely to amuse. This also led to a looser, freer style of cartooning, one again leaning heavily on caricature, as the point increasingly became that of being funny in the drawing as well as in the joke of the cartoon. Such humorists as Sam Gross and Jack Ziegler, both of whom are included in this volume, have pursued this tradition with a high degree of effectiveness in their down-to-essentials, minimalist cartoons.

The humor magazine in turn contributed to the universal popularity of the cartoon by spreading its technique beyond the confines of journalism. Illustrators, who were also heavy contributors of magazine art, took notice and learned from the cartoonists' armory of tricks, just as the cartoonists had earlier learned the lessons of the popular illustrators. There was now a commingling of genres, and it was sometimes hard to determine when illustration ended and cartooning began (or vice versa). This situation can still be said to be, if not a dominant, at least an important trend in modern illustrations; such illustrators as *Contemporary Graphic Artists,* Volume 1, listees Randall Enos and R. O. Blechman can readily attest to this, in pictures as well as words.

Conversely, many books and articles in magazines and newspapers are illustrated with drawings that can only be called "cartoons," and the art of cartoon illustration is now well established as a separate discipline. *Contemporary Graphic Artists* biographees Tom Eaton and Syd Hoff are skilled practitioners of the genre, while Jack Kent has refined it into a high and stylized form; and, of course, Edward Sorel, who also has an entry in this volume, is in a class by himself in his unique fusion of cartoon and illustration into one telling visual image.

It was inevitable that the ubiquitousness of the cartoon form would lead to growing specialization. There have always been cartoons devoted to a single issue or a single interest, or to universal themes—fashion, medicine, money, the courts, etc.—dear to satirists of whatever time or country. There are also cartoons aimed at a specialized public—whether stamp collectors, jogging enthusiasts, or rock 'n' roll fanatics. Sports cartoons have long been a staple of American newspapers, but despite their respected history, they have been steadily losing ground to sports photographs. The genre still exists, however, and has found in Bill Gallo not only a dynamic practitioner, as can be seen in the illustrations accompanying his entry in this volume, but an ardent and eloquent advocate as well.

Another form of the cartoon is the cartoon series—drawings sequentially arranged to tell a story—which eventually led to the appearance of the newspaper and magazine panel feature, exemplified by such well-known creations as Ted Key's *Hazel* and Bil Keane's *The Family Circus.* In this field the boundaries between cartoon and comic strip become blurred as more and more cartoonists (political cartoonists included) use multi-panel compositions to amplify or extend the point they want to make, and many comic strip artists sometimes reduce their features to one gigantic panel.

A weekly panel feature: *Hazel* by Ted Key, ca. 1965. (© 1985, Ted Key. Reprinted with permission.)

Comics—Funny and Otherwise

Toward the end of the nineteenth century, cartoon sequences, already well established, were organized into progressively more complex and more extended stories. They still made use of text separated from the drawings, and this distinguishes them from the comics proper, of which they were the early antecedents. The stirrings of a new art form can be traced to this period. Particularly significant were the growth and popularity in the United States of the illustrated humor magazine, of which *Puck, Judge,* and *Life* were the recognized leaders. At the same time, the daily city newspapers in their quest for an ever-expanding readership were putting out Sunday supplements (despite the outcries of religious groups opposed to publishing on the Sabbath) that made increasing use of illustration and color. In addition, young talent was attracted to the rapidly growing field of newspaper cartooning, and the enthusiasm and vitality of these newcomers, some of them barely out of their teens, made up for their crudeness and lack of technique.

The oft-recounted struggle between publishers Joseph Pulitzer and William Randolph Hearst, the two titans of turn-of-the-century American journalism, provided the final catalyst for the birth of what would come to be called—for want of a better term—"the comics." Among such artists as James Swinnerton, Rudolph Dirks, and R.F. Outcault, who have now become associated with the birth of the form,

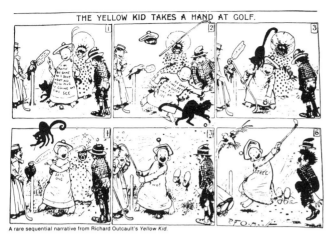

THE YELLOW KID TAKES A HAND AT GOLF.

A rare sequential narrative from Richard Outcault's *Yellow Kid.*

The birth of the comics: *The Yellow Kid* **by R. F. Outcault, 1897.**

Outcault, whose biographical entry can be found in this volume, must take pride of place with his epochal creation of *The Yellow Kid,* regarded as the seminal influence on comics for decades to follow.

In the times of Outcault and Swinnerton and Dirks, the comics were heavily dependent for their style on the contemporary magazine cartoons. Indeed, many artists were working in both media. From the magazine cartoon this new form also borrowed many of its themes and its approach, which was overwhelmingly humorous—hence the terms "comics" and "funnies," often applied in a derisive way. If the comics did not differ markedly or at all from the cartoons in style, they looked radically different in presentation (often using a whole newspaper page to tell a story) and exhibited a number of unique features. The definition given by Coulton Waugh in *The Comics* (Macmillan, 1947) still remains largely in force. The comics, he wrote, consist of "a continuing character [or group of characters] . . . ; a sequence of pictures . . . complete in themselves or part of a longer story; speech in the drawing, usually in blocks of lettering surrounded by 'balloon' lines."

The comics remained "cartoony" for a long time. Winsor McCay was the first artist to bring to them techniques borrowed from illustration, fantasy, and fine art. His use of imagery was astonishing, and his utilization of perspective vastly innovative. His achievements are detailed in his entry in this volume. Yet McCay's innovations remained the exception, and the comics went on their merry way, developing a style of caricature that has come, for obvious reasons, to be called "bigfoot." Many of today's comic strip artists still belong to that respected tradition, and probably none is as skillful and as representative in this regard as Dik Browne, whose *Contemporary Graphic Artists* entry discusses his work as the artist on the *Hi and Lois* comic strip and the creator of the universally beloved *Hagar the Horrible.*

Only in the 1920s did a growing number of comic strip artists become disenchanted with the limitations of traditional cartooning, and they started moving closer to magazine illustration in their style of drawing. During that period, poster and advertising art also exercised a marked influence on the artists of the comics and led them into the direction of greater realism. The introduction of Edgar Rice Burroughs's Tarzan character to the comic pages marked a decisive

turning point in 1929. In order to draw the jungle adventures of the ape-man, the artist would have to know not only anatomy, but also classical illustration to be able to depict in a convincing manner all the complex happenings of the tale. Thus classical realism—or idealism—came to the comics, first with Harold Foster's *Tarzan,* then with Alex Raymond's *Flash Gordon,* followed by Burne Hogarth's version of *Tarzan,* regarded by most critics as the definitive one. "In a few years," wrote Pierre Couperie in *A History of the Comic Strip* (Crown, 1968), "the comic strip absorbed the entire tradition of classical painting and draftsmanship."

An adventure strip realistically drawn: *Drago* **by Burne Hogarth, 1946.** (© Burne Hogarth. Reprinted with permission.)

The success of the comic strip spawned a new kind of publication widely known as the comic book. This a double misnomer since these publications are rarely comic, nor are they books in the accepted sense of the term. They are usually magazines, about seven by ten inches in size, printed in color on pulp paper. The first genuine comic book is considered to be *Funnies on Parade,* distributed as a promotional giveaway by the Procter & Gamble Company in 1933. It was shortly followed by the first commercial comic book, *Famous Funnies,* in 1934. These early publications were made up exclusively of reprints from newspaper strips. The first comic book to contain only original features was a collection of humorous stories, *New Fun,* which came out in 1935. But it was adventure that definitively established the comic book as a viable medium. In 1937 *Detective Comics* was the first such publication entirely devoted to a single protagonist, and it was followed the next year by *Action Comics,* in which *Superman* first appeared and immediately soared to unprecedented success with its youthful audience.

The early comic book drawings were crude and primitive. They were mostly done by teenage cartoonists whom the comic book companies could hire at a cheap salary. (Fred Schwab's early experience in the field, which is fairly typical, is recounted in his entry in this volume.) In time, however, the comic book developed its own themes and its own brand of draftsmanship. Little by little humor disappeared in favor of costumed superheroes, whose progenitor was Superman, boasting of powers out of the reach of ordinary humans— such as flying in the air, changing into a human torch, or making oneself invisible. The superhero has become the staple of the medium, but there have been cartoonists who have preferred to devote themselves to more mature themes, such as peace and war and the testing of character under stress. One such comic book artist, whose entry is included in this volume, is Joe Kubert, justly hailed for his stylistic contributions to the medium, as well as for his handling of sometimes controversial themes.

In a category by himself in the gallery of original and innovative comic book creators is Will Eisner, who in 1940 brought out *The Spirit,* a comic book insert not sold at newsstands but carried as a supplement by a number of newspapers. This was the newspapers' answer to the growing threat of comic books, which were taking a large chunk of their youthful readers away from the Sunday supplements. On the whole it proved successful and gave rise to a number of imitators. It was also an artistic and critical success, and this fact assured *The Spirit* of wide renown and longevity. (It is still being published today, though in a different format and no longer in newspapers.)

The 1960s saw the liberation of comic book theme, style, and treatment. The so-called underground cartoonists enjoyed a tremendous success throughout the decade, despite censorship, harassment, and lawsuits. The comic book format petered out somewhat ingloriously in the next decade, but in the interval it had given fresh impetus to a whole new generation of artists. Among these can be counted Richard Corben, who began his career drawing for underground comics but has in recent years developed his own brand of adult graphic storytelling. Another such artist also included in this volume is Frank Thorne, a defector from mainstream comic books, who has evolved a much-imitated style and initiated a welcome return to humor in his often bawdy stories.

In the last three decades the comics have become a universal form, as popular in Japan, Argentina, or Italy, as in the United States. Foreign countries have produced their own masters of comic strip and comic book art, many of whom have published in this country and have in turn influenced American artists. Let us mention Guido Crepax from Italy, Osamu Tezuka from Japan, and the Spanish artists Jordi Bernet and Fernando Fernandez, all of whom are represented in these pages.

Graphic Art in Motion: The Animated Film

From time immemorial man has tried to animate images, from the Chinese shadow theater and the early flip-books to the magic lantern of the seventeenth century. As the phenomenon known as persistence of vision (the persistence of an image on the retina after the object has disappeared)

came to be understood by scientists, ingenious inventors tried to build devices aimed at producing the optical illusion of movement. The phenakistiscope, for instance, was invented by the Belgian Joseph Plateau in 1832. It was a viewing device fitted with mirrors and through which passed drawings painted on a cardboard disc. Emile Reynaud went further with his praxinoscope, another mirrored device, and organized shows consisting entirely of skits enacted with animated drawings. He could not keep pace with the rapid development of the movie camera, however, and animation ultimately went in the direction of the motion picture.

The identification of animation with film has led many historians to catalogue it as one of many sub-groups that make up the movies. It is definitely much more. Most animation is still produced manually and one frame at a time; this alone would distinguish it from the movie process where sequences are photographed and produced as part of one continuous process. The animated film is part of the cinema only in a mechanical and superficial way—it is preserved on film stock and generally projected onto a screen. The animated cartoon, the most prevalent form of animation, is derived from the print cartoon, in spirit and technique as well as in etymology. Its development and subsequent acceptance owe much to the early newspaper cartoonists. It is, therefore, fitting to include animation among the graphic, not the photographic, arts.

The flowering of the animated film can be credited to James Stuart Blackton, who was both a newspaper cartoonist and a filmmaker, and thus ideally suited to fuse the two techniques together. He was the first to apply the simple technique of "one turn [of the camera crank], one picture" to

A frame from the celebrated *Gertie the Trained Dinosaur* by Winsor McCay, 1914.

cartoon filmmaking. The first cartoon film he produced in this manner, *Humorous Phases of Funny Faces,* undisputably earned him the title "father of modern animation."

While Blackton and his colleagues here and in Europe—Earl Hurd, J. R. Bray, Walter Booth, Emile Cohl—were perfecting the cartoon as a technical innovation, it fell upon Winsor McCay to develop it as an art form. The showing in 1914 of his film *Gertie the Trained Dinosaur* caused a sensation among laymen and professionals alike. Emile Cohl, who happened to be in New York at the time and saw the film, wrote: "On the stage, in front of the screen, McCay stood, in evening dress, whip in hand. He started a little speech; then, going back to the screen, like a lion tamer he gave an order to the beast, which came out from behind the rocks. Always under the command of the tamer, it gave an exhibition of acrobatic skill; the dinosaur jumped, danced, uprooted trees and finally took a bow in front of the wildly applauding audience."

Gertie had been created by the painstaking process of drawing by hand each one of the more than five thousand drawings that went into making the film. Other animators at the same time sought ways to alleviate the staggering workload and thus make animation into a viable commercial enterprise. Gradually economies were realized through the introduction of a system of pegs to keep every drawing in the same position relative to the camera, the adoption of transparent celluloid sheets (or "cels") on which to draw or paint animation scenes, and other technical innovations.

The decisive development that gave the animated cartoon its final impetus was the introduction of sound. Walt Disney was the first animator to understand and exploit the possibilities of dialogue and sound effects in his short films, starting with *Steamboat Willie* in 1928, the first Mickey Mouse cartoon. Later Disney produced the first animated film entirely shot on color stock (the earlier efforts had been colored by hand), and the release in 1937 of *Snow White and the Seven Dwarfs* signaled a new direction in filmmaking: for the first time an animated feature received the same kind of popular and critical attention accorded the most successful live-action films. The 1930s were indeed "the reign of Disney."

The next two decades saw a flowering of American animation. Warner Brothers, Columbia, and all the major movie studios kept pouring out films that competed in quality and popularity with the Disney productions. Among the most successful was Metro-Goldwyn-Mayer (MGM), which, under the direction of Joe Barbera and Bill Hanna, turned out the widely acclaimed *Tom and Jerry* series. Hanna and Barbera later went on to become the pioneers of television animation. At the same time, a new studio, United Producers of America (UPA), made up largely of former Disney staffers, released the innovative *Mr. Magoo* and *Gerald McBoing Boing* cartoons, under the direction of such talented artists as Peter Burness and John Hubley.

The American domination of the animation field is no longer going unchallenged. Nor is animation flourishing only in its traditional European bastions—France, Great Britain, Italy—but it has spread all over the continent where recognizable national schools, such as the Zagreb school in Yugoslavia, have imposed their own identity on the medium. The most dramatic case may be that of Japan, where from the ashes of an industry in total ruin at the end of World War II has sprung a mighty phoenix that is now challenging American animators on their own ground.

The Jetson family from the animated television series *The Jetsons*, created by Joe Barbera and Bill Hanna. (© 1983, Hanna-Barbera Productions, Inc.)

Osamu Tezuka, for instance, took the television kiddie audience by storm with such creations as *Astroboy* and *Kimba the White Lion,* and his techniques have influenced a whole generation of American animators.

Outside of the confines of the major studios, American animators have themselves made strides toward a more personal art of animation. Sally Cruikshank is noted for imparting her own, often irreverent, vision of the animated cartoons of the 1930s and 1940s. Others have extended the boundaries of animation further, in computer animation, for example, or, as in the case of David Ehrlich, into the field of holography.

Thus are the parameters of the graphic arts as applied in this series, described in their broad outlines. The bio-bibliographical entries for the individual artists covered in *Contemporary Graphic Artists* will provide the reader with a wealth of additional information.

—*Maurice Horn*

Contemporary
Graphic Artists

Contemporary Graphic Artists

ALDER, Jamie   1951-
   (Bill Shut)

PERSONAL: Born October 30, 1951, in Detroit, Mich.; son of James Raymond, Jr. (a horseman) and Patricia (a horsewoman; maiden name Murphy) Alder. *Education:* University of Michigan, Ann Arbor, B.F.A., 1974. *Home and studio:* 24816 Aden Ave., Newhall, Calif. 91321.

CAREER: Assistant trainer, Stoney Ridge Farm (a horse-training farm), Chelsea, Mich., 1975-82; trainer, Paradise Farm, Sacramento, Calif., 1982-83; head of hunter/jumper department, Pacific Horse Center (a post-secondary school), Elk Grove, Calif., 1983-84; trainer, Quest's End (a rider training school), 1984—; freelance cartoonist and artist, 1973—. *Awards, honors:* First place for sculpture in University of Michigan Undergraduate Show, 1973.

EXHIBITIONS: University of Michigan Undergraduate Show, Rackham Gallery, Ann Arbor, Mich., 1973; University of Michigan B.F.A. Show, Art School Gallery, Ann Arbor, 1974; International Mail Art Show, 1982.

A page from "Home Movies." (© 1980, Bill Shut. Reprinted with permission.)

21

A spread from "Exquisite Corpse Comix." (© 1984, Bill Shut and Michael Roden. Reprinted with permission.)

WORK IN PROGRESS: Currently working on "Exquisite Corpse Comix," which is a jam comix based on the surrealist "exquisite corpse" game/experiment, but with a slight variation.

SIDELIGHTS: While gainfully employed as a horse-trainer in various parts of the country, Jamie Alder, under the nom de plume Bill Shut, has been in the forefront of the so-called "Newave" movement in comics. The Newave artists are the spiritual heirs to the underground comic movement of the 1960s, but their emphasis is on aesthetic experimentation rather than social and political protest. Among the many comic books to which Alder has contributed over the years are *Babyfat, City Limits Comix, Comix Wave, Fried Brains, Tales Too Tough for TV* and *Queen of Hairy Flies.* Alder's current project is "Exquisite Corpse Comix" in which he and other cartoonists collaborate to produce a series of comics that, upon completion, will look like one immense and continuous drawing. Five issues of this experimental work were published by mid-1985, with ten more in the planning stage.

In his article for the *Comics Journal* Dale Luciano noted that Alder used a "non-linear, surreal approach to comics and image making." Writing of a particular Alder story, "Flash Sage," he judged it to be "a bizarre series of visual transmogrifications that are something like hallucinatory test patterns: in some vague, mysterious way, Alder/Shut's

images begin to resemble the unconscious, psychic mish-mash of years of accumulated TV viewing—no recollection of content, just shape, juxtaposition, and transformation."

Alder wrote *CGA:* "While attending the University of Michigan I enjoyed the freedom of the fine arts field, but became very disillusioned with the elitism of the fine arts gallery scene. Shortly after graduating I subscribed to *Clay Geerdes' Comix World.* Clay at this time was writing on how easy it was for someone to self-publish through the use of cheap offset or photocopy. Clay covered and plugged the alternative publishers in his newsletter and basically is the father of the network of alternative publishers and artists that exists today. Self-publication allows me the freedom of the fine arts and gets exposure and feedback for my art without all the elitism and 'Bill Shut' of the fine arts gallery scene. Steve Willis coined the term 'folkomix' and I think it accurately describes the motivation and spirit of my work."

BIOGRAPHICAL/CRITICAL SOURCES: Clay Geerdes, "The Independent Comics Movement," San Diego Comic Convention souvenir program book, 1978; Jay Kinney, "Comix," *Heavy Metal,* December, 1980; Clay Geerdes, "Newave 1980's: Comix in Revolution," *Fanfare,* summer, 1981; Jay Kennedy, *The Official Underground and Newave Comix Price Guide,* Boatner Norton, 1982; Dale Luciano, "The Newave Comics Survey," *Comics Journal,* March, 1985.

B

BARBERA, Joe
    See BARBERA, Joseph Roland

        *   *   *

BARBERA, Joseph Roland   1911-
  (Joe Barbera)

PERSONAL: Born March 24, 1911, in New York City; son of Vincente and Frances Barbera; married Sheila Holden; children: Lynn Meredith, Jayne Earl, Neal Francis. *Education:* Attended American Institute of Banking, Pratt Institute, Art Students League. *Office:* Hanna-Barbera Productions, 3400 Cahuenga Blvd., Hollywood, Calif. 90068.

CAREER: Banking clerk, Irving Trust Company, New York City, 1930-32; animator, Van Beuren Studios, New York City, 1932-37; story man, director and producer, Metro-Goldwyn-Mayer (MGM), Hollywood, Calif., 1937-57; president, Hanna-Barbera Productions, 1957—. Member, board of directors, Taft Broadcasting Company, Hollywood, Calif. President, Southern California Theatre Associations; Greek Theatre Association (former president); St. Joseph's Medical Center (on advisory board); Greater Los Angeles Visitors and Convention Bureau (on advisory board); Children's Village (on advisory board); Los Angeles Earthquake Preparedness Committee (co-chairman); Wildlife Waystation (honorary board member); Cousteau Society. *Member:* National Academy of Television Arts and Sciences, Academy of Motion Picture Arts and Sciences.

AWARDS, HONORS: Seven Academy Awards for animated short subjects from Academy of Motion Picture Arts and Sciences, all with William Hanna, all for cartoons featuring the characters Tom and Jerry: "Yankee Doodle Mouse," 1943; "Mouse Trouble," 1944; "Quiet, Please," 1945; "The Cat Concerto," 1946; "The Little Orphan," 1948; "The Two Mouseketeers," 1951; "Johann Mouse," 1952. Seven Emmy Awards from National Academy of Television Arts and Sciences, all for outstanding achievement in children's programming, unless otherwise noted; all animation, unless otherwise noted: *Huckleberry Hound*, 1960; *Jack and the Beanstalk* (live action and animation), 1966; *The Last of the Curlews*, 1973; *The Runaways* (live action), 1974; *The Gathering* (for outstanding special—drama or comedy; live action), 1978; *The Smurfs*, 1982; *The Smurfs*, 1983. Golden Globe Award from Hollywood Foreign Press Association for outstanding achievement in international television cartoons, *The Flintstones*, 1965; Annie Award, *Charlotte's Web*, 1977; Christopher Award, *The Gathering*, 1978; Golden

Reel Award, for animation sound editing, *The Smurfs Springtime Special*, 1982.

FILMS—Producer; all animated features, unless otherwise noted: *Hey There, It's Yogi Bear*, 1964; *A Man Called Flintstone*, 1966; *Charlotte's Web*, 1973; *C.H.O.M.P.S.* (live action), 1979; *Heidi's Song*, 1982; *Forever Like the Rose* (in production).

TELEVISION—All live-action movies, unless otherwise noted: *Hardcase*, ABC, 1972; *Shootout in a One-Dog Town* (animated), ABC, 1974; *The Gathering*, ABC, 1977; *The Beasts Are in the Streets*, NBC, 1978; *KISS Meets the Phantom of the Park*, NBC, 1978; *The Gathering, Part II*, NBC, 1979; *Belle Starr*, CBS, 1980; *Rock Odyssey* (in production); *P.K. and the Kid* (in production).

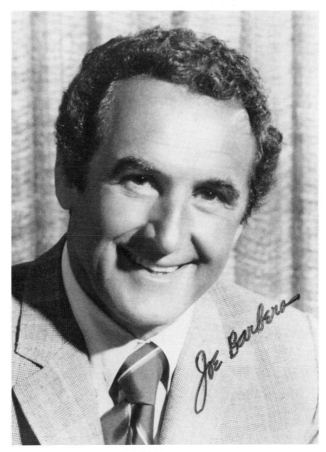

JOE BARBERA

Live-action series: *Banana Splits*, NBC, 1968-70; *Danger Island*, NBC, 1968-70; *The New Adventures of Huck Finn*, NBC, 1968-69; *Korg: 70,000 B.C.*, ABC, 1974-75; *Skatebirds*, CBS, 1977-78; *Mystery Island*, CBS, 1977-78; *Benji*, CBS, 1983-84; *Going Bananas*, 1984-85.

Animated series: *Ruff and Reddy*, NBC, 1957-60; *Huckleberry Hound*, syndicated, 1958-62; *Pixie and Dixie*, syndicated, 1958-62; *Snooper and Blabber*, syndicated, 1959-62; *Augie Doggie & Doggie Daddy*, syndicated, 1959-62; *Quick Draw McGraw*, syndicated, 1959-62; *Yakky Doodle*, syndicated, 1960-62; *Yogi Bear*, syndicated, 1960-62; *Hokey Wolf*, syndicated, 1960-62; *The Flintstones*, ABC, 1960-65; *Snagglepuss*, syndicated, 1960-62; *Top Cat*, ABC, 1961-62; *Lippy the Lion*, syndicated, 1962; *Touche Turtle*, syndicated, 1962; *Wally Gator*, syndicated, 1962; *The Jetsons*, ABC, 1962-63, syndicated, 1984-85; *Magilla Gorilla and Peter Potamus*, syndicated, 1963-67; *Punkin' Puss*, syndicated, 1963-67; *Breezly and Sneezly*, syndicated, 1963-67; *Yippee, Yappee and Yahooey*, syndicated, 1963-67; *Ricochet Rabbit*, syndicated, 1963-67.

Johnny Quest, ABC, 1964-65; *Secret Squirrel*, NBC, 1965-67; *Precious Pupp*, NBC, 1965-67; *Hillbilly Bears*, NBC, 1965-67; *Atom Ant*, NBC, 1965-67; *Winsome Witch*. NBC, 1965-67; *Squiddly Diddly*, NBC, 1965-67; *Sinbad, Jr* (distributed by AIP), 1965; *Laurel and Hardy* (distributed by Wolper), 1966-67; *Space Kidettes*, syndicated, 1966-67; *Space Ghost*, CBS, 1966-68; NBC, 1981-82; *Dino Boy*, CBS, 1966-67; *Frankenstein, Jr.*, CBS, 1966-67; *The Impossibles*, CBS, 1966-67; *Abbott and Costello* (distributed by RKO and Jomar), 1967-68; *Herculoids*, CBS, 1967-68, NBC, 1981-82; *Samson and Goliath*, syndicated, 1967-68; *The Fantastic Four*, ABC, 1967-68; *Mightor*, CBS, 1967-68; *Shazzam*, CBS, 1967-68; *Moby Dick*, CBS, 1967-68; *Birdman*, NBC, 1967-68; *Cattanooga Cats*, ABC, 1967-70; *Three Musketeers*, NBC, 1968-70; *Arabian Knights*, NBC, 1968-70; *Micro Ventures*, NBC, 1968-70; *Adventures of Gulliver*, ABC, 1968-69; *Wacky Races*, CBS, 1968-69; *Penelope Pitstop*, CBS, 1969-70; *Motormouse and Autocat*, ABC, 1969-70; *It's the Wolf*, ABC, 1969-70; *Scooby-Doo*, CBS, 1969-74, ABC, 1976-79; *Dastardly & Muttley*, CBS, 1969-70; *Around the World in 79 Days*, ABC, 1969-70.

Characters from the *Top Cat* television series. (© 1961, Hanna-Barbera Productions, Inc. Reprinted with permission.)

Tom and Jerry in their later version. (© 1983, Hanna-Barbera Productions, Inc. Reprinted with permission.)

Josie and the Pussycats, CBS, 1970-71; *Where's Huddles?*, CBS, 1970; *The Harlem Globetrotters*, CBS, 1970-72; *Pebbles and Bamm Bamm*, CBS, 1971-73; *Help! It's the Hair Bear Bunch*, CBS, 1971-72; *The Funky Phantom*, ABC, 1971-72; *Sealab 2020*, NBC, 1972-73; *Roman Holidays*, NBC, 1972-73; *The Amazing Chan and the Chan Clan*, CBS, 1972-73; *The Flintstones Comedy Hour*, CBS, 1972-73; *Josie and the Pussycats in Outer Space*, CBS, 1972-73; *The New Scooby-Doo Movies*, CBS, 1972-74; *Wait Till Your Father Gets Home*, syndicated, 1972-74; *Jeannie*, CBS, 1973-74; *Speed Buggy*, CBS, 1973-74; *The Addams Family*, NBC, 1973-74; *Inch High Private Eye*, NBC, 1973-74; *Butch Cassidy*, NBC, 1973-74; *Goober and the Ghost Chasers*, ABC, 1973-74; *Superfriends*, ABC, 1973-74, 1979-83; *Yogi's Gang*, ABC, 1973-74; *Peter Puck*, NBC, 1973-74; *Hong Kong Phooey*, ABC, 1974-75; *These Are the Days*, ABC, 1974-75; *Devlin*, ABC, 1974-75; *Valley of the Dinosaurs*, CBS, 1974-75; *Wheelie and the Chopper Bunch*, NBC, 1974-75; *The Partridge Family: 2200 A.D.*, CBS, 1974-75; *The Great Grape Ape*, ABC, 1975-76; *Tom and Jerry*, ABC, 1975-79.

Dynomutt, ABC, 1976-78; *Jabberjaw*, ABC, 1976-77; *Mumbly*, ABC, 1976-77; *Clue Club*, CBS, 1976-77; *CB Bears*, NBC, 1977-78; *Shake, Rattle and Roll*, NBC, 1977-78; *Undercover Elephant*, NBC, 1977-78; *Robonic Stooges*, CBS, 1977-78; *Woofer and Wimper Dog Detectives*, CBS, 1977-78; *Blast-Off Buzzard*, NBC, 1977-78; *Heyyy, It's the King*, NBC, 1977-78; *Posse Impossible*, NBC, 1977-78; *Wonder Wheels*, CBS, 1977-78; *Captain Caveman and the Teen Angels*, ABC, 1977-79; *The New Superfriends Show*, ABC, 1977-79; *Scooby-Doo's All Star Laff-A-Lympics*, ABC, 1977-

79; *Yogi's Space Race*, NBC, 1978-79; *Galaxy Goof-ups*, NBC, 1978-79; *Challenge of the Superfriends*, ABC, 1978-79; *Galloping Ghost*, NBC, 1978-79; *Buford Files*, NBC, 1978-79; *Jana of the Jungle*, NBC, 1978-79; *Godzilla*, NBC, 1978-80; *The All-New Popeye Show*, CBS, 1978-82; *Dinky Dog*, CBS, 1978-81; *The New Schmoo*, NBC, 1979-80; *Super Globetrotters*, NBC, 1979-80; *Casper and the Angels*, NBC, 1979-80; *The Thing*, NBC, 1979-80; *The Flintstones*, NBC, 1979-80; *Scooby and Scrappy Doo*, ABC, 1979-82; *The New Fred and Barney Show*, NBC, 1979-80.

Flintstone Family Adventures, NBC, 1980-82; *Pebbles, Dino and Bamm Bamm*, NBC, 1980-82; *The Bedrock Cops*, NBC, 1980-82; *Dino and the Cavemouse*, NBC, 1980-82; *The Frankenstones*, NBC, 1980-82; *Captain Caveman*, NBC, 1980-82; *Drak Pak*, CBS, 1980-81; *Fonz and the Happy Days Gang*, ABC, 1980-82; *Richie Rich*, ABC, 1980-83; *Space Stars*, NBC, 1981-82; *Astro and the Space Mutts*, NBC, 1981-82; *Teen Force*, NBC, 1981-82; *Crazy Claws*, CBS, 1981-82; *Kwicky Koala*, CBS, 1981-82; *Dirty Dawg*, CBS, 1981-82; *Bungle Brothers*, CBS, 1981-82; *The Smurfs*, NBC, 1981-85; *Laverne and Shirley*, ABC, 1981-82; *Private Olive Oyl*, CBS, 1981-82 *The Trollkins*, CBS, 1981-82; *Mork and Mindy*, ABC, 1982-83; *Laverne and Shirley/Fonz*, ABC, 1982-83; *The Little Rascals*, ABC, 1982-83; *Scooby, Scrappy and Yabba Doo*, ABC, 1982-83; *Pac-Man*, ABC, 1982-84; *Shirt Tales*, NBC, 1982-84; *The Gary Coleman Show*, NBC, 1982-83; *The Dukes*, CBS, 1983-84; *The Little Rascals/Richie Rich*, ABC, 1983-84; *Monchhichis*, ABC, 1983-84; *Scooby and Scrappy Doo*, ABC, 1983-84; *Baskitts*, CBS, 1983-84; *The Snorks*, NBC, 1984-85; *The Pink Panther and Sons*, NBC, 1984-85; *The New Scooby-Doo Mysteries*, ABC, 1984-85; *Superfriends: The Legendary Super Powers Show*, ABC, 1984-85; *GoBots*, syndicated, 1984-85; *The Funtastic World of Hanna-Barbera* (consisting of three segments: "Paw Paws," "Galtar and the Golden Lance," and "Funtastic Treasure Hunt"), syndicated, 1984-85; *The Bible*, Home Video, 1985.

The main characters from *The Flintstones* television series. (© 1983, Hanna-Barbera Productions, Inc. Reprinted with permission.)

TELEVISION SPECIALS—All animated, unless otherwise noted: *Alice in Wonderland*, ABC, 1966; *Jack and the Beanstalk*, NBC, 1966; *The Thanksgiving That Almost Wasn't*, syndicated, 1971; *Love American Style* (consisting of three segments: "Wait Till Your Father Gets Home" pilot, "Love and the Private Eye," "Melvin Danger"); *A Christmas Story*, syndicated, 1971; *The Last of the Curlews*, ABC, 1972; *Yogi's Ark Lark*, ABC, 1972; *Robin Hoodnik*, ABC, 1972; *Oliver and the Artful Dodger*, ABC, 1972; *Here Come the Clowns*, ABC, 1972; *Gidget Makes the Wrong Connection*, ABC, 1972; *The Banana Splits in Hocus Pocus Park*, ABC, 1972; *20,000 Leagues Under the Sea*, syndicated, 1973; *The Three Musketeers*, syndicated, 1973; *Lost in Space*, ABC, 1973; *The Count of Monte Cristo*, syndicated, 1973; *The Runaways* (live action), ABC, 1974; *Cyrano de Bergerac*, ABC, 1974; *Crazy Comedy Concert* (live and animated), ABC, 1974; *The Last of the Mohicans*, syndicated, 1975; *Phantom Rebel* (live action), NBC, 1976; *Davey Crockett on the Mississippi* (live action), CBS, 1976.

Taggart's Treasure (live action, ABC, 1976; *Five Weeks in a Balloon*, CBS, 1977; *Yabba-Dabba-Doo!* (live and animated), CBS, 1977; *The Flintstones' Christmas*, NBC, 1977; *Energy: A National Issue*, syndicated, 1977; *Beach Girls* (live action), syndicated, 1977; *It Isn't Easy Being a Teenage Millionaire* (live action), ABC, 1978; *Hanna-Barbera's Happy Hour* (animated mini-series), NBC, 1978; *Hanna-Barbera's All Star Comedy Ice Revue* (live and animated), *The Funny World of Fred and Bunni* (live and animated), both CBS, 1978; *The Flintstones' Little Big League*, NBC, 1978; *Black Beauty*, CBS, 1978; *Yaba-Dabba-Doo II*, CBS, 1978; *Superheroes Roast* (live action), NBC, 1979; *Challenge of the Superheroes* (live action), NBC, 1979; *America vs. the World* (live action), NBC, 1979; *Scooby Goes Hollywood*, ABC, 1979; *Casper's First Christmas*, NBC, 1979; *Sgt. T.K. Yu* (live action), NBC, 1979; *Popeye: Sweethearts at Sea*, CBS, 1979; *Gulliver's Travels*, CBS, 1979; *Casper's Halloween Special: He Ain't Scary, He's Our Brother*, NBC, 1979.

The Harlem Globetrotters Meet Snow White (serialized in *Fred and Barney* series), NBC, 1980; *The Flintstones Meet Rockula and Frankenstone*, NBC, 1980; *The Flintstones' New Neighbor*, NBC, 1980; *Fred's Final Fling*, NBC, 1980; *The Gymnast* (live action), ABC, 1980; *B. B. Beagle*, syndicated, 1980; *Hanna-Barbera Arena Show* (live action), NBC, 1981; *Jogging Fever*, NBC, 1981; *Wind-Up Wilma*, NBC, 1981; *The Great Gilly Hopkins* (live action), CBS, 1981; *Daniel Boone*, CBS, 1981; *The Smurfs*, NBC, 1981; *The Smurfs' Springtime Special*, NBC, 1982; *The Jokebook*, NBC, 1982; *The Smurfs' Christmas Special*, NBC, 1982; *Christmas Comes to Pac-Land*, ABC, 1982; *Yogi Bear's All-Star Christmas Caper*, CBS, 1982; *My Smurfy Valentine*, NBC, 1983; *The Secret World of Og*, ABC, 1983; *The Amazing Bunjee Venture*, CBS, 1984; *The Smurfic Games*, NBC, 1984; *Smurfily-Ever-After*, NBC, 1985; *Johnny Yune Variety Special* (in preparation).

SIDELIGHTS: Joe Barbera's fifty-year career in animation is one of the most productive and acclaimed in the field. As Gerald and Danny Peary wrote in *The American Animated Cartoon*, "In 1976 William Hanna and Joseph Barbera placed their star in front of 6753 Hollywood Boulevard on the Walk of Fame in honor of over one hundred television series since 1957 and eight [Barbera lists seven] Emmys." While Barbera's name is usually linked with that of his long-

A scene from the award-winning *Charlotte's Web.* (© 1973, Hanna-Barbera Productions, Inc. Reprinted with permission.)

time associate, Bill Hanna, it is well to remember that his career goes back much earlier, to the early days of sound animation.

Barbera had at first contemplated a career in accounting, but the coming of the Depression cut his ambitions short. He contributed cartoons to various magazines of the day with some success, but discovered his real calling after he joined the animation staff of the Van Beuren studio in 1932. He went from in-betweener to director, working notably on the *Tom and Jerry* series (this one involved the zany doings of a mismatched pair of human characters, not the cat and mouse of later fame).

Following the lead of so many other animators, Barbera migrated to the West Coast in 1937 in order to set up a new animation unit for Metro-Goldwyn-Mayer (MGM). "It was a horrible experience trying to start up a studio for MGM," Barbera later recalled in *Continental*. "The man in charge didn't have the faintest idea what he was doing. Just as MGM was going to close the studio, another story man, Bill Hanna, and I did a cartoon on our own about a cat chasing a mouse. But an MGM executive felt people were tired of cats chasing mice and told us not to make any more. Luckily, a letter came from one of the big exhibitors in Texas requesting more cat-and-mouse cartoons. If not for that letter, Bill Hanna and I would not have made *Tom and Jerry*."

The cartoon was "Puss Gets the Boot," and its release won it an Academy Award nomination in 1940, and assured the success not only of the *Tom and Jerry* series, but also that of the Hanna-Barbera partnership. Barbera usually contributed the lion's share of creation, while Hanna's talent lay more in timing and organization. In his book *Of Mice and Magic*, Leonard Maltin wrote: "The stories were almost entirely the

A montage of Hanna-Barbera characters. Clockwise from upper left: Huckleberry Hound, Quick Draw McGraw, Yogi Bear, the Flintstones, and Top Cat (center). (© 1985, Hanna-Barbera, Inc. Reprinted with permission.)

work of Barbera, one of the most creative minds ever to function in the animation field. That one person could develop so many variations on a basic theme is astounding. In addition to comedy, Barbera worked with characterization, which added fuel to his story repertoire. Thanks to his animators' skills, Tom and Jerry developed into full-blooded characters, with thoughts and feelings. Barbera learned to channel these nuances into effective story ideas."

After more than two hundred cartoons and no fewer than seven Oscars to their credit Barbera and Hanna saw their long association with MGM abruptly come to an end in 1957, when the studio disbanded its animation unit in an economy move. The two partners than created their own animation company, Hanna-Barbera Productions (now part of Taft Communications) and specialized in cartoons made for television. They pioneered the use of limited animation and were successful to such an extent that they soon became the major purveyors of animation for the small screen, dubbing themselves "the largest producer of animated entertainment in the world." The studio later branched out into full-length animated features, making some notable contributions to the field, such as *Charlotte's Web* and *Heidi's Song*. The company is now heavily involved in theme amusement parks in Ohio, Virginia, California, and in Canada.

Even into his seventies, Barbera still kept a hand in every facet of the studio's activities. "I'm still involved with plotting or kicking off ideas, which is the part I like," he told a reporter for the *Los Angeles Times* in 1985. "But I'm trying to get out of doing all the work . . . getting involved so much in every story."

BIOGRAPHICAL/CRITICAL SOURCES: Roger Manvell, *The Animated Film*, Hastings House, 1955; Ruth Harbert, "Mr. Tom and Mr. Jerry," *Good Housekeeping*, March, 1956; Ralph Stephenson, *Animation in the Cinema*, A.S. Barnes, 1967; Bruno Edera, *Full-Length Animated Feature Films*, Hastings House, 1977; *The World Encyclopedia of Cartoons*, Chelsea House, 1980; George and Danny Peary, *The American Animated Cartoon*, Dutton, 1980; Leonard Maltin, *Of Mice and Magic: A History of American Animated Cartoons*, McGraw-Hill, 1980; Joseph Barbera, "Suspended Animation," *Continental)*, July, 1984; Ellen Farley, "Saturday Morning Turf Now Being Invaded," *Los Angeles Times*, March 8, 1985.

* * *

BASS, Saul 1920-

PERSONAL: Born May 8, 1920, in New York City; son of Aaron and Pauline Bass; married Elaine Makatura, September 30, 1961; children: Jennifer, Jeffrey; (children by previous marriage) Robert, Andrea. *Education:* Studied with Howard Traffon at Art Students League, New York City. 1936-38; with Gyorgy Kepes at Brooklyn College, New York City, 1944-45. *Office:* 7039 Sunset Blvd., Los Angeles, Calif. 90028.

CAREER: Freelance graphic designer, New York City, 1936-46; proprietor, Saul Bass & Associates (design consultants), Los Angeles, Calif., 1946-80; Saul Bass/Herb Yager &

Associates, Los Angeles, 1980—. Designer and developer of trademarks and identification systems for many commercial corporations, including AT&T, Bell, Alcoa, Celanese, Quaker Oats, United Airlines, Minolta, United Way, Rockwell International, and Warner Communications. Designer of commercial packages and government symbols, including President's White House Council for Energy Efficiency, 1981; U.S. Post office Art and Industry commemorative stamp, 1983. Architect and designer of world-wide network of Exxon/Esso gasoline stations, 1983. Designer of graphic symbols for over sixty motion pictures; creator of over forty motion picture titles; director of motion picture special sequences, short films, and feature films.

MEMBER: International Design Conference (board member); Alliance Graphique Internationale; American Institute of Graphic Arts; Academy of Motion Picture Arts and Sciences; National Humanities Faculty; National Society of Art Directors; Sundance Film Institute (board member); Society of Typographic Arts (Chicago); Association of Graphic Designers (Sweden).

AWARDS, HONORS: Awards for artistic and professional excellence from numerous museums and organizations, including Museu de Arte Moderno, Rio de Janeiro, Brazil, 1959; Philadelphia Museum of Art, 1960; New York Art Directors Hall of Fame, 1977; and American Institute of Graphic Arts, 1982. Received honorary fellowship from Bezalel Academy, Jerusalem, Israel, 1984, and honorary doctorates from the Philadelphia Museum College of Art and Los Angeles Art Center College of Design. Appointed honorary faculty member of Royal Designers for Industry by the Royal Society of Arts, England, 1965.

SAUL BASS

Poster for the film *The Man with the Golden Arm*, 1955.
(© Saul Bass. Reprinted with permission.)

Film honors include Grand Award from Venice Film Festival, 1965, for *Searching Eye;* Gold Hugo from Chicago Film Festival, 1966, for *From Here to There;* Academy Award from the Academy of Motion Picture Arts and Sciences, 1968, for *Why Man Creates;* Gold Medal from Moscow Film Festival, 1970; nominated for Academy Award, 1980, for *Solar Film,* and 1984, for *Quest.* Film retrospectives include Rotterdam Film Festival, 1981; Cinamatheque Francaise, Paris, 1982; and Zagreb Film Festival, Yugoslavia.

FILMS—Director: *The Searching Eye* (short film), 1965; *From Here to There* (short film), (1966); *Why Man Creates* (short film), 1968; *Phase IV* (feature film), 1974; *Notes on the Popular Arts* (short film), 1977; *The Solar Film* (short film), 1980; *Quest* (short film), 1984. Director of special sequences, including shower sequence in *Psycho,* 1960; final battle in *Spartacus,* 1960; races in *Grand Prix,* 1966. Also director of animated epilogue for *Around the World in Eighty Days,* 1956; live action epilogue for *West Side Story,* 1961.

Designer of graphic symbols: *Carmen Jones,* 1954; *Bonjour Tristesse,* 1956; *Saint Joan,* 1957; *Anatomy of a Murder,* 1959; *Advise and Consent,* 1962; *The Victors,* 1964; *Seconds,* 1966; *Such Good Friends,* 1974; *The Shining,* 1980.

Creator of motion picture titles: *The Man With the Golden Arm,* 1955; *The Seven Year Itch,* 1955; *The Big Country,*

1958; *Vertigo,* 1958; *North by Northwest,* 1959; *A Walk on the Wild Side,* 1962, *It's a Mad, Mad, Mad, Mad World,* 1963; *That's Entertainment, Part II,* 1974.

EXHIBITIONS: Represented in permanent collections of Museum of Modern Art, New York City; Library of Congress, Washington, D.C.; Smithsonian Institution, Washington, D.C.; Cooper-Hewitt Museum, New York City; Prague Museum, Czechoslavakia; Stedelijk Museum, Amsterdam, Netherlands. Participated in many one-man shows and group exhibits in the Unites States, Europe, South America, and the Far East.

SIDELIGHTS: According to Herb Yager, a friend of Saul Bass's from their East Bronx boyhood days, when Bass was still in his early teens, he constructed a mobile which promptly went on permanent exhibit in the living room of the family apartment. It received generally good reviews from neighbors and friends, but when the inevitable reservation was at last expressed by one visiting critic, the artist's

Poster for the 1984 Olympics. (© Saul Bass/Olympic Committee.)

proud mother was ready with a retort: "What did you expect?" she reportedly demanded; "It's not finished yet!" In many respects, Bass's subsequent career as a designer has been a continuation of that mobile—made up of an artist's creativity, an engineer's grasp of equipoise, a philosopher's sense of logic—and a constantly evolving creation in its own right.

Bass studied at the Art Students League at night and was working on the staff of a New York ad agency when, at age twenty-two, he came across a new book by Gyorgy Kepes called *Language of Vision*. The visual span and humanism of the book moved him deeply and thus when he heard that the book's author was giving a night-school course in design at Brooklyn College, he enrolled. This was to prove the turning point in his career. Impressed by his young student's eagerness, Kepes invited Bass to work with him on several projects after the coursework was completed. During the resulting association, Bass learned by practical application that truly effective design—that which is seamless, natural, obvious, and apparently the result of flash inspiration—is often the result of a difficult process of trial and error, and a careful piecing together of disparate elements into a meaningful mosaic.

In 1946, Bass moved to Los Angeles to take over direction of art activities for the west coast branch of Buchanan & Co., subsequently moving on to Foote, Cone & Belding in a similar capacity before striking out on his own in 1952 with the founding of Saul Bass & Associates, a design consulting firm. In the more than three decades since, Bass has worked successfully in such traditional design areas as space advertisements, package design, point-of-purchase displays, direct mail campaigns, and eventually in film and the development of corporate identity programs, counting among his clients some of America's largest corporations. The kindly, smiling gentleman in the broad-brimmed hat adorning the Quaker Oats box is a Bass creation, as is the narrow-waisted Wesson Oil bottle, and the new, high-tech AT&T globe.

In an insightful article in *Novum Gebrauchs*, Bass explained the process of developing corporate identities for two of the world's largest consumer concerns by analyzing the peculiar difficulties he faced in each instance. For United Airlines, he pointed out, the governing considerations were the highly competitive nature of the market and the importance of safety to the consumer; in the case of the Bell System, it was necessary to counteract the tendency of the consumer to associate the communications giant's semi-monopoly position with indifference and technological lag. In each case, Bass applied the Bauhaus dictum that design is as much a social as an artistic discipline to come up with the appropriate imagery for his clients. At this end of the design scale, artistic flair is clearly defined by logical analysis, but there is an area in which the name Saul Bass is synonymous with inventiveness and inspired achievement; film design.

Bass has produced posters, title sequences, multiple-image sequences within the narrative itself, and other elements of filmmaking. His association with the film industry began traditionally enough; he designed ad campaigns (poster and print ad art) for films. His work in this area was notable from the start for its effort to find the most succinct and reductive image to evoke the mood of a film and express its basic theme. In the course of doing this work for such films as Otto Preminger's *The Moon Is Blue*, he got the idea of

Trademark for AT&T.

making the heretofore unimaginative opening credits sequence a part of the film's narrative and using it to set the mood for what was to follow, much as he tried to do with his poster art. It was while working on the ad campaign for Preminger's 1954 release *Carmen Jones* that he came up with the rose-and-flame motif (beauty and consuming passion) and, as he recalls, presented it to Preminger with the suggestion "Why not make it move?" The adventurous director gave Bass the go-ahead and as *Life* noted in its February 7, 1964, issue, the result "set the movie world on its ears, and titles haven't been the same since."

Among Bass's most highly praised early achievements were his title sequences for *The Man With the Golden Arm* and *The Seven Year Itch*. These were essentially animated graphics. The stalking black cat montage at the beginning of *A Walk on the Wild Side* was his first live-action sequence, and it was so successful that it made the rather ordinary movie that succeeded it seem even more so to most critics, many of whom (like the *New Yorker*'s Brendan Gill) specifically singled his work for praise despite their general damnation of the film as a whole. As his skill and reputation grew, Bass inevitably was given the opportunity to work his multiple-image magic in the actual narrative portion of films. It is to Saul Bass that we also owe one of modern cinema's single most memorable sequences: the shower murder scene in Hitchcock's *Psycho*. Bass not only did the original storyboards for the sequence, but was allowed by Hitchcock to direct the shooting of the action that was to make movie history.

Bass had himself written and directed a number of short features, including the critically acclaimed *Why Man Creates,* and in 1974 he directed a full-length science-fiction feature entitled *Phase IV.* Of all his activities, his film-related works seem to sum up his strengths, both as a creator and a synthesizer, a problem solver and an artist. As a writer in *Film Comment* put it in a 1982 assessment of Bass's contribution to the cinema: "Every filmmaker must be an artist/salesman. Saul Bass is the medium's Bach and Barnum combined."

BIOGRAPHICAL/CRITICAL SOURCES: C. Sullivan, "The Work of Saul Bass," *American Artist,* October, 1954; "Movie (Titles) Mogul," *New York Times Magazine,* December 1, 1957; "The Man With the Golden Arm," *Time,* March 16, 1962; "Seen Any Good Titles Lately?" *Life,* February 7, 1964; E. Aison, "Saul Bass: The Designer as Film-Maker," *Print,* January, 1969; "The Complete Film-Maker; From Titles to Features," *American Cinematographer,* March, 1977; Herb Yager, "Saul Bass," *Graphis* No. 193, February-March, 1978; *Novum Gebrauchs,* December, 1978; *Film Comment,* May-June, 1982.

—*Sketch by Richard Calhoun*

BASSET, Gene   1927-

PERSONAL: Born July 24, 1927, in Brooklyn, N.Y.; married Ann Komatz, December 11, 1981; children: Darien Geraghty, Roger, Brian. *Education:* Brooklyn College, B.A., 1950; attended University of Missouri, Cooper Union, Art Students League, Pratt Institute. *Home:* 3210 Beechwood Dr., Marietta, Ga. 30067. *Office:* Atlanta Journal, 72 Marietta St., Atlanta, Ga. 30302.

CAREER: Editorial cartoonist, *Honolulu Star-Bulletin,* 1961-62; Scripps-Howard Newspapers, Washington, D.C., 1962-81; United Feature Syndicate (now United Media Services), 1972—; *Atlanta Journal,* 1982—. *Military service:* U.S. Coast Guard, 1944-46. *Member:* Association of American Editorial Cartoonists (president, 1973-74); National Cartoonists Society. *Awards, honors:* Best Editorial Cartoon, from Population Institute, 1974.

SIDELIGHTS: Since the early 1960s Gene Basset has enjoyed a career remarkable for its consistency and eclecticism. He has commented with smiling humor, even amounting at times to serenity, on all the major and minor mishaps, accidents, and catastrophes of the last quarter of a century, from the Vietnam war to the strength of the dollar abroad in the early 1980s. Perhaps newspaper readers in this shock-filled period in history need Basset's mildly disbelieving

"Okay Shultz, you drive. Weinberger, Clark and I will navigate."

Editorial cartoon. (© 1982, Gene Basset–United Feature Syndicate. Reprinted with permission.)

worldview. There is an amiability—almost a jauntiness—about his cartoons that make us consider even the worst outrages, such as civil-rights violations or international terrorism, with a deprecating smile.

To suit his argument Basset has perfected his own drawing style, a style, wrote Richard Marschall in *The World Encyclopedia of Cartoons*, which "seems at once derivative and startlingly original: there is something of the zaniness of *Mad* magazine in his concepts, and his lines are very loose without being sketchy or superfluous." Marschall noted that the artist draws "in the now-standard horizontal format on doubletone paper."

Basset often makes use of speech balloons instead of captions in his cartoons, and sometimes devises multi-panel cartoons (in comic-strip fashion) in order to build on a given situation and thus make the punch line in the last panel the more striking. The neatness and humor of Basset's cartoons have made them natural candidates for reprinting in such national magazines as *Newsweek* and *Time;* and they have often been broadcast (with a narrator's voice-over) on the *Mac-Neil-Lehrer News Hour's* Friday recap of the news of the week "as the cartoonists see it."

Gene's son, Brian Basset, is also an editorial cartoonist (with the *Seattle Times*) and the creator of the *Adam* newspaper strip about a "house husband."

BIOGRAPHICAL/CRITICAL SOURCES: The World Encyclopedia of Cartoons, Chelsea House, 1980; *Who's Who in American Art*, 16th edition, Bowker, 1984.

* * *

BEA (I FONT), Josep Maria 1942-
(Sanchez Zamora)

PERSONAL: Born March 11, 1942, in Barcelona, Spain; son of Jose (in business) and Modesta (Font) Bea; married Mariana Bellido Martinez (a publishing executive). *Education:* Attended Escuela Superior de Artes, Barcelona; Academie Julian, Paris, France; Universidad Central de Barcelona. *Home:* Calle Paris, 45-47, Barcelona, Spain. *Studio and office:* Ronda San Antonio, 49, Barcelona, Spain.

CAREER: Illustrator, cartoonist, and scriptwriter, 1956—; co-publisher, *Rambla* (a comic magazine), 1982-84; founder and publisher, Intermagen, 1984—. *Military service:* Spanish Army, 1963, served in infantry. *Awards, honors:* Warren Publishing Company annual award, New York City, 1973; Club de Amigos de la Historieta annual award, Barcelona, 1980; "1984" Award, Barcelona, 1980, 1981.

WRITINGS—All books of comics: *Les nuits de l'epouvante* (title means "The Nights of Terror"), Dargaud, France, 1978; *Historias de Taberna Galactica* (title means "Tales from the Galactic Tavern"), Toutain, Barcelona, 1981; *En un lugar de la mente* (title means "In a Place of the Mind"), Garcia & Bea, Barcelona, 1983; *En un lugar de la mente-II*, Garcia & Bea, 1984; *La esfera cubica* (title means "The Cubic Sphere"), Garcia & Bea, 1984.

Under the pseudonym Sanchez Zamora; all published by Intermagen, Barcelona, in 1985: *Once nombres* (title means

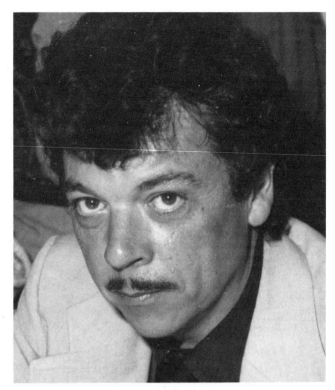

JOSEP MARIA BEA

"Eleven Names"); *El estado de Joey* (title means "Joey's Estate"); *Mediterraneo.*

EXHIBITIONS—All of paintings: Gallery Ten Flowers, U.S., 1970; Colegio de Arquitectos de Barcelona, 1970; Sorbonne, Paris, 1971; Ayuntamiento de Bagur, Gerona, Spain, 1972.

WORK IN PROGRESS: A didactic series in twelve weekly pamphlets on the techniques involved in the production of comics, to be published in 1985.

SIDELIGHTS: Josep Bea started work in the comics field with Josep Toutain's agency in Barcelona, Selecciones Ilustradas, with comics designed for the British market, and later (1971-75) for James Warren's magazines in New York. He can be considered to have come into his own with the series *Sir Leo,* published in the Spanish magazine *Dracula* in 1971, and later translated into French and English. Immediately afterwards he became a notable influence in the fields of horror and fantasy as a scriptwriter as well as an artist with his contributions to Warren's magazines *Creepy, Eerie,* and *Vampirella.* After creating the short series *Peter Hipnos* (1973-74), he started his acclaimed series of science-fiction tales *Historias de Taberna Galactica* in the Spanish magazine *1984* (some of these tales have been published in the United States by *Heavy Metal*).

Historias de la Taberna Galactica is Bea's major accomplishment. From George Lucas's movie, *Star Wars,* he took the idea of a science-fictional tavern in which beings from different species and morphologies would meet. Each of these tales is framed by the Galactic Tavern locale, in which a different patron contributes one tale for the edification and

entertainment of all. Started in 1979, the series ended in 1981 with the closing of the tavern on account of financial difficulties. A double perspective informs this series, with the habitual use of the tale-within-a-tale technique, and its frequent satire of science-fiction comics.

As an author with a high intellectual tact and a perverse sense of humor, Bea has developed a series of tales that reflect social and psychological contexts present in the modern world, and that lend themselves to all kinds of interpretations. The formula of having such a disparate assembly of beings in a tavern, all narrating their experiences, recalls group therapy. The tavern clients, however, arrive not at catharsis, but at a general skepticism, in which each of them glamorizes his own nostalgias, and puts down those of the others. It is significant that the series ends on a sarcastic note, with the characters all protesting the hermetism of the last tale.

Bea's next series, *En un lugar de la mente,* also first published in *1984* (1981-82), consists of a number of tales as well, but without a common framework. These stories are told with a high sense of satire and poetry, and combine humor with dream-like narrative. As the co-publisher of *Rambla,* Bea could give vent even more to his personal fantasizings and the extremes of his imagination, with such creations as *La esfera cubica* (1982), *La Muralla* ("The Wall," 1983), *Siete vidas* ("Seven Lives," 1984), the last two in the form of animal strips having as protagonist the cat Gatony.

A page from *Historias de Taberna Galactica.* (© 1980, Josep Maria Bea. Reprinted with permission.)

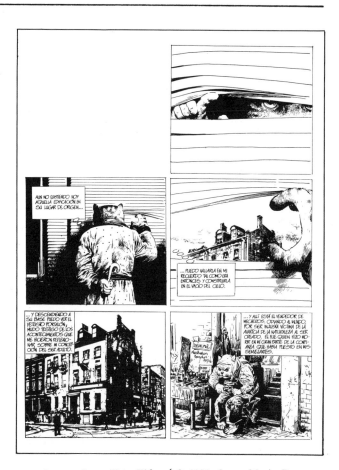

A **page from** *Siete Vidas.* (© 1984, Josep Maria Bea. Reprinted with permission.)

In 1983 Bea embarked on a new direction, with a much simpler graphic line (inspired by the French woman cartoonist Chantal Montellier) and themes centered on everyday life, with emphasis on the erotic. In these works he used the pen name "Sanchez Zamora." *El estado de Joey,* based on the formula of the continuity strip, has been his most interesting creation in this genre. With this departure, Bea temporarily forsook what had been one of his major virtues: the rich density of his compositions made of complex images subject to different interpretations. On this score the author offered the following comment about his work: "There exist half-open doors that are the consequence of ignorance, error or inaccuracy, and which give us the possibility of witnessing the palpable presence of other realities. I have occasionally passed through those doors. Beyond them lies the material with which I have organized my stories."

BIOGRAPHICAL/CRITICAL SOURCES: The World Encyclopedia of Comics, Chelsea House, 1976; Javier Coma, ed., *Historia de los Comics,* Toutain, Barcelona, 1983.

—*Sketch by Javier Coma*

* * *

BEIMAN, Nancy 1957-

PERSONAL: Surname is pronounced "Bee-man"; born September 20, 1957, in Jersey City. N.J.; daughter of

33

Melvyn (a computer programmer) and Frances (a librarian; maiden name Rubin) Beiman. *Education:* California Institute of the Arts, B.F.A., 1979. *Home:* 14 Horatio St., New York, N.Y. 10014.

CAREER: Animator, Zander Associates, 1979-82; designer, Walt Disney Productions, merchandising department, 1983-84; freelance animator, Rick Reinert Productions, 1982—; freelance designer, Henson Associates, 1983—; illustrator, Angelsoft Inc. 1985—. *Member:* Motion Picture Screen Cartoonists, Local 841, National Cartoonists Society, ASIFA-East, Cartoonists Guild, Graphic Artists Guild, "Sons of the Desert" society.

FILMS: (Animator and director) *Your Feet's Too Big*, 1984; (animator) *Gnomes*, 1980; *Winnie the Pooh and a Day for Eeyore*, 1983; *The Bollo Caper*, 1984. Also animator of many television commercials and of opening title for *Bugs Bunny Show*, Warner Bros. video, 1985.

EXHIBITIONS: Permanent collection of Museum of Cartoon Art, Port Chester, N.Y.

WORK IN PROGRESS: An animated film entitled *Hitchhikers from Mars*.

SIDELIGHTS: Nancy Beiman wrote *CGA:* "I became an animator because of stage fright. I've always loved film and have wanted to work in the business for as long as I can remember. Animation's advantage over live film is obvious: you can do absolutely anything with it. I'm not restricted to female parts (or human ones for that matter). Everything is planned meticulously in advance, and the set always stays up. You don't even need to be at a studio to do it—I work out of a walk-in closet in my apartment. It's the ultimate fantasy; you can become 'something' other than what you are.

"Animals are my favorite subjects, not only because of their potential as caricatures of humans, but also because of the fascinating ways in which they move. I contribute to nearly all the major wildlife foundations. The nice thing about animation, however, is that literally any field of study, no matter how exotic, can be useful when doing it.

"Animation is considered 'kid stuff' in this country, which is a pity. Nearly everyone likes cartoons, but no one ever lists a film like *Pinocchio* on a list of ten best films of all time (and it certainly belongs there). In addition, the storylines of most current productions often make me wonder why I spent four years in college to make pacifiers for feebleminded children. I have been fortunate enough to work on some excellent films, but they are the exception not the rule.

"There are many talented people in the U.S. who would love to work on worthwhile productions, but the Saturday morning stuff pays the bills. Although it still has bright spots, American animation appears to have progressed from infancy directly to senility. The only way out is to make your own films, which I have done and will continue to do in the future."

In her junior year of high school, Nancy Beiman made a cut-out animated film for her English class. "I decided there

Self-portrait of Nancy Beiman with Harry the Elephant. (© 1984, Nancy Beiman. Printed with permission.)

and then, that I liked the field and I wanted to do it for a living", she told *Cartoonist Profiles*. Her love and talent for animation led to a scholarship at the California Institute of the Arts.

Enrolled in the newly formed character animation program, sponsored by Walt Disney Productions, she learned her craft under Disney veterans Jack Hannah, T. Hee, Elmer Plummer, Bill Moore, and Ken O'Connor. Her first paying job in the animation industry came during her summer vacation in her third year of college. For Ralph Bakshi she worked in various capacities on the film *Lord Of The Rings*.

Returning to the New York area in 1979, Beiman joined Zander Associates as staff animator, lending her talents to many television commercials, including spots for Dime Savings Bank and Hamm's Beer. She was principal animator for Zander's television special *Gnomes* (1980).

Leaving Zander in 1982 to freelance, she completed her personal film *Your Feet's Too Big* in 1983. This musical short, featuring the song of the same title by "Fats" Waller, has run on television and in festivals, winning the best animation award at ASIFA-East's festival in 1984 and a CINE Golden Eagle from the U.S. government.

California-based Rick Reinert Productions has farmed out much freelance work to Beiman in recent years, including commercials featuring Dr. Seuss's characters and award-winning public service spots starring Cap'n O.G. Readmore.

Reinert's company produced animation for Walt Disney Productions, and Beiman was principal animator for the

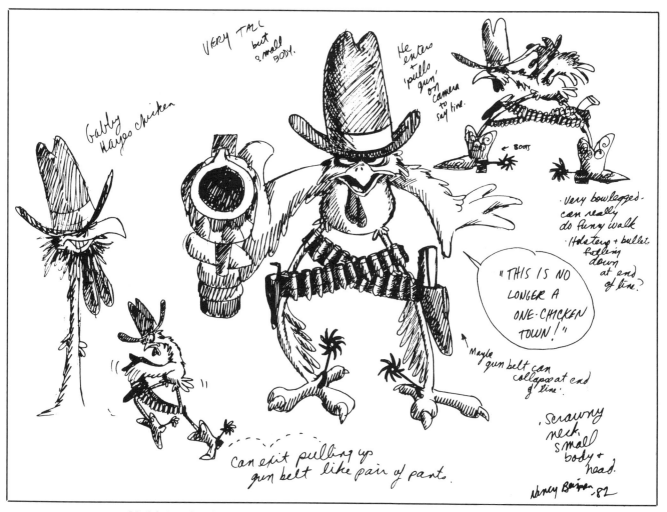

Model sheet for *Cowboy Chickens*. (© 1982, Nancy Beiman. Printed with permission.)

theatrical short *Winnie the Pooh and a Day for Eeyore* (1983). In addition, she animated station breaks for cable television's Disney Channel and a series of educational films featuring Donald Duck for Disney World's EPCOT Center. Beiman's recent work includes the television special *The Bollo Caper* for the American Broadcasting Company and the latest Bugs Bunny titles for video.

In addition to her animation work, Beiman has designed characters for Walt Disney Productions' character merchandise division, and has designed products using Jim Henson's Muppets. She also does book and magazine illustration.

AVOCATIONAL INTERESTS: Books, comedy films (particularly silent comedies), fine wood furniture, caricature.

BIOGRAPHICAL/CRITICAL SOURCES: Cartoonist Profiles, June, 1982; Leonard Maltin, *The Disney Films* (revised edition), Crown, 1985.

* * *

BERG, Dave
    See BERG, David

BERG, David   1920-
(Dave Berg)

PERSONAL: Born June 12, 1920, in Brooklyn, N.Y.; son of Morris Isaac (a builder) and Bessie (a dressmaker; maiden name Friedman) Berg; married Vivian Lipman (an artist, writer, and agent), March 3, 1949; children: Mitchel Ian, Nancy Ann Iva. *Education:* Studied at Pratt Institute, New School for Social Research, Cooper Union, and Art Students League. *Politics:* Registered Democrat. *Religion:* Hebrew. *Home:* 14021 Marquesas Way, No. 3070, Marina Del Rey, Calif., 90292. *Office: Mad*, 485 Madison Ave., New York, N.Y. 10022. *Agent:* S. Minanel Agency, 14021 Marquesas Way, Marina Del Rey, Calif. 90292.

CAREER: Background artist, Will Eisner Productions, New York, N.Y., 1940-41; writer/artist, Captain Marvel Comics, New York, N.Y., 1941; writer/artist, Marvel Comics, New York, N.Y., 1946-56; writer/artist, Archie Comics, New York, N.Y., 1950; writer/artist, *Mad*, New York, N.Y., 1956-; creative consultant, NBC-TV, New York, N.Y., 1978. Field commissioner, Boy Scouts of America, 1950-1975; Little League coach, 1962. *Military service:* U.S. Army Air Forces, 1942-46, served in Chemical Warfare unit; served as war correspondent on Iwo Jima, Guam, and

Self-caricature of Dave Berg. (Printed with permission.)

Saipan, and in Japan; became sergeant. *Member:* Authors Guild, Writers Guild West, National Cartoonists Society, Marina Del Rey B'nai B'rith Lodge (president, 1985-86).

AWARDS, HONORS: Th.D. (Hon.), Reconstructionist Rabbinical College, 1973; "Chair of Great Cartoonists" from University of California, Los Angeles, student body,

1975; B'nai B'rith Youth Services Award, 1978; David Berg Day proclaimed in Westchester County, N.Y., 1978.

WRITINGS: Mad's Dave Berg Looks at the USA, New American Library, 1964, reissued, Warner, 1977; *Mad's Dave Berg Looks at Things*, New American Library, 1967, reissued, Warner, 1974; *Mad's Dave Berg Looks at People*, New American Library, 1966; *Mad's Dave Berg Looks at Modern Thinking*, New American Library, 1969, reissued, Warner, 1976; *Mad's Dave Berg Looks at Our Sick World*, New American Library, 1971; *My Friend God*, New American Library, 1972; *Mad's Dave Berg Looks at Living*, Warner, 1973; *Roger Kaputnik and God*, New American Library, 1974; *Mad's Dave Berg Looks Around*, Warner, 1975; *Mad's Dave Berg Takes a Loving Look*, Warner, 1977; *Dave Berg's Mad Trash*, Warner, 1977, reissued, 1981; *Mad's Dave Berg Looks, Listens and Laughs*, Warner, 1979; *Mad's Dave Berg Looks at You*, Warner, 1982; *Mad's Dave Berg Looks at the Neighborhood*, Warner, 1984.

EXHIBITIONS: Permanent collections of Ohio State University and Museum of Cartoon Art, Port Chester, N.Y. One man show in New Rochelle, N.Y.; New York Public Library exhibition, 1974; *Mad* Art Exhibit, Rockefeller Plaza, New York, N.Y., 1984.

WORK IN PROGRESS: Mad's Dave Berg Looks at Our Planet.

SIDELIGHTS: At the age of three, Dave Berg reportedly returned home from a family get-together, took up a pencil, and began to attempt to draw the day's events as he had seen them. "My parents thought they had a talented child," he remembers; "That shows what kind of judges they were." All self- and filial-deprecation aside, he firmly credits his eastern European immigrant parents and the poor Brooklyn ghetto into which he was born (and which as a boy he was so determined to escape) with affording him the encouragement and support, both emotional and intellectual, that

"The Lighter Side of ... Divorce." (© *Mad Magazine.*)

"The Lighter Side of . . . Sports." (© *Mad Magazine*.)

would ultimately make him one of America's best known graphic humorists. Indeed, it is the influence of these early days that Berg cites in explaining his success, as one who not only amuses with his witty commentary on middle-class, suburban culture but instructs and enlightens as well. This reputation has won him an honorary theological degree, an honorary professorial chair in cartooning, and made him a perennial favorite on the college lecture circuit.

Given the appropriate foundations at home and in the public schools, Berg began early to develop his talents as an artist, and more importantly, as he sees it, as a writer. At the age of twelve, he won a scholarship to Pratt Institute where he attended Saturday morning classes with other talented students. He continued his concentration on art, even after his father died and he was forced to drop most of his other extracurricular activities in order to help support his family by after-school work. He drew cartoons for his high school newspaper and wrote humorous poems and stories for the literary magazines. Upon graduation, Berg parlayed these experiences into a job in the fledgling comic book industry as a background artist for Will Eisner's seminal *Spirit* series, which featured one of the finest of the early comic book detective heroes. It was while working for Eisner that Berg learned what he believes to have been his key lesson: "I realized that there are many good artists, but good writers are at a premium. So I concentrated on what was once a hobby, writing." With time out for military service during World War II, he continued his work on comic books as writer/illustrator between 1940 and 1956. His assignments included such features as *Captain Marvel, Combat Kelly,* and *Archie.*

In 1956, however, following several years of coaxing by editor Al Feldstein, he moved to *Mad,* the zany satire magazine. There he developed his signature "Berg's Eye View" feature entitled *The Lighter Side of . . .* "[*Mad*'s contributors] were satirizing commercials, movies and TV programs," Berg explains. "I added something new—

People. That's when 'The Lighter Side' was born. It was more than just gags, it was a psychological and sociological study of the human condition, and truth in humor." His material for the almost thirty-year-old series has come from personal experience, observations of friends and associates, books, and the media. His style has been gentle mockery rather than Swiftian satire.

The true test of Berg's success is to measure how consistent he has been over the years in capturing the changing moods and preoccupations of that segment of American society that, for better or worse, defines our national culture. Thus, two treatments of *The Lighter Side of TV,* separated by almost twenty years, allow one to contrast the naive, innocent, family-style fascination with the tube characteristic of the 1950s and early 1960s, when the most erotic material was to be found in cosmetic commercials, with the technological sophistication (not to say jadedness) of the "wired" 1980s, when cable television supplies music videos to adolescents, X-rated erotica to adults, and sex and violence to all ages.

Berg's artwork is clean and carefully drafted, and employs the device of caricature—by which he means "slightly exaggerated realism"—to illustrate substance he describes as "slightly exaggerated truth." There are frequent appearances by Berg's bespectacled, pipe-smoking alter ego, "Roger Kaputnik," and a full-bearded, pudgy, and eccentric figure suspiciously resembling *Mad* publisher William M. Gaines can often be found wandering through the panels of an installment. Additionally, his loving rendering of the female form—long-legged, wasp-waisted, high-busted—has resulted in invitations to serve as judge at the annual Miss America Pageant. But it is his homelier asides on the joys and miseries of such subjects as summer camp, adolescence, dating, parents, and school that have kept two generations of *Mad*'s youthful readership devoted fans of *The Lighter Side of . . .* feature, and made of its creator something of a campus oracle.

"So much is written about abnormal psychology and nothing is said about being normal," he has said, speculating on the sources of his widespread popularity. "Very few books are about normal people and I am writing about normalcy—that which is average." More than that, he is careful not to take sides, but prefers to play the role of an often baffled, generally harassed "everyman," observant, to be sure, but not necessarily wiser than any other thoughtful human being when it comes to providing explanations and solutions. Still, someone has to ask the relevant questions, and this Berg sees as his function. Art and humor, he insists, are not ends in themselves, but merely tools which he hopes to use to heighten the awareness of his fellow-man to the dangers he sees as inherent in the human condition, to proclaim to all, as he puts it, "Hey, world, cut it out!" Observing (as befits the grandson of a rabbi) that people have rarely listened to the rantings of the traditional prophets, Berg has settled upon a less direct way of disseminating his teachings. "I'm an angry man," he declares, "but by the time I get through drawing these things, I've sugar coated them and the anger is no longer there." The lesson that mankind is more prone to foible than perfection, however, continues to come through loud and clear.

BIOGRAPHICAL/CRITICAL SOURCES: Cartoonists Profiles, February, 1970; *The World Encyclopedia of Comics*, Chelsea House, 1976; *Something About the Author*, Vol. 27, Gale, 1982; *Contemporary Authors*, New Revision Series, Vol. 10, Gale, 1983; *Who's Who in America*, 1984-85; *Who's Who in the World*, 1984-85; *Who's Who in World Jewry*, 1984-85.

—Sketch by Richard Calhoun

* * *

BERNET (CUSSO), Jordi   1944-
(Jordi)

PERSONAL: Born June 14, 1944, in Barcelona, Spain; son of Miguel (a humor strip cartoonist under the pseudonym Jorge, his son's name translated from Catalan to Spanish) and Carmen (Cusso) Bernet; married Amalia Royo Valls; son: Arnau. *Education:* Primary school. *Home and studio:* Burriana 1, 08030 Barcelona, Spain. *Agents:* Rafael Martinez, Agencia Norma, Alí Bey 11, 08010 Barcelona, Spain; Josep Toutain, Selecciones Ilustradas, Diagonal 325, 08009 Barcelona, Spain.

CAREER: Humor cartoonist, continuing the comic strip created by his father, *Doña Urraca,* 1960-61; freelance cartoonist and illustrator, 1962—. *Military service:* Spanish Army, 1965, served in artillery. *Awards, honors:* Critics Award "1984," Barcelona, Spain, 1982; Club de Amigos de la Historieta, Barcelona, 1983; "1984" Award, 1984.

WRITINGS—All books of comics: *Andrax-Experiment des Grauens* (title means "The Experiment in Terror"), Rolf Kauka (West Germany), 1974; (under pseudonym Jordi) several titles in the *Paul Foran* series, Dupuis (Belgium), 1976; *Torpedo 1936-I,* Catalan Communications (United States), Toutain (Spain), 1984; *Sarvan,* Norma (Spain),

1984; *Torpedo 1936-II,* Catalan Communications, Toutain, 1985; *Kraken,* Toutain, 1985.

EXHIBITIONS: 8° Convegno Internazionale del Fumetto e del Fantastico, Prato, Italy, 1985.

WORK IN PROGRESS: A series on scripts by the Argentine writer Carlos Trillo; further volumes of *Torpedo 1936.*

SIDELIGHTS: The necessity for Jordi Bernet to start working at an early age, following his father's untimely death in 1960, caused him to serve a long apprenticeship unmotivated by aesthetic considerations. On the other hand his interest pointed in the direction of the American story strips, and this led him away from his father's teachings in the field of graphic humor. In consequence he developed his artistic abilities in a quasi-didactic manner, coming above all under the influence of Frank Robbins, to which was added much later that of Joe Kubert. Working on other people's scripts, Bernet focused his objective on the narrative line—more than on the drawing as such—especially in the way he arranged his images in sequence, following the example of Milton Caniff and his disciples. In the drawing of his characters he started to adopt Kubert's anatomical models, but in his editing, as well as in his use of black and his lighting, he remained faithful to Robbins's strip structure and graphic technique. Bernet is currently the Spanish artist who comes closest to the classicism of the story strips published in American newspapers. The skillful breakdown of his pages into panels can be likened to the movement of the camera in filmmaking.

JORDI BERNET

Bernet's professional apprenticeship found its outlet in works done for other lands, in a period—the 1960s—when various Spanish agencies supplied an abundant production of comics on scripts provided by foreign publishers. Bernet first illustrated numerous stories for such British publishers as Fleetway and Thomson, through the Barcelona agency Bardon Art. In 1967 he received an offer from Dupuis publishers to collaborate on the Belgian magazine *Spirou*, where for the first time he signed his work (as "Jordi"). That was the time of *Paul Foran*, of *Dan Lacombe* (on scripts by his uncle Miguel Cusso), and others. He later returned to Bardon Art, doing for the German magazine *Pip* a series with a sexy protagonist, *Wat 69*, and taking charge of the sword-and-sorcery strip *Andrax* (1972) to which he brilliantly imparted his own stamp. Despite this, Bernet mainly turned out potboilers for the rest of the decade; aside from *El cuervo* (title means "the Raven") which he drew along with Jose Ortiz on scripts by Andreu Martin for Selecciones Ilustradas, he contributed countless Western and crime stories to Italian publications. At the beginning of the 1980s he was practically unknown in Spain, the country where he had lived from birth. Then a great opportunity presented itself, in the aftermath of the prestige—cultural and critical—acquired by the comics after dictator Francisco Franco's death and the end of his regime's very strict censorship system.

The Spanish agent and publisher Josep Toutain had been producing a series of comics on a criminal theme, *Torpedo*

A page from *Torpedo 1936*. (© 1985, Jordi Bernet. Reprinted with permission.)

1936, which took place in the America of the 1930s and had a professional criminal as its protagonist; it was written by the Spaniard Enrique Sínchez Abulí and drawn by the American Alex Toth. After the first two episodes, published in February and March 1982 in Toutain's magazine *Creepy*, Toth left and was replaced by Bernet who gave this series of hard and cynical tales a notable sense of time and place and a brilliant narrative dynamism, endowing his panels with great expressive intensity, an enormous inner drive, and an unrelenting sense of movement.

Without abandoning *Torpedo 1936*, Bernet has in recent years increased his creative activity through other series that were first published in Spanish comics magazines before being translated in other countries. With the scriptwriter Antonio Segura and in the pages of *Cimoc* he finished *Sarvan* (1982-83), with an attractive female character and in a climate of fantastic adventure reminiscent of *Andrax*; with the same writer he created *Kraken*, a series which took place in the immense sewer system of a great city run by a suicidal technology, and which had for its protagonist the police lieutenant Dante, always under the menace of the monster that gave the work its title (this was published in the short-lived magazine *Metropol* in 1983-84). In that latter year he developed *De vuelta a casa* (title means "Coming Home"), on scripts by Sanchez Abuli, for the magazine *Zona 84:* it is a futuristic thriller that starts with an escape from a prison-planet and involves the subsequent manhunt for the fugitives led by a relentless dwarf.

A page from *Kraken*. (© 1984, Jordi Bernet. Reprinted with permission.)

"I believe I do well with strong, hard themes, in which there is much movement," Bernet told *CGA*. "In this field I think that, in my already long career, I have played on all possible variations of the action and adventure genres." He further explained the motives of his transition from hired hand to *auteur* in the 1980s: "Only for economic reasons could I endure working for Italian publications with no artistic ambitions. In the end I decided that I had already spent too much time working for foreign publications, while I was a complete unknown in my own country. At the same time, Spain had changed; there no longer existed the suffocating censorship of a dictatorial regime. One could create important works of comics there. Twenty years had elapsed since the last time I had published my drawings in Spain, and I had the desire to come back."

An exile, in a professional sense, for two decades, Bernet, since his return to Spanish publication, has successfully acquired an international following and world-wide acclaim. In the United States he has been known and appreciated for years by readers of *Heavy Metal*; and the publication in this country of his first two *Torpedo 1936* books has been greeted with both popular and critical kudos. The American public can therefore expect to hear even more from Jordi Bernet in the future.

BIOGRAPHICAL/CRITICAL SOURCES: The World Encyclopedia of Comics, Chelsea House, 1976; Javier Coma, ed., *Historia de los Comics*, Toutain, 1983.

—*Sketch by Javier Coma*

* * *

BERRY, William A(ugustus) 1933-

PERSONAL: Born September 29, 1933, in Jacksonville, Tex. *Education:* University of Texas at Austin, B.F.A., 1955; University of Southern California, M.F.A., 1957; attended Universita per i Stranieri, Perugia, Italy, 1955, and Il Circolo Artistico Internazionale, Rome, Italy, 1955-56. *Home:* 908 Edgewood Ave., Columbia, Mo. 65201. *Office:* Department of Fine Arts, University of Missouri, Columbia, Mo. 65211.

CAREER: Acting curator of the Art Gallery, University of Southern California, Los Angeles, Calif., 1957; freelance illustrator and painter, New York City, 1959-68; assistant professor of art, University of Texas at Austin, 1968-74; associate professor of art, Boston University School of Visual Art, 1974-78; professor of art, University of Missouri, Columbia, Mo., 1978—. Graphic artist, writer, lecturer. *Member:* American Institute of Graphic Arts, College Art Association of America.

AWARDS, HONORS: Citation of Merit from New York Society of Illustrators, 1965, 1967, 1970; third prize for drawing, Art Annual, Tulsa, Okla., 1980; Meritorious Award, Boulder Center for the Visual Arts, 1982; Active Sponsor Award, Mid-Four, Kansas City Art Institute, 1983; Weldon Spring Award, University of Missouri, 1984; second prize for drawing, Montana Institute of the Arts, 1984; and many others.

WRITINGS: (With Norman Krinsky) *Paper Construction for Children*, Reinhold, 1966; *Drawing the Human Form*, Van Nostrand, 1977.

Illustrator and/or designer: *The Book of Knowledge Annual*, Grolier, 1962; Tom Wicker, *Kennedy Without Tears*, Morrow, 1964; Gene Smith, *Still Quiet on the Western Front*, Morrow, 1965; Lael Tucker Wertenbaker and Maude Basserman, *The Hotchkiss School: A Portrait*, Hotchkiss School, 1966; Carter Wilson, *On Firm Ice*, Education Development Center, 1967 (new edition, Thomas Y. Crowell, 1969); Israel Rogosin, *The Quest for the Righteous*, Yeshiva University, 1968; *A Journey to the Arctic*, Education Development Center, 1969; Kelly Fearing, et al., *The Creative Eye*, W. S. Benson, 1969; Kelly Fearing, et al., *Art and the Creative Teacher*, W. S. Benson, 1971.

Also author of many papers and articles.

EXHIBITIONS—One-man shows: Galleria Schneider, Rome, Italy, 1956; USIA Gallery, Athens, Greece, 1959; AFME Gallery, New York City, 1964; Middle East House, Washington, D.C., 1967; Gallery of Southwest Texas State University, San Marcos, Tex., 1971; Southwestern University Art Gallery, Georgetown, Tex., 1972; Luther College, Decorah, Iowa, 1982; Muscarelle Museum of Art, College of William and Mary, Williamsburg, Va., 1984. Group exhibitions include: Philadelphia Museum of Art, 1955; Dallas Museum of Fine Arts, 1957; Galeria Senatore, Stuttgart, Germany, 1959; Hammer Gallery, New York City, 1960; Janet Nessler Gallery, New York City, 1961; "American Drawings IV" (a Smithsonian Institution traveling exhibition), 1983-84; Nelson-Atkins Museum of Art, Kansas City, Mo., 1983; Altos de Chavon, Dominican Republic, 1983.

SIDELIGHTS: A successful university art teacher for close to twenty years, and an outstanding artist and illustrator for over twenty-five, William Berry has never lost his love for drawing. "I believe that there is an even deeper satisfaction in drawing from life, which is felt before the drawing is completed," he wrote in the preface to his book, *Drawing the Human Form*. "During the intense period of concentration required by drawing, thoughts unrelated to the activity of drawing temporarily disappear. I have noticed, for instance, that as I become more aware of the model and of my drawing, I become less aware of myself. And the contemplation of the form of the model, a fellow human being, may be compared to an act of humility in which the artist temporarily forgets his or her physical frailties and imperfections and marvels at the diversity possible within the human form."

Berry has traveled extensively to Italy, Latin America, and the Middle East. His drawings and photographs of people and places of the latter region were widely exhibited, and many were reproduced in *Al-Majal*, the Arabic-language publication of the U.S. Information Agency. The artist has also contributed a great number of cover and interior illustrations for such leading publications as *Newsweek, Esquire, Harper's, TV Guide*, the *New York Times*, the *Reporter*, and *Holiday*, as well as dust-jacket designs for Random House, Doubleday, Scribner's, Van Nostrand and other book publishers. In addition, he was the first art director of *Texas Monthly* in 1972-73, during which time it was awarded the best magazine prize in the category of specialized journalism by the Columbia University School of Journalism.

Teaching, however, has been Berry's principal occupation for most of the past two decades, and he has given college courses in drawing from the model, illustration, basic and graphic design, lettering and typography, painting, and color theory. His years of teaching and lecturing culminated in the publication of *Drawing the Human Form*, a guide to drawing from life and a manual that seeks to integrate the theory and history of drawing with its step-by-step practice.

BIOGRAPHICAL/CRITICAL SOURCES: "Bill Berry Paints the Arab World," *Al-Majal*, No. 2, 1967; Susan E. Meyer, "William A. Berry, Illustrator/Painter," *American Artist*, March, 1970; *Illustrators '70 (The Annual of American Illustration)*, Society of Illustrators, 1970; William A. Berry, *Drawing the Human Form*, Van Nostrand, 1977; Cynthia Wehling, "The Creative Mr. Berry," *Search*, (University of Missouri magazine) winter, 1984; *Who's Who in American Art*, 16th edition, Bowker, 1984.

* * *

BINDIG, Bob
    See BINDIG, Robert Kuhn

* * *

BINDIG, Robert Kuhn   1920-
    (Bob Bindig)

PERSONAL: Born December 21, 1920, in Buffalo, N.Y.; son of Otto Robert (a grocer) and Julia (Kuhn) Bindig; married Dorris Krull, December 27, 1941; children: David Alan, Terry Lynn Bindig Skura, Mark Scott, Wendy Sue Bindig McCormick, Amy Elizabeth. *Education:* Graduated from Buffalo Technical High School, 1939; completed Raye Burns correspondence course in cartooning, 1940. *Politics:* Registered Republican ("leans toward conservatism"). *Religion:* Protestant. *Home:* 6166 Powers Rd., Orchard Park, N.Y. 14127.

CAREER: Art department trainee, *Buffalo Evening News*, Buffalo, N.Y., 1939-40; artist, advertising department, E. W. Edwards department store, Buffalo, 1940-43; advertising artist, Roizen Advertising Agency, Buffalo, 1946-53 (chief art director, 1948-53); assistant art director, Landscheft & Barber (later Barber & Drullard) Advertising Agency, Buffalo, 1953-57; freelance advertising artist and illustrator, 1957-82; instructor in cartooning, University of Buffalo, 1979-81; creative director, Flagler & Nelson Advertising Agency, Buffalo, 1982—. *Military service:* U.S. Army, 1943-46, became staff sergeant. *Member:* Boy Scouts of America (Scout leader, 1957-74), Campfire (instructor, 1957-74), National Cartoonists Society, Art Directors Club of Buffalo. *Awards, honors:* Inkpot Award for Outstanding Achievement in Fandom Projects/Services, San Diego Comics Convention, 1982.

WRITINGS—Illustrator; children's books: Donald Lewis Edwards and Shirley Edwards, *What the Fox Did Not Know*, Kenworthy Educational Service, 1959; D. L. Edwards and

Bob Bindig as Ludwig von Digbin, drawn by Milton Caniff. (© Milton Caniff.)

S. Edwards, *A Coat for Gray-One*, Kenworthy, 1959; published together in one volume as *Animal Stories for Beginning Readers*, Kenworthy, 1967. Creator of features for periodicals, including "Trivia Quiz" for *Menomonee Falls Gazette*, 1967-75, "Robert's Ramblings" and "Inspector Close Presents . . ." for *The Funnies Paper*, 1984—. Associate editor of *Strip Scene*, 1977-84; consulting editor of *Nemo*, 1983-84.

SIDELIGHTS: Bob Bindig's name and advertising art have been a familiar part of the Buffalo business scene for almost half a century. Fresh out of high school, in 1939, Bindig's art career began with an offer of fifty-three dollars a week from the *Buffalo Evening News*—a munificent sum in those just-post-Depression days. He leaped at the chance, only to learn that he was to be paid "three dollars in cash and fifty dollars in experience." He profited from that experience, however, and within the year rose to the princely salary of eight dollars a week.

The rigorous training of this year with the *News* prepared him for his first job in advertising, and he spent the next three years doing newspaper layouts and illustrations for the E. W. Edwards department store in Buffalo. He learned every aspect of commercial art, including, when business was slack, window decoration.

But a three-year stint in the army focused his ambitions and interests. A correspondence-course in cartooning he had taken after high-school prompted him to seek out art work in the army, and in Korea he was assigned to do a

The Mischievous Twin Bears, a comic strip drawn in Korea, 1946. (© Bob Bindig. Reprinted with permission.)

pantomime comic strip for a Seoul newspaper. *The Mischievous Twin Bears*, a lively eight-panel animal strip, entertained Korean children and adults alike for several months before he was discharged in 1946 and returned to the commercial art scene in Buffalo.

His old boss at Edwards had opened his own agency, and Bindig had sold some freelance work to him while he was still doing department-store window displays; so when he left the army, he joined Roizen and soon became its art director. Four years later, he took a cut in title but a raise in pay to become assistant art director with a much larger firm,

and after four years with Landscheft & Barber he felt he was ready to make it on his own. For the next twenty-six years, Bob Bindig ranged through the western New York area as one of its most versatile and imaginative freelance commercial artists.

During this period, Bindig designed the logo for the Buffalo Bisons baseball team (his very determined-looking bison swinging a baseball bat remains their emblem), created advertising campaigns for many of the major industries of the Niagara Frontier, and did two covers for the *Buffalo Courier-Express Magazine* (June 8 and September 7, 1975).

His work appeared in such national magazines as the *Saturday Evening Post* and *Organic Gardening*, as well as in innumerable trade journals such as the steel industry's magazine *Iron Age*. Over the years, Bindig has incorporated every aspect of commercial art in his work—layout, lettering, package design, slide presentations—but his favorite has always been cartooning.

It is Bindig's love of cartooning and cartoons that has given him his greatest contact with the national art scene. A prominent collector of comic art and an authority on the history of cartooning, he has contributed both art and expertise to the field for many years. He is a dealer on a national scale of newspaper comics pages as well as individual comic strips and cartoon panels and has handled some of the country's largest collections. He has also taught cartooning at the University of Buffalo.

Bob Bindig has been widely associated, as both writer and artist, with the literature of cartooning in the United States and has contributed important research to the fanzines in the field. He has been a consulting editor of *Nemo* and was an associate editor of *Strip Scene* for its last eight years. The latter magazine carried many articles of his, and his covers were a popular feature. The original of the *Strip Scene* cover for the issue celebrating the fiftieth anniversary of *Tarzan* in the comics was acquired by the Edgar Rice Burroughs archive for their permanent collection. Columns and features have flowed from his pen for other periodicals as well: *The Menomonee Falls Gazette* carried his "Trivia Quiz" for the five years before they ceased publication, and *The*

Funnies Paper still runs his "Robert's Ramblings" and "Inspector Close Presents. . . ." As Inspector Close, he reveals discrepancies and repetitions in cartoons, illustrations, and comic strips from his large personal collection.

Long a fan of Milton Caniff's *Steve Canyon*, Bindig was paid a special compliment in that strip in November, 1981. His face was used (as that of "Kommandant Ludwig von Digbin") in a dream sequence flashback to World War I. The episode was reported in a *Cartoonist Profiles* article in June, 1982.

The cartoon industry recognized Bindig's service to the field with an Inkpot Award at the San Diego Comics Convention in 1982. For many years a highly successful commercial cartoonist in advertising, Bob Bindig has extended his influence beyond New York's Niagara Frontier area. His name is well-known nationally for his informed appreciation and wide-ranging scholarship in the field of cartooning, and for his many services to it.

BIOGRAPHICAL/CRITICAL SOURCES: Cartoonist Profiles, June, 1982.

—Sketch by Dennis Wepman

* * *

BLECHMAN, R. O. 1930-

PERSONAL: Born October 1, 1930, in Brooklyn, N.Y.; son of Samuel (in business) and Mae (Braunstein) Blechman; married Moisha Kubinyi, June 2, 1960; children: Nicholas, Max. *Education:* Oberlin College, B.A., 1952. *Home:* 1 W. 64th St., New York, N.Y. 10023. *Studio:* 2 W. 47th St., New York, N.Y. 10036.

CAREER: Assistant animator, Storyboard Inc., 1954-55; freelance cartoonist, animator, and illustrator, 1955—; president, R. O. Blechman, Inc. 1962—; president, The Ink Tank, New York City, 1978—. Instructor at the School of Visual Arts, 1960—; lecturer and guest speaker. *Military service:* U.S. Army, 1952-54; served in Korea. Swann Foundation (on advisory board). *Member:* Alliance Graphique Internationale, American Institute of Graphic Arts. *Awards, honors:* Clio Award, twice in 1968, in 1969 for best animation design of a television commercial, in 1973 for best animated commercial; Gold Medal, Cannes Film Festival, 1977, for Funk & Wagnall's "Great Artists" commercial; selected "Illustrator of the Year," *Adweek*, 1983; Emmy Award from National Academy of Television Arts and Sciences for *The Soldier's Tale*, 1984.

WRITINGS: The Juggler of Our Lady, Henry Holt & Co., 1953; *Onion Soup and Other Fables*, Odyssey, 1963; *The Potato Book*, Morrow, 1972; *R. O. Blechman: Behind the Lines*, Hudson Hills, 1980.

FILMS—All animated cartoons: *The Juggler of Our Lady*, CBS-Terrytoons, 1958; *Abraham and Isaac*, 1971; (producer of animated segments) *The Great American Dream Machine*, Public Broadcasting System (PBS), 1972; *Exercise*, 1974; *Simple Gifts*, R. O. Blechman, Inc., 1978 (drew the "No

Emblem by Bob Bindig for the Buffalo Bisons.

Room at the Inn" segment and directed the entire film); *The Soldier's Tale* (animated version of Igor Stravinsky's "L'Histoire du Soldat"), R. O. Blechman, Inc., 1980.

EXHIBITIONS: One-man shows at Galerie Delpire, Paris, 1968; Graham Gallery, New York City, 1978; Gallerie Bartsch & Chariau, Munich, 1982; collective shows in West Berlin, 1964; "The Poison Pen," School of Visual Arts, New York City, 1965; Mead Gallery, New York City, 1972.

WORK IN PROGRESS: "The Golden Ass," an animated feature scheduled for 1987.

SIDELIGHTS: Born into a cultured and artistic family (brother Burt is a novelist), R. O. Blechman spent much of his childhood drawing, and attended the High School of Music and Art in New York City. Later he went on to Oberlin College, graduating in 1952. Some two years later he embarked upon a successful career as a cartoonist, illustrator, and animator (spurred on, no doubt, by the critical acclaim that his first book, *The Juggler of Our Lady*, had received).

Blechman's well-recognized wiggly, amorphous style is his trademark. He has carried it into countless cartoons and illustrations for such publications as *Look, Graphis*, the *New York Times*, the *New Yorker, Punch, McCall's, Fortune*, and *Esquire;* and through a number of award-winning animated

"**Washington Crossing the Delaware.**" (© 1977, R. O. Blechman. Reprinted with permission.)

cartoons, not to mention such memorable television commercials as "the talking stomach" for Alka-Seltzer and "the attack of the car" for Volvo. The books he has written and illustrated are as well remembered for their witty comments as for his unforgettable line. To those who think that he works only in miniature format Blechman has come back with a vengeance by executing such giant murals as those for the U.S. Pavilion at Expo '67 in Montreal and for the Museum of Natural History in New York City.

In his foreword to *R. O. Blechman: Behind the Lines* Maurice Sendak commented feelingly that, "There is one aspect of Blechman's art that touches me personally and is something of an obsession; I would even suggest it is the unconscious bond that ties us together as artists. It is something I fleetingly mentioned earlier on: Blechman's child view. *Child view* is often translated into *creative view*, but they are not the same thing. There is a fierce, first freshness implied in the former that is part of an elaborate sensibility in the other." It is perhaps this directness and freshness of vision that impress themselves on the viewer of a Blechman television commercial or the reader of a Blechman book, this simple gift (to paraphrase the artist) of child-like wonder and whimsy.

"I set on the road again," Blechman wrote of his career after making the film *Simple Gifts*. "No, it was not a road. There was no road because nobody had preceded me on the journey I was to take—I simply set out, that is all, with a staff that I hoped would not fail me every fourth step of the way." All of his admirers are grateful that Blechman's staff hasn't failed him yet—and hopeful that it never will.

BIOGRAPHICAL/CRITICAL SOURCES: R. O. Blechman: Behind the Lines, Hudson Hills, 1980; *The World Encyclopedia of Cartoons*, Chelsea House, 1980; *Who's Who in Graphic Art*, Vol. 2, De Clivo, 1982; *Who's Who in America*, 42nd edition, 1983.

R. O. BLECHMAN

"Uncle Sam." (© 1977, R. O. Blechman. Reprinted with permission.)

* * *

BOIVIN, Jacques 1952-
(Jacques)

PERSONAL: Born April 7, 1952, in Montreal, Quebec, Canada; son of Bernard (a botanist) and Cosette (an administration agent; maiden name Marcoux). Boivin; *Education:* University of Ottawa, B.A. (honors), 1974. *Religion:* Roman Catholic. *Home:* 4531 Bordeaux, Montreal, Quebec, Canada H2H 1Z9.

CAREER: Technical illustrator and lab research assistant, 1969; illustrator of children's games for an educational research group, 1973; staff comic strip artist for *La Pulpe,* 1974; freelance cartoonist, illustrator, and graphic designer, 1975—.

AWARDS, HONORS: Third prize in cartooning, San Mateo County Fair, 1981.

WRITINGS: (Under name Jacques) *The Heart Single-Field Theory,* privately printed, 1978; (under name Jacques) *Jacques,* privately printed, 1979; *Beastie and the Boo,*

privately printed, 1982; *Dinosaur Comics,* Phantasy Press, 1983; *Fluffhead Vol. 1* and *Fluffhead Vol. 2,* Phantasy Press 1983; *Aliens,* Phantasy Press, 1983; *Land of Consciousness,* Phantasy Press, 1984.

FILMS: Produced, directed, and edited *New Age Video,* twenty-one half-hour weekly television shows on experimental film and performance, for Skyline Cablevision, 1980.

EXHIBITIONS: Group shows include "Rétrospective de la bande desinée québécoise", Musée d'Art Contemporain de Montreal, 1976; one-man exhibition at Galerie Duguay-Mathieu, Montreal, 1985.

WORK IN PROGRESS: Inking *Northguard* series for *New Triumph* starting with No. 3, published by Matrix Graphic Series; contributing to *Cartoon Loonacy* No. 5 and subsequent issues; cover art for *Mélody,* published by Editions Mélody of Montreal; editing and drawing *Love Fantasy,* a romance comic book to be published by Renegade Press in 1986.

SIDELIGHTS: Jacques Boivin enjoyed the advantages of growing up in a bilingual environment. As a child he was able to enjoy fantasy in both French and English, in European *bandes dessinées* and American Marvel Comics.

JACQUES BOIVIN

He began drawing in early childhood, producing illustrated epics of his own devising that often ran for hundreds of pages.

However, when he entered the University of Ottawa with a four-year scholarship, it was to study computer science. In 1972, midway through the curriculum, despite high grades, he abruptly switched to visual arts, wherein he received his degree in 1974.

Since then, he has been working in a wide variety of applications of the graphic arts. His first professional job in the comics field was as a staff artist for the French-Canadian comic magazine *La Pulpe*. Thanks to the freedom of the magazine, he produced some notable work, including the mildly erotic fantasy "Flora", which was later translated into English and included in his privately published collection *Jacques*.

After leaving *La Pulpe* he went freelance, and has continued to work for a variety of markets and in a variety of styles ever since. His work has appeared in the prestigious European weekly *Tintin*, and in *Saturday Night, Books in Canada, Enterpriser, Canadian Consumer, Canadian Heritage, Speculations in Science and Technology*, Marvel's *Crazy*, and elsewhere, in addition to his small-press solo projects, printed privately or through Phantasy Press. From 1978 to 1981 he used only his first name, Jacques.

In 1978, the comic strip *Fluffhead*, which he both wrote and drew, was syndicated by Miller Services of Toronto. This

A page from "Dinosaur Days." (© 1985, Jacques Boivin. Reprinted with permission.)

"Descent into Lower Realms," an illustration. (© 1985, Jacques Boivin. Reprinted with permission.)

"**Electronic Facemask.**" (© 1985, Jacques Boivin. Reprinted with permission.)

strip displayed his warm, "cuddly" art and bizarre, original wit to good advantage, but unfortunately does not appear to have found its audience in time to survive. More successful was a venture into drawing and publishing his own extensive line of note and greeting cards in 1979. He sold over ten thousand cards despite very limited distribution. In 1980 he took on the production, direction, and editing of *New Age Video* for Skyline Cablevision, a cable-television series of performances in dance, theatre, and music, and experimental animated films.

After that he felt the need of a change of pace, and left his native Canada for California, where his drawing career continued, as he found new outlets and directions, such as rubber-stamp companies, and political cartooning. Now back in Montreal once again, he has begun to settle into the growing field of Canadian comics, with the short feature "Scene in an Alien Discotheque" in *Neil the Horse* No. 10 and various work for the Matrix Graphics Series.

Boivin reports his major interests to be comic art, dance, video, animation—and physics, which is rather unusual in a cartoonist, all the more so because he incorporates his interest into his work. Much of his work is satirical in tone, and covers a wide range from the esoterica of *Land of Consciousness* to the direct commentary of "Dinosaur

Days". Boivin has a knack for seeing things from unusual viewpoints, for making unexpected analogies, and for bringing out the absurdity in the world around us, often simply by taking what we say literally. His humorous work has a warmth and a charm all its own, and manages to appear naive while actually being quite sophisticated—much more so than the work of many more pretentious and flashy artists.

—Sketch by Lawrence Watt-Evans

*　　*　　*

BOSCH PENALVA, Jordi　1927-
(Jordi Penalva)

PERSONAL: Born July 22, 1927, in Barcelona, Spain; son of Anton and Remei (Penalva) Bosch; married Julia Arolas Sivill; children: Norma. *Education:* Attended Escuela Superior de Bellas Artes (Higher School of Fine Arts), with courses in painting and anatomy, 1954-56. *Home:* Avenida Hospital Militar 252, Barcelona, Spain. *Agent:* Josep Toutain, Selecciones Ilustradas, Diagonal 325, 08009 Barcelona, Spain; Bernd Metz, Selecciones Ilustradas, 43 E. 19th St., New York, N.Y. 10003.

CAREER: Jewelry designer, Barcelona, 1941; designer, department stores, 1942; designer, glass manufacturer, Barcelona, 1945; freelance illustrator, 1945—; designer, publishing company, Rio de Janeiro, Brazil, 1952; supervisor, advertising department, textile factory, Sao Paulo, Brazil, 1953-54. *Military service:* Spanish Army, 1949-50, served in Quartermaster Corps.

SIDELIGHTS: Jordi Penalva chose his maternal name as his professional signature so as to avoid confusion with his brother, Antonio Bosch, a noted comic book artist who drew the series *Silver Roy* and *Erik, el enigma viviente* (title means "Erik, the Living Enigma") in the late 1940s. By that time Penalva was already a professional illustrator and cover designer, two specialties into which he was initiated at age eighteen, thus laying the foundation of his now vast experience in these fields. His style is grounded in his long practice of the art, but also in his studies of the human form in painting, not to mention classes in architecture which have given him a solid knowledge of perspective and proportions.

In 1945 Penalva began his career as a book cover illustrator for such publishing companies as Bruguera, Juventud, Reguera, Janes, and others. He painted urbanization models for what was then known as "Greater Barcelona" prior to his being called to military service. Like many other Spanish artists who felt artistically and politically oppressed at the time, he emigrated overseas: from 1952 to 1954 he resided in Brazil where he worked as a designer. After his return to Spain he embarked on a successful international career in illustration.

While he has made—and still makes—abundant use of photographs, Penalva works first and foremost with natural models. This attitude may have helped him distance himself from hyperrealism, and has made him look for greater freedom of expression and greater diversity of style in the

Illustration for a historical novel, ca. 1980. (© Jordi Penalva. Reprinted with permission.)

tradition of the great American illustrators, from Howard Pyle and Norman Rockwell to Frank Frazetta and Richard Corben. Starting from pencil sketches, he adds more and more detail until the application of color, then tries out different lighting schemes with the help of photographs. His pictures are finally rendered in acrylics, watercolors, oils, or other painting mediums, whatever the case requires. Penalva displays a vigorous and elegant romanticism, joined to a solid knowledge of the human figure and an exacting care for period and background. His illustrations bear the mark of the true draftsman, as well as the touch of the gifted painter.

Penalva's illustrations and covers met with great success in Britain in the latter half of the 1950s, and in the course of the 1960s and early 1970s their fame spread to other European countries, including the Netherlands, Sweden, Norway, and Germany. In 1974 Penalva started to work for U.S. clients, painting covers for books published by Berkley, Popular Library, Fawcett, Avon, Dell, Signet, Bantam, Ace, Playboy, and others. He also drew covers for the comic magazines put out by Warren Publishing Company. Recently he contributed the covers to the Hardin series of western novels, published by Berkley.

Penalva is highly eclectic as to his themes: he has treated practically every subject, and he sees in versatility the best safeguard against artistic stagnation. Of late, however, he

seems to have become fascinated with the imaginative freedom afforded by science-fiction.

BIOGRAPHICAL/CRITICAL SOURCES: Comix International, No. 18, Barcelona, 1982.

* * *

BROWNE, Dik
    See BROWNE, Richard Arthur Allen

* * *

BROWNE, Richard Arthur Allen   1917-
    (Dik Browne)

PERSONAL: Born August 11, 1917, in New York, N.Y.; son of William Joseph (a cost accountant) and Mary (a wardrobe mistress; maiden name Slattery) Browne; married Joan Marie Therese Hosey Haggerty Kelly (treasurer, Browne Creative Enterprises, Inc.), May 11, 1942; children: Robert, Christopher, Sally (adopted, 1961). *Education:* Attended Cooper Union, New York City, 1934. *Politics:* Registered Democrat ("votes independent"). *Religion:* Roman Catholic. *Home:* Sarasota, Fla. *Office:* c/o King Features Syndicate, 235 E. 45th St., New York, N.Y. 10017.

CAREER: Copyboy, staff artist, *New York Journal-American*, New York City, 1936-41; staff artist, *Newsweek*, New York City, 1941-42; advertising artist, Johnstone & Cushing Art Agents, New York City, 1946-54; comic strip artist on *Hi and Lois*, 1954—; comic strip artist and writer, *Hagar the Horrible*, 1973—. *Military service:* U.S. Army, 1942-46, became sergeant. *Member:* National Cartoonists Society (president, 1963-65), National Comics Council.

AWARDS, HONORS: Named Best Comic Strip Cartoonist by National Cartoonists Society, 1959, for *Hi and Lois*; Reuben Award for Best Cartoonist in All Categories from National Cartoonists Society, 1962, for *Hi and Lois*, 1973, for *Hagar the Horrible*; Banshee Silver Lady from the Banshees press club, 1962; named Best Humor Strip Cartoonist by National Cartoonists Society, 1969, 1972, 1977, and 1985; Elzie Segar Award, 1975; Best Non-British International Cartoon Award from British Cartoonist Society, 1984, for *Hagar the Horrible*; first annual Max und Moritz Preis for best comic artist from Comic Salon, Erlangen, West Germany, 1984, for *Hagar the Horrible*.

WRITINGS: (Self-illustrated) *The Wit and Wisdom of Hagar the Horrible*, Windmill Press, 1974.

All *Hagar the Horrible* books of comics: *The Best of Hagar*, Simon & Schuster, 1981; *The Very Best of Hagar*, Simon & Schuster, 1982; *The Best of Hagar*, Holt, 1985; *Hagar the Horrible's Very Nearly Complete Viking Handbook*, Workman, 1985.

All *Hagar the Horrible* books of comics; all published by Ace: *Hagar the Horrible*, 1977; *Hagar the Horrible No. 2*, 1978; *Animal Haus*, 1983; *Born Leader*, 1983; *Bring 'em Back Alive*, 1983; *The Brutish Are Coming*, 1983; *Helga's Revenge*, 1983; *Midnight Munchies*, 1983; *My Feet Are Really Drunk*, 1983; *Hagar on the Loose*, 1983; *Excuse Me*, 1984; *Hagar Hits the Mark*, 1984; *Hagar's Knight Out*, 1984; *Happy Hour*, 1984; *The Simple Life*, 1984; *Hagar on the Rocks*, 1985; *Sack Time*, 1985.

All *Hagar the Horrible* books of comics; all published by Berkley: *Have You Been Uptight Lately?*, 1980; *Big Bands Are Back*, 1981; *Hagar the Horrible and the Basilisk*, 1981; *Hagar the Horrible's Activity Book*, 1982.

Self-portrait of Dik Browne. (Printed with permission.)

A *Hi and Lois* daily strip. (© 1960, King Features Syndicate. Reprinted with special permission of King Features Syndicate.)

All *Hagar the Horrible* books of comics; all published by Tor Books: *Hagar and the Golden Maiden*, 1983; *Hagar at Work*, 1983; *Sacking Paris on a Budget*, 1983; *Hear No Evil*, 1984; *Room for One More*, 1984.

All with Mort Walker; all *Hi and Lois* books of comics; all published by Ace: *Hi and Lois: Family Ties*, 1978; *Suburban Cowboys*, 1982; *Father Figure*, 1983; *American Gothic*, 1983; *The Bright Stuff*, 1984; *Mama's Home*, 1984.

All with Mort Walker, all *Hi and Lois* books of comics: *Trixie*, Dell, 1960; *Hi and Lois: Beware, Children at Play*, Putnam, 1968; *Is Dinner Ready?*, Tor, 1984; *Mom, Where's My Homework?*, Tor, 1984.

Illustrator: Bishop Fulton J. Sheen, *Life Is Worth Living* (a series), Doubleday, 1950-54; Mort Walker, *Most* (juvenile), Windmill, 1971; Mort Walker, *Land of Lost Things* (juvenile), Windmill, 1973.

SIDELIGHTS: As the son of a cost accountant who worked often in the stone trade, Dik Browne had early dreams of being a sculptor, but his mother's work as a wardrobe mistress on Broadway nurtured in him the instinct to entertain. The product of these two influences—being an entertainer in the graphic medium—was a natural result. It was not until he was fifty-seven that he found the ideal form for his talents, but his success since then has been meteoric.

After a year at the Cooper Union Art School in New York, Browne began his career as a copyboy with the *New York*

Journal-American. He was captivated by the glamor of the newsroom and vaguely hoped to become a journalist, but decided he had no talent for it. "I got lost on the streets of New York," he explains, "I couldn't spell or remember phone numbers, I had a short attention span, and I was too shy to ask people questions." But his co-workers began noticing his clever doodles and caricatures, and he was sent out to do courtroom sketches. From there it was a short step to the art department doing maps and illustrations for the war that had just begun.

An offer from *Newsweek* to do the same thing for three times the money gave Browne the first taste of financial security he ever had, and he married. Shortly afterward, in 1942, he was drafted and spent the next four years in the U.S. Army Engineering Corps, where he drew maps, charts, and posters.

When he was discharged as a technical sergeant in March, 1946, he found his job on *Newsweek* gone ("an absolute blessing," he now calls it) and work of any kind hard to get. At last he landed a job doing straight advertising art for the now legendary Johnstone & Cushing agency, where such noted cartoonists as Leonard Starr, Milton Caniff, and Stan Drake also served their apprenticeships. During the five years he spent with this agency, Browne's work become known for its warmth, imagination, and humor. He redesigned the lovable Campbell Soup kids, created Chiquita Banana, and, significantly, did the art for five different candy companies at the same time.

His growing success in advertising never stifled Browne's dream—a dream he had cherished since before the war—to be a cartoonist. While still at the *Journal-American* he collaborated with a fellow copy boy on a Yiddish comic strip called *Muttle the Gonif* ("Muttle the Thief"), based on Shalom Aleichem's stories transposed to New York, but the strip never sold. During the war, he offered a strip called *Rembrandt*, "about street kids," to the New York Herald-Tribune Syndicate, but it was turned down too ("also a blessing," according to Browne). From 1950 to 1960 he drew *The Tracy Twins*, written by Al Stenzel, for *Boy's Life*. The expressive faces and stylish composition of this strip were to earn it a devoted audience, and inevitably Browne's name became known beyond the narrow world of advertising.

In 1954, cartoonist Mort Walker (whose *Beetle Bailey* had begun four years earlier) noticed an ad for Peter/Paul Mounds. It was one of Browne's rare signed drawings, and Walker made a mental note of the name. Talking with King Feature Syndicate cartoon editor Sylvan Byck soon after, he learned that Byck had noticed the very different *Tracy Twins* and been similarly impressed. The two invited Browne to collaborate with Walker on *Hi and Lois*, a family strip which began as a spin-off about Beetle Bailey's sister and brother-in-law. It began in October of that year, and Browne has been drawing it ever since.

Hi and Louis Flagston are a typical suburban couple, more realistic than Dagwood and Blondie but confronting much the same situations. Hi works in an office and Lois tries to sell real estate and keep house at the same time. Their disheveled teenaged son Chip resists discipline like all teenagers, and their twins Dot and Ditto have the usual competitive instincts and animal cunning of first-graders. The Flagstons' baby, Trixie, engages in an endless struggle to make sense of the adult world and conducts long one-sided conversations with a sunbeam.

The daily gags of *Hi and Lois* show this likable family often bewildered by life but never outraged or really pained by it, and no violence, physical or emotional, ever intrudes. The popularity of this gentle, sensitively drawn comic strip, which appears in over one thousand newspapers in fifty countries, owes much to Browne's economical line, simplicity of format, and uniformly pleasing composition.

Having come from a broken home and grown up in the Great Depression, Browne has always felt concerned about his own family's security, and when he suffered a detached retina in 1973 he decided, as he reports, that "it was time to do something new." In February of that year he started his own strip, *Hagar the Horrible*. "[It] was the first idea I tried," Brown says, "and I got lucky."

Hagar's phenomenal success—it was the fastest-growing new strip in the history of the comics, with more than six hundred papers in its first two years—was more than just luck. Browne's unerring sense of the comic, coupled with his vigorous artwork, has struck a responsive chord all over the world. His extensive use of sight-gags makes his creation especially accessible to foreign markets, and *Hagar* has been translated into dozens of languages, and is read by an estimated one hundred million in the United States alone.

Although traditional in its broad, often vaudeville-based daily gags, *Hagar* has a cast which is truly original. Its titular hero, a shaggy, bearded ninth-century Viking bearing a suspicious resemblance to its creator, is an endearingly naive barbarian who views his work ("I'm in sacking and looting," he explains) as matter-of-factly as Hi Flagston. His formidable wife Helga labors as tirelessly and as fruitlessly to civilize him as Maggie does with Jiggs in *Bringing Up Father*, but she holds her own against him far better. Their young son Hamlet worries his father by wearing his hair short, bathing, and aspiring to be a dentist, while their sexy sixteen-year-old daughter Honi intimidates her suitors by being more a Viking than they are. Her favorite dress is stainless steel, with mace, sword, and battle-axe for accessories. Even Helga's pet duck and Hagar's nondescript dog Snert wear horned helmets. Lucky Eddie, Hagar's loyal but dimwitted sidekick, sports a funnel as headgear.

Hagar is irresistible because he is universal. Like Huckleberry Finn, he is an archetype, the greedy, anarchic spirit we all bear within ourselves. When Hagar goes to tell his warrior band he wants more blood and thunder, Helga must gently remind him to leave his teddy bear with her. He fights against his annual bath, eats faster than his wife can cook, and when a priest says he goes wherever sin and vice hold sway, he innocently asks, "Hey—can I go along?"

In all of Browne's graphic work, an element which contributes to the universality of its appeal is the harmonious simplicity of his line. Nothing is wasted or superfluous in Browne's work. An early and profound influence on his drawing was Kimon Nicolaides, whose book *The Natural*

Hagar the Horrible **strips.** (From top: © 1981, 1984, 1983, King Features Syndicate. Reprinted with special permission of King Features Syndicate.)

Way to Draw calls for just such clean economy as Browne displays. Hagar's creator had what he still regards as "the great good fortune" to meet Nicolaides in the early 1930s and continues to consider *The Natural Way to Draw* "a great book." It continues to inspire him to simplify his work.

Although Browne's work in all media reveals a pleasing simplicity and naturalness of line and composition, it is by no means uniform. An important feature of his style is the harmony of style and subject. The drawing of *Hagar* has

from the beginning been more robust than that of *Hi and Lois*, as befits the character, and the characters, of the strip. Browne explains, "In *Hi and Lois*, the line is clean and round, and that somehow suits a clean, round, tight, warm family. . . . When you get to someone as raunchy as Hagar, I like the line a lot cruder and bolder." As his eyesight has worsened, Browne's drawing has become heavier and clearer and his shading less delicate, giving the strip the attractive effect of an older, more spontaneous style of cartooning.

Browne's abundant imagination enables him to write about thirty gags a week. He makes rough pencil sketches on tracing paper for his family's rating, and then he selects six dailies and a Sunday from them for the week. His son Chris, a cartoonist whose work appears in *Playboy* and the *National Lampoon*, helps him with *Hagar*, and his second son Bob, a musician performing under the name of Chance Browne, works with him on *Hi and Lois*. His wife Joan provides a keen critical eye as well as serving as the official treasurer of Browne Creative Enterprises, Inc.

The family co-operation this close group have established—a "cottage industry," as Browne calls it—has freed him to explore other avenues of expression, such as illustration and oil painting. Together with Mort Walker, Dik Browne has produced two children's books, *Most* and *The Land of the Lost Things*, in recent years, and he has increasingly turned his attention to the production of full-length Hagar stories for the European book market. In these diverse genres, as in the seemingly inexhaustible flow of his genial comic strip, Dik Browne's exuberant virtuosity and gentle, humane vision continue to bring new vitality to his medium.

BIOGRAPHICAL/CRITICAL SOURCES: Hartford Courant, November 11, 1974 (reprinted in *Authors in the News*, Vol. I, Gale Research Co.); *The World Encyclopedia of Comics*, Chelsea House, 1976; *Cartoonist Profiles*, March, 1978; *Sarasota Herald Tribune*, May 11, 1980; *American Artist*, Vol. 1, No. 1, 1984; *Who's Who in America*, Marquis, 1984.

—*Sketch by Dennis Wepman*

* * *

BUSINO, Orlando 1926-

PERSONAL: Born October 10, 1926, in Binghamton, N.Y.; son of Frank (a tailor) and Rose (Clemente) Busino; married Ann Louise Darlington, November 3, 1951; children: Linda, Chris, Michele, Andrea, Robert, Frank. *Education:* Iowa State University, B.A., 1952; attended School of Visual Arts, 1954. *Home:* 12 Shadblow Hill Rd., Ridgefield, Conn. 06877. *Office:* P.O. Box 463, Ridgefield, Conn. 06877.

CAREER: Advertising artist, Macmillan Publishing Co., 1954; free-lance cartoonist, 1954—. *Military service:* U.S. Army Air Corps, 1945-47. *Awards, honors:* Best Magazine Gag Cartoonist award, from National Cartoonists Society, 1966, 1967, 1968.

WRITINGS: Good Boy!, Andor, 1980; *Oh, Gus!*, Andor, 1981.

SIDELIGHTS: Orlando Busino is known for the crispness of his drawings and his economy of line, which puts him in the tradition of such old-school cartoonists as Otto Soglow and Carl Anderson, a predilection he is quick to acknowledge. "I draw a big nose and big foot type cartoon," *The World Encyclopedia of Cartoons* reports him as saying, "and I enjoy it." He likes to draw funny-looking characters and slightly absurd situations, which make his wordless cartoons specially appealing; for instance, one shows a giant frog

waiting patiently at a kissing booth. When Busino does use dialogue (always sparingly), it is still the drawing that carries most of the punch. In one cartoon, for example, a mischievous-looking boy tells the customs inspector going through his parents' luggage, "You're getting warmer." It is not the line that is most funny, but the expressions, ranging from gleeful to irate, on the characters' faces—they are hilarious.

Busino was already cartooning in high school, and while in college he drew cartoons for the *Daily Iowan*. After a short stint in the advertising department of Macmillan Publishing Co. in New York, he decided to become a professional cartoonist, and was able to sell on his first try to the *Saturday Evening Post*. During the 1960s, Busino was a top seller of cartoons to the now defunct *Saturday Evening Post*, *Collier's*, *American Magazine*, *True*, and *Argosy*. Today his work appears in the *Ladies' Home Journal*, *Good Housekeeping*, *Family Circle*, *Readers Digest*, *Working Mother*, *Scouting Magazine*, and other magazines. He draws a monthly cartoon panel for *Boys' Life* called *Gus*, a feature about a large, friendly dog.

As an artist Busino stresses discipline, the willingness to discard fruitless ideas, no matter how funny they might have first appeared. He mentally pictures situations that appeal to him, and then sketches them in rough form from every possible angle. His advice to aspiring cartoonists is to stay fresh and current, and to get as much education as possible.

BIOGRAPHICAL/CRITICAL SOURCES: Cartoonist Profiles, winter, 1969; *The World Encyclopedia of Cartoons*, Chelsea House, 1980; *Scouting Magazine*, October, 1984; *Who's Who in America*, 1984-85; *Japan/New York*, January-February, 1985.

Self-portrait of Orlando Busino surrounded by his cartoon creations. (© Orlando Busino. Reprinted with permission.)

C

CANEMAKER, John 1943-

PERSONAL: Born May 28, 1943, in Waverly, N.Y.; son of John F. (in hospital maintenance) and Rose (a nurse's aid; maiden name Laux) Cannizzaro; name legally changed. *Education:* Marymount Manhattan College, B.A., 1974; New York University, M.F.A., 1976. *Office and studio:* 120 W. 70th St., New York, N.Y. 10023.

CAREER: Worked as actor, singer and dancer on television commercials and on stage, 1961-71; freelance animator, 1971—; teacher of animation at workshops in New York City, 1973-76, Nassau County Arts Development Center, Long Island, 1976, William Paterson College, Wayne, N.J.,

Photo by Grace Alexander-Greene.

JOHN CANEMAKER

1978-80, New York University, 1981—. Lecturer in animation at School of Visual Arts, New York City, 1976, New York University, 1977-78, Adelphi University, 1978, Los Angeles International Film Exposition (Filmex), 1978, and Yale University, 1979-80. Host for CBS *Camera Three,* 1975-77; master of ceremonies at New York International Animation Festival, 1975; coordinated the first U.S. retrospectives of the animated films of Winsor McCay, 1975; held cartoon screenings at New York Film Festival, Museum of Modern Art, Carpenter Center for Visual Arts, John F. Kennedy Center, Smithsonian Institution, and others. *Military service:* U.S. Army, 1965-67; specialist 4th class.

AWARDS, HONORS: Award for best film in nostalgia category for *Lust,* Association of Animators, 1973; third prize for *Greed,* Association of Animators, 1973; grants from: American Film Institute, 1974, National Education Association, 1981, Public Broadcasting System, 1983 and 1984; "Cineprobe" retrospective, Museum of Modern Art, 1984.

WRITINGS: The Animated Raggedy Ann & Andy: An Intimate Look at the Art of Animation—Its History, Techniques and Artists, Bobbs-Merrill, 1977; (contributor) Gerald Peary and Danny Peary, eds., *The American Animated Cartoon,* Dutton, 1980; (introduction) *Treasures of Disney Animation Art,* Abbeville, 1982. Contributor to magazines and periodicals, including *Horizon, Variety,* and *Film Comment.*

FILMS—All animated short subjects: *Animation: Its History and Uses,* 1959; *Lust,* 1973; *The 40's,* 1974; *Street Freaks,* 1974; *Remembering Winsor McCay,* 1976; *Otto Messmer and Felix the Cat,* 1977; *Confessions of a Stardreamer,* 1978.

Programs for *Camera Three,* CBS-TV: "The Boys from Termite Terrace," 1975; "Felix the Cat," 1977; "The Art of Oskar Fischinger," 1977, "Bottom's Dream," 1983. Also animator of many commercial films, titles, and opening sequences.

WORK IN PROGRESS: Winsor McCay, publication by Abbeville Press expected in 1986.

SIDELIGHTS: John Canemaker is among that rare breed of artists who can both do and teach. As an animator he has produced a number of award-winning cartoons, notably *Confessions of a Stardreamer,* which the artist described as having been animated "to an improvised spoken track in a variety of styles and techniques (including cel, Xerography,

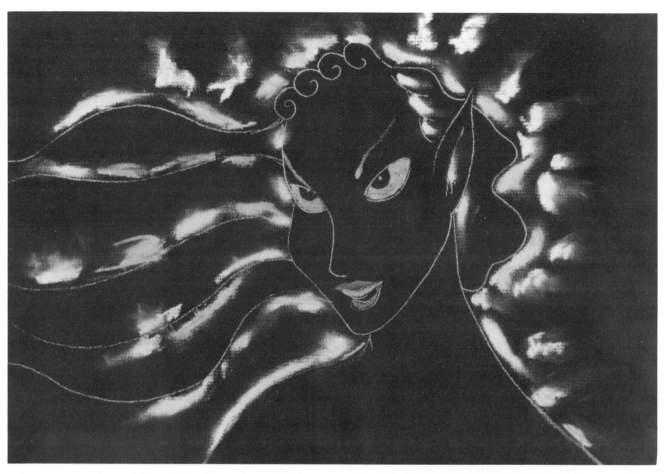

A frame from "Bottom's Dream." (© 1983, John Canemaker. Printed with permission.)

and child-like crayon and watercolor sketches)." He is also responsible for some of the most interesting compilations and documentaries devoted to great animators of the past, such as Winsor McCay, Otto Messmer, and Oskar Fischinger. Lately he has contributed animated sequences to a number of entertainment spectacles, from the Broadway musical *Woman of the Year*, about the romance between a cartoonist and a television hostess, which also included *The World Encyclopedia of Cartoons* as a plot element, to the movie *The World According to Garp*, in which he gave life to the titular hero's childhood drawings in a symbolic display of action and fantasy dream-sequences.

Canemaker is also a prolific writer about animation, and his contributions to such varied periodicals as *Connoisseur, Horizon, Millimeter, Variety,* and *Film Comment,* now numbering over one hundred, cover a wide range of subjects and themes. His book, *The Animated Raggedy Ann & Andy,* goes well beyond its stated subject, into the history of the form and a general discussion of the art of animation, as it is and as it could become.

Canemaker has also widely lectured and taught at institutions of higher learning here and abroad, and has brought to his lessons a practical knowledge added to a broad understanding of theory and history. All these activities have definitely made him animation's number one fan, spokesman and ambassador-at-large.

BIOGRAPHICAL/CRITICAL SOURCES: Film News, November and December, 1976, summer, 1977; *Hollywood Reporter,* August 12, 1977; *Los Angeles Times,* May 26, 1978; *Atlanta Journal-Constitution,* November 18, 1978; *Cartoonist Profiles,* March, 1983; *The Complete Kodak Animation Book,* Eastman-Kodak Company, 1983; *Print,* March-April, 1984.

A frame from *What Do Children Think of When They Think of the Bomb?* (© 1983, Icarus Co. World rights reserved.)

CANTONE, Vic 1933-

PERSONAL: Born August 7, 1933, in New York, N.Y.; son of Victor and Mary Cantone. *Education:* Graduated from School of Art and Design, New York City, 1952; Nassau College, Garden City, N.Y., A.A. (cum laude), 1978; Hofstra University, B.A., 1979. *Politics:* Independent. *Office:* New York Daily News, 220 E. 42nd St., New York, N.Y. 10017. *Agent:* Rothco Cartoon Syndicate, 40 Minerva Dr., Yonkers, N.Y. 10710.

CAREER: Cartoonist, *Newsday* (a daily newspaper), Garden City, N.Y., 1954-59; political cartoonist and caricaturist, *New York Daily News*, 1959—; editorial cartoonist, *Editor & Publisher* (a weekly magazine), 1973-78; syndicated cartoonist, Rothco Cartoon Syndicate, 1980—. *Member:* Association of American Editorial Cartoonists, New York Press Club.

AWARDS, HONORS: Fourth Estate Award and Bicentennial Trophy from Auxiliary American Legion, 1976; Valley Forge Honor Certificate from Freedoms Foundation, 1976; Patriotic Service Award from U.S. Department of Treasury, 1978; George Washington honor medal from Freedoms Foundation, 1978; Golden Press Award from Women's Auxiliary of American Legion, 1979.

SIDELIGHTS: Vic Cantone once stated that the political cartoon is a weapon able to shape public image and opinion, and that, therefore, "the burden of responsibility rests heaviest upon the political cartoonist to triumph in common

VIC CANTONE

ARMS TALK

Editorial cartoon, ca. 1983. (© *New York Daily News/* Rothco Cartoon Syndicate.)

sense over myths and hysteria, over nostalgia or paranoia." In his long career, first with the respected suburban daily newspaper *Newsday*, and now with the giant *New York Daily News*, Cantone has demonstrated that he could indeed handle the weapon of editorial satire with restraint as well as vigor. His drawings tend to the humorous, both in line and treatment, but his comments are often telling. Being nationally syndicated, Cantone keeps for the most part to national and international issues, although he has also lampooned local and/or regional figures on occasion. His cartoons for *Editor & Publisher* were especially funny, perhaps because they were aimed at a smaller and more "inside" audience—an audience made up of newspeople and editors would could catch Cantone's point more quickly and with greater empathy. He has also done a number of caricatures for *The Wall Street Journal Report*, a financial program for television; and his work has been frequently telecast on such news programs as *The Independent Network News* and *From the Editor's Desk*.

BIOGRAPHICAL/CRITICAL SOURCES: Who's Who in American Art, 16th edition, Bowker, 1984; *Who's Who in America*, Marquis, 1984.

HAWKERS

Editorial cartoon, ca. 1984. (© *Editor & Publisher*/Rothco Cartoon Syndicate.)

CATHERINE, Susan 1951-
(Francesca Valentine)

PERSONAL: Born May 11, 1951, in Ann Arbor, Mich.; daughter of Bernard Polishuk (a librarian and professional storyteller) and Orabelle Connally (a college instructor). *Education:* Attended Banff School of Fine Arts, 1968; Chichester School of Drama, 1969; Fairhaven College, 1970-71; Evergreen State College, B.A., 1972; San Francisco State University, 1973-77. *Politics:* Liberal. *Religion:* Agnostic. *Residence:* 1412 Taylor Ave. N., Seattle, Wash. 98109. *Agents:* (Newspaper syndication) West Coast Syndicate, 320 Vista Linda Drive, Mill Valley, CA 94941; (book distribution) Cornucopia, P.O. Box 85627, Seattle, Wash. 98145-1627.

CAREER: Artist's model, Kyoto, Japan, San Francisco, Vancouver, Canada, 1972-76; professional dancer (under name Francesca Valentine), toured with nightclub show through Japan, Canada, United States, 1976-80; professional actress, San Francisco, Seattle, 1980-83; freelance cartoonist and illustrator, 1976—. Organizer, United Farm Workers; organizer, Poetry in the Prisons Program; volunteer reader, Washington State Library for the Blind. *Member:* Northwest Cartoonists Association, YWCA Women Artists Support Group.

WRITINGS: Entendu dans les Restaurants d'Amerique (title means: "Heard in America's Restaurants"), Editions Fungus, Bordeaux, France, 1984.

Contributor of art work: *Because You Speak,* Panjandrum, 1976; *Backbone Four: Humor by Northwest Women,* Seal Press, 1982; *The 1984 Wimmen's Comix Book,* Last Gasp, 1984.

Contributor of cartoons and illustrations to many publications in Canada, Finland, and France.

EXHIBITIONS—One-woman shows: Ground Zero Gallery, Seattle, Wash., 1983; Ethnic Cultural Center, Seattle, 1983; Washington Hall Performance Gallery, Seattle, 1983; Two Bells Tavern, Seattle, 1984; QAE Gallery, Seattle, 1984. Group shows: TEMBI Gallery, San Francisco, Calif.; 1974 Revere Gallery, San Francisco, 1975; Women's Cultural Center, Seattle, 1983.

WORK IN PROGRESS: Quarterly books of collected cartoons, to be published by Cherry Stone Press; a second book of cartoons to be published in France by Editions Fungus.

SIDELIGHTS: Susan Catherine started her career as a dancer and actress (under the professional name Francesca Valentine) and, like so many other aspiring performers, she had to take up occasional waitressing jobs between engagements. That's where she got the inspiration for her cartoon panel, *Overheard at America's Lunch Counters.* In an article in the *Comics Journal,* Dale Luciano said of these cartoons, "These are witty, clever, and sophisticated snapshots of the American psyche."

Susan Catherine wrote *CGA:* "I am working on *one* project and all my work of the past two years has centered on it: a one-frame cartoon titled *Overheard at America's Lunch Counters* which has appeared in over twenty publications in four countries (Canada, Finland, France, The United States). My cartoon is a combination of actual overheard conversation and drawings of people who frequent public places. I consider myself a culture-bearer. With this project I am exploring the rhythms and eccentricities of working-class speech and the way in which it offers simultaneously funny and revealing glimpses into the texture of everyday American life."

BIOGRAPHICAL/CRITICAL SOURCES: Magnolia News, August 31, 1983; *Uncle Jam International,* November, 1984; Dale Luciano, "Newave Comics Survey," *Comics Journal,* March, 1985.

SUSAN CATHERINE

* * *

CATROW, David Johnson III 1952-

PERSONAL: Born December 16, 1952, in Fort Lee, Va.; son of David J. (a financial officer) and Patricia (Sullivan) Catrow; married Deborah Budinsky, June 16, 1973; children: Hillary Elizabeth, David Johnson IV. *Education:* Attended Kent State University, 1976-78. *Home:* 1023 Woodlawn Ave., Springfield, Ohio 45504. *Office:* Springfield Newspapers, 202 N. Limestone St., Springfield, Ohio 45501.

CAREER: Illustrator, 1978—; editorial cartoonist, *Springfield News-Sun,* 1984—. *Military service:* U.S. Navy, 1972-

"There's the hitchhikers group and the bus group and the plane group. I'm in the hitchhikers group."

"You can't really meet anyone at a bar anymore. Hell, if its not murder its herpes."

"I was going to Mexico for my vacation, but they all talk in Spanish all the time."

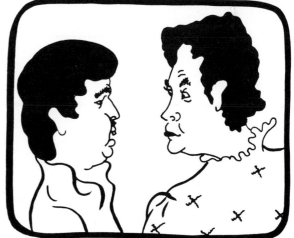

"I was set-up, I know I was set-up. My urine is clean, man."

Panels from *Overheard at America's Lunch Counters.* (© 1984, Susan Catherine. Reprinted with permission.)

75, served as hospital corpsman. *Member:* Association of American Editorial Cartoonists. *Awards, honors:* First Place in editorial cartooning, Associated Press Society of Ohio, 1984.

WRITINGS—Illustrator; all by R. Conrad Stein; "Cornerstones of Freedom" series; published by Children's Press: *Little Big Horn*, 1982; *Wounded Knee*, 1982; *Oregon Trail*, 1983; *Apollo 11*, 1985; *Trail of Tears*, 1985; *Johnstown Flood*, 1985.

WORK IN PROGRESS: Developing illustrations for *Treasure Island* and *Robin Hood* classic novels.

Self-portrait of David J. Catrow. (Printed with permission.)

SIDELIGHTS: Only thirty-three years old in 1985, David J. Catrow has already acquired a certain artistic reputation in southwestern Ohio, where he draws editorial cartoons for the *Springfield News-Sun.* His political cartoons show a conservative position that reflects well not only his own opinions but also those of his newspaper readers. This is the case, for instance, in his biting representation of the vulturous and evil Ayatollah Khomeini of Iran perched on the crown of the Statue of Liberty.

On the other hand, his social drawings have a more whimsical, even absurd, irony, as he gently pokes fun at human foibles, such as our irrational infatuation with the English royal family or the jet-set world. Especially amusing is his cartoon of an old lady, dressed in a housecoat, her hair

Editorial cartoon. (© 1985, *Springfield News-Sun.*)

in curlers, about to jump off a ledge because there would no longer be "sex, greed and Claus von Bulow" on television, although "Richard Dawson and *Family Feud* " will always be here, solaces her husband.

In addition, Catrow has illustrated several historical children's books in the "Cornerstone of Freedom" series. These illustrations depict with a wonderfully dramatic liveliness and detail the important events and figures of the Battle of Little Big Horn or the 1889 Johnstown flood. Catrow should enjoy still greater artistic freedom and unconstrained imagination when conveying the exciting adventures of the heroes of fictional classics.

As he seeks to combine social and political commentary with "the grace and permanence of fine arts," David J. Catrow is slowly freeing himself from the influence of fellow cartoonists, like Raymond Osrin and Mike Peters, to develop his own graphic style—an original style that is at once direct, uncluttered, and vigorous.

Editorial cartoon. (© 1984, *Springfield News-Sun.*)

CELLI, (Joseph) Paul 1935-

PERSONAL: Surname is pronounced "ch-elli"; born May 8, 1935, in Boston, Mass.; son of Joseph F. (a management executive with Boston Edison) and Katherine (Connolly) Celli; married Mary Skinner (a registered nurse), July 5, 1970; children: Peter, Bernard, Jonathan. *Education:* Massachusetts College of Art, B.F.A., 1960; Rhode Island School of Design, M.F.A., 1962. *Home:* 162 Walpole St., P.O. Box 109, Dover, Mass. 02030.

CAREER: Instructor, studio, art history, foundation program, Art Institute of Boston, 1964-69; associate professor, art history, drawing, and painting, Massachusetts College of Art, Boston, Mass., 1970—. Painter and cartoonist, 1963—.

WRITINGS: Foundation Handbook (curriculum material), Art Institute of Boston, 1968; *Time and Art: Anthology*, Massachusetts College of Art, 1973; *Ink Comics Nos. 1* and *2*, privately printed, 1984.

EXHIBITIONS: Collective shows at North-East Contemporary Artists Association, Boston, Mass., 1963, Berkshire Museum, Springfield, Mass., 1966; one-man show, Carpenter Center, Harvard University, Cambridge, Mass., 1976.

WORK IN PROGRESS: Paintings; *Ink Comics*, comic-book art; narrative drawing; a drawing course using comic-strip form to integrate second with fourth dimension.

SIDELIGHTS: In addition to a busy career in painting, drawing, and teaching, Paul Celli has devoted a fair amount of time and talent to furthering the artistic aspect of the comic strip form. His major effort in this direction is *Ink Comics*, a series of comic books with two issues in print by 1985, that aim to integrate, according to the author, bi-dimensional space and time. To this effect the artist draws himself into the story, and from a simple self-portrait proceeds to create, in his own words, "a version of the whole world but only one picture at a time."

The story, full of nonsense humor and whimsical incidents, is reminiscent of Edward Lear and Lewis Carroll, while the black-and-white drawings, done in an arresting broad brush style, display graphic effects (reverse images, negative space) that proceed very much along the lines of such stylistic pioneers as the Belgian etcher James Ensor. Yet Celli remains faithful to the spirit of the classic strip, and in his narrative, dialogues, and, above all, in his primitive-looking linework, he stays close to such masters of the medium as George Herriman and Elzie Segar. This is an interesting experiment which should be followed with interest.

The artists wrote *CGA:* "I think my art is autobiographical, an attempt to know something essential about myself, find a center, a fixed point. This attempt is a continuing process, successive and sequential. So the law of modern art that recognizes the use of opposites such as constancy and change is of great interest to me."

In a latter postscript to his comments Celli further elaborated on his creation: "*Ink Comics* is a series of books about an artist who accidentally draws himself into his story. His attempts to remove himself from his drawing and return to

Self-portrait of Paul Celli. (Printed with permission.)

'reality' send him on a series of adventures and encounters with a variety of characters.

"*Ink Comics* is an amusing way of showing how an artist thinks about a picture. It is an introduction to esthetics. The series focuses on ideas about art by using the components of a picture, such as line, shape, and pictorial space as its subject. Situations are developed by playing opposite definitions of the pictorial component against one another.

"The idea for *Ink Comics* came from three sources: an awareness, since childhood, that the comic strip does communicate ideas about art; a growing familiarity with the function of these ideas through continued practice of painting; and the attempt to communicate these ideas as a teacher.

"One of the incentives for presenting this idea in the form of a comic book was prompted by the unique way that the comic strip and comic book define time: a definition located half-way between the moving time of film and the 'fixed' time of a painting. Time in a comic strip brings the development of a literary narrative together with the development of pictorial events represented by each panel.

"The graphic effects of the black and white drawings are based on paintings in which a form of severely reduced chiaroscuro had evolved. The emphasis is placed on the way light and dark interact to form an image. The edge of an object is secondary to the edge of its shadow. The object 'blends' with its background, making composition the essential factor.

"Baroque painting and paintings of the modern masters, especially Giorgio Morandi, served as models for this effort. Milton Caniff, Noel Sickles, Alex Toth, Harvey Kurtzman,

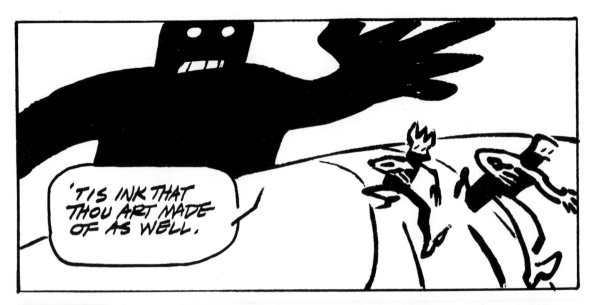

A page from *Ink Comics, No. 1.* (© 1984, Paul Celli. Reprinted with permission.)

George Herriman, Cliff Sterret, and many other comic artists contribute to the inspiration of this work."

BIOGRAPHICAL/CRITICAL SOURCES: Who's Who in American Art, 16th edition, Bowker, 1984.

* * *

CLAMPETT, Bob
    See CLAMPETT, Robert

* * *

CLAMPETT, Robert   1914(?)-1984
    (Bob Clampett)

OBITUARY NOTICE: Born May 8, 1914 (some sources say 1910), in San Diego, Calif.; died May 2, 1984, in Detroit, Mich. Cartoonist, animator, writer, and director of animated films, lecturer, and author. Clampett began his career in 1931 working for Rudolph Ising and Hugh Harman on the early *Looney Tunes* and *Merrie Melodies* cartoons for Warner Brothers. He became a director in 1936, and directed a number of memorable Porky Pig and Bugs Bunny cartoons. He also directed *Horton Hatches the Egg* from a Dr. Seuss story. Clampett left Warner in 1946, formed his own studio, and in the late 1940s created the highly popular *Time for Beany* puppet show for television. Beany and his seafaring friends, Captain Huffenpuff, Cecil the Seasick Sea Serpent, as well as his arch-enemy, the villainous Dishonest John became favorites of the public and lasted for five years, succeeded by the animated cartoon series *The Beany and Cecil Show*, which in turn lasted in syndication into the 1960s. Clampett then took his puppet characters on tour, and featured them in a self-illustrated book, *Beany*. In the course of his career he received many awards, including three Emmys and an Annie Award from ASIFA. He has always been ranked high among animators. "Of all the WB animators none drew so imaginatively from his batch of comic topics more madness and savage wit than Robert Clampett," wrote Mitchell S. Cohen.

BIOGRAPHICAL/CRITICAL SOURCES: Mitchell S. Cohen, "Looney Tunes and Merrie Melodies," *Velvet Light Trap*, fall, 1975; Gerald Peary and Danny Peary, *The American Animated Cartoon*, Dutton, 1980; *The World Encyclopedia of Cartoons*, Chelsea House, 1980.

OBITUARY SOURCES: Los Angeles Times, May 4, 1984.

* * *

CORBEN, Richard V(ance)   1940-
    (Corbou, Darvc, Gore, Harvey Sea)

PERSONAL: Born October 1, 1940, in Anderson, Mo.; son of farmer parents; married wife, Donna; children: one daughter. *Education:* Kansas City Art Institute, B.F.A., 1965. *Studio:* 27 W. Bannister Rd., Kansas City, Mo. 64114.

CAREER: Animated cartoonist, Calvin Communications, 1963-72; cover and poster artist and illustrator, 1967—; comic book artist, 1968—. *Awards, honors:* Golden Eagle

Award for work in animation, 1971; Japan Cultural Society Award, 1975; many awards from fan organizations.

WRITINGS—All books of comics: *Bloodstar*, Morning Star Press, 1976; *Neverwhere*, Ballantine, 1978; (with Jan Strnad) *New Tales of the Arabian Nights*, Heavy Metal Books, 1979; (with Jan Strnad) *Mutant World*, Fantagor Press, 1983; *Den*, Catalan Communications, 1984; *Muvovum (Den II)*, Catalan Communications, 1984; *Werewolf*, Catalan Communications, 1985; *Edgar Allan Poe*, Catalan Communications, 1985.

FILMS—All animated cartoons: *Neverwhere*, 1971; "Den" segment of *Heavy Metal—The Movie*, 1981 (based on Corben's story and character).

SIDELIGHTS: Richard Corben is a very private person, which is the reason why his "personal" section is so bare. He himself stated: "I'm not used to interviews and certainly not comfortable through them. I'm generally a nonverbal person. I don't respond well to fast-paced questions; I like to organize my thoughts before answering."

After graduation from the Kansas City Art Institute and a stint in the Army, Richard Corben returned to Calvin Communications—where he had started as an assistant in 1963—to work as a full-fledged animator on advertising cartoons. In the meantime he started contributing to fanzines—amateur fan magazines—, and it is in the pages of these publications that his comic book work first appeared. In the early 1970s he moved to underground comic books, and in the magazine *Up from the Deep* he did his first color story, "Cidopey." It was an immediate success, and from

Self-portrait of Richard Corben. (© 1985, Richard Corben. Printed with permission.)

A page from *Rowlf*. (© 1971, 1979, Richard Corben. Reprinted with permission.)

there he moved to established publications, first to magazines from Warren Publications, later to *Heavy Metal*. There he reworked his early fanzine creations, such as *Rowlf* and *Den*, into elaborate tales of horror, sex, and fantasy. Yet later many of these were again elaborately reworked into book form.

In *Rowlf* (1969), Maryara, a splendidly beautiful maiden, is abducted by a ruthless horde of alien invaders. The girl is rescued by her dog Rowlf who has magically assumed half-human shape. Outwitting and outrunning the invading armies they find a remote and unspoiled plot of land where to live out their strange idyl. Humor and irony are not absent from this twist on the Beauty and the Beast motif; a decrepit sage wryly comments on the action.

In Corben's latest version of *Den* (1984), the theme of man's innate bestiality and woman's embodiment of god (and conversely vessel of evil) is revisited. The hero is transported by electronic means to a strange land called Neverwhere in which barbarity and technology go hand in hand. There he finds his beloved, Kath, and after many battles and perilous encounters retires to live a free life of love and contentment with her (at least until the next adventure; as readers are well aware—there is no rest for heroes). The reverse image of Kath is represented by the black queen of Neverwhere who tries to seduce and trick Den away from his beloved. *Den II* is a further exploration of Corben's obsessive themes, with Den leaving his sky-island paradise and Kath to embark again on his never-ending quest. Rather than a sequel to the first book, *Den II* is a further refining and purifying of the initial tale: all of the artist's narrative strands—heroic fantasy, speculative fiction, horror play—are in fact gathered in this volume, which is perhaps Corben's most representative work.

Corben's book *Werewolf* is a collection of horror stories, abundantly laced with the salt of ribald humor. As in all of Corben's works, the men in this book are models of virility and the women embodiments of sexuality—both primeval earth figures. This aspect has often aroused criticism from ill-informed detractors. Corben has always maintained that there was subtle humor, as well as symbolic validity, in his depiction of the human form. He went so far as to aver in a letter, that his drawings show "a heroic idealism developed to such an extreme degree as to be slightly satirical and tongue-in-cheek."

Corben has garnered critical praise almost from his first efforts. In *Masters of Comic Book Art* P. R. Garriock wrote: "Corben has developed a characteristic style that is unmistakable. He is a graphic artist rather than a cartoonist and is continually experimenting with new effects. His concern with obtaining a sculptural quality, a three-dimensional roundness to his objects, has led him to explore the potential of shading, hatchwork, linear and aerial perspective . . . Perhaps the most striking feature of his work is the colour. His dazzling washes of ink and paint jump out from the page, giving a striking immediacy to his pictures."

Corben's art and themes have always appealed to authors of science-fiction who could recognize in the artist a kindred spirit. "The art traditions which Richard Corben drew on," wrote Fritz Leiber, "go back thirty thousand years and

more—to Late Paleolithic man's cave paintings of hunters and their weapons, witchdoctors and their rituals, and a profusion of animals feared and revered: the mammoth and the aurochs, the reindeer, wild horse, bison, rhinoceros, and elephant, and perhaps by way of dimly recalled racial experience the sabertooth tiger, the dire wolf, the dragon, and kindred monsters." Philip Jose Farmer concurred, stating: "A Corben illustration is unique. Once you've seen your first one, you instantly recognize the next, even if it's unsigned. Part of the style is the subtle . . . blend of the paleolithic and the modern, of magic, black and white, and science. Half a million years form a compressed chronological spectrum in both character and background."

Corben's work in animation has been the object of just as much praise as his work in comics. His feature film *Neverwhere* received an impressive number of awards, and his contribution (in the form of story and character) to the animated movie *Heavy Metal* was usually hailed as the most worthwhile segment of the film. In addition, Corben has won more acclaim and awards for his incredible airbrush renditions for book covers and posters, as well as for his distinctive works of illustration. His pictures for various novels of science-fiction, for an anthology of Edgar Allan Poe's tales, and for such magazines as *Eerie* and *Heavy Metal* have become classics.

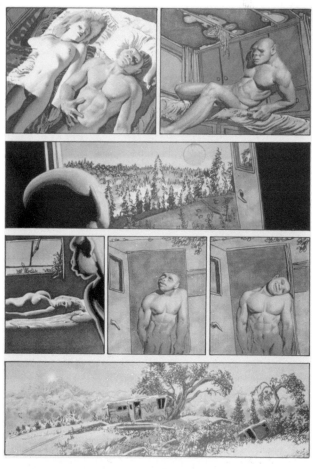

A page from *Mutant World.* (© 1982, Richard Corben and Jan Strnad. Reprinted with permission.)

BIOGRAPHICAL/CRITICAL SOURCES: The World Encyclopedia of Comics, Chelsea House, 1976; P. R. Garriock, *Masters of Comic Book Art,* Images Graphiques, 1978; Fritz Leiber, foreword to *Neverwhere,* Ballantine, 1978; Fershid Bharucha, *Flights into Fantasy,* Thumb Tack, 1981; *Heavy Metal,* June, July, and August, 1981; Philip Jose Farmer, prologue to *Den,* Catalan Communications, 1984.

—*Sketch by Maurice Horn*

* * *

CORBOU
      See **CORBEN, Richard V(ance)**

* * *

CRAFT, Kinuko Yamabe 1940-

PERSONAL: Born January 1, 1940, in Kanemaru, Rokusei, Japan; daughter of Naoyoshi (in business) and Sugi Morita Yamabe; married Mahlon Frederick Craft (a photographer and designer), March 21, 1965; children: Marie Charlotte. *Education:* Kanazawa Municipal College of Fine and Industrial Arts, B.F.A., 1962; attended the School of the Art Institute of Chicago, 1963-65. *Home and studio:* Litchfield Rd, R.F.D. 1, Box 286, Norfolk, Conn. 06058. *Agent:* Fran Seigel, 515 Madison Ave., New York, N.Y. 10022.

CAREER: Illustrator, Handelan Pederson, Inc., Chicago, Ill., 1966-67; illustrator, Stephens, Biondi, DiCicco, Inc., Chicago, Ill., 1967-69; freelance illustrator, 1969—. *Member:* Society of Illustrators, American Portrait Society.

AWARDS, HONORS: Citation for Merit, Society of Illustrators; Certificate of Excellence, Insides, 1974; Award of Distinctive Merit, Illustration Chicago, 1974; Certificate of Distinction, Creativity, 1975; Award of Excellence, Communi Graphics 1971; Certificate of Excellence (twice), Chicago 4, 1972; Citation for Merit, Society of Illustrators, 1972; Certificate of Excellence (twice), Chicago, 1974; Certificate of Merit, Society of Publication Designers, 1974; Certificate of Excellence (four times), Chicago, 1976; Citation of Merit, Society of Illustrators, 1977; Certificate of Distinction, Creativity, 1977; Certificate of Merit, Book Binders West Show, 1977; Certificate for Merit, Society of Illustrators,

Book jacket illustration for *American Illustration 3,* **ca. 1982.** (© Kinuko Y. Craft. Reprinted with permission.)

"Wolf in sheep's clothing," done for Infodata Systems Inc., ca. 1984. (© Kinuko Y. Craft. Reprinted with permission.)

1978; Award of Merit, Society of Publication Designers, 1978; Certificate of Excellence, Chicago, 1978; Award of Excellence, STA 100 Show, 1979; Award of Merit (four times), Society of Publication Designers, 1979; Certificate of Excellence, Communicating with Children; Certificate for Merit, Society of Illustrators 21; Certificate for Merit, Society of Illustrators 22; Award of Excellence (twice), The Art Annual 1981; Certificate of Distinction, Creativity 81; Merit Award (twice), Art Directors Club 60th, 1981; Award of Merit, Society of Publication Designers, 1981; Merit Award, Art Directors Club 61st, 1982; Award of Merit (twice), Society of Publication Designers, 1982; Award of Excellence (three times), International Editorial Design, The Art Annual, 1983; Award of Excellence, CA-83, 24th Annual Exhibition; Merit Award, Art Directors Club 62nd Annual Exhibition, 1983; Certificate of Merit (three times), Society of Illustrators, 25th Annual National Exhibition.

EXHIBITIONS: Columbia College, Chicago, Ill., 1981; one woman shows at Society of Illustrators, New York, N.Y., 1983; Norfolk Public Library, 1985.

SIDELIGHTS: Kinuko Yamabe Craft was born and raised in the small Japanese town of Kanemaru, set among the hills and forests of central Honshu. As a child she was encouraged in her artistic pursuits both by environment and temperament. Her grandfather was a student of art as well as a collector, and his house was filled with museum catalogs from all over the world, reproductions, and prints of great masters, classical and modern. Indeed, she spent her youth expanding her imagination among these books and prints and sharpening her technique by painting and sketching scenes from the local countryside. Upon graduating from secondary school, she attended the Kanazawa College of Fine and Industrial Arts, from which she earned a Bachelor of Fine Arts degree in 1962. In 1963 she came to the United States and enrolled at the School of the Art Institute of Chicago to continue her studies in illustration and commercial design. In 1966 she took her first job as a staff illustrator with a Chicago art studio, and in 1969 she set out upon a freelance career. Today Kinuko Craft counts among her clients any number of prestigious editorial accounts, including *Time*, *Newsweek*, and *Forbes*, as well as major advertising and packaging clients. She has illustrated everything from *Playboy* articles to children's books, and has worked with Doubleday, Berkley, and other publishing companies.

Mrs. Craft's success in the trendy world of commercial design and illustration owes as much to her scholarly grounding in world art history as it does to her mastery of the format's production techniques. Her approach to editorial illustration, for which she is perhaps best known, has its roots in her youth, when she looked at her grandfather's books and prints and made up stories from them. Now, however, the process is reversed, as she explained in an interview in *Communication Arts:* "Since I am telling the visual side of the story, I must create an atmosphere that fits the flavor of the story. When I'm assigned a historical subject I research for costume and environment, but mainly I search for the style of the artists who existed at the period and try to paint with their procedures." From a personally assembled library of art books and clipping files, she can find inspiration for almost any assignment, and in a metier where creative impulses are often attributed to "the muse" she is not ashamed to declare, "Books are my best friends."

Once she has nailed down an appropriate style—say early Sienese Renaissance a la Duccio (complete with gesso and gold leaf surfacing) to portray Adam and Eve bobbing for apples in the garden of Eden (cover art for *National Lampoon*'s "Sin" issue)—she faces a production schedule no Renaissance master working for the most impatient of Popes could ever have confronted. To achieve the luminescence characteristic of this style, she must reject acrylics; while fast drying, they are too flat for the effect she wants. Oils would be a logical medium except that she must mix in large amounts of drier, and this detracts from the finished tone. Thus she has settled for egg tempera, built up in washes, as the best means of getting the desired lambency in combination with the quick-curing properties demanded. Using the yolk of the egg as a binder for the medium, she finds the resulting work has both delicacy of effect and toughness and durability once cured—even if, as she cheerfully admits, a piece "smells funny for a few weeks."

Her insistence on durability is another idiosyncrasy not generally encountered in the evanescent milieu of commercial art; but because of the care with which she addresses herself to the planning of an assignment and the intensity with which she executes it, Craft always tries to retain ownership of her work, and (where possible) the balance of the reproduction rights. Fortunately her status among illustrators is such that most of her clients agree to retain only reproduction rights, while she keeps physical possession, exhibition rights, and right to sale of the original art work.

A review of Craft's editorial work—and a representative portfolio is provided in the *Communication Arts* article—underlines her scholarly versatility and unimpeachable workmanship. In addition to the cleverness of her Renaissance conceits, she demonstrates mastery of a wide range of historically and culturally diverse styles. The portfolio includes a Michelangelo-like chalk line drawing that could serve as a cartoon for her own version of a chapel-ceiling Titan; a Magritte-style surrealist comment on the computer age (which is perhaps less benign in tone than its commissioner, AT&T, might have wished); a naif painting, "Picnic with Death," of a turn of the century steamship disaster; a scene from Dickens's *A Christmas Carol* (pen and ink, color wash) that faithfully echoes the esthetic of Boz's contemporary illustrators, H. K. Browne (Phiz) and John Leech; and various fantasy pieces recalling illustrators as varied as those from the Marvel Comics and *Heavy Metal* schools. Nor is her work devoid of sharp political content, as in a piece for *Cosmopolitan* which portrays woman as a yielding jazz-age flapper in the arms of a Valentino-like vampire/exploiter.

Drawing upon six centuries of art history not merely with knowledge and discipline but with respect and wit as well, Kinuko Y. Craft is clearly one of the most imaginative and least predictable of the top commercial illustrators working today.

BIOGRAPHICAL/CRITICAL SOURCES: Communication Arts, September/October, 1981.

—*Sketch by Richard Calhoun*

"Einstein at computer terminal," done for Infodata Systems Inc., ca. 1984. (© Kinuko Y. Craft. Reprinted with permission.)

CREAMER, David H.   1957-

PERSONAL: Born November 29, 1957, in Winchester, Mass.; sone of Harold David (a hardware store owner) and Judy Hayden (Hewitt) Creamer. *Education:* Graduated from Joe Kubert School of Cartoon and Graphic Art, 1981. *Office:* Modern Drummer Publications, 870 Pompton Ave., Cedar Grove, N.J. 07009.

CAREER: Art director, Modern Drummer Publications (a publisher of music magazines), 1981—; freelance cartoonist and illustrator, with clients including DC Comics, Fisher-Price, McDonald's, Peter Pan Records.

SIDELIGHTS: David Creamer wrote *CGA:* "I am currently the art director of two international magazines, and the main aspect of my career has been in the commercial art field. The most interesting thing about commercial art is that you never stop learning. There is always room to improve as long as you are willing to remain open to new ideas." As a postscript he adds that *Modern Drummer* has just won an award in its field.

A graduate of the Joe Kubert School in New Jersey, Creamer started freelancing illustrations and cartoons to miscellaneous companies even before he graduated in 1981. Among his early contributions were several comic book stories, some on war themes, an inclination he may have picked up from his mentor Joe Kubert. In these stories he displays a flair for dramatic effect and a good sense of page composition, as well as an imaginative use of irregularly shaped and elongated panels.

After graduation Creamer joined the Modern Drummer Publications (which publishes the monthly *Modern Drummer* and the quarterly *Modern Percussionist*) as art director.

A page from a war comic book. (© 1981, David Creamer. Reprinted with permission.)

His chores on the magazines (for which he also writes occasional articles) leave him little time at present for illustration work, though he continues drawing and cartooning mainly for his own enjoyment.

* * *

CREPAX, Guido   1933-

PERSONAL: Born July 15, 1933, in Milan, Italy; son of Gilberto (a cellist) and Maria Crepax; married wife, Luisa; children: Caterina, Antonio, Giacomo. *Education:* Politecnico di Milano, School of Architecture, graduated 1958. *Residence:* 45, Via de Amicis, Milan, Italy.

CAREER: Designer of record and book covers, 1953-57; commercial and advertising artist, 1957-65; comics artist and writer, 1965—. *Awards, honors:* Salone Internazionale dei Comics di Lucca, 1967; Yellow Kid and Gran Guinigi, Lucca, 1972; First Prize, American International Congress of Comics, 1972; Svenska Sereakademin, Gotheberg, Sweden, 1973; Nettuno, ANAF, Italy, 1984.

WRITINGS—All books of comics: *L'Astronave Pirata*, Rizzoli, 1968; *Valentina*, Milano Libri, 1968; *Valentina con*

DAVID CREAMER

gli Stivali, Milano Libri, 1970; *Bianca*, Edizioni Morgan, 1972; *Valentina nella Stufa*, Milano Libri, 1973; *Anita*, Edizioni Morgan, 1974; *Diario di Valentina*, Milano Libri, 1975; *Histoire d'O* (from Pauline Réage's novel of the same title), Franco Maria Ricci, 1975, published as *Story of O*, Grove, 1979; *Valentina in Giallo*, Milano Libri, 1976; *Valentina Assassina?*, Milano Libri, 1977; *L'Uomo di Pskov*, Edizioni Cepim, 1977; *Emmanuelle* (from Emmanuelle Arsan's novel of the same title), Olympia Press, 1978, Grove, 1980; *Lanterna Magica*, Edizioni d'Arte Angolare, 1978; *L'Uomo di Harlem*, Edizioni Cepim, 1979; *Justine* (from the Marquis de Sade's novel of the same title), Olympia Press, 1979, Grove, 1981; *Il Ritratto di Valentina*, Milano Libri, 1979; *Valentina Pirata*, Milano Libri, 1980, *Valentina Sola*, Milano Libri, 1981; *Venere in Pelliccia*, Olympia Press, 1984.

EXHIBITIONS: La Colonna, Como, Italy, 1968; Centro Arte, Turin, 1975; Galleria dell'Obelisco, Rome, 1975; Galleria Angolare, Milan, 1977; Gallerie Abras, Brussels, 1980, 1983; Il Vicolo, Genoa, 1981.

WORK IN PROGRESS: Another *Valentina* graphic novel in which Rembrandt comes back to Valentina; contribution to an encyclopedia of comics; short stories; a play featuring Valentina.

SIDELIGHTS: Guido Crepax's school years were filled with drawing and music; his father was a professional musician, and one of his schoolmates was the future orchestra conductor Claudio Abbado. It is hardly surprising, therefore, that his first professional works should be covers for record albums. Crepax started his cartooning career in 1959 with drawings for the medical magazine *Tempo Medico* (he still draws the covers to the magazine after twenty-five years). In 1965 Giovanni Gandini, founder of the magazine *Linus*, approached Crepax with an offer to draw and write a comic strip for his new magazine. Crepax, an avid reader and collector of comics, accepted with alacrity.

In the initial stories of the series titled *Neutron,* the hero was an enigmatic American criminologist and art critic, Philip Rembrandt—in actuality Neutron, a mutant endowed with super-powers. Valentina Rosselli made her appearance in the strip after a couple of months, became Neutron's companion, and soon took over the strip. In 1968 she appeared alone for the first time, and the next year the strip was officially renamed *Valentina*.

At the very core of Crepax's universe are his women ("Women attract me very much and frighten me very much," he once confessed). In addition to Valentina, he has conjured up many more small-chested, long-limbed beauties with delicate, patrician faces and plaintive names: Anita, Bianca, Belinda. These predilections have made Crepax the ideal illustrator for some of the most celebrated novels of erotic literature, such as the Marquis de Sade's *Justine* and Pauline Réage's *Story of O.* (It should be noted that Crepax is also the author of a children's adventure story, *L'Astronave Pirata*.)

Valentina, however, remains Crepax's most acclaimed feature. No fewer than twelve books have already been compiled from her adventures, and in 1983 the author wrote

A page from *Valentina in Giallo*. (© 1976, Guido Crepax. Reprinted with permission.)

the screenplay for *Baba Yaga*, adapted from Valentina's adventures. A devoted family man (his wife Luisa was the model for Valentina, and his children often appear in his drawings) Crepax is little impressed by the fame that has come his way with the success of *Valentina.* He shuns invitations and parties, and his life, as ordered as Valentina's is disheveled, revolves almost completely around his work.

Crepax's detractors have charged that his *Valentina* stories carry no discernible plot. This is somewhat of an exaggeration, although it is true that Crepax took greater liberty with conventional plotting as *Valentina* progressed. In the beginning (when the feature was still known as *Neutron)* it was a straightforward tale of science-fantasy. After Valentina assumed the dominant role the feature veered towards pure fantasy, with stories derived from myth, folklore, or the movies. In these latter episodes all semblance of plot does indeed disappear in favor of a stream-of-consciousness narrative, but there still remains a thematic link.

Crepax's themes are incredibly varied in their inspiration, as well as in their expression. They may be freely derived from myth (Heracles and Atalanta, Orpheus in the underworld), folklore (in some of her adventures Valentina is pitted against the legendary witch of Russian legend, Baba Yaga) or fairy tales (some of his stories are modern-dress retellings of *Snow White* or *Hansel and Gretel*). The artist also draws on movies (notably those of directors Ingmar Bergman and Michelangelo Antonioni), works of literature (*Moby Dick, Faust*), pieces of music (Richard Wagner's *Tristan and Isolde*, Modest Mussorgsky's *Pictures at an Exhibition*), and, above all, from the comics.

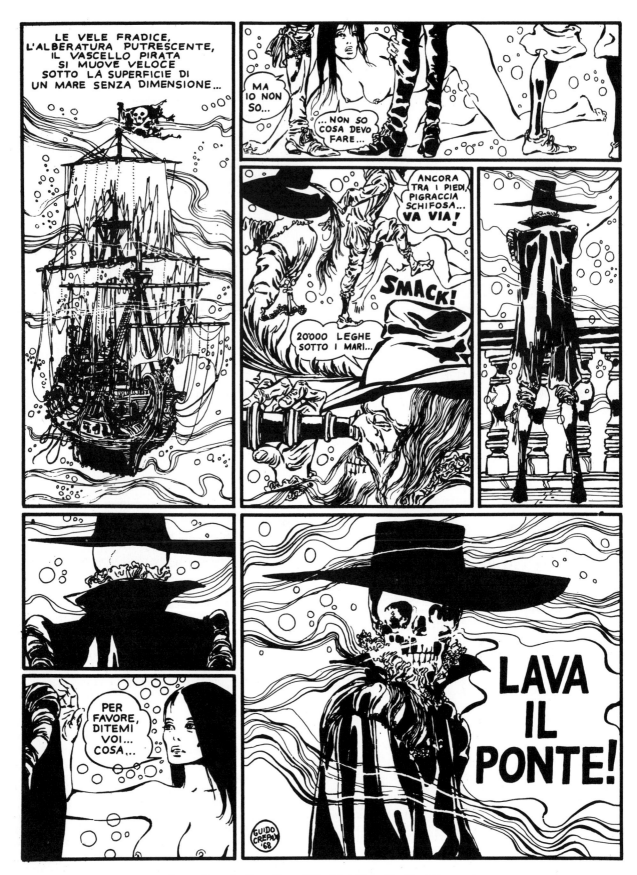

A page from *La Casa Matta* ("The Mad House"). (© 1970, EDIP.)

"Ciao Valentina," one of the most entertaining of the *Valentina* stories, is a tale of mystery that comes to its denouement in the course of a "comics party" where the guests come dressed as comic characters (Valentina in a blonde wig makes herself up as *Lil' Abner's* Daisy Mae). In other episodes Valentina fantasizes herself as "Valentina Arden" rescued from the Hawkmen by Flash Gordon, as "Princess Valda" hypnotized into willing submission by Mandrake the Magician, and as "Valentina Palmer" locked into fiery embrace with the Phantom (who leaves his famous mark—a skull—on her right buttock). There are in other Crepax works besides *Valentina* many instances of famous characters from the comics, such as Dick Tracy, Popeye, and Krazy Kat popping up in the most unexpected situations.

Crepax's fame reached the United States well before some of his books were translated here. His works are most often featured in the pages of the magazine *Heavy Metal*, and his following here is vocal and articulate. Among Crepax's admirers in this country former movie star Louise Brooks occupies a special place: she was the initial inspiration for the figure of Valentina, to whom she lent her famous hairdo and her film persona, and has kept up an active correspondence with the artist through the years.

BIOGRAPHICAL/CRITICAL SOURCES: The World Encyclopedia of Comics, Chelsea House, 1976; *Heavy Metal*, April, 1980; Vincenzo Mollica and Mauro Paganelli, *Guido Crepax*, Editori del Grifo, 1980.

—Sketch by Maurice Horn

* * *

CROFUT, Bob
See CROFUT, Robert Joel

* * *

CROFUT, Robert Joel 1951-
(Bob Crofut)

PERSONAL: Born April 20, 1951, in Danbury, Conn.; son of Marvin Robert and Dorothy (Niemeyer) Crofut. *Education:* Tufts University, B.F.A., 1974; attended Boston Museum School of Fine Arts, 1970-74. *Home and studio:* 225 Peaceable St., Ridgefield, Conn. 06877.

CAREER: Professional illustrator and painter, 1975—. Professor of illustration, Sacred Heart University, 1984-86. *Member:* Society of Illustrators, American Portrait Society, *Awards, honors:* Received sixteen awards from the Society of Illustrators, 1978 through 1985.

EXHIBITIONS: Bridgeport Museum of Art and Science, Bridgeport, Conn., 1980-85; Greenwich Workshop Gallery, Greenwich, Conn., 1983, 1984. Represented in the permanent collections of the New Britain Museum of American Art, Museum of American Illustration of the Society of Illustrators, and New York University Medical Center.

WORK IN PROGRESS: A fine art print publication scheduled for 1986; is preparing a poster and a one-man show.

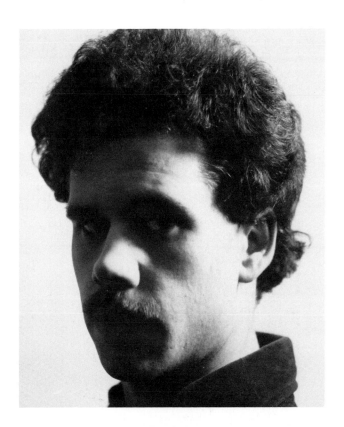

BOB CROFUT

SIDELIGHTS: Bob Crofut discovered his talent for art at age five, when he drew an amazingly accurate likeness of his favorite uncle. There was no stopping him after that. At home he found inspiration in the works of his grandmother, a remarkable self-taught artist; and in Ridgefield, where he grew up, he was an assiduous visitor to the museum made from Western artist Frederic Remington's home. After graduation from Tufts and four years of study at the Boston Museum School of Fine Arts (where he won the Sigma Nu award for best painting), Crofut performed odd jobs as a sign painter, waiter, and salesman, while pondering his future and honing his artistic skills. "My friends worried that I was becoming a hermit," he says, "but it was an important time for me as an artist. I had the time to experiment. I could select a story line and then create a variety of illustrations for it to see which one was best."

One year later, in 1975, Crofut took the plunge into the world of professional illustration, and he has never looked back again. In the next ten years he did illustration work for NBC, Exxon, IBM, Bristol Babcock, and other American corporations. He has designed posters for MGM, and illustrated classic works of literature for the Franklin Library, the Easton Press, and the Heritage Press. His art has appeared in *Reader's Digest, Outdoor Life, Field and Stream, Seventeen*, and other magazines; and it has adorned the covers of books published by Avon, Pocket Books, Signet, Berkley, Prentice-Hall, Viking, and many others. Crofut's portraits of great writers, from Feodor Dostoevski to Henry James, have been justly hailed for their deep psychological perception and their nobility of expression. He has also endowed with just the right touch of mood, mystery, and atmosphere classic adventure tales like Alexandre Dumas's *The Count of Monte Cristo.* But his forte is the American West, for which he feels a special affinity. He has painted the book covers for several Zane Grey novels, and in 1979 the Heritage Club commissioned him to paint a limited-edition print, *The Virginian*, inspired by Owen Wister's novel of the same name.

Crofut is also an established canvas painter, mainly of Western scenes, and his paintings have been bought by collectors in the United States and Europe. Of these pictures the bulletin of the Heritage Club, the *Easel*, said: "The artist invariably shows people in conflict, managing to survive against great hardships. It is a viewpoint that emerges through a wide variety of subjects: from the swashbuckling exploits of a hero to the besieged dignity on the face of an old Indian."

BIOGRAPHICAL/CRITICAL SOURCES: "The Old West Lives On," *Easel* (bulletin of the Heritage Club), 1979; Walt and Roger Reed, *The Illustrator in America: 1880-1980*, Madison Square, 1984.

Portrait of Feodor Dostoevski by Bob Crofut for *The Brothers Karamazov*, 1980. (© Heritage Press MBI Inc.)

* * *

CRUIKSHANK, Sally   1949-

PERSONAL: Born June 24, 1949, in Chatham, N.J.; daughter of Ernest (an accountant) and Rose (Swindell) Cruikshank; married Jon F. Davison (a film producer), March 17, 1984. *Education:* Smith College, B.A., 1971, *Studio:* 15143 Hartsook St., Sherman Oaks, Calif. 91403.

CAREER: Animator, Snazelle Films, San Francisco, Calif., 1972-82; independent animator, 1982—. *Awards, honors:* Grant from the Southwest Creative Film Center, 1972, to make *Chow Fun*, an animated short subject; grant from the National Endowment for the Arts, 1980, to develop *Quasi's Cabaret*, an animated feature; many film festival awards.

*FILMS—*All as director and producer: *Ducky*, 1971; *Fun on Mars*, 1971; *Chow Fun*, 1972; *Quasi at the Quackadero*, 1975; *Make Me Psychic*, 1978; *Quasi's Cabaret Trailer*, 1980 (produced as a sample for a proposed animated feature).

Animation work on other productions: *Twilight Zone: The Movie*, Warner, 1983 (designed and directed the animation in Joe Dante's episode of the movie); *Anijam*, Marv Newland, 1984 (one of twenty-two animators who each did a connected, but separate, sequence in this animation experiment); *Top Secret*, Paramount, 1985 (designed and directed the "Pacman" sequence).

Portrait of Edmond Dantes from *The Count of Monte Cristo.* (© Illustrators 27.)

SALLY CRUIKSHANK

WORK IN PROGRESS: An animated cartoon titled *Spectral Spree*; screenplays for *Quasi's Cabaret, Crooner, Your Cartoon Eyes, Love That Makes You Crawl,* and *20th Century Blues.*

SIDELIGHTS: "There is more to animation than good design and nice backgrounds," Sally Cruikshank told *CGA.* "Motion can express emotion, can create magical moods. This may seem obvious, but turn on the television set and you'll see its being too often ignored." Television directors may ignore the psychodynamics of screen motion, but Cruikshank certainly does not. Her films are filled with all kinds of incredible rotations, gyrations, permutations, and transformations that engulf characters and scenery alike.

Her first cartoon was made while she was still a student at Smith. Entitled *Ducky,* it showed both Cruikshank's love of motion for its own sake and her endless fascination with duck characters, a passion, she claims to have acquired in childhood reading *Donald Duck* and *Uncle Scrooge* comic books. Her second effort, *Fun on Mars,* was already more professional, but involved the same swirling, crazy, kaleidoscopic motion that has now become her trademark. *Chow Fun* (1972) completes the trio of early films that earned Cruikshank a reputation as a promising animator. Mixing drawings on paper and cut-out figures glued on animation

cels, it recreated the bounciness and abandon of the early *Silly Symphonies* cartoons.

Her next cartoon took two years to draw and lasted ten minutes. Her most ambitious effort to date, it introduced the two duck characters with whom she would become identified, the pudgy, guileless Quasi and Anita, a sophisticated, flirty female duck. The story took place at the Quackadero, an amusement park featuring some bizarre attractions, and was called, naturally enough, *Quasi at the Quackadero.*

The short film garnered numerous plaudits and won many theatrical bookings, thereby returning a profit on Cruikshank's initial investment of six thousand dollars. Quasi and Anita were teamed again in her next film, *Make Me Psychic,* which featured a great many sight gags in quick succession. With a ten-thousand-dollar grant from the National Endowment for the Arts, she next produced a three-minute sample for a proposed feature film that would again star Quasi and Anita. *Quasi's Cabaret Trailer* opens with Anita, Quasi, and a Cab Calloway-type character named Snozzy proposing to set up a tropical nightclub and making a sales pitch to potential producers for financial backing. By 1985 Cruikshank had completed the screenplay for the feature.

Cruikshank's cartoons have been called "bizarre," "off-the-wall," "crazy," and worse. She only modestly admits to having "a sense of motion that makes for an offbeat view of the world." Her imagery comes from underground comics, the psychedelic posters of the 1960s, Art Deco designs, and funny-animal comic books. She blends it all with the inspired craziness of early Warner Bros. and Max Fleischer cartoons. Sally Cruikshank is obviously one animator to watch.

BIOGRAPHICAL/CRITICAL SOURCES: J. Hoberman, "The Kwazy World of Sally Cruikshank," *American Film,* December, 1981; Kyle Counts, "The Short Life of Sally Cruikshank," *Comics Scene,* January, 1982.

A frame from *Make Me Psychic,* 1978. (© Sally Cruikshank. Printed with permission.)

A frame from *Quasi at the Quackadero,* **1975.** (© Sally Cruikshank. Printed with permission.)

* * *

CRUSE, Howard 1944-

PERSONAL: Born May 2, 1944, in Birmingham, Ala.; son of Jesse Clyde (a minister, journalist, and photographer; died 1963) and Irma (a telephone company executive; maiden name Russell) Cruse. *Education:* Birmingham-Southern College, B.A., 1968. *Religion:* "Free form cosmic potpourri." *Home and studio:* Jackson Heights, N.Y.

CAREER: Assistant to art director, WAPI-TV (now WVTM-TV), Birmingham, Ala., 1964-65; staff artist, *Birmingham News,* 1967; paste-up artist, Mag Computer Corporation, New York City, 1969; art director and puppeteer, WBMG-TV, Birmingham, Ala., 1969-72; actor and scenic design assistant, Atlanta Children's Theatre, 1972-73; photostat operator and staff artist, Art Service, Inc., Atlanta, Ga., 1973-74; staff artist, Luckie & Forney Advertising,

Birmingham, Ala., 1975-76; art director, *Starlog* and *Future Life,* New York City, 1977-78; freelance illustrator, cartoonist, and writer, 1963—; founding editor of *Gay Comix,* 1980-84.

MEMBER: Cartoonists Guild, Graphic Artists Guild, New York Theatre Bridge Playwright's Circle. *Awards, honors:* Shubert Playwriting Fellowship, 1968.

WRITINGS: (Illustrator) H. William Stine and Megan Stine, *How to Succeed in Sports Without Ever Playing,* Scholastic, 1981; (illustrator) Steven Bloom, *Video Invaders,* Arco, 1982; *Wendel,* Gay Presses of New York, 1985 (collection of comic strips from the *Advocate).* Contributor of cartoons and illustrations to periodicals, including *American Health, American Photographer, Success, Crawdaddy, Geo, Playboy, Heavy Metal, Village Voice,* and *Advocate.* Author of "Loose Cruse" column on cartooning in *Comics Scene,* 1981-83. Writer and illustrator of daily cartoon panel *Tops & Button* in *Birmingham Post-Herald,* 1970-72.

Self-portrait of Howard Cruse. (© 1985, H. Cruse. Printed with permission.)

Also author of seven short plays and one long play, all unpublished, non-professionally produced in Alabama, Georgia, Pennsylvania, and New York City; author of two short teleplays broadcast on Alabama Educational Television.

SIDELIGHTS: Howard Cruse has been fascinated by comics from his earliest age. "When he was 6 years old, the preacher's son drew his first comic book," wrote Clarke Stallworth in the *Birmingham News.* "It was an adaptation of *Alice in Wonderland,* and little Howard Cruse showed the crude drawings to his parents Clyde and Irma Cruse." They liked them and encouraged their son to develop his drawing abilities. From then on Cruse doggedly kept on drawing comics in his spare time, while pursuing a more conventional career as staff artist and illustrator.

Cruse's comic strip work started appearing regularly in the 1970s in the pages of underground comics such as *Yellow Dog, Snarf, Alien Encounters,* and *Dope Comix*; he was also featured alone in three issues of *Barefootz Funnies* (1975-79). Cruse came into his own, however, in *Gay Comix* (of which he is the founding editor) with such stories as "Billy Goes Out," which the author said, "got more response. . . than anything else I've done." Since then he has gone on to develop more features in the same vein, including *Wendel,* a humorous strip about gay people in an unnamed city.

Cruse wrote *CGA:* "When I'm drawing a book or magazine illustration, my goal is to create a visual moment that is funny or interesting. I want it to invite the reader to slow down and spend some time with the text. My sense of humor will be on display, but not necessarily my own philosophy of life. When I write and draw comic strips, though, communicating my own philosophy becomes my central concern.

Excerpt from *Wendel* comic strip. (© 1984, H. Cruse. Reprinted with permission.)

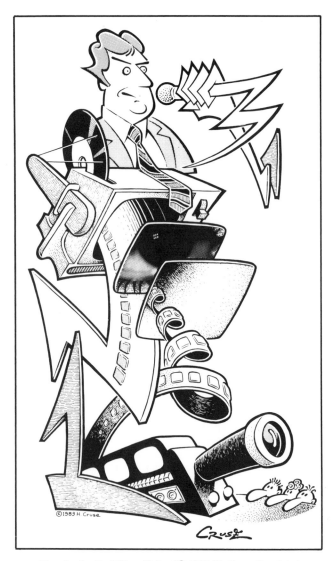

Drawing for the *Village Voice*. (© 1983, H. Cruse. Reprinted with permission.)

"The comic strip still needs to be funny or dramatically involving; and the philosophy I am talking about is almost never badly stated. The point of view of the artist surfaces eventually, implied by his or her choices of style, form and content over the years that make up a creatively productive life.

"Hopefully, someone who reads many of my strips and stories will gain a sense of what my values are. Ideally, that person will ultimately be moved emotionally to care about some of the things I care about. Comics that only deal in fantasy rarely interest me. Comics that wield satire in a spirit of arrogance repel me.

"I enjoy the company of comics that reflect concern about the real feelings people have about real life. I admire the work of cartoonists who dare to explore the harshest of life's truths without evasions and euphemisms. I'm drawn to satire which is skeptical but humane, in which the satirist points the finger of ridicule at his own behavior as well as at the behavior of others.

"These are the kinds of comics I like to read, and these are the kinds of comics I try to draw."

BIOGRAPHICAL/CRITICAL SOURCES: Howard Cruse, "Me, Barefootz, and Underground Comix," *Cartoonist Profiles*, June 1980; Clarke Stallworth, "Cruse's Comics: Wonderland to Underground," *Birmingham News*, July 31, 1983; Gillian G. Garr, "Cartoons and Coffee with Howard Cruse," *Washington Cascade Voice*, August 10, 1984; "Howard Cruse News," *Comics Buyer's Guide*, March 15, 1985.

*   *   *

CUCCIO, David   1956-

PERSONAL: Surname is pronounced "Kooshe-ō"; born July 30, 1956, in Columbus, Ohio; son of Paul S. (a truckdriver) and Louise E. (Ross) Cuccio; married Sandra K. Johnson (an elementary art teacher), August 11, 1979. *Education;* Graduate of Joe Kubert School of Cartoon and Graphic Art, Dover, N.J., 1984. *Home and studio:* 168 Woodcliff Dr., Columbus, Ohio 43213.

CAREER: Sanitation crew, Rainbo Bakery, Albuquerque, N.M., 1979-1980; salesman, Office Outfitters, Columbus, Ohio, 1980; forklift operator, Allied Farm Equipment, Columbus, Ohio, 1981; illustration, production, and camera work, Brewster-Nock Advertising, Landing, N.J., 1982-83; advertising and commercial artist, 1984—. *Member:* Columbus Society of Communicating Arts.

WORK IN PROGRESS: Research for magazine editorial illustrations, work for advertising agencies.

Self-portrait of David Cuccio, drawn specially for *Contemporary Graphic Artists*.

SIDELIGHTS: David Cuccio's first artistic job came in 1978 when, for about a year, he did ink portraits of sales personnel as well as watercolor renditions of homes under contract for Century 21, a national real-estate company. After the real estate market came to a virtual standstill in 1979, he supported himself in various jobs while saving money for college. Since graduating from the Joe Kubert School, Cuccio has been busy doing illustrations and design for various corporate clients, creating presentation manuals and brochures, and submitting editorial illustrations to various magazines.

David Cuccio commented to *CGA*: "The opportunity to bring a client's vision to life is always exciting and challenging, and it's that kind of reward that makes illustration enjoyable to me. The desire to learn and a love for the expression afforded an artist is what keeps me going when things are the roughest.

"While in college, I found that a montage allows me more freedom of movement and expression than one illustration generally does. I like to experiment with shapes and shades, tearing away and building images until, finally, I know I have what I want to say on the board.

"I enjoy working with diluted inks, watercolor, and pencil most of all, although I think you should always keep yourself open to new media experimentation. I draw inspiration and enthusiasm from artists such as Bob Peak, Jim Sharpe, and Ken Dallison. They continually amaze me with their skill and knowledge. Looking at their accomplishments only makes me want to work that much harder, to please my own creative drive."

Cuccio's illustrations show him to be in possession of a clear, uncluttered line and a neat, straightforward style that should grow more personal as he matures and develops. One last personal note: a small, stylized raccoon adorns David Cuccio's professional letterhead, because, "I have a special affinity for raccoons," the artist says. "Their curiosity and impetuous nature made them an obvious choice to include in my logo design."

BIOGRAPHICAL/CRITICAL SOURCES: "Showcase Feature Artist," *Art Product News*, September, 1985.

D

D'ALESSIO, Hilda   1914-
(Hilda Terry)

PERSONAL: Born June 25, 1914, in Newburyport, Mass.; daughter of Charles (a barber and male nurse) and Annie (a shoe factory worker; maiden name Aronson) Fellman; married Gregory d'Alessio (an artist, cartoonist, and writer) June 11, 1938; children: none ("by choice"). *Education:* High school equivalency diploma, 1972; attended National Academy of Design, 1932; Art Students League, 1939; New York University, 1965. *Religion:* Jewish. *Home and studio:* 8 Henderson Place, New York, N.Y. 10028.

CAREER: Cartoonist 1935-; creator of "Teena," 1941-64; director, Hilda Terry Gallery, 1964—; computer animator for electronic scoreboards, 1969—; also worked at various times as Varitype operator, designer, caterer; taught cartooning at Phoenix School of Design, New York City, and New School for Social Research, New York City Camp Fire Girls, volunteer leader, 1944-61; member of the board, Prescott Neighborhood House, early 1950s—; youth leader, Police Athletic League. *Member:* National Cartoonists Society, Association Internationale du Film d'Animation (ASI-FA; name means "International Association of Animated Film"), "numerous computer societies." *Awards, honors:* Best "Waste Not" cartoon award, New York Times, 1943; Camp Fire Girls WOHELO Award, 1956: award for best animator, National Cartoonists Society, 1980.

WRITINGS: "Teena," King Features Syndicate, 1941-64; Teena comic book series, Magazine Enterprises, 1948-49; *Originality in Art*, Art and Cartoon, 1954.

FILMS: Computer animation for *Turk 182*, Twentieth Century-Fox, 1985.

WORK IN PROGRESS: A book about computerized electronic scoreboards tentatively titled *Scoreboard Lady;* an autobiography ("never ending"); a book tentatively titled *The IRS and Me.*

SIDELIGHTS: Hilda Terry is best known as the creator of the comic strip *Teena,* which is still fondly remembered today. Of the feature Coulton Waugh wrote in *The Comics:* "*Teena*. . . originated in a panel that ran in the *Saturday Evening Post*, and now is a King Features feature, a star of the Saturday color section of the New York *Journal-American.* Hilda Terry . . . knows young girls at first hand and her drawings of them have an uncanned, juicy quality . . . " Endearing and whimsical, her strip about typical American teenagers endured for almost a quarter-century.

HILDA D'ALESSIO (Hilda Terry)

After her feature folded, Terry, who had her cartoons published as early as 1938 in such magazines as the *New Yorker, Saturday Evening Post*, and *College Humor*, went back to school and took courses in computer science. This led directly to her present position as one of the preeminent creators of animation for huge computerized scoreboards in stadiums and arenas. As *The World Encyclopedia of Cartoons* summed it up: "As a cartoonist, Hilda Terry has always been a pioneer. In the field of syndicated comics, where successful women cartoonists are the exception rather than the rule, she enjoyed a long career. Now she is possibly the only cartoonist so intimately involved with the newest technological cartooning medium."

Of her current work Terry stated in a 1978 interview in *Cartoonist Profiles:* "As a creative medium, it's extremely fulfilling. There has to be a future for it as a fine art, which has never been profitable for artists, but has always been the ultimate in satisfaction. There aren't enough walls in the world to accommodate the accelerated production as more and more people have more and more time for self-expression, and since, in my belief, cartoonists—on the highest level—are the purest of fine art expressionists,

A *Teena* Sunday page by Hilda Terry. (© 1959, King Features Syndicate.)

observing, reporting and recording the sense and mood of their generations, these expressions must be increasingly preserved on tape, film, microfilm, and computer disk-packs." As a postscript Terry wrote *CGA:* "Jim Mitschele and I created a peripheral system for the Kansas City Royals that allows graphic input from the Apple computer, making it possible for others to do the work, so after this season I'm going to stay home and write."

BIOGRAPHICAL/CRITICAL SOURCES: Coulton Waugh, *The Comics*, Macmillan, 1947; "Hilda Terry's Scoreboard Animations," *Cartoonist Profiles*, September, 1978; *The World Encyclopedia of Cartoons*, Chelsea House, 1980; *Who's Who in American Art*, 16th edition, Bowker, 1984; "Computer Wizards Improve Animation," *Kansas City Times*, April 2, 1984.

* * *

DARVC
   See CORBEN, Richard V(ance)

* * *

DE CESARE, John A.   1935-

PERSONAL: Surname is pronounced "Dee-Caesar"; born August 13, 1935, in the Bronx, N.Y.; son of Louis A. and Marjorie (Chism) de Cesare; married Moira K. O'Dea, August 11, 1956; children: John L., Paul A., Michael P. *Education:* Attended Brown University, 1953-54; University of Buffalo, A.A.S., 1956, *Home:* 15 Waverly Rd., Darien, Conn. 06820. *Studio and office:* De Cesare Design Associates, 22 Thorndal Circle, Darien, Conn. 06820.

CAREER: Art director, Macmillan (a publishing company), New York, N.Y., 1960-63; senior art director, BBDO Communications Design Center, New York, N.Y., 1964-67; executive art director, Geigy (a pharmaceutical company), Ardsley, N.Y., and Summit, N.J., 1967-78; president, De Cesare Design Associates, 1978—; vice-president and managing director, the Illustrators Workshop, 1979—. *Member:* Society of Illustrators, American Institute of Graphic Arts.

JOHN DE CESARE

A John de Cesare design.

AWARDS, HONORS—Numerous awards, including: Gold Medal from New Jersey Art Directors Club, 1973, 1978, and 1980; Gold Medal from Society of Illustrators, 1978; Gold Medal, Society of Publication Designers, 1979; Gold Medal, New York Art Directors Club, 1978 and 1979.

WRITINGS: Contributor to *Graphis* and *Advertising Techniques.*

EXHIBITIONS: Albright Art Gallery, Buffalo, N.Y., 1970; University of Buffalo, 1970.

SIDELIGHTS: John de Cesare is one of the most successful art directors and designers of the so-called post-modernist era. As the art director for Geigy he had graphic responsibility for all advertising, direct mail, sales promotion materials, publications, and exhibits. His design and packaging of both old and new products earned him numerous citations and inclusion in a ten-year retrospective of the best in packaging design by *Graphis*. His designs for publications and brochures have also been much praised.

In 1978 de Cesare left Geigy to form his own design firm, and rapidly established himself as a leading design consultant. His clients include Mobil Oil, Hitachi, McGraw-Hill, International Thomson, Volvo, the Cousteau Society, AGIP-USA, and the National Association of Home Builders. As can be expected he also works extensively with pharmaceutical and medical concerns, such as Johnson & Johnson, Roche Laboratories, Parke-Davis, Dupont Pharmaceuticals, and Ciba-Geigy. He is also a former consultant to the New York State Council on the Arts, and is listed on the Federal Registry of the National Endowments for the Arts.

In addition de Cesare also lectures extensively at universities, art schools, and graphic art societies. In 1979 he assumed the position of vice-president of the Illustrators Workshop, and has presented programs yearly at locations that include Monterey, Calif., and Paris, France.

AVOCATIONAL INTERESTS: Travel to Europe ("to be exposed to graphics there, see historical places and works") and to the Caribbean islands ("for relaxation"). Appreciates all sports, both as participant and spectator.

BIOGRAPHICAL/CRITICAL SOURCES: Communication Arts, autumn, 1978; *Idea Magazine,* Tokyo, 1979; *Graphis,* January-February, 1981.

*   *   *

DEDINI, Eldon Lawrence   1921-

PERSONAL: Born June 29, 1921, in King City, Calif.; son of Grutly S. (a rancher) and Oleta (a teacher; maiden name Loeber) Dedini; married Virginia Conroy (a painter), July 15, 1944; son: Giulio. *Education:* Hartnell College, Salinas, Calif., A.A., 1942; attended Chouinard Art Institute, Los Angeles, Calif., 1942-44. *Religion:* Episcopalian. *Office:* Box 1630, Monterey, Calif., 93942.

CAREER: Editorial cartoonist, *Salinas Index-Journal* and *Salinas Morning Post,* 1940-41; staff artist, Universal Studios, Universal City, Calif., 1944; artist in story department, Walt Disney Studios, 1944-46; staff cartoonist and gag writer, *Esquire,* 1946-50; contract cartoonist, *The New Yorker,* 1950—; contract cartoonist, *Playboy,* 1960—; freelance contributor to various magazines since 1942, including *Judge, Art in America, Punch, Collier's, Look, Saturday Evening Post, Sports Illustrated, True, Holiday. Member:* National Cartoonists Society, Cartoonists Association.

AWARDS, HONORS: Best Magazine Cartoonists Award from National Cartoonists Society, 1958, 1961, 1964; Best Color Cartoon from *Playboy,* 1978.

WRITINGS: The Dedini Gallery, Holt, 1961; (illustrator) Yvette de Petra, *La Clef,* Holt, 1970; (contributor) Bob Abel, editor, *The Great American Cartoon Gallery,* Dodd, 1974; (contributor) *20th Anniversary Playboy Cartoon Album,* Playboy Press, 1974; (contributor) *New Yorker Album of Drawings 1925-1975,* Viking, 1975; *A Much, Much Better World,* Microsoft Press, 1985.

EXHIBITIONS: Richmond Museum of Art, Richmond, Calif., 1968; Monterey Peninsula Museum of Art, Monterey, Calif., 1983.

ELDON DEDINI

WORK IN PROGRESS: A cartoon book of political humor.

SIDELIGHTS: At age twelve Eldon Dedini became intrigued by the watercolor cartoons he saw in a certain magazine and tried to copy them. Intrigued by the process, he bought a book on the art of cartooning by Lawrence Lariar and studied particularly the sections on roughing out and captioning. Five years later, he sold his first cartoon to the very magazine that had inspired those first emulations, *Esquire,* and the career of one of the more successful and (in his own right) widely emulated of modern cartoonists was launched.

Having focused on a career in art early on, Dedini was singularly dedicated to the advancement of his prospects. As a student at a junior college in Salinas, California, he took a portfolio of drawings to the editor of the local newspaper and not only got a job as an editorial cartoonist but arranged to receive college credit for his experience as well. Winning a scholarship to the prestigious Chouinard Art Institute in Los Angeles in 1942, he spent the next two years formally studying art by day and freelance cartooning by night for *Esquire, Judge,* and other contemporary magazines. In 1944, he left school and went to work in the story department at the Walt Disney Studios and there, he recalls, his education really began.

"Maybe I'd spend days working on a background sketch . . . and still not get it to my satisfaction," he told an interviewer in 1973, "Finally a messenger girl would take my sketch down to the background department and half an hour later she'd come back with a great big finished rendering of the scene that would knock my eyes out. When I saw it, I felt about two inches tall, but yet I studied the drawing to see how the background artist did it. One certainly learned humility there." To this day, Dedini freely admits that the painterly quality of his humorous art is an outgrowth of the opportunity he had to work with the Disney staff, whose members constituted the core of what would become known as the Southern California Watercolor Group. Among cartoonists, Dedini mentions as inspirational figures two rather obvious stylistic influences—Peter Arno, the *New Yorker*'s cynical recorder of Jazz Age excesses and E. Simms Campbell, watercolorist supreme of statuesque femininity for *Esquire* and *Playboy*—and one gifted gagster, the *New Yorker*'s Whitney Darrow, Jr.

In 1946, he received a call from the editor of *Esquire* offering him two times his salary at Disney to become the magazine's staff humorist. He accepted and during 1946-50 worked exclusively for *Esquire*, under contract to produce a certain number of finishes as well as gag ideas for the magazine's stable of contributing artists. During this period he regularly came up with one hundred gags a month, farming them out to the likes of E. Simms Campbell, Barbara Shermund, and Paul Webb. But an artist and humorist as prolific and versatile as Dedini was not likely to remain exclusively connected to one outlet; thus in 1950, he received a "first look" contract from the *New Yorker*'s cartoon editor, Jim Geraghty, and embarked upon a full-time freelance career. Since that time his cartoons have appeared regularly in the most prestigious of the few remaining showcases for comic art.

As a superior artist and a very funny man, Dedini has learned that creation is a constant struggle between the painter and the clown. Full-page watercolors, for example, often become so involved as artistic productions, they tend to lose the humor that Dedini regards as his bread and butter. The urge to illustrate, he maintains, "is death to humor," and so he must wage a never-ending war "to keep the eyes beady and the nose bulgy, or vice versa." When he fails, he finds it best to tear up the over-production and begin anew. In his chosen metier, Dedini acknowledges that the most important skill to possess is that of the humorist. A clown can always learn to draw well enough if he has something genuinely amusing to say, but the most gifted technician cannot learn to be funny.

When all is said and done, however, it is his signature style that has elevated Dedini to his current standing as a graphic artist—the bold, curving lines, the bright colors, the lush backdrops that taken altogether define the "Dedini style." As he tells it, he first became aware that he was held worthy of emulation in the late 1950s when a fellow cartoonist told him about a sale to a daring new magazine whose "hands on" publisher had suggested a color finish "in the Dedini style." "I figured if they were going to teach people to work in my style, I'd better get in on some of it." As a result, his colorful, funny, and ever-tastefully risque panels have been a staple in *Playboy* since 1960. (Incidentally, his rule of thumb as a contributor of cartoons to both *Playboy* and the *New*

Yorker: "It may have the same essence in both magazines, but in the *Playboy* version the men's eyes will bug out and the women will weigh an extra seventy-five pounds.")

From a purely technical standpoint, Dedini attributes his success to hard work, openness to new impressions, and wide and varied reading. In a highly competitive milieu, that means twelve hour days, the ability to replenish one's stock of types through random observation, and a voracious curiosity. He reads chiefly novels, memoirs, news magazines, and papers, but no area is too abstruse in pursuit of a good gag. Recalling one line he came across and particularly liked—"I think he's a little weak with his potentiometers, but the oscillating feedback is inspired."—he recounts doing the cartoon and after it had been rejected in his main markets selling it to the magazine in which he had originally come across the line in an article about Moog synthesizers. Ultimately, however, grueling work schedules, attention to faces in the street, and literary tastes running from Faulkner to *Motor Trend* do not of themselves make every practitioner of comic art a Dedini. As to the source of his creative impulses, he expresses a comfortable ignorance. "Maybe if I knew more about it, I'd lose the touch."

Perhaps the key to Dedini's originality can be found in his ultimate goal as a cartoonist. He is on record as wanting to produce a belly laugh—not merely a chuckle or a smile—every time out; but even beyond this formidable task, his main concern is the thought the reader is left with after the laugh. A case in point is found in the history of one of his *New Yorker* cartoons. He had read an article on guided tours in the Sunday *New York Times* and was reading some recipes in another section when he started free associating. The result was a drawing of an elderly American couple in a Parisian restaurant, wearing earphones and eating a "guided

"You're retired now. Relax." A magazine cartoon, 1976.
(© *New Yorker*.)

"This is all very well for you Roman soldiers, but what we Sabine women really need is a children's day-care center!"

A magazine cartoon by Eldon Dedini, 1982. (© *Playboy*.)

meal" of Choucroute a l'Alsacienne. Beyond the absurdist premise, Dedini had a more profound point to make, i.e., that in our media-conscious society people are so attuned to the notion of authority that they have lost the knack of experiencing a thing to its fullest unless there is some reinforcing commentary from an exterior, presumably expert source. Several weeks after the cartoon's appearance, Dedini was pleased to read an article in the *Times* Travel Section that picked up his point and, using the drawing as a point of reference, expanded upon it. This article in turn was followed by an exchange of letters by readers, and the artist was gratified to have provoked the sort of response an artist always hopes for but is seldom aware of getting. And, as if the personal satisfaction weren't enough, he reports: "IBM in New York bought the original."

BIOGRAPHICAL/CRITICAL SOURCES: Cartoonist Profiles, June, 1973; *Contemporary Authors*, Vol. 65-68, Gale, 1977; *The World Encyclopedia of Cartoons*, Chelsea House, 1980; *Who's Who in America*, 1984-85, Marquis, 1984.

—Sketch by Richard Calhoun

*   *   *

DEVLIN, Harry   1918-

PERSONAL: Born March 22, 1918, in Jersey City, N.J.; son of Harry George (general manager of Savarin Co.) and Amelia (Crawford) Devlin; married Dorothy Wende (an artist and writer), August 30, 1941; children: Harry Noel, Wende Elizabeth Gates, Jeffrey Anthony, Alexandra Gail Eldridge, Brion Phillip, Nicholas Kirk, David Matthew. *Education:* Syracuse University, B.F.A., 1939. *Politics:* Independent. *Religion:* Congregationalist. *Home and studio:* 443 Hillside Ave., Mountainside, N.J. 07092.

CAREER: Cartoonist, illustrator, and writer, 1939—; editorial cartoonist, *Collier's,* 1945-54. Lecturer in history of fine arts and history of American domestic architecture, Union College, Cranford, N.J., 1962-64. Member of the New Jersey State Council on the Arts (grants chairman, vice-chairman), 1970-79. President, Mountainside Public Library, 1968-69; member of Rutgers University Advisory Council on Children's Literature; chairman, Advisory Board on the Arts, Union County, N.J., vocational and technical schools, 1972-75; trustee, Morris Museum, N.J., 1980—; member, New Jersey Committee for the Humanities, 1984—. *Military service:* U.S. Naval Reserve, 1942-46; served as artist; became lieutenant, Office of Naval Intelligence.

MEMBER: Society of Illustrators (life member); National Cartoonists Society (president, 1956-57); Associated Artists of New Jersey (president, 1983—); Artists Equity Association (New Jersey); Graphic Artists Guild; Dutch Treat Club. *Awards, honors:* New Jersey Teachers of English Award, 1970, for *How Fletcher Was Hatched!;* Award of Excellence, Chicago Book Fair, 1974, for *Old Witch Rescues Halloween;* New Jersey Institute of Technology Award, 1976, for *Tales of Thunder and Lightning;* Arents Award for Art and Literature, Syracuse University, 1977; Chairman's Award for the painting "House on High Street," Society of Illustrators, 1981; elected to Hall of Fame in Literature,

HARRY DEVLIN

Photo by: Lucinda Dowell.

New Jersey Institute of Technology, 1980; elected to Advertising Hall of Fame, 1983; five times winner, Best in Advertising Cartoons, National Cartoonists Society, 1956, 1962, 1963, 1977, 1978; awarded Honorary Doctorate in Humane Letters by Kean College, 1985.

WRITINGS—Juveniles, all self-illustrated: *To Grandfather's House We Go,* Parents' Magazine Press, 1967; *The Walloping Window Blind,* Van Nostrand, 1968; *What Kind of House Is That?,* Parents' Magazine Press, 1969; *Tales of Thunder and Lightning,* Parents' Magazine Press, 1975.

With wife, Wende Devlin: *Old Black Witch,* Encyclopaedia Britannica Press, 1963; *The Knobby Boys to the Rescue,* Parents' Magazine Press, 1965; *Aunt Agatha, There's a Lion Under the Couch,* Van Nostrand, 1968; *How Fletcher Was Hatched!,* Parents' Magazine Press, 1969; *A Kiss for a Warthog,* Van Nostrand, 1970; *Old Witch and the Polka Dot Ribbon,* Parents' Magazine Press; *Cranberry Thanksgiving,* Parents' Magazine Press, 1971; *Old Witch Rescues Halloween,* Parents' Magazine Press, 1973; *Cranberry Christmas,* Parents' Magazine Press, 1976; *Hang on Hester,* Lothrop, 1980; *Cranberry Halloween,* Four Winds, 1982.

FILMS—Author and host, all for New Jersey Public Broadcasting Corp. (now New Jersey Network): four films collectively entitled *Fare Thee Well, Old House,* 1976, 1979, 1980, 1981; *Houses of the Hackensack,* 1976; *To Grandfather's House We Go,* 1981.

The Winter of the Witch (adapted by Gerald Herman from *Old Black Witch*), Parents' Magazine Films, 1972.

EXHIBITIONS—All one-man shows: Morris Museum, Morristown, N.J., 1979; World Headquarters, General Electric, Fairfield, Conn., 1980; Union League Club, New York City, 1981.

WORK IN PROGRESS: A book on American architecture, with sixty-six paintings, to be published David Godine.

SIDELIGHTS: Harry Devlin wrote *CGA:* "While a member of the New Jersey State Council on the Arts I was able to get funding for the founding of the Rutgers University Collection of Children's Art and Literature, now a thriving entity of the Voorhees Zimmerli Museum of Rutgers University." Looking further back on his durable and varied career, he commented: "As I have survived as an artist and writer, I

"A House at Waverly," illustration for *Portraits of American Architecture.* (© Morris Museum of Arts & Sciences.)

can say that diversity is the key to survival. I have illustrated magazines, novels, children's books, painted portraits and murals, and was an editorial cartoonist. I am now devoting much of my time to writing and painting."

Devlin's career really took flight after World War II when, as an editorial cartoonist for *Collier's,* he made a name for himself as a shrewd and clear-headed commentator. He also created two newspaper strips of unfortunately short duration, *Fullhouse* and *Raggmopp.* The latter was a child strip of more than passing charm, which Jerry Robinson in *The Comics* described as "stylishly drawn with a tasteful use of white space."

The same stylishness characterizes Devlin's later book illustrations. The clear line, solid black masses, and detailed background of his drawings endow them with a down-to-earth quality that agreeably contrasts with the whimsical treatment of the characters. The books illustrated on texts by his wife Wende have often been best-sellers, and many of them are now recognized as children's classics.

BIOGRAPHICAL/CRITICAL SOURCES: New York Times Book Review, May 9, 1965, January 4, 1970; *Library Journal,* May 15, 1969, May 15, 1970; Jerry Robinson, *The Comics: An Illustrated History of Comic Strip Art,* Putnam, 1974; *Who's Who in American Art,* 16th edition, Bowker, 1984.

*   *   *

DORE, (Louis Christophe Paul) Gustave   1832-1883

PERSONAL: Surname is pronounced Do-*ray,* was originally Dorer; given name sometimes listed as Louis Auguste; born January 6, 1832, in Strasbourg, France; died, January 23, 1883, in Paris, France. *Education:* Attended Lycee Charlemagne, Paris, France.

CAREER: Painter, sculptor, book illustrator. Started professional career at age fifteen; regular contributor, *Le Journal pour Rire,* 1848; began to exhibit pen-and-ink drawings, at the Paris Salon, 1848; with Charles Philippon, established the periodical, *Musee Anglo-Francais,* 1856; instrumental in founding of Dore Galley, London, 1869. Among his well-known works (aside from his illustrations) are: "Christ Leaving the Praetorium," 1867-72; "L'Ange et Tobie," ("The Angel and Tobias"), 1876, now at the Luxembourg Gallery in Paris; "La Vigne" ("The Vine," a sculpture of a colossal vase) exhibited at the Universal Exhibition in Paris, 1878. *Awards, honors:* Honorable mention for the painting "The Battle of Inkerman" at the Paris Salon, 1857; made Chevalier of the Legion of Honor, 1892.

WRITINGS—All as illustrator: *Les Travaux d'Hercule* (title means "The Labors of Hercules"), Aubert, 1847: *Desagrements d'un Voyage d'Agrement,* Arnaud de Vresse, 1849: *Trois Artistes Incompris, Meconnus et Mecontents: Leur Voyage en Province et Ailleurs, Leur Faim Devorante, et Leur Deplorable Fin* (French wit and humor), Arnaud de Vresse, 1849; *Histoire Pittoresque, Dramatique et Caricaturale de la Sainte Russie,* J. Bry aine, 1854, translation by

Cover for Dore's *Les Travaux d'Hercule*, **1847.**

Daniel Weissbort published as *The Rare and Extraordinary History of Holy Russia*, reprinted Library Press, 1971; *Two Hundred Sketches, Humorous and Grotesque*, Warne, 1867; *Historical Cartoons; or, Rough Pencillings of the World's History, from the First to the Nineteenth Century*, Hotten, 1868.

Other illustrated works: Francois Rabelais, *Oeuvres de Rabelais*, J. Bry aine, 1854, translation by Thomas Urquhart and Peter A. Motteux published as *Works of Rabelais*, Hotten, 1871; Honore de Balzac, *Les Contes Drolatiques Colligez ez Abbayes de Touraine*, [Paris], 1855, translation by Alec Brown published as *Droll Stories Collected in the Monasteries of Touraine*, Elek Books, 1958; Cecile Jules Gerard, *La Chasse au Lion*, [Paris], 1855, translation published as *Lion Hunting in Algeria*, [London], 1874; Hippolyte A. Taine, *Voyage aux Eaux des Pyrenees*, L. Hachette, 1855, translation by J. Safford Fiske published as *A Tour Through the Pyrenees*, Holt, 1874; Mary Lafou, translator, *Histoire du Chevalier Jaufre et de la Belle Brunissende: Legende Nationale*, Librarie Nouvelle, 1855, English translation published as *Sir Geoffrey the Knight: A Tale of Chivalry*, Nelson & Sons, 1869.

M. Lafou, translator, *Fierbras d'Alexandrie: Legende Nationale* Librarie Nouvelle, 1856; Pierre Dupont, *La Legende du Juif Errant*, Michel Levy freres, 1856, translation by G. W. Thornbury published as *The Legend of the Wandering Jew*, [London], 1857; Benjamin Gastineau, *La France en Afrique et l'Orient a Paris*, [Paris], circa 1856; *Historie Complete de la Guerre d'Italie*, [Paris], 1959; Victor Adolphe Malte-Brun, *Geographie du Theatre de la Guerre et des Etats*

Circonvoisins, [Paris], 1859; George Pardon, *Boldhearts the Warrior and His Adventures in the Haunted Wood: A Tale of the Times of Good King Arthur*, [London], 1859.

(With Birket Foster) William Shakespeare, *The Tempest*, Bell & Daldy, 1860; *L'Histoire des Environs de Paris*, [Paris], 1860; *Les Figures du Temps*, [Paris], 1861; Edmond Francois About, *Le Roi des Montagnes*, [Paris], 1861, translation by C.F.L. Wraxall published as *The Greek Brigand: or, The King of the Mountains*, J. & R. Maxwell, 1881; Charles Perrault, *Les Contes de Perrault*, edited by J. Hetzel, [Paris], 1861, translation by Charles Welsh published as *The Tales of Mother Goose*, D. C. Heath, 1902, new translation by A. E. Johnson published as *Perrault's Fairy Tales*, Dover, 1969.

C. Vincent and E. Plouvier, *Les Chansons d'Autrefois* (French ballads and songs), Coulon Pineau, 1861; Leon Godard, *L'Espagne: Moeurs et Paysages, Histoire et Monuments*, A. Mame, 1862; Leon de Laujon (pseudonym of Joseph Louis Duponnois), *Contes et Legendes*, [Paris], 1862; Victor Adolphe Malte-Brun, *Les Etats-Unis et le Mexique*, [Paris], 1862; Manuel (pseudonym of Ernest Louis L'Epine), *Histoire du Capitaine Castagnette*, L. Hachette; 1862, translation by Austin Dobson published as *The Authentic History of Captain Castagnette*, Beeton, 1866; X. B. Saintine (pseudonym of Joseph Xavier Boniface), *La Mythologie du Rhin*, L. Hachette, 1862, translation by M. Schele DeVere published as *The Myths of the Rhine*, Scribner, Armstrong, 1875, reprinted, Tuttle, 1957; Francois René de Chateaubriand, *Atala, ou les Amours de Deux Sauvages dans le Desert*, L. Hachette, 1863, translation by James Spence Harry, Cassell, 1867.

Benjamin Gastineau, *Chasses au Lion et a la Panthere*, [Paris], 1863; E. L. L'Epine, *La Legende de Croque Mitaine*, L. Hachette, 1863, translation by Tom Hood published as *The Legends of Croquemitaine and of the Chivalric Times of Charlemagne*, Cassell, 1866; Miguel de Cervantes Saavedra, *History of Don Quixote*, translated by Charles Jarvis, edited by J. W. Clark, Cassell, 1864-67, reissued as *The Adventures of Don Quixote de la Mancha*, Heron Books, 1969; Adrien Marx, *Histoires d'une Minute*, Denton, 1864.

(With Robert Dudley) John George Edgar, *Cressy and Poictiers; or, The Story of the Black Prince's Page*, Beeton, 1865; Thomas Hood, Jr., *The Fairy Realm*, Ward, Lock, 1865; Thomas Moore, *L'Epicurien* (poem), translated by Henri Butat, [Paris], 1865; Theophile Gautier, Sr., *La Capitaine Fracasse*, Charpentier, 1866; John Milton, *Milton's Paradise Lost*, Cassell, 1866; Baron Munchausen (pseudonym of Rudolf Erich Raspe), *The Adventures of Baron Munchausen*, [London], 1866; Dante Alighieri, *The Divine Comedy*, Leypoldt & Holt, 1867, new translation by Lawrence Grant White, Pantheon Books, 1948, reissued, 1965; Emile Gigault de la Bedolliere, *La France et la Prusse*, [Paris], 1867.

Henry G. Blackburn, *The Pyrenees: A Description of Summer Life at French Watering Places*, Sampson, Low, 1867; Victor Adolphe Malte-Brun, *Pays Bas Belgique*, [Paris], 1867; Jean de La Fontaine, *Fables de la Fontaine*, L.

Hachette, 1867, translation by Walter Thornbury published as *The Fables of de La Fontaine*, [London], 1867-70; Alfred Tennyson, *Idylls of the King*, Moxon, 1868; Jose Zorrilla, *Ecos de las Montanas: Leyendas Historicas*, [Barcelona], 1868; Thomas Hood, Sr., *Thomas Hood* (poems), edited by J. B. Payne, [London], 1870.

William Blanchard Jerrold, *The Cockaynes in Paris; or, Gone Aboard*, [London], 1871; *Fairy Tales Told Again*, [London], 1872; W. B. Jerrold, *London: A Pilgrimage*, Unwin, Grant, 1872, reprinted, Newton Abbot, 1971; Jean Charles Davillier, *L'Espagne*, L. Hachette, 1874, translation by John Thomson published as *Spain*, Sampson, Low, 1876; Louis Énault, *Londres*, L. Hachette, 1875-76; Samuel Taylor Coleridge, *The Rime of the Ancient Mariner*, Harper, 1876, reissued, Dover, 1970; Joseph Francois Michaud, *Histoires de Croisades*, Furne & Jouvet, 1877; Lodovico Ariosto, *Roland Furieux*, translated by A. J. DuPays, L. Hachette, 1878-79; *Aladdin; or, The Wonderful Lamp*, revised by M. E. Braddon, J. & R. Maxwell, 1880; Edgar Allan Poe, *The Raven*, Harper, 1883; Georgiana M. Craik, *Twelve Old Friends: A Book for Boys and Girls*, Sonnenschein, 1885; Charles Dickens, *The Life of Our Lord*, United Feature Syndicate, 1934; Olivia Coolidge, *Tales of the Crusades*, Houghton, 1970; Sophie Rostopchine Segur, *The Enchanted Forest*, retold by Beatrice Schenk De Regniers, Atheneum, 1974; Joseph McHugh and Latif Harris, *Journey to the Moon*, Celestial Arts, 1974.

"At the Seashore," illustration, 1849.

Portrait of composer Jacques Offenbach, 1861.

Religious: *The Holy Bible*, [London], 1866, later edition edited by the Daughters of Saint Paul, St. Paul Editions, 1963; *Daily Devotion for the Household*, Cassell, 1873; *The Dore Bible Gallery*, Fine Art Publishing, 1879, reissued, Dover, 1974; Edmund Ollier, *A Popular History of Sacred Art*, Cassell, 1882; Eric Christian Matthews, *Stars of the Bible*, New Era Studio, 1963.

Collections: *A Dozen Specimens of Gustave Doré*, [London], 1866; *The Dore Gallery*, Cassell, 1870, reissued, Spring Books, 1974; *A Dore Treasury: A Collection of the Best Engravings of Gustave Dore*, edited by James Stevens, Bounty Books, 1970; *Selected Engravings*, edited by Marina Henderson, St. Martin's Press, 1973; *Illustrations to Don Quixote*, edited by Jeannie Ruzicka, St. Martin's Press, 1975; *Dore's Illustrations for the Divine Comedy by Dante*, Dover, 1976; *Dore's Illustrations for Rabelais*, Gannon, 1978; *Dore's Illustrations for Rabelais: A Selection of 252 Illustrations*, Dover, 1978; *Dore's Illustrations for Ariosto's "Orlando Furioso,"* Dover, 1980; *Dore's Illustrations for Don Quixote: A Selection of 190 Illustrations by Gustave Dore*, Dover, 1982.

ADAPTATIONS—Movies and filmstrips: "The Raven" (motion picture; a visualization of Poe's poem through reproductions of drawings by Dore), American Art and History Films, 1953; "The Rime of the Ancient Mariner" (motion picture; based on the engravings by Doré for the poem by Samuel Taylor Coleridge), University of California at Los Angeles, 1953.

SIDELIGHTS: A very precocious child, Gustave Dore drew several lithographs for various newspapers of eastern France, where he was going to school. Having presented his portfolio to Charles Philipon, the publisher of *Le Journal pour rire*, the fifteen-year-old Gustave moved to Paris with his mother to attend the Lycée Charlemagne and begin a professional career as a weekly contributor of drawings that satirized French foibles and fashions in the manner of fellow artist "Cham" (pseudonym of Amedee, Comte de Noe).

That some year (1847), at Philipon's urging, he published his first sketchbook, titled *Les Travaux d'Hercule*, which made fun of the heroic myth. Through black and white he was able to emphasize not only an earthy humor but also a sense for action and composition. This became particularly evident, first, in his *Histoire pittoresque, dramatique et caricaturale de la Sainte Russie* (title means "Picturesque, Dramatic and Caricatural History of Holy Russia"—quite a program!) and then in his book illustrations to which he now turned full-time. After several albums of his cartoons all devoted to

"Dancing Girl in Seville," illustration, 1866.

Parisian scenes and Parisian types (*Ces Chinois de Parisiens, La Ménagerie parisienne, Les Différents Publics de Paris*), he came out in 1854 with a volume attaching the unpopular Czar Nicholas and his bloodthirsty ancestors, based in part on Toepffer's *Album des caricatures*. For his purpose Dore invented a brilliant comic-strip device using irregular white squares to depict uninteresting periods or an enormous black stain to represent the rule of Ivan the Terrible. Moreover, he also illustrated Rabelais's story of *Gargantua et Pantagruel*. This work contained one hundred and four illustrations, later expanded to sixty-one plates and six hundred and fifty-eight illustrations. While the early edition is full of verve and variety, the 1873 version captures, according to Stanley Appelbaum, "a gaiety and an appreciation for the absurd that had long been absent from Dore's art" and ranges "from highly finished and shaded studies to brilliant sketches of eiderdown lightness."

Dore once declared that his idea "was to produce in a uniform style an edition of all the masterpieces in literature of the best authors—epic, comic, and tragic." Indeed, he illustrated more than two hundred books, among which are Dante's *The Inferno* (1861), Cervantes's *Don Quixote* (1863), and the Bible (1866). In all he shows a predilection for a hallucinatory, even visionary, style that owes much to Hieronymus Bosch and Pieter Brueghel for its themes and images. He loves to depict the more terrifying aspects of a foreboding nature, where lightning tears gloomy skies, haunted forests hide dark secrets, and roaring waterfalls drown harmonious sounds. His characters evolve in a nightmarish world, full of gothic horror and cruelty that uncover many of childhood's most frightening fears, as in the case of the Charles Perrault fairy tales (1862). Ogres with bulging vicious eyes abound, along with animals devoid of cuteness and charm, children about to have their throats slit. Men and women are being whipped, tortured, hanged, eaten alive, while gigantic evil creatures, monsters, and angel-vultures strike menacing poses, further exaggerated by full close-ups. Everywhere there are skulls and skeletons, whether of animals and humans or of the Grim Reaper himself.

Thanks to plunging perspectives, bizarre medieval towns and streets dwarf a heretofore egocentric man and project a claustrophobic and vertiginous malaise reminiscent of Giambattista Piranesi's moody architectural studies, *Prisons*. Dore's lithographs for *The Inferno* are eerie in their fantastic, chiaroscuro presentation of the netherworld: in fact, the tonal effects seem to suggest painting more than drawing. Despite his melodramatic subject matter (for instance, wandering Jews, ancient mariners, *héros manqués*, infernal shades), many of his illustrations maintain a grotesque and boisterous kind of black humor which Nigel Gosling ascribes to a juxtaposition of neo-gothic and neo-rococo attributable to his Franco-German childhood and early environment (Gustave was born in Strasbourg, a very Germanic city in the early nineteenth century).

Gustave Dore abandoned myth, legend, and fantasy when in 1872 he undertook to illustrate *London: A Pilgrimage*, accompanied by a text by Blanchard Jerrold. Beside being an incisive social commentary on life at the top and bottom, *London* is an awesome, realistic record of the great English city. Furthermore, the subtitle suggests the quasi-religious seriousness of the enterprise: this is no mere account of their trip to a foreign land and of its touristic highlights. It is rather a gripping portrait of an overpowering misery. Through his use of cinematographic techniques (e.g., daring camera angles) and of white and black, we feel the poverty, the grime, the smells, the despair; by squeezing a lot of people and things in a small space Dore emphasizes the hellish overcrowding of the new slaves of industrial progress. Not all is bleak, however. He also shows the busyness of the city, including amusing street scenes and insoluble traffic jams, and offers an uncritical picture of the upper-classes at play.

In addition to his prodigious output of over ten thousand lithographs for which he sometime employed a hundred and thirty-seven engravers, chief among them being Heliodore Pisan (Théophile Gautier, the French poet and art critic, joked that, if some publisher commissioned Dore to illustrate a book on the influence of fleas on female sentimentality, he would find a way of crafting five hundred drawings), Dore also painted, mainly portraits (see his very pleasing *Sarah Bernhardt*), etched, and sculpted: his most famous sculpture is of D'Artagnan the Musketeer, which he did as a memorial to Alexandre Dumas (Place Malesherbes, Paris).

Dore's own influence is quite noticeable on Expressionists and Surrealists (especially Max Ernst and Salvador Dali), as

Frontispiece for *London*, 1872.

Illustration for Ludovico Ariosto's *Orlando Furioso*, 1879.

well as on filmmakers, comic-strip artists, cartoonists, and of course modern book illustrators (Maurice Sendak is one who immediately comes to mind). His work should become even better known as more and more reprints of his illustrations are available in paperbound editions (Dover alone lists eight titles).

The last of the Romantics, as David Bland calls Gustave Dore, died in Paris, a very rich man, on January 23, 1883.

BIOGRAPHICAL/CRITICAL SOURCES: Blanche Roosevelt Macchetta, *Life and Reminiscences of Gustave Dore*, Cassel & Co., 1885; William Blanchard Jerrold, *Life of Gustave Dore*, W. H. Allen, 1891 (reprinted, Singing Tree Press, 1969); Millicent Rose, *Gustave Dore*, Pleiades Books, 1946; Thieme-Becker, *Kunstler-Lexikon*, Seemann, 1970; Eric De Mare, *The London Dore Saw; A Victorian Evocation*, St. Martin's, 1973; Nigel Gosling, *Gustave Dore*, Praeger, 1974; *The World Encyclopedia of Cartoons*, Chelsea House, 1980.

—Sketch by Pierre Horn

Dore's frontispiece for ''The Raven'' by Edgar Allan Poe, 1883.

DRUCKER, Mort 1929-

PERSONAL: Born March 22, 1929, in Brooklyn, N.Y.; son of Edward (in business) and Sarah (Spielvogel) Drucker; married Barbara Hellerman, August 28, 1948; children: Laurie Bachner, Melanie. *Education:* Erasmus Hall High School, Brooklyn, N.Y. *Politics:* Democrat. *Religion:* Jewish. *Home and studio:* 42 Juneau Blvd., Woodbury, N.Y. 11797.

CAREER: Staff artist, National Periodicals, New York, N.Y., 1948-50; freelance commercial artist, 1951—; *Mad*, contributing artist, 1956—. *Member:* Graphic Artists Guild, National Cartoonists Society.

AWARDS, HONORS: Certificate of Merit, Art Directors Club of New York, 1968; Award of Excellence, San Francisco Society of Communicating Arts, 1973; Gold Award, San Francisco Society of Communicating Arts, 1980; Andy Award, Art Directors Show for Consumer Advertising, 1983; Booth Newspaper Award of Excellence, Advertising Club of New York, 1981; Best Cartoonist, Barcelona Comics and Illustration Fair, 1985.

WRITINGS: (With Paul Laikin) *JFK Coloring Book*, Kanrom, 1961; (with Jerry Dumas) *Benchley* comic strip, Cowles Syndicate, 1984—; *Mort Drucker's Showstoppers*, Warner, 1985.

EXHIBITIONS: Society of Illustrators, New York, N.Y., 1975; cartoons in permanent collections of Museum of Cartoon Art, Port Chester; N.Y., and covers painted for *Time* in National Portrait Gallery of Smithsonian Institute.

A promotion piece. (© Mort Drucker. Reprinted with permission.)

MORT DRUCKER

SIDELIGHTS: Caricaturist par excellence Mort Drucker has been delighting the readers of *Mad* for almost three decades with his inspired graphic satire of popular movies and television shows, done in association with some of that journal's redoubtable staff of writers. With a lucrative parallel career as a commercial artist and as a contributing artist for *Mad*, in July, 1984 he and writer Jerry Dumas launched the syndicated daily strip, *Benchley*, as a vehicle which allows him to exercise his considerable gift for caricature on some of the best known of contemporary Americans.

Born and bred in Brooklyn, Drucker was a recreational doodler as a high school student, but he had no particular aspirations to an artistic vocation. Then in 1947, having just graduated, he was hired by Bert Whitman to do backgrounds for Whitman's strip *Debby Dean, Career Girl*. He was only with Whitman for six months, but it introduced him to cartooning as a career. In 1948 he went to work for National Periodicals, where his job was to make minor corrections in the artwork. In the process he was able to study and learn first hand the art as well as the business of cartooning. After three years there his artwork had improved to the point that he felt ready to embark upon a freelance career. His early assignments were mainly comic books, including a series featuring comedian Bob Hope. This assignment clearly afforded him a matchless chance to practice his gifts on the likes of old "Ski-nose" and constant pal Bing Crosby, both of whom are great subjects for caricature.

A *Benchley* daily strip. (© 1985, Cowles Syndicate.)

In 1956 he saw an ad for freelance artists run by *Mad*. He applied and was hired. His first assignment was a cigarette ad parody, and shortly thereafter he become the magazine's resident specialist in movie and television satire. With writers like Larry Siegel, he waged a war of merciless hilarity against Hollywood moguls like Joseph E. Levine, Cecil B. De Mille, and Dino De Laurentiis, while taking particular delight in deriding the "spectacular" and skewering the cinematic cliche. For example, he imagined De Laurentiis's forty-five million dollar remake of "Paddy Chafedknee's *Mardy*," in which the East River is parted to give the butcher (played in this version by Charlton Heston) access to Manhattan (and to his homely girlfriend, played by Sophia Loren). Only one of the extras feels moved to ask, "Wouldn't it have been easier to take the Williamsburgh Bridge?" Popular television series also came in for their share of satirical abuse, but it is Drucker's continual dismantling of cinematic icons like Burt Reynolds, Charles Bronson, Gregory Peck, and Barbra Streisand, with occasional starring roles for non-thespians such as President John Kennedy and Adlai Stevenson (as the finger-popping leaders of a gang opposed to a rival gang headed by Soviet premier Krushchev and Cuban leader Fidel Castro in a UN-inspired musical entitled *East Side Story*) that is his hallmark.

Stylistically, Drucker's work hails back to the comic book art of the fifties—carefully drawn, fine lined, densely detailed, voluptuous in character, and excellent in portraying action sequences—and his way with the features of the famous is more that of the illustrator than of the parodist. And yet the parody is unmistakably there. As he explains his technique, "I look for those unique facets that separate individuals. A head may be round, long and thin, square, etc. I study how the features float within the head's outline and their proportion to one another." In addition, he has a knack for capturing subtleties of physical attitude—Adlai Stevenson's scholarly slouch, Barbra Streisand's myopic forward thrust—and exaggerating them to produce likenesses that are at once faithful portraits *and* caricatures. These can be, according to intent, either flattering or devastating.

With the high recognition his work has gained in the pages of *Mad*, Drucker has also enjoyed a highly successful run as a commercial artist. In addition to the usual ad work he has been responsible (oddly enough, considering his reputation as a film critic) for a number of movie posters, among them the one for *American Graffiti*. He has also been commissioned by *Time* to execute a number of cover portraits. One of his more lucrative ventures was *The JFK Coloring Book*, on which he collaborated in 1962 with *Mad* writer Paul Laikin. On the *New York Times*'s best seller list for twenty-six weeks, the volume sold over two million copies.

In a recent interview in *Cartoonist Profiles*, Drucker confessed a long standing urge to do political cartooning, but as a *Mad* satirist of pop culture and a successful advertising and editorial illustrator, he was unable to pursue it until joining forces in the spring of 1984 with Jerry Dumas to create *Benchley,* a comic strip currently syndicated by the Cowles service. Having earlier rejected the daily grind of strip work because of other commitments (he once turned down an invitation to draw *Li'l Abner* from Al Capp), he finally accepted the *Benchley* challenge because the character was a presidential assistant and thus gave him the opportunity to do pure social and political satire.

He calls the strip, which began appearing in July of 1984, a "mild roast" of the presidency, and revels in the chance it gives him to draw Ronald Reagan, George Bush, Thomas "Tip" O'Neill, Geraldine Ferarro, and other politicians, and celebrities from industrialist Lee Iacocca to television personality Mr. T. The purely fictional Benchley is a short, pudgy, cherubic character—a genuine cartoon presence among the real-life figures he encounters as a member of the Presidential staff—with whom Drucker reports himself on excellent terms. "I know him as a friend," he says. The strip itself has no political slant, and Drucker promises that should it last until a Democrat wins the White House, he and Dumas will prove that their purpose is to offend (mildly) the office, not the man.

Considering his background at *Mad*, where not even page margins are immune from the plagues of scribbling and doodling, it is not surprising that Drucker's chief complaint about syndicated strip work is "the lack of space given for drawing."

BIOGRAPHICAL/CRITICAL SOURCES: The World Encyclopedia of Cartoons, Chelsea House, 1980; *Who's Who in America*, 1984-85; *Cartoonist Profiles*, March, 1985.

—Sketch by Richard Calhoun

Three *Benchley* daily strips. (From top: © 1984, 1985, 1985, Cowles Syndicate.)

E

EATON, Tom 1940-

PERSONAL: Born March 2, 1940, in Wichita, Kan.; son of Newton A. (an engineer) and Betty (Cooper) Eaton; married Shara Pinkley (a designer for Hallmark Cards), June 24, 1967. *Education:* University of Kansas, B.F.A., 1962. *Home and studio:* 911 W. 100th St., Kansas City, Mo. 64114.

CAREER: Artist and writer, Contemporary Cards department, Hallmark Cards, Kansas City, Mo., 1962-66; art editor and cartoonist, Scholastic Magazines, Inc., New York City, 1966-68; freelance writer, artist, and cartoonist, 1968—. *Military service:* U.S. Army, Medical Field Service School, 1963-65.

WRITINGS—All self-illustrated; published by Scholastic Book Services, except as indicated: *Chicken-Fried Fudge and Other Cartoon Delights,* 1971; *Flap* (a novel), Delacorte, 1972; *Captain Ecology, Pollution Fighter,* 1974; *Otis G. Firefly's Phantasmagoric Almanac,* 1975; *Popnut* (illustrated novel), 1976; *Tom Eaton's Book of Marvels,* 1977; *Rufus Crustbuster and the Earth Patrol* (illustrated novel), Saturday Evening Post Co., 1978.

Also creator of specialty books: *Holiday Greeting Cards* (greeting cards to detach and mail); *Super Valentines to Cut and Color* (cards to detach and mail); *Monster Stand-Up Greeting Cards; Monster Mazes.*

Illustrator; all juveniles: Richard L. Penney, *The Penguins Are Coming!,* Harper, 1969; William J. Cromie, *Steven and the Green Turtle,* Harper, 1970; Edward R. Ricciuti, *An Animal for Alan,* Harper, 1971; *The Big Time Book,* Mulberry, 1971; W. Harmon Wilson and Roman F. Wormke, *Life on Paradise Island,* Scott, Foresman, 1970; Z. S. da Silva, *Nuestro Mundo,* Macmillan, 1970; Robyn Supraner, *A Sea Parade,* Nutmeg, 1971; Supraner, *Surprises!,* Nutmeg, 1971; M. Gerrard and J. McInnes, *Hickory Hollow ABC,* Thomas Nelson, 1977.

Illustrator; all published by Garrard: Donna Pape, *Leo Lion Looks for Books,* 1972; Pape, *Count On, Leo Lion,* 1973; Pape, *The Sleep-Leaping Kangaroo,* 1973; John McInnes, *Have You Ever Seen a Monster?,* 1974; McInnes, *Leo Lion Paints It Red,* 1974; Emily Hearn, *TV Kangaroo,* 1975; Howard Goldsmith, *What Makes a Grumble Smile?,* 1977; Nancy L. Robison, *Where Did My Little Fox Go?,* 1977; Pape, *Where Is My Little Joey?,* 1978; Pape, *Doghouse for Sale,* 1979; Leonard Kessler, *Tricks for Treats on Halloween,* 1979; Pape and Kessler, *Play Ball, Joey Kangaroo!,* 1980.

Illustrator; all published by Scholastic Book Services: *Laugh Your Head Off,* 1969; LaVinia Dobler, *It's Your World: Don't Pollute It!,* 1972; Bud Delaney and Lolo Delaney, *The Daily Laugh,* 1973; Jim Razzi, *Mad, Mad Puzzle Parade,* 1975; Mosesson, *The Perfect Put-Down,* 1975; B. Delaney and L. Delaney, *The Laugh Journal,* 1975; Donna Pape and Jeanette Grote, *Pack of Puzzles,* 1976; Leonore Klein, *Mazes & Mysteries,* 1976; *The Organized Week,* 1976; Dick Hyman, *Crazy Laws,* 1976; Pape, *Puzzle Panic,* 1977; B. Delaney and L. Delaney, *The Beastly Gazette,* 1977.

Also illustrator of many other titles, including children's books, humor books, primers, puzzle books, datebooks, workbooks, and novelty books.

Contributor of cartoons to *Look, Saturday Evening Post, Playboy,* and other publications. Writer and artist, *Dink and Duff* and *Webelos Woody,* five-page cartoon features for *Boy's Life,* 1984—.

WORK IN PROGRESS: A humor novel and a science-fiction novel.

Self-portrait of Tom Eaton. (Printed with permission.)

Illustration for *The Organized Week*. (© 1976, Scholastic Book Services.)

SIDELIGHTS: Tom Eaton wrote *CGA:* "As a child my interests developed early—science, the future, fantasy and cartoons—and I wrote and drew for the amusement of myself and my classmates. As I grew older, it dawned on me that I was expected to buy my own groceries and gasoline, and I began drawing cartoons professionally. They weren't any better necessarily, but now someone was paying me for them. I have loved cartoons and comic strips all my life, and spent much of my early childhood sprawled on the floor reading the funnies that overflowed the pages of the *Wichita Eagle* and the *Wichita Beacon* like a cornucopia. The greatest influences on my own work came from those funny papers and from comic books, from luminaries like Carl Barks (artist and writer on the *Donald Duck* comic books), Walt Kelly (creator of *Pogo*), George Herriman (creator of *Krazy Kat*), and others. I also liked the little cartoon ads in the Sunday funnies in the 1940s and 1950s, especially those for Ben-Gay ointment starring Peter Pain. The image of that green devil, bewhiskered jaw a-twitch with malice, leaping upon some poor wretch's shoulder to jab him with the pitchfork of neuralgia, has always seemed to me the symbol of all the irritations that plague mankind. That and Congress.

"My working habits are simple—I begin each job when it cannot possibly be put off any longer, and try to get it over with as quickly as possible. I feel this makes my work more spontaneous, and also assures that my mind will be free when *Let's Make a Deal* comes on. As a freelancer I work in a studio in my home, at a long drawing board which seats me and my three dogs comfortably. Contrary to malicious rumors, they do not 'ghost' my work for me to then sign and send out. I do the main portion myself, employing them only for lettering and filling in black spaces. My greatest ambition is to someday illustrate the National Debt in cartoon form."

As can be seen from the foregoing, Tom Eaton freely indulges in what is commonly known as "cartoonist banter,"

a blend of self-deprecating humor, true confession, and jibes at the establishment that allows its practitioners to face the world and all its indignities (such as answering publishers' questionnaires) with some semblance of fortitude—the cartoonist's equivalent of the British stiff upper-lip. His ability to laugh at the world and at himself is typical of Eaton, who also states that he is now in "his late late childhood."

The same whimsicality can be found in Eaton's cartoon work and in many of his illustrations for children's books. In *The Organized Week*, which outwardly purports to be a datebook, for instance, he actually illustrates (in hilarious miniatures) all sorts of irrelevant data pertaining to history, astrology, and psychology. He is at his best when illustrating everyday crazy happenings, as in *The Laugh Journal*, or looney legislation, as in *Crazy Laws*, but even his workbooks and puzzles present the same winsome, light-hearted quality. After all, a man who can (and did) title a chronicle of odd facts and plausible fictions *Otis G. Firefly's Phantasmagoric Almanac* (with a conspiratorial wink in the direction of Groucho Marx's memorable screen character, Rufus T. Firefly, the would-be dictator of *Duck Soup*) clearly shows where his humor comes from.

BIOGRAPHICAL/CRITICAL SOURCES: Contemporary Authors, New Revision Series, Vol. 15, Gale, 1985.

*   *   *

EHRLICH, David 1941-

PERSONAL: Born October 14, 1941, in Elizabeth, N.J.; son of Max (a physician) and Jeannette (Gordon) Ehrlich; married Marcela Rydlova (a professor of engineering), July 17, 1975. *Education:* Cornell University, B.A., 1963; University of California, Berkeley, M.A. (dramatic arts), 1966; Columbia University, M.F.A. (film), 1975. *Home:* R.D. 2, Randolph, Vt. 05060.

CAREER: Instructor in English, Pachaiyappa's College, Madras, India, 1963-64; adjunct assistant professor of interdisciplinary arts, State University of New York at Purchase, Purchase, New York, 1970-75; lecturer in art, University of Vermont, Burlington, Vt., 1976-84; certified psychotherapist. Artist-in-residence for Vermont elementary schools, Vermont Council on the Arts, 1975—; film instructor at Governor's Institute for the Arts, Vermont, 1983—. *Member:* ASIFA-International, American Association for Artists-Therapists, Association of Independent Video and Filmmakers, ASIFA-East.

AWARDS, HONORS: Second prize, non-sponsored film for *Metamorphosis*, ASIFA-East, 1976; all for *Precious Metal*, 1980, Certificate of Merit, Chicago International Film Festival; First Prize, animation, and Second Prize, design, ASIFA-East, New York City; Gold Medal, animation, Houston International Film Festival; all for *Fantasies: Animation of Vermont Schoolchildren*, 1981, Silver Plaque, Chicago International Film Festival; Special Award, ASIFA-East Animation Festival; Second Prize, animation, Marin County National Film Competition; all for *Dissipative Dialogues*, 1982, First Prize, experimental animation, Espinho International Animation Festival, Portugal; Silver Award, experimental animation, Houston International

A frame from *Precious Metal*. (© 1980, David Ehrlich. Printed with permission.)

Film Festival; Special Mention, Murcia Short Film Festival, Spain; all for *Precious Metal Variations*, 1983, Third Prize, design, ASIFA-East Animation Festival; Silver Award, experimental animation, Houston International Film Festival. Fulbright Fellowship to India, 1963; Scholar of Arts Award, Columbia University Program in the Arts, 1965; Animated Holography Grant, Cabin Creek Center, New York City, 1978; Individual Artist Grant, Vermont Council on the Arts, 1978, 1979, and 1984; Animated Holography Grant, Holographic Film Foundation, New York City, 1983 and 1984.

WRITINGS: The Bowel Book, Schocken, 1981.

Contributor of articles to many animation and film publications in the United States and abroad.

FILMS—All animation shorts: *Metamorphosis*, 1976; *Robot*, 1977; *Vermont Etude*, 1977; *Robot Two*, 1979; *Vermont Etude, No. 2*, 1979; *Precious Metal*, 1980; *Fantasies: Animation of Vermont Schoolchildren*, 1981; *Dissipative Dialogues*, 1982; *Precious Metal Variations*, 1983; (producer) *Albert Bridge Presents Olympics*, 1984; *Point*, 1984; (co-directed with A. Petringenaru) *Perpetual Revival*, 1985. All animated holograms: *Oedipus at Colonus*, 1978; *Ranko's Fantasy*, 1983; *Phallacy*, 1983; *Stabila*, 1984.

EXHIBITIONS: Retrospective shows and other exhibitions, including Triangle Theatre, New York City, 1970, 1971, 1972, and 1974; Neuberger Museum, State University of New York at Purchase, 1972; ML Gallery, New York City, 1976; 112 Greene Street Gallery, New York City, 1977; Museum of Holography, New York City, 1978; Umwelt Gallerie, Stuttgart, Germany, 1979; Animators' Gallery, New York City, 1981; all 1982—Boston Museum School Gallery; Centre d'Art Plastique Contemporain de Bordeaux, France; Musee du Saguenay, Lac St. Jean, Canada; Montreal Museum of Modern Art; Brattleboro Museum, Vermont.

WORK IN PROGRESS: "Dissipative Monologues," an animated short on social commitment; *The Creativity Book*, publication by Schocken, expected in 1986.

Photo by David Ehrlich, 1981.

DAVID EHRLICH

SIDELIGHTS: A certified psychotherapist, David Ehrlich has garnered many credits in the field of multi-media therapy: he has been a consultant to the Psychoanalytic Institute in Linz, Austria, and to the Alcoholism Ward at Manhattan State Hospital in New York City, as well as the director of neuro-science films at Mt. Sinai School of Medicine, also in New York. He has pursued at the same time a fifteen-year academic career, and is a distinguished multi-media artist whose work has been exhibited widely in the U.S. and overseas. It is for his experimental films, however, that he is best known.

Ehrlich's abstract animated shorts have been shown at film festivals and on television stations throughout the world. They have won for their author many awards and distinctions, and have been exhibited in a number of American and foreign retrospectives. He has experimented widely with colors, patterns, rhythms, and shapes, and the resulting films have been hailed as major artistic achievements.

Ehrlich has also worked with holographic processes. His first hologram, *Oedipus at Colonus*, was the first work of its kind ever shown at the international festivals of Annecy, France, and Zagreb, Yugoslavia. This has encouraged

A frame from *Dissipative Dialogues.* (© 1982, David Ehrlich. Printed with permission.)

A frame from *Precious Metal Variations.* (© 1983, David Ehrlich. Printed with permission.)

Ehrlich to continue his experiments with holography, and has led him to organize the first International Animated Hologram Symposium at the Zagreb animation festival in 1984.

In addition to his experimental work, Ehrlich has created, under a grant from the Vermont Council on the Arts, the film *Fantasies*, in collaboration with twenty-five Vermont schoolchildren. His work in the field of animation extends to teaching the subject in Vermont, and to writing articles for animation journals here and abroad. Finally, as the director of an International Exchange Program, he has brought animators from Yugoslavia, Romania, China, Denmark, Brazil, and France to Vermont to collaborate on animation workshops and tour the state, screening their countries' animation.

BIOGRAPHICAL/CRITICAL SOURCES: Susan Green, "Randolph Filmmaker Teaches Animation," *Burlington Free Press*, January 20, 1978; David Dupont, "The Free-Flowing David Ehrlich," *Vermont Vanguard Press*, August 14, 1981; Jean Latham, "Filmmaker Uses Animation as an Educational Tool," *Barre Times-Argus*, August 24, 1981; Sarah Seidman, "Hot Shots: David Ehrlich," *Moving Image*, December, 1981; "Vermont's Animated Shorts," *Leisure*, May 24, 1984.

* * *

EISNER, Will(iam Erwin) 1917-
(Will Erwin, Willis Rensie)

PERSONAL: Born March 6, 1917, in Brooklyn, N.Y.; son of Samuel (a furrier) and Fanny (Ingber) Eisner; married Ann Louise Weingarten (a director of volunteer hospital services), June 15, 1950; children: John David, Alice Carol (deceased). *Education:* Attended Art Students League, 1935. *Office:* 8333 W. McNab Rd., Suite 114, Tamarac, Fl. 33321.

CAREER: Staff artist, *New York American*, 1936; founder and partner, Eisner & Iger, 1937-40; founder, publisher, Eisner-Arnold Comic Group, New York City, 1940-46; author and artist, *The Spirit* (newspaper feature), 1940-52; founder and president, American Visuals Corp., 1949—; president, Bell-McClure North American Newspaper Alliance, 1962-64; executive vice-president, Koster-Dana Corp., 1962-64; president, Educational Supplements Corp., 1965-72; chairman of the board, Croft Educational Services Corp., 1972-73; president and publisher, Poor House Press, 1974—; instructor in sequential art, School of Visual Arts. *Military service:* U.S. Army, Ordnance, 1942-46. *Member:* National Cartoonists Society, Princeton Club (New York City).

AWARDS, HONORS: Recipient of many honors, including being named best comic book artist by National Cartoonists Society, 1967-69, and 1979; award for quality of art in comic books, Society of Comic Art Research, New York City, 1968; best foreign artist, International Convention of Comics, Angouleme, France, 1974; award for best comic book for *A Life Force*, International Conference of Comics and Illustration, Barcelona, Spain, 1984.

WRITINGS: A Pictorial Arsenal of American Combat Weapons, Sterling, 1960; *America's Space Vehicles: A Pictori-*

al Review, Sterling, 1962; *Gleeful Guides* series, all published by Poor House, including *Communicating with Plants*, 1972, *Occult Cookery*, 1974, *Living with Astrology*, 1974, *Amazing Facts, Statistics & Trivia*, 1974, and *How to Avoid Death and Taxes. . . and Live Forever*, 1974; *A Contract with God, and Other Tenement Stories*, Baronet, 1978; *Odd Facts*, Ace Books, 1978; *Life on Another Planet (Signal from Space)*, Kitchen Sink, 1981; *A Life Force*, Kitchen Sink, 1983; *Comics and Sequential Art*, Eclipse/Poor House, 1985.
For children and young adults; all Baronet, 1979: *Dating and Hanging Out*; *Funny Jokes and Foxy Riddles*; *Ghostly Jokes and Ghastly Riddles*; *One Hundred and One Half Wild and Crazy Jokes*; *Spaced-Out Jokes*.

Also creator of comic book and newspaper features: *Uncle Sam*; *Muss'em Up Donovan*; *Sheena*; *The Three Brothers*; *K-51*; *Hawk of the Seas*, 1937-40; *The Spirit*, 1940—; *Odd Facts*, 1975.

WORK IN PROGRESS: "New and innovative projects in process. . . "

WILL EISNER

A page from *The Spirit,* **1947.** (From *Comix & Sequential Art* by Will Eisner. © Will Eisner. Reprinted with permission.)

SIDELIGHTS: While he may be known in more conservative circles as a pioneer in the use of comics in administrative and classroom instruction, Will Eisner is generally regarded by comic fans and the public at large as the creator of the mystery-and-humor feature, *The Spirit*. This was a weekly seven-page feature, part of a comic-book sized Sunday supplement (that also included two back-up series not by Eisner, *Lady Luck* and *Mr. Mystic*) carried in the comics section of a number of newspapers. *The Spirit* section bridged the gap between comic books and newspaper comics (there also was a short-lived daily *Spirit* newspaper strip, 1941-44).

A year after its first appearance, Eisner recalled the creation of his already famous series for the *Philadelphia Record*. "When I decided upon the Spirit," he declared, "I worked from the inside out, you might say. That is, I thought first of his personality—the kind of a man he was to be, how he would feel about life, the sort of mind he would have. When that was worked out, I didn't have to imagine him as a person. I began to see him. Handsome obviously, and powerfully built, but not one of those impossibly big, thick-legged brutes. He was to be the kind of man a child could conceive of seeing on the street.

"Then I gave him a mask, as a sort of fillip to his personality. And he had to be on the side of the law, of course, but I believed it would be better if he worked a little outside of the law. In that way he acquires some of the sympathy most of us feel for adventurers who are absolutely on their own. And for a necessary tie-up with the regular police I gave him Commissioner Dolan. Then, we needed humor, hence Ebony, and, of course, there had to be a girl. The kind of girl, pretty and clean-cut and brave, whom a man like the Spirit would like."

As a newspaper feature *The Spirit* ended in 1952, at a time when adventure and action were beginning to wane from the comic pages. Gone, but not forgotten, its spirit (so to speak) was kept alive by a small but appreciative public in the form of comic books and other reprints. In 1965 Jules Feiffer, Eisner's one-time assistant, devoted a whole chapter of his book *The Great Comic Book Heroes* to *The Spirit*. In it he gave expression to his long-felt nostalgia for the feature. "Alone among mystery men the Spirit operated," he wrote, "in a relatively mature world in which one took stands somewhat more complex than hitting or not hitting people. Violent it was—this was to remain Eisner's stock in trade—but the Spirit's violence often turned in on itself, proved nothing, became, simply, an existential exercise; part of somebody else's game. The Spirit could even suffer defeat in the end: be outfoxed by a woman foe—stand there, his tongue making a dent in his cheek—charming in his boyish, Dennis O'Keefe way—a comment on the ultimate ineffectuality of even super-heroes."

A *Joe Dope* instruction strip, ca. 1950. (From *Comix & Sequential Art* by Will Eisner. © Will Eisner. Reprinted with permission.)

After *The Spirit* was revived for a unique piece in the now-defunct *New York Herald-Tribune* in 1966, the floodgates really opened to a full-fledged reappraisal of the feature and of its creator. Thus Les Daniels wrote in *Comix:* "Will Eisner occupies a unique place among comic book men as an innovator of unparalleled ingenuity. Equally skilled as a writer and an artist, he brought a dramatic flair to everything he touched, and left an indelible mark on every series he created, even though he often remained with a series only long enough to get the thing launched."

In *The Comic-Book Book* Maggie Thompson, hardly less laudatory in her appraisal, stated: "Eisner viewed life with a creative approach previously unseen in comics. The art was stunning and experimental—to such an extent that other comic-book artists studied his work. The influence of the strip was enormous in the world of cartoonists—and many fledgling artists studied the techniques that Eisner's work-force developed over the strip's dozen years." To which P.R. Garriock added a foreign (British in this case) perspective in *Masters of Comic Book Art.* "Will Eisner synthesized in pen and ink two modern art forms, the movie and the popular short story," he wrote. "He was perhaps the first artist to perceive the analogy between the film frame and the comic book panel, and applied the principle of cutting between camera angles to the rapidly shifting viewpoints of his own panels. Lighting effects such as throwing deep shadows, enshrouding a scene in mist, or revealing a face with a lighted match all reflect a cinematic influence."

Last but not least, *The World Encyclopedia of Comics* summed up Eisner's masterpiece thusly: "In its seven-page narrative each *Spirit* episode constituted a self-contained short story, but the weekly unfolding of the tales revealed a peculiar rhythm, a cadence evoking not so much the prose narrative as the prose poem (even down to the suggestion of blank verse in the text). In this aspect *The Spirit* probably has few counterparts in comic history."

Since the early 1970s the *Spirit* stories have become again widely available, as a number of publishers rushed to print with the old episodes and an occasional new story (they can currently be seen in *The Spirit* and *Will Eisner's Quarterly*). Eisner is also devoting his talents to more thoughtful pieces, "graphic" stories and novels as he calls them, of which *A Contract with God* is probably the best known. Writing in *The Art of Will Eisner*, Catherine Yronwode gave a sensible evaluation of the tales: "The four short stories which comprise *A Contract with God* are universal in scope but personal in the sense that they arise from Eisner's own experiences. Set in the 1930s in a tenement, they are what Will calls 'eyewitness fiction.' The fictional veil is thinnest of all in the last story of the quartet, *Cookelein*, which relates in detail the events which transpire during the fifteenth summer of an introspective boy named Willie."

Eisner still keeps ebulliently busy, and his recent work, *Comics and Sequential Art*, a treatise that encapsulates all his experiments and thoughts on a subject to which he has devoted a substantial part of his life, should prove stimulating as well as inspirational.

BIOGRAPHICAL/CRITICAL SOURCES: Philadelphia Record, October 13, 1941; Jules Feiffer, *The Great Comic*

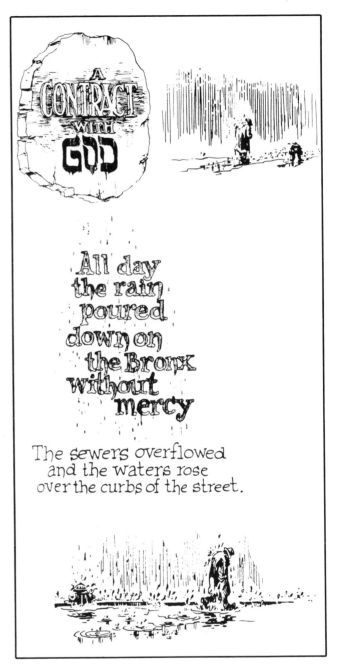

Title page of *A Contract with God* by Will Eisner. (From *Comix & Sequential Art* by Will Eisner. © Will Eisner. Reprinted with permission.)

Book Heroes, Dial Press, 1965; *New York Herald-Tribune*, January 9, 1966; Les Daniels, *Comix: A History of Comic Books in America*, Outerbridge and Dienstfrey, 1971; James Steranko, *The Steranko History of Comics*, Vol. 2, Super-graphics, 1972; Don Thompson and Dick Lupoff, eds., *The Comic-Book Book*, Arlington House, 1973; *The World Encyclopedia of Comics*, Chelsea House, 1976; P.R. Garriock, *Masters of Comic Book Art*, Images Graphiques, 1978; *The Art of Will Eisner*, Kitchen Sink, 1982; *Contemporary Authors*, Vol. 108, Gale, 1983; *Something About the Author*, Vol. 31, Gale, 1984.

—Sketch by Maurice Horn

EMMETT, Bruce   1949-

PERSONAL: Born October 7, 1949, in Greenwich, Conn.; son of Robert A. (a chemical engineer) and Jean (Bertram) Emmett; married Lisa Smith (a fashion illustrator), June 9, 1973 (divorced); married Jo Keim (an employee of the Brooklyn Botanical Gardens); children: Agatha. *Education:* Syracuse University, B.F.A., 1973. *Home and studio:* 285 Park Pl., Brooklyn, N.Y. 11238. *Agent:* Frank and Jeff Lavaty, 50 E. 50th St., New York, N.Y. 10022.

BRUCE EMMETT

CAREER: Freelance illustrator, poster designer, cover and advertising artist, 1973—. Contributor to *Cosmopolitan*, *Woman's Day*, and other publications. *Member:* Society of Illustrators, Graphic Artists Guild.

WRITINGS: (Self-illustrated) *Rooftop Wizard* (juvenile), Prentice-Hall, 1974.

EXHIBITIONS: Work included in many of the annual shows of Society of Illustrators, New York City.

WORK IN PROGRESS: "Paperbacks, portraits."

SIDELIGHTS: In the course of his twelve-year career Bruce Emmett has garnered an impressive list of credits in a variety of illustration endeavors. On the commercial and advertising side, he has been commissioned to execute ads or posters for such prestigious clients as Seagram's, Estee Lauder, Ralph Lauren, Burlington, as well as the Churchill Downs racetrack. He has also illustrated many book covers, in a rich, lush style, for publishers such as Avon, Berkley, Dell, and Warner; and worked for magazines as diverse as *Woman's Day* and *High Times*.

Emmett has also contributed some striking posters for a number of recent movies produced by the likes of Columbia, RCA, and United Artists. His renderings, done in rich colors, with minutely detailed foreground characters, and elaborate, lavish backgrounds, place him squarely in the tradition of the great American illustrators of the past, from Norman Rockwell to J. C. Leyendecker. This has made him a natural choice when it comes to evoking the atmosphere and zeitgeist of the Depression and World War II years. Whether designing the videocassette covers for such period films as the classic *Gold-Diggers* series of the 1930s, painting posters for the backward-directed 1975 movie version of *Farewell, My Lovely* and the nostalgia-drenched *Sugar Babies* Broadway musical, or depicting a bucolic scene for Ralph Lauren, Emmett has always risen to the task with gusto.

The Rockwellian influence is particularly apparent in Emmett's ads for Van Heusen Sportswear, with its rugged adult character and its all-American kid character, and (oddly) in one of his covers for *High Times*, depicting a devil-like character on a background of demons and fallen creatures. Yet the artist can also be strikingly modern, as in his iconic rendition of the quintessential 1980s woman (beautiful, self-assured, hard) for Estee Lauder.

BIOGRAPHICAL/CRITICAL SOURCES: Art Direction, October, 1973; *Swank*, May, 1975; *American Showcase* (Japan), 1981, 1984.

Illustration for "French Hashish Heads," a story in *High Times*, **1979.** (© *High Times*.)

ENG—, Tom
See ENGELHARDT, Tom

* * *

TOM ENGELHARDT

ENGELHARDT, Tom 1930-
(Tom Eng—)

PERSONAL: Born December 29, 1930, in St. Louis, Mo.; son of Alex F. (an office manager) and Gertrude (Derby) Engelhardt; married Katherine Agnes McCue (an administrative assistant), June 25, 1960; children: Marybeth, Carol Marie, Christine Leigh, Mark Thomas. *Education:* Attended Music and Arts College (no longer in existence), St. Louis, 1949-50; Denver University, 1950-51; Ruskin School of Fine Arts, Oxford, 1954-56; School of Visual Arts, New York City, 1957. *Office and studio:* St. Louis Post-Dispatch, 900 N. Tucker Blvd., St. Louis, Mo. 63101.

CAREER: Freelance commercial artist and cartoonist, New York City, 1957-60; editorial cartoonist, Newspaper Enterprise Association (a newspaper syndicate), Cleveland, Ohio, 1960-61; freelance graphic artist, Cleveland, 1961-62; editorial cartoonist, *St. Louis Post-Dispatch*, 1962—. *Military service:* U.S. Air Force, 1951-53; became staff sergeant. *Awards, honors:* Award from Missouri Committee for Firearm Safety, 1977, "in support of programs to prevent handgun misuse"; award from Ozark Chapter of the Sierra Club, 1981, for environmental and anti-pollution cartoons.

Photo by Jim Rackwitz, St. Louis Post-Dispatch.

EXHIBITIONS: One-man show at Fontbonne College Gallery, St. Louis, Mo., 1972; "Decade of the Environment: 1970-1980," one-man show, Old Courthouse, St. Louis, 1981.

SIDELIGHTS: When Bill Mauldin stepped down as the editorial cartoonist for the *St. Louis Post-Dispatch* in 1962 to join the *Chicago Sun-Times*, there was some suspense in newspaper circles as to who would succeed the legendary Mauldin, and whether the new man would uphold his predecessor's liberal point of view. As it turned out, Tom Engelhardt was picked for the prestigious post, on the strength of his former tenure as editorial cartoonist for Newspaper Enterprise Association (where he signed his work "Tom Eng—"). He proved to be the right choice, both in terms of graphic excellence and of editorial preference.

Engelhardt has termed the delicate balance between a newspaper and its editorial artist as "a marriage between publisher and cartoonist." The marriage of the *Post-Dispatch* and its new cartoonist proved a happy one, at any rate: it has lasted well over twenty years, and gives all indication of lasting many more. Engelhardt himself allowed that he had no trouble adjusting to the Midwestern daily's liberal viewpoint (which coincides with his own) and editorial outlook, "having," as he says, "grown up with it and practically cut my cartoonist's teeth on Daniel R. Fitzpatrick's powerful work."

One of Engelhardt's steadiest targets has been the military establishment, whose power he has castigated in many forceful cartoons. "Just give us the tools and we'll get the job done," piously intones an American general as he reviews rows of flag-draped coffins arriving from Vietnam (1967); "The Great Seal of the Military-Industrial Complex" (1969) depicts the American eagle with a big cigar in his beak, a wad of money bills in one claw, a pile of nuclear missiles in the other, and a shield reading "profits" on his chest, while a streamer behind him proclaims in Latin "Pecunia Omnia Vincit" ("Money Conquers All"). The cartoonist has remained true to his principles to this day, as he consistently flays President Ronald Reagan for sacrificing social concerns to military expenditures.

Another of Engelhardt's cherished causes has been the environment, and the depredations visited upon it by what he perceives to be special interests with ties to the White House, as can be seen in the cartoon depicting the proposed Alaska Parklands Bill being crushed by the "oil and mining interests." These concerns have won him an award from the Ozark Chapter of the Sierra Club, and praise from many other conservation and ecology groups.

The World Encyclopedia of Cartoons said of Engelhardt, "His cartoons are drawn in vertical format, handsome and tightly rendered, with a sense of reserve rather than exaggeration." The cartoonist's meticulous attention to detail and painstaking care of execution match his strongly-held convictions in consistency and lucidity. In a 1969 article for *Cartoonist Profiles* he expressed his views on the subject this way: "Once upon a time some character with a mathematical bent launched a fable to the effect that the idea was 90% of an editorial cartoon, the remainder apparently being set aside for the drawing. Having been buffeted too many times by algebra and other forms of the old math, I'm not going to argue figures, but—to put it another way—there doesn't seem to be much sense wasting a Rolls-Royce engine in a Kaiser body . . . If an idea is so great, the cartoonist should want to cherish it with his best composition, his best drawing, his best attention to detail, such as props, drapery, etc. . . . If the medium is the message, it seems logical that the better designed and executed the medium, the more effective the message. Catch the reader's eye with a first-rate picture and there's a much better chance that the message is going to get across."

Engelhardt's careful rendering is noticeable in all his drawings, but it is especially apparent in his foreign-policy oriented cartoons, be it French President Charles De Gaulle trying to keep a sailboat labeled "the franc" afloat on a sea of trouble by sheer dint of willpower (and legwork), a Russian jackboot brutally trampling down the Czech "spring" of 1968, or former Secretary of State Henry Kissinger delivering one of his strongly-accented homilies on the balance of power to a crowd of bemused newspeople.

Nuclear Giant And Humanitarian Midget

Editorial cartoon, 1984. (© Engelhardt-*St. Louis Post-Dispatch*. Reprinted with permission.)

Engelhardt concedes that before the drawing, before the idea, there comes the general background information in which an editorial cartoonist must immerse himself in order to get his inspiration in the first place. This he does by reading the news and determining which article or story deserves a comment, in addition to a large amount of supplementary reading which, he says, "goes on continuously." While national and international issues may be more glamorous, he strongly believes that local problems should be given equal emphasis and that it is the "closer-to-home cartoons that evoke the biggest reaction."

In *Editorial and Political Cartooning*, Engelhardt is quoted as saying that he is never satisfied with any given day's finished cartoon as it appears on the page, always vowing to do better the next day. This constant perfectionism has gradually led him to move away from Mauldin's influence—an influence apparent as late as his 1969 drawing of an American soldier leaning over a trench, which is very close in concept and execution to Mauldin's immortal World War II cartoons—and to evolve his own style, characterized by a strong sense of design, a harmonious flow of penlines, and a keener eye for artistic effect (probably sharpened by his art training) than can be found in the work of most editorial cartoonists.

'Now, Let's See — Who'll I Play On The Next Campaign Swing?'

Editorial cartoon, 1984. (© Engelhardt-*St. Louis Post-Dispatch*. Reprinted with permission.)

Bigfoot

Editorial cartoon, 1985. (© Engelhardt-*St. Louis Post-Dispatch*. Reprinted with permission.)

BIOGRAPHICAL/CRITICAL SOURCES: John Chase, *Today's Cartoon*, Hauser, 1962; Tom Engelhardt, "Editorial Cartoonist for the *St. Louis Post-Dispatch*," *Cartoonist Profiles*, spring, 1969; Syd Hoff, *Editorial and Political Cartooning*, Stravon, 1976; *The World Encyclopedia of Cartoons*, Chelsea House, 1980; *Who's Who in America*, Marquis, 1985.

—*Sketch by Maurice Horn*

* * *

ENOS, Randall   1936-

PERSONAL: Born January 30, 1936, in New Bedford, Mass.,; son of Eugene (an insurance executive) and Elizabeth (a factory worker; maiden name Dacosta) Enos; married Leann Walker (an actress and gymnastics teacher) June 23, 1956; children; Kristan, Timothy. *Education:* Boston Museum School of Fine Arts, 1954-55. *Politics:* Democrat. *Religion:* "None." *Home and studio:* 11 Court of Oaks, Westport, Conn. 06880.

CAREER: Instructor, Famous Artists School (correspondence art course), Westport, Conn, 1956-64; freelance illustrator, part-time, 1956-66, full time, 1966—; film designer, Pablo Ferro Films, 1964-66; instructor, Parsons School of Design, New York City, 1974-84. *Member:* Shoshin Society (a group of graphic designers dedicated to world peace). *Awards, honors:* TV Film Award from Cannes Film Festival, 1964, for a John Hancock commercial that was never aired; award for illustration from Boston Art Directors Club, 1985, for illustration in *Byte* (a computer magazine); "Desi" Award from Graphic Arts U.S.A., 1985, for cover of *Tennis Magazine*.

WRITINGS—All as illustrator: Robyn Supraner, *It's Not Fair,* Frederick Warne, 1976; Judy Reiser, *And I Thought I Was Crazy,* Simon & Schuster, 1980. Also illustrator of many other small books for Harper, Simon & Schuster, and other publishers as well as hundreds of children's textbooks for various publishers.

Contributor to the *New York Times, Boy's Life,* the *National Lampoon, Playboy,* and many other periodicals.

FILMS—(Designer of titles) *Mickey One* (1964); (designer of titles) *The Russians Are Coming, the Russians Are Coming* (1966). Also animated spots for the "Johnny Carson Show" and many commercials, including the Burlington criss-cross television signature.

EXHIBITIONS: One-man shows at Art Directors Club, New York City, 1981; Wooster School, Danbury, Conn., 1985. Included in many shows organized by the American Institute of Graphic Arts (AIGA), the Society of Illustrators, and the Art Directors Club, in New York City.

WORK IN PROGRESS: A suite of linocuts illustrating Edgar Allan Poe's comic short stories, completion expected in early 1986.

Linocut gag drawing, ca. 1980. (© Randall Enos. Printed with permission.)

Illustration for *New York Times* "Living Section," ca. 1982. (©*New York Times*.)

SIDELIGHTS: Randall Enos commented for *CGA:* "My medium is the linocut; my medium is also humor. In my work I am trying to create a kind of merger between the cartoon and painting. I am very committed to working for the press, whether newspapers or magazines, and communicating with the public on a large scale. I am committed to an art of ideas and social significance; I am very proud of my work in such publications as the *Nation* and the *Progressive.*

"When I talk of creating a merger between painting and cartooning, I mean using the attitude or frame of mind of the painter, and merging it with the things I love in the world of cartooning and comic strips, such as the poignant, crude artistry of Billy DeBeck's *Barney Google* and the beautiful *Krazy Kat* by George Herriman.

"Lately I have been striving more and more towards imbuing my work with a social consciousness; I am trying to make statements about injustice, world peace, and the preservation of the environment. I feel that a 'reporter-artist' such as myself has an obligation to uplift man's spirit and to expose injustices and inequities in every way possible. My hope is to leave behind a legacy testifying to these causes: good, powerful statements can be made very effectively through the medium of humor.

"In another respect I am endeavoring to contribute statements of an esthetic nature: by the expressionistic use of color and form, I am trying to continue and improve on—

inasmuch as I can—a tradition of art that has evolved through the work of the great designers, painters, animators, and cartoonists of the past. *Good design* coupled with a *meaningful statement* is the ideal end product."

Given Enos's artistic and social credo, as expressed in his comments, it is not surprising that he adopted the linocut as his medium of choice. The process was popularized (and refined upon) in the 1920s and 1930s by Pablo Picasso, Henri Matisse, Joan Miro, and other famous Cubist and Surrealist artists, as a means of protest or persuasion more immediately powerful than painting. By marrying such a typically European form of social and political expression with the very American tradition of cartoon slapstick and humor, Enos has given it a new vigor and possibly a new direction.

The linocut (or linoleum block) print process is fairly simple, and consists in inking a previously cut and grooved piece of linoleum, then transferring the inked image to paper. This is quite similar to the woodblock technique, and an uninitiated eye may not be able to tell the subtle differences between the two methods. To his *Print* magazine interviewer Enos explained that he preferred linoleum over wood, because it was easier to work with and did not present the restriction of wood grains, thus giving him any texture he might want. To add color to his prints Enos does not use several linoleum cuts with inks of different colors—as his fine-art predecessors were wont to do—but superimposes cut collages over the original print for a more spontaneous effect. (Many pieces from different colored prints are used to create a full-color illustration.)

All those who have commented upon Enos's work have stressed the artist's close affinity to and freely expressed love of cartoons. Ellen-Jane Opat pointed out, for instance, that "stylistically, Enos often uses sequential repeats or multiples of the same figure in his illustrations—an obvious spin-off from cartooning." In this respect it is worth noting that he was an instructor at the Famous Artists School at a time when this institution extensively drew upon the talents (and reputations) of celebrated cartoonists like Al Capp and Milton Caniff, while also boasting such illustration luminaries as Norman Rockwell and Austin Briggs. It is conceivable—indeed probable—that during his years with the School, Enos was already thinking in terms of a synthesis between the two disciplines. "I function as an illustrator," he

has said, "but I'm always caricaturing, working in satire." This self-confession has been duly noted in several quarters. In *The Illustrator in America* the Reeds called Enos "a satirist in the guise of a primitive"; while in *Graphis* Steve Heller elaborated further: "Randall Enos is a showman, a P.T. Barnum of the graphic arts; his art is his circus."

The bulk of Enos's work is done in color, and there is no doubt that color adds immensely to the zaniness of the artist's visual comments on, say, the art of filmmaking, the history of transportation, or the rules of tennis one-upmanship, all subjects Enos has handled with ease and his usual flippancy of approach. In the same vein, his small color illustrations for a 1980 tennis horoscope are nothing short of riotous, and his depiction of New York's sleazy porno district is an eye-opener (in more ways than one). As for his outrageous "Guernixa" poster, wherein Enos spoofs with a vengeance Picasso's most famous masterpiece in what

Illustration of "Peter and the Wolf" for *New York Times* children's page, ca. 1983. (© *New York Times*.)

is at once a loving parody and a knowing homage, its put-down of modern art's more meretricious pretensions is so telling that one may easily forget how excruciatingly funny the whole thing also is.

Yet his black-and-white prints are in some ways even more inventive and personal. His picture of Shakespeare playing with alphabet blocks not only weighs in with yet another learned comment on the Bard for future English Ph.D. candidates to ponder, but it also gives new and sardonic meaning to the old cliche, "a picture is worth a thousand words." Enos has also done a series of illustrations for the food pages of the *New York Times* that so accurately pinpoint the cuckoo aspirations of the Big Apple's *nouveaux gourmets* that it must have made more than one *Times* reader wince. In these and similar confections he is in a direct line with such otherwise different visual humorists as S. J. Perelman (for the deadpan looniness of his concepts) and John Held, Jr. (for the stylishness of his drawings and the with-it cynicism of his humor).

It is moreover in his black-and-white illustrations that Enos comes closest to the comic strip form, with his frequent use of multiple panels to make a point, and his witticism-filled speech balloons that aptly parallel the visuals. In the mid-1970s his love for the comic strip format overcame even his devotion to the linocut medium, when the *National Lampoon* gave him the opportunity to draw a monthly comic page, *Chicken Gutz*, a funny strip done in pen-and-ink in the style of the old cartoonists he so admires.

Enos has stated that he would never work for a publication whose views he dislikes, nor illustrate any article running contrary to his convictions. His originality and talent have so far assured that he did not have to breach his principles, while at the same time giving him a broad range of publications to work for: his illustrations have appeared in a variety of periodicals, from the *New York Times* to the *National Lampoon,* and from *Boy's Life* to *Playboy.* Yet his work, for all the exposure it has received, has never enjoyed the public recognition that it so obviously deserves. Perhaps the artist's very eclecticism, his wide cultural knowledge have done him a disservice with the general public. In a time of rampant illiteracy and philistinism, his subtle allusiveness (in the manner of some of Marguerite Yourcenar's short stories, some of Enos's prints could be titled "After Durer," "After Callot," "After Goya") may be just a little too scholarly, too esoteric, too "elitist." Perhaps also is he closer than this age will permit its satirists to be to the great artists of the past whom he so often lampoons, but whom he never seeks to debunk.

BIOGRAPHICAL/CRITICAL SOURCES: Ellen-Jane Opat, "Art Today, Gone Tomorrow," *Print,* May-June, 1976; Steve Heller, "Randall Enos," *Graphis,* November-December, 1980; *Who's Who in Graphic Art,* De Clivo, 1982; Walt and Roger Reed, *The Illustrator in America: 1880-1980,* Madison Square, 1984.

—Sketch by Maurice Horn

*   *   *

ERNST, Ken(neth) 1918-1985

OBITUARY NOTICE: Born 1918, in Illinois; died August 6, 1985, in Salem, Ore., where he had been visiting his son, Kenneth Ernst, Jr.; of a heart attack. Cartoonist, best known as the artist on the *Mary Worth* newspaper strip. Ernst studied at the Chicago Art Institute; his first occupation, however, was that of a stage magician. In 1936 he joined the Harry "A" Chesler comic book shop, and also worked for a number of other comic book publishers, drawing *Clyde Beatty* and *Buck Jones* for Western, and *Larry Steele* for National (now DC Comics). In 1940 he went on to the newspaper strip field, as an assistant on *Don Winslow of the Navy.* His long association with *Mary Worth* started in 1942, when he took over the drawing of the strip from Dale Conner. Along with scriptwriter Allen Saunders, he was the man most responsible for taking the feature away from its initially shabby surroundings (when, as Apple Mary, the heroine was a street-corner apple vendor) and putting her in more affluent circumstances. John Saunders, son of Allen Saunders, who currently writes the strip, commented to a United Press reporter that Ernst's "comments on the plots and his acute sense of propriety were invaluable assets to the production of the feature and helped mold the character of Mary Worth."

BIOGRAPHICAL/CRITICAL SOURCES: Stephen Becker, *Comic Art in America,* Simon & Schuster, 1959; *The World Encyclopedia of Comics,* Chelsea House, 1976.

OBITUARY SOURCE: New York Daily News, August 9, 1985.

*   *   *

ERWIN, Will
See EISNER, Will(iam Erwin)

F

FARRIS, Joseph 1924-

PERSONAL: Born May 30, 1924, in Newark, N.J.; son of George (a confectionary store owner) and Adele (Najjoum) Farris; married Rosine Mims, July 9, 1951 (divorced 1969); married Cynthia Cox (an art teacher), May 20, 1971; children: Christine Andersen (first marriage); stepchildren: Michael, Stephen, Peter Aron. *Education:* Attended Art Students League, 1942; Whitney School of Art, 1946-49 (certificate). *Politics:* Democrat. *Religion:* Unitarian-Universalist. *Home and studio:* Long Meadow Lane, Bethel, Conn. 06801.

CAREER: Freelance cartoonist, 1950—. *Military service:* U.S. Army, 1943-46, served in infantry; became staff sergeant; received Bronze Star, Combat Infantryman's Badge, and other decorations. *Member:* Cartoonists Association. *Awards, honors:* Emily Lowe Award for Painting, 1965.

EXHIBITIONS: One man show, Ward Eggleston Gallery, New York City.

SIDELIGHTS: As Joseph Farris tells it, he was in his early teens when he read an intriguing piece on the well-known American painter and cartoonist Richard Taylor in *Collier's.* Shortly thereafter, he learned from his local Danbury, Connecticut, paper that Taylor, a resident of nearby Bethel, was teaching an art class there. Enrolling in that class, he began an association that was to continue all through his high school days. "He gave me the basics in art," Farris told his profiler for *The World Encyclopedia of Cartoons;* "I was impressed by the quality of his life style and with his ability to see things freshly." While the emphasis in Taylor's classes was more on art than cartooning, Farris must have seen his teacher's comic contributions to the *New Yorker* and *Esquire* as the chief supporters of the life style he admired, for to this day he separates his cartooning form his "fine arts side" as a painter/sculptor "completely free of commercialism."

JOSEPH FARRIS

World War II service in the 100th Infantry Division not only gained Farris a Bronze Star for combat services; it saw publication in *Stars and Stripes* of his first cartoons. While awaiting discharge in 1946, he spent three months studying art at the University of Biarritz, France, and upon demobilization returned to Connecticut to study at the Whitney School of Art in New Haven. In 1949, he began his career as an illustrator, and a year later sold his first panels to a Roman Catholic periodical called, somewhat dauntingly from a cartoonist's point of view, *The Victorian.* Today a regular contributor to such magazines as *Playboy, Pent-* *house, Barron's* and *Crain's New York Business* and a contract artist with the *New Yorker,* Farris considers himself primarily a social commentator, generally eschewing the subjects of sex and politics to concentrate on social class, family status, and the communications media. Favorite targets include stuffiness, sculptors (self parodying?), and suburbia. He is not without a sense of the absurd, but the bulk of his work is firmly based in the day-to-day experience of middle class America. Stylistically, Farris is an accomplished visual communicator and seems equally proficient with the sight gag and the captioned drawing. In executing

"*How sweet of you!*"

Gag cartoon, ca. 1982. (© *The New Yorker*.)

Farris's work its individual identity. By frequently removing the focal point of a panel from its geometric center, he provides the viewer with a sense of looking at it from over the original observer's shoulder and, as such, exhibits a technique that has more in common with the positioning and lighting of a piece of sculpture than with the execution of a gag cartoon.

A productive cartoonist—between 1971 and 1974 he drew a daily cartoon feature, *Farriswheel,* for the Chicago Tribune-New York News Syndicate—Farris still finds time for serious painting and sculpture. His work is represented in many private collections. His painting tends to be representational and humorous in genre, but his sculpture is in the abstract mode.

BIOGRAPHICAL/CRITICAL SOURCES: Who's Who in the East, 1978; *Who's Who in American Art,* 1980; *The World Encyclopedia of Cartoons,* Chelsea House, 1980.

—*Sketch by Richard Calhoun*

the former he often employs serial drawings (three to nine panels) in which action is the basis for humor, while the latter tend to revolve around situations or cliches. While his drawings—chiefly ink line and an occasional wash—can be as busily detailed as a paisley print (usually when "busyness" is the basis for humor), Farris is quite capable of making his points as deftly as any of his minimalist colleagues: a drawing is set in Washington, D.C., by the simple expedient of making the Washington Monument visible beyond an office window, a quartet of gloomy faces is glimpsed through the partly open door of "Misery Loves Co."

Much can be said for the fineness of line and the superiority of the draftsmanship in a Farris cartoon, but the critic comes away from a cumulative appraisal of his work impressed by a mastery of perspective more characteristic of a sculptor (which he is) than of a graphic artist. It is not a detail that is thrust upon the viewer, but one which is subtly revealed, only becoming apparent after concentrated study. Most often, the view is from slightly above and off to one side—the sort of an angle a sculptor might take on a virgin block of marble—though when he wants to emphasize height, as in a drawing featuring an exchange between two elephants, he will choose an upward line of sight. It is this touch that gives

Gag cartoon, ca. 1980. (© *The New Yorker*.)

"*I've called the family together to announce that, because of inflation, I'm going to have to let two of you go.*"

Gag cartoon by Joe Farris, ca. 1980. (© *The New Yorker*.)

FERNANDEZ (SANCHEZ), Fernando   1940-

PERSONAL: Born February 7, 1940, in Barcelona, Spain; son of Rafael (a taxi driver) and Micaela (Sanchez) Fernandez; married Maria Rosa Lleida Sabater (a painter), May 29, 1964; children: Eva, Hector. *Education:* Attended business school, Barcelona, 1953-55. *Home:* Calle Industria, 89, Barcelona. *Studio:* Calle Castillejos, 280, Barcelona. *Agent:* Josep Toutain, Selecciones Illustradas, Diagonal 325, Barcelona; Bernd Metz, 43 E. 19th St., New York, N.Y. 10003.

CAREER: Illustrator and cartoonist, 1956—; contributed science-fiction comics to Artima, France, 1956-58; romance and war comics for Fleetway, United Kingdom, 1959-65; illustrator for European and American publications, 1966-73; poster and advertising artist for Spanish agencies, 1966-73; author of comics, cover artist, book illustrator, and painter, 1972—. *Military service:* Enlisted, health services, 1960-62. *Awards, honors:* Warren Publishing Company Award, New York City, 1975; Semana Nacional de Publica-

ciones Infantiles y Juveniles (as illustrator), Spain, 1977; Club de Amigos de la Historieta, Spain, 1980; "1984" Award, from the public (as scriptwriter), Spain, 1982. *Member:* Organizing Committee, Comics and Illustration Fair, Barcelona, Spain.

WRITINGS—Author of texts and illustrator; all published by Afha, Barcelona: *Los invasores del cuerpo humano* (title means "The Invaders of the Human Body"), 1975; *Viaje al mundo secreto de los insectos* ("Travel to the Secret World of Insects"), 1976; *Viaje a la Prehistoria* ("Travel to Prehistoric Times"), 1977; *Viaje a las estrellas* ("Travel to the Stars"), 1979.

Author and illustrator; books of comics: *L'Uomo di Cuba* ("The Man from Cuba"), Cepim, Milan, Italy, 1979; *Cuando el comic es arte—Fernando Fernandez,* Toutain, Barcelona, 1980; *Zora,* Toutain, 1983, Catalan Communications, 1983, *Firmado por: Isaac Asimov* (from Asimov's stories), Bruguera, Barcelona, 1983; *Dracula* (from Bram Stoker's novel), Toutain, 1984, Catalan, 1984.

EXHIBITIONS: Comics and illustrations shown at Colegio de Arquitectos, Barcelona, Spain, 1972; Museo de Arte Moderno, Sevilla, Spain, 1973; Bologna Book Fair, Italy, 1976; Frankfurt Book Fair, West Germany, 1978; International Salon of Comics, Lucca, Italy, 1982; Angouleme Comics Salon, France, 1982; Comics and Illustration Fair, Barcelona, 1981-85; paintings exhibited in many private galleries in Europe.

WORK IN PROGRESS: Color illustrations for children's and juvenile books published by Random House; paperback covers for Pocket Books; drawings for a series of television animated cartoons to be broadcast world-wide on the occasion of the fifth centennial of the discovery of America; a collection of short stories in comic strip form.

SIDELIGHTS: Fernando Fernandez commented on his work: "I have tried to experiment in an innovative way with the most diverse techniques—ink, watercolor, acrylic, airbrush, oil, etc.—in my comics as well as in my illustrations. My work has been figurative, with the exception of a short period in my painting career. The two 'isms' that interest me most in painting are impressionism and expressionism, and I don't believe that my style can be defined easily, except to say that it is in constant evolution."

FERNANDO FERNANDEZ

Cover illustration for *Cuando Comic Es Arte*, 1980. (© Fernando Fernandez. Reprinted with permission.)

The diversity of Fernandez's artistic directions has added a personal dimension to his comics, that of a permanent plastic experimentation, at the same time that he was innovating in the field of narrative technique as his own scriptwriter. Since 1972 he has imparted a spirit of poetry and humanism that immeasurably adds to the visual spectacle of his compositions.

His stories in black-and-white published between 1972 and 1975 in the American magazine *Vampirella* are rich in lyrical expressions that transcend the simple graphic lines. In *L'Uomo di Cuba* the beauty of the illustrations overwhelms the narrative thread. With great literary and graphic conviction Fernandez undertook *Zora,* a series first published in the Spanish magazine *1984,* and later translated in the United States in the pages of *Heavy Metal.* In *Zora* the artist brought his experiments in graphic expression to their ultimate, as though he had undertaken to display a vast radiograph of his working methods.

A whole panoply of artistic processes, from pencil to oil, find their way in *Zora,* where they blend together in an amazing display of all the resources open to illustration. The panels in turn merge into pages of diverse geometrical shapes, with emphasis given to the curved line, and with an inspiration that goes back to the turn of the century. The plot, which belongs to the science-fiction genre, is secondary to the artistic fireworks, and the futuristic society described in the story is only a pretext for the artist to go back to a fantastic and romantic world. Almost nostalgic in its luxuriousness, *Zora* is reminiscent of the spectacular illustrations of the old space-operas.

In 1982 Fernandez, who had already used color in *Zora*, gave us a pictorial version of *Dracula*, Bram Stoker's famous novel. "Fernandez's most personal expression in *Dracula* resides in his composition, his sense of line, and his use of color," Maurice Horn wrote in his preface to the book. "The painter's touch is apparent at every step, and the painter's eye recognizable in each frame." At the same time that he was using to good effects his skills as a painter, Fernandez, however, was falling back to a more traditional method of storytelling, with his use of a grid made of rectangular panels, in contrast to the curvilinear structure of his previous work. The story was thus predominantly told in cinematic terms, and the color tones all had a deep narrative function. More perhaps than any other author of comics in Spain, Fernandez realizes how much the intelligent staging of narrative sequences can contribute to the art of the comics.

Fernandez's latest comic series, *La leyenda de los cuatro sombras* (title means "The Legend of the Four Shadows"), on a script by the Argentine writer Carlos Trillo, is a fantasy on a medieval theme.

A page from *Dracula*, 1984. (© Fernando Fernandez. Reprinted with permission.)

BIOGRAPHICAL/CRITICAL SOURCES: Javier Coma, *Y nos fuimos a hacer vinetas,* Penthalon, Madrid, 1981; Coma, ed., *Historia de los Comics,* Toutain, Barcelona, 1983; Maurice Horn, "Dracula Lives!", preface to *Dracula,* Catalan Communications, 1984.

—*Sketch by Javier Coma*

* * *

FOSTER, Brad W. 1955-

PERSONAL: Born April 28, 1955, in San Antonio, Texas; son of Byron V. (a U.S. Air Force pilot) and Yvonne (Kirst) Foster. *Education:* Texas A & M University, Bachelor of Environmental Design, 1977; attended University of Texas at Austin, 1977-1979. *Residence:* 4109 Pleasant Run, Irving, Tex. 75038.

CAREER: Freelance illustrator and proprietor of Jabberwocky Graphix, 1975—.

WRITINGS—Illustrator only, unless otherwise noted: *Aesop's Fables Coloring Album,* Troubador Press, 1982; *Monica the Computer Mouse,* Sybex Inc., 1984; *Primarily LOGO,* Prentice Hall, 1984; *A Bit of LOGO Magic,* Prentice Hall, 1984; (also writer) *One Year's Worth,* Jabberwocky Graphix, 1984; (also writer) *The Alpha Beastiary,* Jabberwocky Graphix, 1984.

WORK IN PROGRESS: Illustrating two children's books by Ardath Mayhar, *The Door in the Hill* and *The Jewelled Mouse,* as well as three scripts for children's books of his own; proposal for a comic book series, "Bertram and the Gizmos"; an illustrated book on the history of tarot cards.

SIDELIGHTS: Brad Foster began his career as a cartoonist and illustrator drawing "Tales of the Gigags" for *The Battalion,* the student paper at Texas A & M. This strip featured the adventures of imaginary little humanoids living in the utility tunnels under the campus, and was popular enough to be collected into a magazine. With that as his start, Foster went on to create his own small-press publishing house, Jabberwocky Graphix, which began in 1976 with the publication of *Jabberwocky,* a magazine of Foster's work.

Jabberwocky Graphix has survived ever since, turning out a variety of "alternative comix" by Foster and others. Even while running Jabberwocky, however, Foster has contributed stories and illustrations to science-fiction fanzines and small press comics all over the country, becoming one of the most visible of the many "fan artists" active in science fiction fandom, and has also pursued a career as a professional illustrator, primarily of children's books. He works in a variety of styles, from his simple cartooning to the ornate compositions he calls his "argent" style, and continues to experiment with both the style and content of his drawing.

Foster says of his work, "I draw because it is what I enjoy doing more than anything else—as simple as that. To reply at any greater length would simply be to restate that idea in different ways."

Illustration of "The Twelve Days of Christmas," also used as logo for Jabberwocky Graphix. (© 1984, Brad W. Foster. Reprinted with permission.)

BIOGRAPHICAL/CRITICAL SOURCES: The Comics Journal, April, 1985.

* * *

FURUKAWA, Taku   1941-

PERSONAL: Born September 25, 1941, in Ueno City, Mie Prefecture, Japan; son of Yasushi and Yasuko Furukawa; married wife Michi; children: Shuntaro, Momoko. *Education:* Graduated from Osaka University of Foreign Studies. *Home:* 2-1865 Wakamatsucho, Fuchushi, Tokyo, Japan. *Studio:* 701-7-1-12 Minami Aoyama, Minato-ku, Tokyo, Japan.

CAREER: Animator in Yoji Kuri's company, Kuri Jikken Manga Kobo, Tokyo, 1964-67; formed own studio, Takun Jikken Manga Box, 1970—; established Inc. Inc, a special company to handle animation videos, 1985—. *Member:* Manga Shudan, ASIFA-Japan, Tokyo Designer's Space, NEWZ.

AWARDS, HONORS: Special Jury Award, from Annecy International Animation Film Festival, 1975, for *Odorokiban;* Bungei Shunju Comics Award, 1979, for *The Takun Humor.*

WRITINGS—All collections of cartoons: *Takun Nonsense,* 1976; *The Takun Humor,* 1978; *Dessin d'Humor,* 1982; *Furukawa Taku no Bimyo na Sekai* (title means "The Delicate World of Taku Furukawa"), 1984.

FILMS—All animation shorts: *Head Spoon,* 1972; *New York Trip,* 1972; *Beautiful Planet,* 1974; *Odorokiban* (title means "Phenakistoscope"), 1975; *Coffee Break,* 1979; *Speed,* 1982; *Portrait,* 1984.

SIDELIGHTS: Taku Furukawa is an unusual breed of artist in Japan, in that he defies easy classification. In a culture where most artists are sucked into the gigantic, commercial worlds of comic books and television animation, Furukawa has been able to consistently adhere to his own playful vision, and make a considerable name for himself in the process. Furukawa's main love can perhaps be said to be experimental animation shorts, but he also is known as a cartoonist, an illustrator, a humorist, and a conceptual artist. Almost all of his work is characterized by the same whimsical approach—slices of human life, shown in a new way, gently.

TAKU FURUKAWA

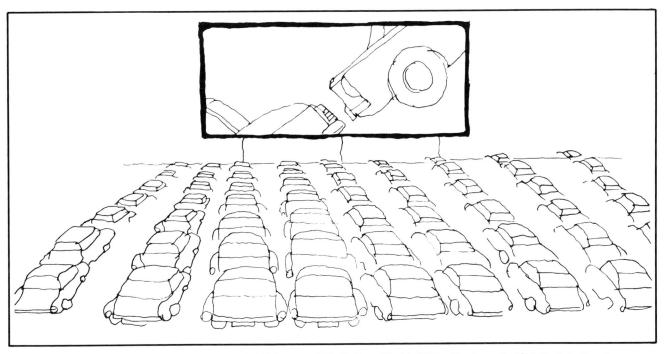

Cartoon from *Furukawa Taku no Bimyo na Sekai* (title means "The Delicate World of Taku Furukawa"). (© 1984, Taku Furukawa. Reprinted with permission.)

Most of Furukawa's drawings and animation are identifiable by their sparse, "squiggly" lines. His animation shorts are also idiosyncratic. *Odorikiban*, which won the Annecy Special Jury Award, was based on the phenakistoscope, an optical toy pioneered by Joseph Plateau, a Belgian, in 1832. *Coffee Break*, a three-minute short, starts off with a man drinking coffee to a countdown; when it reaches zero, everything is blown into the air. His short, single-panel cartoons are particularly outstanding in Japan, where long, dramatic comics have virtually swamped the market.

BIOGRAPHICAL/CRITICAL SOURCES: The World Encyclopedia of Cartoons, Chelsea House, 1980; *Films and TV Graphics*, Graphics Press (Japan), 1982; *Annual Illustration in Japan*, 1984.

Cartoon from *Furukawa Taku no Bimyo na Sekai* (title means "The Delicate World of Taku Furukawa"). (© 1984, Taku Furukawa. Reprinted with permission.)

Cartoon from *Furukawa Taku no Bimyo na Sekai* **(title means ''The Delicate World of Taku Furukawa'').** (© 1984, Taku Furukawa. Reprinted with permission.)

G

GALLO, Bill
See GALLO, William

* * *

GALLO, William 1922-
(Bill Gallo)

PERSONAL: Born December 12, 1922, son of Francisco (newspaperman) and Henrietta (concert pianist; maiden name Cabellero) Gallo; married Dolores Rodriguez (a travel agent) March 13, 1950; children: Gregory, William, Jr. *Education:* Attended Columbia University, two years; graduated from Cartoonists and Illustrators School (now School of Visual Arts), 1954. *Home:* 1 Mayflower Dr., Yonkers, N.Y. 10710. *Office:* New York Daily News, 220 East 42nd St., New York, N.Y. 10017.

CAREER: New York Daily News, 1941—, sports cartoonist and columnist, 1961—, associate sports editor, 1984—. *Military service:* U.S. Marine Corps, 1942-45. *Member:* Baseball Writers' Association, Boxing Writers' Association (president), National Cartoonists Society (president, 1973-77), Society of Illustrators, Turf Writers, Professional Football Writers, Society of Silurians, New York Press Club, International Council of Mayors of New York State.

AWARDS, HONORS: Recipient of eighteen "Page One" awards from New York Newspaper Guild in 1965, 1968, 1969, and 1971; Elzie Segar Award as Outstanding Cartoonist, 1976; Alumni Achievement Award, School of Visual Arts, 1977; James J. Walker Award, Downtown Athletic Club, New York City; named best sports cartoonist by National Cartoonists Society in 1969-1973 and 1984, 1985; named to Yonkers Hall of Fame, 1984; to Westchester Hall of Fame, 1984.

EXHIBITIONS: One-man show, Spectrum Gallery, New York City, 1980.

SIDELIGHTS: The son of a newspaperman, Bill Gallo published his first cartoons while still a high school student. He joined the staff of the *Daily News* in 1941. He joined the Marines in 1942 and after participating in the landings at Roi-Namur, Saipan, Tinian, and Iwo Jima returned to the *News* in 1945. He did various jobs in the paper's art department while attending Columbia University's School of General Studies and the Cartoonists and Illustrators School, but he has been quoted as saying the most important part of his education was the on-the-job training he got at the *News*.

Self-portrait of Bill Gallo. (Printed with permission.)

In 1960 he became the paper's chief sports cartoonist. His model was Willard Mullin (1902-1978), the legendary sports cartoonist of the *New York World Telegram*, whom he regards (as do most of his colleagues in the field) as the preeminent sports cartoonist of the past half century. Like Mullin, Gallo approaches his assignment as columnist, commentator, and (not least) fan, observing and reporting on the world of sport in a fashion both amusing and informative. Indeed, his signature creation, "Basement Bertha," was inspired by Mullins' own raucous, blue-collar Dodgers baseball fan, the "Brooklyn Bum." Bertha, whom Gallo once described as a "pixie washerwoman . . . with some of the philosophy of Sancho Panza," first appeared in 1962 as the number one fan of the just-formed and hopelessly inept New York Mets baseball team, then piloted

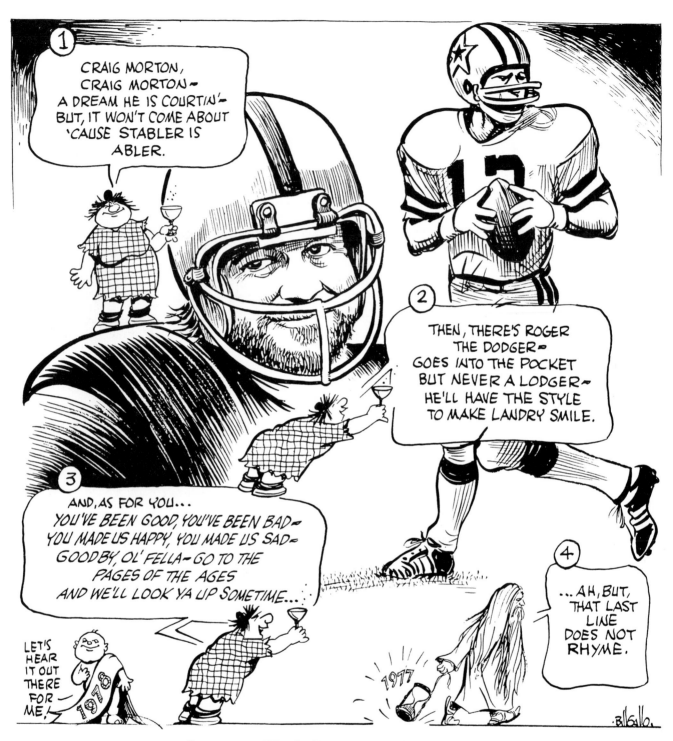

Sports cartoon, 1977. (© Bill Gallo. Reprinted with permission.)

by the colorful Casey Stengel. As he explained in a 1980 interview: "Basement Bertha symbolizes the 'loser,' though she doesn't take losing all that seriously. She respects winning, but she realizes she's dealing with a game, when all is said and done, and a game, to all intents and purposes, is to entertain."

In 1981 Gallo took Bertha out of the pages of the Sunday *News,* where she starred in a half-page feature·and put her in

a one man show at the Spectrum Gallery in New York City entitled "Basement Bertha's Friends"—a series of acrylic painting in which the lumpy, knob-nosed Bertha shared the canvas with luminaries from the worlds of sport (Joe DiMaggio, Joe Frazier), politics (Jimmy Carter), entertainment (Zero Mostel, Frank Sinatra), and art (Pablo Picasso). This was a liberating experience for Gallo, who confesses he was once "afraid of colors" to the extent that he thought he might be color-blind, and he recommends it to young pen-

and-inkers as stretching therapy: "It will help their work, and they'll find that they work a lot looser with their cartoons after they've started painting. Working in one medium seems to help in another."

As the regular sports cartoonist for one of the largest circulation daily papers in the world, Gallo is not only the latest in a line of American sports cartoonists that has included T. A. Dorgan and Mullin, but perhaps the genre's most ardent defender. He has repeatedly assailed the tendency of sports editors to excise cartoons in favor of photographs, asserting that each has its place on the sports page. The photo's purpose is to snatch a single frame from the continuity of an action being described in words, while a cartoon, Gallo insists "*should* tell a story—whether it is told with humor or strong emotion, it must *SAY* something." To this end, he chides younger cartoonists who insist upon emulating the noble but passé tradition of pen and ink portraiture, arguing that their inspiration should be the modern editorial cartoonist, not the classic sports illustrators. "If an editor sacrifices a good sports cartoon feature for a whim, or to save a little money, I think it's a crime," Gallo declares; "One way that more space can be made for a sports cartoon is for editors to eliminate some of the wasted words in many of the stories on the page."

BIOGRAPHICAL/CRITICAL SOURCES: "Sports Cartoon—Then and Now," *Cartoonist Profiles*, September, 1974; Gallo interview, *Cartoonist Profiles*, December, 1980; *The World Encyclopedia of Cartoons*, Chelsea House, 1980; *Who's Who in America*, 1984-85.

—*Sketch by Richard Calhoun*

Sports cartoon, 1985. (© Bill Gallo. Reprinted with permission.)

* * *

GIMENEZ (GIMENEZ), Carlos 1941-

PERSONAL: Born March 6, 1941, in Madrid, Spain; son of Vicente Gomez Moratalla (a mechanic and welder) and Marcelina Gimenez Garcia; married, with children. *Education:* Received primary education in the so-called "Hogares" ("Homes") of the Service of Social Assistance, government-sponsored institutions for children unable to afford to go to normal schools. *Home:* Pasaje de Montesa, 5, 28006 Madrid, Spain. *Agent:* Josep Toutain, Selecciones Ilustradas, Diagonal 325, 08009 Barcelona, Spain; Bernd Metz, Selecciones Ilustradas, 43 E. 19th St., New York, N.Y. 10003.

CAREER: Apprentice, porcelain factory, 1957-59; freelance illustrator and cartoonist, 1959—. *Military service:* Spanish Army, 1962-63, served in Signal Corps. *Awards, honors:* Awards from Club de Amigos de la Historieta, Spain, 1977, 1978, and 1983; "1984" Award, Spain, 1980; Saint-Michel Award, Belgium, 1981; Freixas Award, Certamen de Gijon, Spain, 1981 (withdrawn for ideological reasons); Alfred Award from Salon de la Bande Dessinee d'Angouleme, France, 1981; and others.

WRITINGS—All books of comics; published by De la Torre (Madrid), except as noted: *Hom*, Amaika (Barcelona), 1977, reissued by De la Torre, 1979; *Paracuellos* (title means "Daredevils"), Amaika, 1977, reissued by De la Torre, 1979; *Espana, Una* (title means "Spain, One"), 1978; *Espana, Grande* (title means "Spain, Great"), 1978; *Espana, Libre!* (title means "Spain, Free!"), 1978; *Barrio* (title means "Neighborhood"), 1978; *Mano a Mano* (title means "Hand to Hand"), 1979; *Retales* (title means "Remnants"), 1979;

Sports cartoon, 1985. (© Bill Gallo. Reprinted with permission.)

A page from *Los Professionales*. (© 1984, Carlos Gimenez. Reprinted with permission.)

Koolau el leproso (title means "Koolau the Leper," from Jack London's short story), 1980; *Erase una vez en el futuro* (title means "Once Upon a Time in the Future"), 1980; *Paracuellos 2/Auxilio Social*, 1982; *Los profesionales I*, 1983; *Los profesionales II*, 1983.

WORK IN PROGRESS: Producing episodes for the series *Los profesionales;* creating independent stories on critical and sentimental themes; planning a strip set in Spain during its Civil War.

SIDELIGHTS: Carlos Gimenez started his art career in 1959 when he joined the studio of the illustrator Manuel Lopez Blanco. From there he went on to become a comic artist, at first only doing the drawing, and later, starting in 1974, writing his own scripts. In the 1960s and early 1970s he drew comics on command, many of them for the foreign market. His contributions in this period include *Drake & Drake* (1961), *Gringo* (1963), *Delta 99* (1968), and a work of higher caliber, *Dani Futuro*, a likable science-fiction series on scripts by Victor Mora.

From 1974 on, a progressive awakening, affecting his ethical, esthetic, and professional values, took place, resulting in a major change in his activities. It was then that, taking his inspiration from a Brian Aldiss novel, he started work on a very personal story, *Hom*. The lonely protagonist of the tale falls under the domination of a parasitic fungus, in an analogy with enslaved and exploited man, then falls prey to a pseudo-prophet, till the final annihilation of both dictators. Only after Franco's death could *Hom* be published in Spain, while appearing in the meantime in the Italian magazine *Alter Alter*.

Contrary to the image commonly held abroad when it comes to Spanish comic artists, Gimenez does not display in *Hom*—nor in his subsequent series—any spectacular graphic abilities. The artist's characteristic look is based on a slightly humorous line (which owes much to American cartoonists as well as to Andre Franquin and other Belgian and French artists) and on a preoccupation with the storyline first and foremost. Above all else there exists in the artist an eagerness to express his own passionate convictions, and in this respect it is no surprise that Gimenez has amply drawn upon his fund of personal memories.

What can be termed an autobiographical saga opened with Gimenez's series *Paracuellos* (1976). The different episodes of this strip, short and self-contained, refer directly to the author's childhood in the "Hogares" of the Social Assistance administration and, aside from their political charge, include deeply lyrical sketches about an unusual juvenile world subjected to the cruelties of a dictatorial regime. When this work was anthologized in a book, its success caused Gimenez to continue the series under the title *Auxilio social* ("Social Assistance"). In the meantime the author had proceeded with recollections of his latter life in other interrelated series of short duration, *Barrio* (1977) and *La saga de los Menendez* (1978, later collected in the book *Mano a mano*).

Gimenez used the same formula to retrace his career as an artist for Josep Toutain's agency Selecciones Ilustradas, in his already ample series, *Los profesionales*, created in 1982. In it there are numerous allusions to famous Spanish artists, as well as to Toutain himself (seen, like the other characters,

in a humorous key). In addition to his more personal work, Gimenez has produced a number of stories dealing with sexual-sentimental problems, and especially a series, solidly combative, on the political circumstances that led to the establishment of democracy in Spain. First published in the magazine *El Papus* (1976), the different episodes received their general appellation from the titles of the three books into which they were later collected, *Espana Una, Espana Grande, Espana Libre!*

Paralleling these works of social and political protest (whose moods range from compassionate humor to debunking aggression), Gimenez has followed *Hom* with other adaptations from famous authors, namely Jack London and Stanislaw Lem. A tale from the former gave rise in 1979-80 to *Koolau el leproso*, which again dealt with the theme of domination by one class over another; and stories by both inspired the different episodes, with no tie between them, of *Erase una vez en el futuro*, a science-fiction series published in 1980. There exists no great distance, however, between these works based on other writers' outlines and those that have an autobiographical mainspring: ever since the time that, starting with *Hom*, Gimenez decided to write his own stories, his entire oeuvre exhibits a remarkable ideological and expressive unity.

A number of Gimenez's stories have appeared in the United States in the pages of comic magazines such as *Heavy Metal*, and more particularly in James Warren's publications. *Hom* has recently been serialized in the comic book *Echo of Futurepast*, published by Continuity Comics.

BIOGRAPHICAL/CRITICAL SOURCES: The World Encyclopedia of Comics, Chelsea House, 1976; Javier Coma, *Y nos fuimos a hacer vinetas*, Penthalon (Madrid), 1981; *Carlos Gimenez*, Norma (Barcelona), 1982; *Historia de los comics*, Toutain (Barcelona), 1983.

—*Sketch by Javier Coma*

* * *

GLASER, Milton 1929-

PERSONAL: Born June 26, 1929, in the Bronx, N.Y.; son of Eugene (a tailor) and Eleanor (Bergman) Glaser; married Shirley Girton (an art gallery director), August 13, 1957. *Education:* Graduated from Cooper Union Art School, 1951; Fulbright scholar, Academy of Fine Arts, Bologna, Italy, 1952-53. *Religion:* Hebrew. *Studio:* 207 E. 32nd St., New York, N.Y. 10016.

CAREER: President and founder, with Reynold Ruffins, Edward Sorel, and Seymour Chwast, Push Pin Studio, New York City, 1954-74; founder, with Ruffins, Sorel, and Chwast, *Push Pin Graphic* (a magazine), 1957; president, design director, and founder, with Clay Felker, *New York* (a magazine), 1968-76; vice-president and design director, *Village Voice* (a magazine), 1975-77; president, Milton Glaser Inc., New York City, 1974—. Member of faculty of School of Visual Arts, New York City; lecturer at Pratt Institute, Brooklyn, N.Y. Board member, Cooper Union; member of board of directors, International Design Conference, Aspen, Colo. *Member:* American Institute of Graphic Arts, Art Directors Club, Alliance Graphique Internationale.

AWARDS, HONORS: Gold Medal, American Institute of Graphic Arts, 1972; Gold Medal, Society of Illustrators, 1979; St. Gaudens Medal, Cooper Union, 1979; 1984 Medal of the Society of Industrial Artists and Designers, 1985. Honorary doctorates from Minneapolis Institute of Arts, 1971, Moore College, Philadelphia, 1975, Philadelphia Museum School, 1979, School of Visual Arts, 1979. Member of Art Directors Club Hall of Fame, 1979; honorary fellow of Royal Society of Arts, London, 1979.

WRITINGS: (With wife, Shirley Glaser) *If Apples Had Teeth*, Knopf, 1960; (with Jerome Snyder), *The Underground Gourmet*, Simon & Schuster, 1968, revised edition, 1970; Peter Mayer, editor, *Milton Glaser: Graphic Design*, Overlook Press, 1973; *The Milton Glaser Poster Book*, introduction by Giorgio Soavi, Crown, 1977.

Illustrator: Alvin Tresselt, *The Smallest Elephant in the World*, Knopf, 1959; Conrad Aiken, *Cats and Bats and Things with Wings*, Atheneum, 1965; Gian Carlo Menotti, *Help, Help, the Gobolinks*, McGraw, 1970; George Mendoza, *Fish in the Sky*, Doubleday, 1971; (with Seymour Chwast and Barry Zaid) translated by, Ormonde DeKay, Jr., *Rimes de la Mere Oie*, Little Brown, 1971; Isaac Asimov, *The Annotated Don Juan*, Doubleday, 1972; Boris Vian, *J'irai Cracher Sur Vos Tombes*, Andre Sauret, 1982; *The Works of Apollinaire*, Andre Sauret, 1983-84.

MILTON GLASER

EXHIBITIONS: Museum of Modern Art, New York City, 1975; Portland Visual arts Center, Portland, Ore., 1975; Royal Museum of Fine Arts, Brussels, Belgium, 1976; Centre Georges Pompidou, Paris, 1977 (toured Europe and Middle East, 1977-79); Carl Solway Gallery, Cincinnati, Ohio, 1980; Peabody Museum, Harvard University, Cambridge, Mass., 1981; Lincoln Center Gallery, New York City, 1981; with Jean Michel Folon at a two-man show at the Museum of Modern Art in Liege, Belgium, 1982; Houghton Gallery at Cooper Union, New York City, 1984; Art Center, Pasadena, Calif., 1985; Massachusetts College of Art, Boston, 1985. Represented in the permanent collections of the Museum of Modern Art, New York City; Israel Museum, Jerusalem; National Archives, Smithsonian Institution, Washington, D.C.; Chase Manhattan Bank, New York.

SIDELIGHTS: To call Milton Glaser a graphic artist is to limit the career of a man whose first professional undertaking was to design a set of place mats, and whose most recent commission has been to make over, from jar labels to interior layout, the giant Grand Union supermarket chain. Along the way, he has been influential in the design and, through that, the purpose of projects as variable as the Schlumberger Corporation's annual reports, the Childcraft Toy Store in New York, and the Observation Deck of the World Trade Center at the southern tip of Manhattan. He is, in fact, a many-sided philosopher in the art of visual communication, and as such more than the sum of his techniques and tools. Whether one considers his Push Pin Studio a school of design like the Bauhaus or an attempt, in its repudiation of such dicta as "less is more," to deemphasize the very relevance of "schools," with their implied restrictions and rigidities, one must consider Glaser's among the most important and articulate voices of our media-conscious age.

Glaser was born in the Bronx in 1929, the son of Hungarian Jewish immigrants. He told an interviewer from *Art News* (1975) that his ambition to be an artists dated from an encounter at the age of four with his cousin Eddie, who asked " 'Do you want to see a pigeon?' and promptly drew one on a brown paper bag. Now that was a miracle for me." He entered kindergarten considering himself an artist, and a year-long confinement because of rheumatic fever subsequently sharpened this identification. During this period he amused himself by creating clay models of cities, and as a result discovered at age eight the relationship between design and control: "You see you can't control the world, so you try to create a world you can control." The designer's credo has seldom been more succinctly put. This precocious insight was afterwards enhanced by a first rate education at New York City's High School of Music and Art, the Art School of Cooper Union, and two years as a Fulbright scholar at the Academy of Fine Arts in Bologna, Italy. In 1954, Glaser, along with Seymour Chwast, Edward Sorel, and Reynold Ruffins, founded the Push Pin Studio on East 13th Street in New York City and commenced business by turning out a gross of cork place mats. From such humble origins arose a concept of design that would ultimately challenge the dominant Swiss/Bauhaus austerity, and a movement that Harold T. P. Hayes, former editor of *Esquire* and Glaser associate, was to call in a 1977 article the "Push Pin Conspiracy." "I guess the revolutionary thing we did," Glaser recently recalled, "was to take the position that there

"Gallery of Composers," pen-and-ink drawing, 1973. (© Milton Glaser. Reprinted with permission.)

is no single voice capable of expressing every idea, that romance is still necessary, ornament is necessary, and simplification is not better than complexity." In 1957 the Studio launched *Push Pin Graphic*, a magazine/manifesto which it mailed out free-of-charge to various influential designers and design centers in order to support its challenge to the Bauhaus minimalists. Thanks to such proselytization, the Push Pin approach stands today as the chief alternative current in international design.

While Push Pin Studio was changing the vocabulary of design in the 1960s and 1970s, Glaser was impressing its ebullient, witty eclecticism on a wider audience through a series of colorful posters (six million of his Bob Dylan poster

were distributed world-wide in 1966), eccentric experimentations in typography and imagery, and forays into magazine design. It was in this latter area that Glaser gained his reputation as a guru among image-makers. In 1968, with Clay Felker he launched the magazine *New York*, a sophisticated, glossy weekly. Serving as design director (1968-76), Glaser evolved a new symbiosis of substance and presentation ("visually underlining what was said," according to a critic in *Graphis*), and spawned a host of imitators in other cities. So notable was his impact that in 1973 he was asked to redesign the chic French magazine *Paris-Match*. Upon accepting what he estimated would be a three to four month job, he was informed by the publisher he had in fact one day to complete the renovation. He worked up a revised format overnight, and when it was adopted saw his efforts rewarded by an immediate twenty percent jump in circulation. Other magazine/newspaper design projects have included *New West, Cue, Audience, Ramparts,* and *Esquire* in this country, and *L'Europeo, L'Express,* and *Jardin des Modes* abroad. With Walter Bernard, he also contributed designs for the *Washington Post* and *Lire,* a French literary magazine. He served as design director of the *Village Voice* in New York, 1975-77.

As a book illustrator, Glaser has participated in a number of projects, from children's books (with his wife and with the poet Conrad Aiken) to a recent edition of the works of Guillaume Apollinaire. Nonetheless he has never felt comfortable under the restraints imposed by the traditional illustrator's role. This he traces to the influence of George Salter, one of his Cooper Union teachers, who imbued him with a sense of the unity of design and illustration. In addition, he tends to regard illustration as a less challenging field. Having studied etching with Giorgio Morandi in Bologna and become over the years well versed in the history of reproductive techniques, Glaser argues that the transplantation of old, skill-intensive processes by modern photomechanical equipment has decreased the premium once placed on technical competence and has opened the market to mediocrity. When he has had total control of a book project, however, as with his 1968 restaurant guide, *The Underground Gourmet,* the synthesis of style and content has been all one would expect of a Glaser undertaking.

Glaser's interest in food—he has said that if he had not become a designer he would probably have been a cook—has often been reflected in his choice of design projects. These

"Winged Lion," india ink, 1980. (© Milton Glaser. Printed with permission.)

have ranged from whimsical experiments with various breads to restaurant and supermarket design. Restaurant decor has often appealed as a kind of alimentary theater to the creative fancies of artists and designers, but Glaser is perhaps the first to take his interest into the wings, as it were, and deal systematically with the presentation of food in its market setting. "When I travel through Europe, the first thing I do is go to the food markets," Glaser told a *Newsweek* reporter in the summer of 1984; "You really get a sense of what a place is like: they're full of vitality and information."

Thus when Sir James Goldsmith, the British financier for whom Glaser redesigned *L'Express,* solicited proposals for the redesign of his recently purchased Grand Union supermarket chain in the United States in 1978, Glaser eagerly took on the job. As usual the result was more than changes in color and form; it involved a complete alteration in the usages of grocery retailing. Besides the introduction of display islands to highlight what one critic has called "new gourmet chic" items and break up the familiar monotony of aisles, he argued successfully for the de-emphasis of the long enshrined practice of luring customers by plastering the insides of store windows with "special" signs. And retail figures have borne out his thesis that a bright, light space, easily visible through uncluttered windows is more effective than crass appeals to thrift in pulling in trade: industry analysts have reported that business routinely triples in a Grand Union outlet after a Glaser makeover.

As befits a restless soul who values the *ad hoc* far above the routine, Glaser resigned from Push Pin to set up his own design firm in 1974 because, as he observed at the time, the Studio "has too much history." History, in the Glaserian overview, breeds expectation and stagnation in such areas as style, technique, approach, and philosophy. "I'd much rather hear my work referred to as effective than as beautiful," he told a recent interviewer, "although actually what I really like is when you can't tell the difference."

Pen-and-ink portrait of Hermann Hesse, 1974. (© Milton Glaser. Printed with permission.)

BIOGRAPHICAL/CRITICAL SOURCES: *Graphis*, No. 168, 1973-74; *Art News*, September, 1975; H. T. P. Hayes, "The Push Pin Conspiracy," *New York Times Magazine*, March 6, 1977; *Something About the Author*, Vol. 11, Gale, 1977; *Current Biography*, Wilson, 1980; *Newsweek*, July 16, 1984; *Contemporary Authors, New Revision Series*, Vol. 11, Gale, 1984; *Who's Who in America*, Marquis, 1984; H. Duddar, "All the World's a Page to Designer Milton Glaser," *Smithsonian*, February, 1985.

—*Sketch by Richard Calhoun*

* * *

GLEASON, Paul M. 1940-

PERSONAL: Born November 16, 1940, in New York, N.Y.; son of Arthur E. (a teacher and writer) and Joanne (a nurse) Gleason. *Education:* Art Center School, Los Angeles, B.F.A., 1961. *Home and studio:* 2585 Glenneyre St., Laguna Beach, Calif. 92651.

CAREER: Architectural designer, 1962—. *Member:* Society of Illustrators. *Awards, honors:* Award of Merit from Society of Illustrators, 1980 and 1985.

SIDELIGHTS: Paul Gleason wrote *CGA:* "My favorite work is that which requires research with a free rein to create something fresh. Travel is always inspirational, so I travel quite often to Europe and England, and all around the United States. It is always an eye-opener."

As an architectural designer for such prestigious firms as Killingsworth Brady & Associates, William L. Pereira & Associates, and D. Naegle & Associates, Paul Gleason has been responsible for preparing the designs of a number of public and private buildings, as well as for the design of their interior spaces.

This activity requires a combination of technical skill and artistic flair in almost equal parts. Since there are obvious limitations (technological, commercial, statutory, etc.) on the free flow of forms and ideas, tight discipline must go along with creative expression. In this Gleason has been quite successful, as his awards from professional societies well demonstrate.

In addition, Gleason's interest in painting and illustrating, instilled at the Art Center School, has been strong enough to provoke several years of study with the Illustrators Workshop where he worked with Bernie Fuchs, Bob Heindel, Bob Peak, Fred Otnes, Mark English, and Alan Cober, all of whom are considered to be among the finest illustrators in the United States. His drawings and paintings have appeared in *TV Guide, Woman's Day, Golf, Signature, Road & Track,* and other publications.

Gleason has become an avid golf enthusiast who developed an obsession to see and play the great courses of the world. This interest led him to produce the "Twelve Magnificent Golf Courses of the World" calendar, which includes a description of each course along with a painting of the course by Gleason. He is also a sports-car buff, active in the Long Beach MG Club, where he was chairman of the Long Beach Grand Prix Concours d'Elegance in 1984.

GONZALEZ (NAVARRO), Jose 1939-
(Pepe Gonzalez)

PERSONAL: Born March 29, 1939, in Barcelona, Spain; son of Celestino and Encarnacion (Navarro) Gonzalez. *Education:* Self-taught as an artist. *Home:* Valencia 567, 08026 Barcelona, Spain. *Agent:* Rafael Martinez, Agencia Norma, Ali Bey 11, 08010 Barcelona, Spain.

CAREER: Freelance comic strip artist and illustrator, 1953—; drew *Vampirella* horror strip, 1971-80; did art portfolios, 1980—; illustrator of book covers, 1980—. *Military service:* Spanish Army, 1960-61, served in Engineer Corps. *Awards, honors:* Awards from Warren Publishing Co., 1971, 1975, and 1977.

WRITINGS—Books of comics: *Vampirella Special*, Toutain (Barcelona), 1977; *Cuando el comic es arte—Pepe Gonzalez*, Toutain, 1978; *Chantal*, Norma (Barcelona), 1985.

Art portfolios, all published by Norma in the 1980s: *Marilyn Monroe, Humphrey Bogart, James Dean, Greta Garbo, Las chicas de Pepe Gonzalez* (title means: "Pepe Gonzalez's Girls").

SIDELIGHTS: Pepe Gonzalez (Pepe is the friendly equivalent of Jose) started his career as a comic strip artist at an

A drawing from *Herma*. (© 1978, Jose Gonzalez.)

A splash page from *Vampirella.* (From *Pepe Gonzalez*, published by Toutain Editor. © 1976, Warren Publishing Co.)

A page from *Mas alla del alba* **("Far Beyond Dawn").** (From *Pepe Gonzalez*, published by Toutain Editor. © 1978, Jose Gonzalez.)

early age, when he was discovered by Spanish agent Josep Toutain and hired to work in his studio, Selecciones Ilustradas in the early 1950s. In the 1960s he mainly drew romantic-sentimental love stories for British comic books. In the following decade he won great popularity in the United States with his graphic treatment of the mildly erotic character Vampirella. During the same period, Gonzalez (whose first name, Jose, was little by little replaced in his signature by its equivalent, Pepe) embarked on a parallel career in illustration, a creative field that now claims most of his time.

In the Spanish world of comics and illustration, Gonzalez has always enjoyed great prestige for his natural gifts as a draftsman. Internationally he is best known for his splendid graphic depiction of the feminine form, both from a romantic and an erotic perspective. Although he made his initial impact on the British public with an action-mystery series, *The Avengers* (the comic book version of the popular television series of the same name that started in England in 1961, and was later also seen on American television), Gonzalez expressed himself through his creations for romance comic books aimed at young women, by endowing the young protagonists of the love stories that he drew with a notable sentimental glamour. It can be said that in the course of the 1960s Gonzalez built up a certain esthetic

conception of such characters, a model that was later profusely imitated by his European colleagues.

In 1970 Toutain persuaded the American publisher James Warren to entrust the artwork of *Vampirella* (published in Warren's magazine of the same name) to Gonzalez. The first episode that he drew (on a script by Archie Goodwin) was "Death's Dark Angel" in *Vampirella* No. 12, dated July, 1971. He immediately received the award as the best artist from the Warren staff. The character (whose name brings to mind both "vampire" and "vamp," and whose inspiration owes much to the French comic strip heroine Barbarella by Jean-Claude Forest) had been conceived by the horror-fantasy writer, Forrest J. Ackerman, and had been drawn by a succession of artists, Frank Frazetta among them. Gonzalez gave her the look she was to retain throughout the existence of the series, and is regarded as its definitive artist. Thanks to him the heroine's physical endowments (amply revealed by her emblematic if skimpy outfit marked with a bat) were effortlessly displayed within the requirements of the action.

In the mid-1970s Gonzalez drew another internationally-acclaimed story of eroticism, *Herma* (scripts by Toutain; 1974), and a series of gag pages, *Pamela*, also based on "sexy" themes and images, that numbered over one hundred between 1973 and 1975. After that Gonzalez worked more and more in the illustration field, and in consequence his experience with color also increased. The artist has recently stated his preference for the black-and-white medium: "I like black-and-white better than color, mainly because of the techniques that I use: pencil, brush, watercolor, never oil. I therefore feel more at ease with black-and-white illustrations than with colors; the horizons are more ample and I feel I am expressively freer. The background is almost always white." At the same time Gonzalez regards himself as a better illustrator than comic artist. In his portraits of famous movie stars, conceived in black and white, he shows himself a master of the pencil, and at the same time endows his subjects with a romantic and mythical aura.

The same romantic inclination can also be found in the many covers that Gonzalez has been doing since 1980 for such American paperback publishers as Dell, Bantam, and Signet. Using only crayons, watercolors, and acrylics, he achieves effects that resemble those obtained with oils. In 1983 Gonzalez left Selecciones Ilustradas and is now represented by Norma. For his new agent he is now producing yet another comic series of an erotic nature, *Chantal*, on scripts by Ignacio Molina.

BIOGRAPHICAL/CRITICAL SOURCES: The World Encyclopedia of Comics, Chelsea House, 1976; *Historia de los Comics*, Toutain, 1983.

* * *

GONZALEZ, Pepe
    See GONZALEZ (NAVARRO), Jose

* * *

GORE
    See CORBEN, Richard V(ance)

GOULD, Chester   1900-1985

OBITUARY NOTICE: Born November 20, 1900, in Pawnee, Okla.; died May 11, 1985, in Woodstock, Ill., of congestive heart failure. Cartoonist, world-famous for his newspaper strip creation *Dick Tracy*. Chester Gould started his cartooning career while still in college, as the sports cartoonist for the *Oklahoma City Daily Oklahoman;* he later moved to Chicago, and graduated from Northwestern University in 1923. Soon afterwards he began working for W. R. Hearst's *Chicago American*, where in 1924 he created *Fillum Fables*, a spoof of the silent movies of the time. In 1931 he sold one of his comic strip ideas about a no-nonsense plainclothes police detective to Captain Joseph Patterson of the Chicago Tribune Syndicate; the strip, named *Dick Tracy* by the captain, started its long run in October of that same year. For the next forty-six years Gould devoted most of his life to *Tracy*, in which he expressed many of his own views and ideas about crime, punishment, and life in general. His research into police rules and procedures was painstaking, and he spent a great deal of time with the Chicago Police Department, as well as in the crime laboratories of Northwestern University. His "Crime Stoppers," small vignettes he inserted near the strip title on the Sunday page, were designed to draw the reader's attention to some aspect of police procedure or crime prevention. Gould retired in 1977, and the strip was taken over by Allan Collins (script) and Rick Fletcher (art). At the time of its creator's death *Dick Tracy* was being drawn by Dick Locher, yet it is Gould's *Tracy* that people mostly remember. As Jay Maeder put it in his "appreciation" that appeared in the *New York Daily News*, "Chet Gould was one of the 20th century's most widely read storytellers." Maeder pointed out that most of Gould's work is still available in reprint form.

BIOGRAPHICAL/CRITICAL SOURCES: Chester Gould, *The Celebrated Cases of Dick Tracy*, Chelsea House, 1970; *The World Encyclopedia of Comics*, Chelsea House, 1976.

OBITUARY SOURCES: New York Times, May 12, 1985; Jay Maeder, "Chester Gould: An Appreciation," *New York Daily News*, May 19, 1985; *Newsweek*, May 20, 1985; *Time*, May 20, 1985.

* * *

GROSS, Sam(uel)   1933-

PERSONAL: Born August 7, 1933, in the Bronx, N.Y.; son of Max (a certified public accountant) and Sophie (Heller) Gross; married Isabelle Jaffe (a social work supervisor) June 7, 1959; children: Michelle. *Education:* Baruch College, N.Y.C., Bachelor of Business Administration, 1954.

CAREER: Accountant, 1956-62; freelance cartoonist, 1962—. *Military service:* U.S. Army, 1954-56, PFC. *Member:* Cartoonists Guild, 1967-80 (Vice President, 1972-73, President, 1974-75), Cartoonists Association. *Awards, Honors:* Inkpot Award, San Diego Comicon, 1980.

WRITINGS: How Gross, Dell, 1973; *I Am Blind and My Dog Is Dead*, Dodd, Mead, 1977; *An Elephant Is Soft and*

Mushy, Dodd, Mead, 1980; *Ulk* (German-language anthology), Nelson Verlag, 1980; *More Gross*, Congdon & Weed, 1982; (editor), *Why Are Your Papers in Order*, Avon, 1983.

EXHIBITIONS: New Yorker Group Show, Foundry Gallery, Washington, D.C. 1983; Cartoonists Association Group Show, Master Eagle Gallery, New York City, 1984 and 1985.

WORK IN PROGRESS: Collection of drawings of teddy bears; editing two books on cats and dogs.

SIDELIGHTS: Sam Gross was born in the Bronx, N.Y., the son of a certified public accountant. After attending Baruch College and obtaining a degree in business administration, he spent two years in the U.S. Army. Upon discharge he went to work in an accounting firm, intending no doubt to follow in his father's footsteps. But, fortunately for all lovers of graphic humor, somewhere along the line, the doodling in the margins became more compelling than the numbers in the column, and the career of one of the more maniacally-inspired of current active gag cartoonists was launched. His was not an overnight success story, but by 1962 he had achieved sufficient recognition to give up his associate status in the firm for which he had worked since 1956 and turn his hand to full-time cartooning. Today his work appears in all the major magazine showcases of cartoon art, including the *New Yorker, Playboy, Esquire, National Lampoon, Oui, Cosmopolitan,* and *Saturday Review*. During 1974-75 he served as president of the Cartoonists Guild. In addition to his cartoons, Gross designs greeting cards and lithograph prints, has written for the Public Broadcasting System's children's series *Sesame Street* and the comic strip *Genius,* and been a senior contributing artist to *National Lampoon*.

Stylistically Gross works in ink line and wash, using a free linear drafting technique. In its frequent crude minimalism, this can recall the work of Thurber; but where Thurber's crudeness owed to ineptitude, Gross is capable of a much finer line. When it comes to substance, he is a master of the sight gag (a snail with a snazzy recreational vehicle-type shell, a man digging his car out of a snowbank to find a snowman seated behind the wheel). He is particularly adept at working an idea and finding variations on it where a more

Self-portrait of Sam Gross with gingerbread men. (Printed with permission.)

Magazine cartoon. (© 1970, National Lampoon Inc.)

conventional humorist would have failed even to find an initial theme. The resulting recurrence of characters, situations, or props makes his work especially collectible. Familiar fairy tale figures like the gingerbread man and the little match girl become the bases for a series of gags that derive even greater humor from their cumulative effect on the reader. A cartoon presenting two little match girls, for example, standing ragged and shivering in knee-deep snow on a street corner and complaining about the new identities they have been given by the FBI is funny enough on its own; but appearing as the ultimate in a series of match girl gags, the effect is multiplied, and laughter can become well-nigh uncontrollable.

Besides four volumes of his collected drawings, Gross is represented in numerous cartoon anthologies, including *Best Cartoons of the World* (ed. Bob Abel), Dell, 1969; *Post Mortems* (ed. Gerald T. Counihan), Bantam, 1969; *New Cartoon Laughs from "True,"* Fawcett, 1970; *Best Cartoons of the Year* (ed. Lawrence Lariar), Dodd, Mead, 1970; *Absolutely No Personnel Permitted Beyond This Point* (ed. Bill Lee), Delta, 1973; *Best Cartoons from the New Yorker,* 1925-1975, Viking, 1975.

BIOGRAPHICAL/CRITICAL SOURCES: Contemporary Authors, Vol. 45-48; The World Encyclopedia of Cartoons, Chelsea House, 1980.

H

HALL, H. Tom 1932-

PERSONAL: Born June 12, 1932, in Ridley Park, Pa.; son of Harry Thomas, Jr. and Evelyn (Still) Hall; married Helen Janet Scott, September 17, 1956; children: Thomas Richard, Steven James, David Lance. *Education:* Attended Tyler School of Fine Art; Philadelphia College of Art, B.F.A., 1955. *Home and studio:* Warwick Furnace Rd., Pottstown, Pa. 19464.

CAREER: Freelance illustrator and artist, 1957—. *Military service:* U.S. Army, 1955-57; U.S. Army Reserves, 1957-59, became sergeant. *Member:* Society of Illustrators.

WRITINGS: The Golden Tombo (children's book), self-illustrated, Knopf, 1959.

EXHIBITIONS: One-man shows at Philadelphia Art Alliance, 1974; Moore College of Art, Philadelphia, 1979. Represented in many group shows, including Society of Illustrators annual shows, 1972-85; New York City Society of Illustrators Realist Show, 1975; 70th Street Art Gallery, New York City, 1982; Salt Lake City Art Center, 1984; Japan Traveling Show, 1985.

WORK IN PROGRESS: Book covers and paintings.

SIDELIGHTS: As a student at the Philadelphia College of Art in the early 1950s, H. Tom Hall hoped one day to see his illustrations gracing the pages of *Collier's* or *Saturday Evening Post*, like those of his idols Ben Stahl and Robert Fawcett. Other favorite illustrators were Edwin Austin Abbey and N. C. Wyeth. Unfortunately, his entry into the commercial art market came just as the great mass periodical era was coming to an end. In the environment of shrunken opportunity that resulted, adaptability would be the key to survival. The first indication that Hall possessed this necessary quality resulted from his tour of Army service in Japan, 1956-57. Upon his return to civilian life, Hall wrote a children's book, *The Golden Tombo* (dragonfly), and illustrated it after the Japanese manner. The work was published by Knopf in 1959 to generally favorable reviews, which particularly stressed the detailed nature of the illustrations and the keenness of the illustrator's eye, and for the next dozen years Hall enjoyed steady, if unspectacular success as an illustrator of books and magazines for children.

Then in 1971 he got the break he had been seeking—an assignment from Bantam to do the cover for its paperback

H. TOM HALL

reissue of John Steinbeck's *The Golden Cup*. Thus began his steady and increasingly lucrative connection with the publishing industry. The genre of illustration that has made his reputation, and opened other opportunities to him in the process, has been the romance novel cover. Like the fiction it encases, cover art for such novels depends on a relatively few fixed conventions. Here again Hall's adaptability, technical command, and eye for detail have enabled him to transcend the limitations. In the avowedly commercial world of book merchandising, Hall is a proven seller because of his unrivaled knack for manipulating the stock cliches—voluptuous women, craggily handsome men, exotic settings—in such a way as to create variety, and because of his painterly skill in infusing these scenes with the appropriate feelings of romance and, of course, sex. So palpably does he render these scenes, says one art director, "you can almost feel the wind blowing."

A staple of the form—the "clinch" or passionate embrace—is hardly an inexhaustible challenge, and Hall reckons he's done about every variant on it imaginable. One of his favorite covers avoided this overworked image by portraying a couple, post-clinch: she brushing out her suggestively tousled hair preparatory to retying her loosened gown stays; he reclining easily on the grass beside her strumming a lute (which, Hall puckishly suggests, is the "17th century equivalent of lighting a cigarette"). This is the sort of work that demonstrates not only his conviction that illustration is in large part the ability to solve problems through a combination of skill, patience, and technique, but also that the true masters of the form are interpretive artists with excellent senses of color and humor.

Among the attributes of Hall's work applauded by book industry professionals, the most obvious is his success in moving books. Says Gene Light of Warner Books, "his covers sell like no one else's." (It is of interest to note that when Avon won the bid to issue the best-seller *The Thorn Birds* in a mass-paperback edition and huge sales were anticipated, the cover art was entrusted to Hall.) But publishers also mention Hall's competence as an artist, the fact that he works hard at his craft, like most illustrators, and that he is a keen student of past illustration. "I have always been proud to call myself an illustrator," Hall says. "The field is so filled with the names of artists of real quality." He answers all charges of commercialism leveled at the art of illustration by remarking: "I don't recall anyone whose abilities I really respect who looked down on illustration."

Hall never intended to limit himself to doing only paperback book covers. He has illustrated two books with outdoor/action and historical themes for National Geographic—*John Muir's Wild America* and *Into the Wilderness*—as well as *Lord Jim* for Franklin Library, and has done many illustrations for various magazines. His work for *Into the Wilderness*—a series of seven essays on American explorers in the eighteenth and nineteenth centuries—reveals his careful craftsmanship. Action scenes done in flat, light-absorbing acrylics subordinate photographic detail to mood in the classic illustrator's fashion, while managing to convey such broad sensations and ideas as cold, heat, and the clash of European and native cultures.

BIOGRAPHICAL/CRITICAL SOURCES: Cheryl C. Cobb, "The Passionate Palette of Illustrator Tom Hall," *Philadelphia Inquirer Today Magazine*, August 3, 1980; *Philadelphia Inquirer*, May 7, 1981; Rosemary Guiley, *Love Lines*, Facts on File, 1983; Walt and Roger Reed, *The Illustrator in America*, Madison Square Press, 1984.

Cover illustration for *The Great Steamboat Race.* (© 1983, Ballantine Books.)

Cover illustration by H. Tom Hall for *A Valley Called Disappointment.* (© 1983, Ballantine Books.)

* * *

HAMILTON, William   1939-

PERSONAL: Born June 2, 1939, in Palo Alto, Calif.; son of Alexander and Ellen (Ballentine) Hamilton; married Candida Vargas, May 9, 1969 (divorced, 1976); children: Alexandra. *Education:* Yale University, B.A., 1962. *Politics:* Democrat. *Office:* New Yorker Magazine, 25 W. 43rd St., New York, N.Y. 10036. *Agent:* Herb Valen, P.O. Box 8, Westport, Conn. 06880.

CAREER: Cartoonist, *New Yorker,* 1965—. *Military service:* U.S. Army, 1963-65.

WRITINGS—All books of cartoons, unless otherwise noted: *The Antisocial Register,* Chronicle, 1974; *Terribly Nice People,* Putnam, 1975; *Husbands, Wives, and Live Togethers,* Putnam, 1976; *Money Should Be Fun,* Houghton, 1976; *Introducing William Hamilton,* Wildwood (London), 1977; *The Love of Rich Women* (novel), Houghton, 1982; *The Charlatan* (novel), Simon & Schuster, 1985.

Plays: "Save Grand Central," produced at Phoenix Theater, New York City, 1976; "Plymouth Rock," Northlight Repertory, Chicago, 1977; "Happy Landings," American Conservatory Theater, San Francisco, 1981.

Keeping Up, syndicated cartoon feature for Chronicle Features, 1970—.

SIDELIGHTS: In 1980, in its entry on William Hamilton, who has been termed "the most typical *New Yorker* cartoonist since Peter Arno," the *World Encyclopedia of Cartoons* casually observed that, "this consummate New Yorker lives in California." Hamilton has recently moved back to New York, but this piece of paradox is somehow symptomatic of a man whose life, as a matter of fact, is full of paradoxes, which he has used to creative advantage.

In 1973, just eight years after he had virtually talked himself into a position on the *New Yorker* staff, Hamilton was called by *Newsweek* "the most intriguing of a new generation of *New Yorker* cartoonists." It was particularly impressed by his portrayal of a new class of "haves" which it described as "a trendy hybrid a cut above your garden variety *nouveau rich* in both perception and pretension." Considered by no less an authority than Saul Steinberg a throwback to "the original idea of the *New Yorker* cartoonist—civilized, urbane," Hamilton has been most frequently compared to the late Peter Arno, and if differences in their graphic styles are set aside, the comparison is not an inapt one. Both were born into socially prominent families, both were eastern prep-school and Ivy League products, each was fascinated by the foibles of the "establishment" classes, and each expressed this fascination in satirical terms. But like any attempt to draw similarities between individuals from different generations, this one has its obvious limits.

For all the Manhattan/Long Island/Connecticut flavor of his cartoon milieu, Hamilton himself comes of stock he calls "California Gothic"—by which he means San Francisco Social Register eccentric. Growing up in a curious atmo-

WILLIAM HAMILTON

Keeping Up

I don't see why you don't like going to the Wentworths. It's true she refused to marry me, but that was 20 years ago, and in the meantime, I've crushed him in business.

A *Keeping Up* panel. (© 1985, Chronicle Features Syndicate.)

sphere of privilege and deprivation on a country estate named Ethelwild, he passed his youth in something of a time warp because the family's ancestral seat, built by a late uncle for his wife Ethel, had been frozen in time upon her death in 1901 and not allowed to advance one year further into the twentieth century. This had a curious effect on the sensibilities of young William as he grew up in the 1940s and '50s. First of all, the magazines and books found in the Ethelwild library were all nineteenth century in origin, exposing him to the work of the great illustrators of the pen-and-ink era; in fact, he confesses to thinking that Charles Dana Gibson was a contemporary artist. Secondly, as he explains in his foreword to *Terribly Nice People*, a collection of his drawings, the relics of the ink era that surrounded him as a

boy—quills, nibs, pen-holders and -wipers, desk-sets, blotting powder, etc.—instilled in him a life-long preference for ink as a medium of expression. Given youthful exposure to such inspirations and tools, it is not hard to see why Hamilton's style invites comparison with the classic pen-and-ink illustrators of the past; but it was his revolt against the physical isolation and idiosyncratic family setting that explains how he came to focus on eastern seaboard movers and shakers as subjects for his humor.

Considering that his own father had withdrawn from any regular form of employment after World War II in order to devote himself to the life of the imagination, it is scarcely surprising that when Hamilton came east to attend school at

Andover and later Yale he was somewhat taken aback by encountering "a world where everyone's father was an industrialist, an executive, or a partner in a wonderful and mysterious thing called a firm." There, he recalls, "people had English muffins for breakfast every morning and jobs all day long." This environment fascinated him with its order and dynamism, and the fascination in turn bred a preoccupation as artist and humorist with the often unconsciously funny trendiness and smug self-indulgence of its inhabitants.

After graduating from Yale, he was drafted and spent two years in Alaska where he worked hard (for lack of competing interests) on his drawings and began besieging the *New Yorker's* cartoon editor with submissions. For all his persistence, he had no success. Nonetheless, upon separation from active duty in 1965, he went directly to the magazine's office and managed to wangle a position as a staff artist at a salary of one hundred dollars per week. The hand-to-mouth existence this enforced on him was somewhat brightened, however, by the opportunity it provided him to move once again in the circles that offered both inspiration and material. Before long his panels were appearing regularly in the *New Yorker*, and since 1970 he has drawn a syndicated feature for Chronicle Features. In addition, by 1985 he had published five books of drawings, three plays, and two novels—all of these works drawn from his observations of upper-class society in New York and San Francisco where he resided for a long time.

Hamilton gets most of his humorous mileage out of cliches one imagines being delivered in a breathless Katherine Hepburn rush, a bored Ronald Coleman drone, or with a confident, Cary Grant suaveness. His subjects include such chic, upper-class preoccupations as ecology, crafts, food trends, summer houses, social climbing, and business. Females are slim and have names like Muffy and Amanda, while males are fashionably hirsute, impeccably dressed, and partial to bourbon—in short, a quintessentially *New Yorker* crowd. Renderings are almost fussily fine ink line and washes, nicely detailed but rarely action-oriented, focusing almost always on figures, their facial expressions, and their physical attitudes. The most obvious shortcomings of his work are its rather static quality and the limited cast of characters appearing in his scenarios, but these tend to be faults more noticeable when looking through collections of his drawings than at individual panels as they appear weekly in the *New Yorker*.

Among that of his contemporaries, Hamilton's work might be said to stand out because of its apparently contradictory melding of style and substance—a "now" society executed in a "then" medium and manner. Yet he would argue there is no contradiction at all in portraying evanescence thus: "Ink," he has written, "is too mortal. Your pen starts out overloaded, becomes just right, and then runs out in a rhythm completely oblivious to your train of thought." In this sense, it is a technique peculiarly suited to his purposes.

BIOGRAPHICAL/CRITICAL SOURCES: Newsweek, October 8, 1973; *People*, August 20, 1979; *Time*, March 17, 1980; *The World Encyclopedia of Cartoons*, Chelsea House, 1980; *Who's Who in America*, Marquis, 1984; *Contemporary Authors, New Revisions* series, Vol. 15, Gale, 1985.

—*Sketch by Richard Calhoun*

HANSEN, Doug(las Christopher) 1952-

PERSONAL: Born September 20, 1952, in Fresno, Calif.; son of Robert Noel (a Navy pilot) and Janice (an artist; maiden name Baker) Hansen; married Susan Pool, May 5, 1974; children: Nathaniel, Wyeth. *Education:* California State University at Fresno, B.F.A., 1974. *Office:* Flying Pyramid Enterprises, P.O. Box 2027, Fresno, Calif. 93718.

CAREER: Artist, Meeker Advertising, Fresno, Calif., 1974-77; sole proprietor, Flying Pyramid Enterprises (a freelance art business), Fresno, Calif., 1976—; stripping department, Dumont Printing, Fresno, 1977-79; staff artist, *Fresno Bee* (a daily newspaper), 1979—. Instructor, California State University at Fresno, 1975. *Awards, honors:* Winner of a design contest of the Fresno Alliance for the Arts, 1984, for Fresno Centennial Calendar cover artwork; Award of Excellence from Society of Newspaper Design, 1985, for a travel-page cover design.

WRITINGS—All comic books: *Frezno Funnies* No. 1, Commonwealth Graphics, 1973; *Animal 8-Pager*, Flying

DOUG HANSEN

A page from "China Clipper." (© 1985, Doug Hansen. Reprinted with permission.)

Pyramid Enterprises, 1974; *Frezno Funnies* No. 2, Flying Pyramid Enterprises, 1975; *Valley Fever,* (a collection of works from his comic class), CSUF Comix, 1975. Contributor to comic books, including *Amabolis Insania, Animal Bite Comix, Beastiality, Cap'n Retro, Commies from Mars, Deadspawn, Dope Comix, Forbidden Knowledge, Heebie Jeebie Funnies, Jerry the Polar Bear, Juice City, Moon Comix, Slow Death, Snarf, Zero.* Also contributor to the *Journal of Popular Culture.*

EXHIBITIONS: California State University at Fresno Library, 1973; Manchester Cinema, Fresno, Calif., 1974; First Savings and Loan, Fresno, 1980.

WORK IN PROGRESS: Writing and drawing a children's book on ships; completing a page on British historical ships for the *Fresno Bee*; a horror tale for *Death Rattle* comic book, to be published by Denis Kitchen.

SIDELIGHTS: Doug Hansen wrote *CGA:* "My childhood and growing-up years have been a constant source of ideas and inspiration for my artwork. As the son of a Navy pilot, I lived in California, Texas, Hawaii, and Maryland before starting college in Fresno, our family 'home.' The joy of growing up in a family with four brothers and one sister (I being the eldest child) has slanted my outlook in life towards the sunny and the childlike. Some of my earliest memories are of my parents helping me to draw. I have had nothing but encouragement from my parents all through the years.

"I have always loved planes and ships. In Hawaii I could stand in my frontyard and watch aircraft carriers, destroyers, and submarines entering and leaving Pearl Harbor; our house was directly in the flight path to a nearby airbase, and we learned to identify all the planes that passed overhead. In elementary school I loved to draw huge murals and detailed sketches of old sailing ships on odd pieces of paper. In high school I was captivated by the dazzling, cryptic, psychedelic poster art and the freewheeling, irreverent comic art that appeared in underground newspapers. I admired and imitated the work of Peter Max and other poster artists, whose names I only learned after we moved to Fresno in 1970.

"That same year I enrolled as an art major at college. Through my four years at Fresno State I carried out my intent to sample as many of the art classes offered there as I could. Ironically it was the work I did for the college paper, the *Daily Collegian,* that had the most lasting effect on my career, though it was not even part of my curriculum. The daily challenge of creating cartoons and comic stories was stimulating and rewarding. After my first full-page cartoon story appeared in December, 1970, I decided to become a cartoonist, and read and studied the work of all the great artists of the past. I also began collecting and studying the underground comics (or comix) which had just reached their zenith.

"I imagined a rosy future drawing underground comics; but, while a livelihood was not possible drawing for the undergrounds, I continued to do comics over the next six years, and eventually my work appeared in print. This wide-open forum for personal expression gave me a matchless opportunity to tell stories, and to create my own mythology and imagery. Almost all of my stories involve animal characters, whose appearance makes a humorous counterpoint to their

Cover for Christmas advertising section. (© 1981, *Fresno Bee*.)

human-like behavior. Sea cows are my favorites, their dull lumpishness contrasting wildly with the heroic and dramatic situations in which I place them. I have also returned to the lore of planes and ships, which I often incorporate into my work."

Doug Hansen also admits to a partiality for the great illustrators of the past, starting with Howard Pyle, and continuing with N. C. Wyeth after whom one of his children is named. His work at the *Fresno Bee* affords him a great variety of drawing opportunities, as he may follow a humor cartoon with an historically accurate rendering, or a topical news illustration. At the same time, he has been pursuing a career as a comic book artist and writer, with themes of childhood and fantasy and recreations of historical scenes running through his work.

Hansen's most original creations are probably his adventure/funny-animal comics, an unlikely brand of straightforward action narrative carried on by animal characters in recognizable human dress and uniforms. The juxtaposition of realistic backgrounds, situations, and dialogue, *a la* Milton Caniff, and characters that seem to have come out from a Walt Disney strip, may look jarring at first, but the very improbability of the concept somehow brings the whole thing off. "China Clipper," for instance, recreates the aircraft, machines, and props, as well as the attitudes, of the 1930s with such convincing nostalgia that it makes the era appear as remote as Herodotus's time—after a short while one is no longer surprised to watch large sea mammals in pilot's uniforms as they attempt the first trans-Pacific crossing in a seaplane.

Doug Hansen is only in his early thirties at the time of this writing (1985), and more should be heard from him in the future.

BIOGRAPHICAL/CRITICAL SOURCES: "Doug Hansen!," *Daily Collegian* (daily newspaper of California State University at Fresno), February 22, 1973; "Comics: History and Technique," *Insight* (weekly newspaper of CSUF), March 12, 1975; "Fresno Comic Connection," *Valley Life Review*, March 4, 1982; "Newave Comics Survey," *Comics Journal*, May, 1985.

* * *

HIGDON, Bruce 1950-

PERSONAL: Born November 28, 1950, in Murfreesboro, Tenn.; son of George Franklin (a laborer) and Lillian (Spence) Higdon; married Yong Cha Kim (a seamstress) December 16, 1976; children: Kim Suki. *Education:* Middle Tennessee State University, B.A., 1972, graduate study, 1981-84. *Religion:* Church of Christ. *Home and studio:* Route 11, Box 315 B, Murfreesboro, Tenn. 37130.

CAREER: Captain, U.S. Army, 1972—; instructor in cartooning, Middle Tennessee State University, 1982-84. Murfreesboro Executive Club (president), McFadden Parent Teacher Organization. *Member:* National Cartoonists Society, Cartoonists Guild, Graphic Artists Guild, Kappa Delta Pi, Sigma Delta Chi, Delta Tau Delta, Reserve Officers Association. *Awards, honors:* Cartoonist of the Year (Europe), Department of Defense, 1982-83 and 1983-84, honorable mention for Keith L. Ware Award, Department of Defense, 1984, all for cartoons and illustrations appearing in *The Courier*, Pirmasens, Germany; received National Defense Medal for military service.

WRITINGS—Collections of cartoons: *Empire Goatrope*, Redditt & Associates, 1980; *Go for It, Eltee*, Redditt & Associates, 1982.

EXHIBITIONS: Galerie Cote, Rockville Centre, N.Y., 1983; Emery's Gallery of Fine Art, Murfreesboro, Tenn., 1983; Middle Tennessee State University, 1983.

WORK IN PROGRESS: A book of collected cartoons from *Army Times, Soldiers*, and *Army Magazine*; developing a strip to be syndicated; a book on experiences as courtroom artist for Nashville television station WTVF; a book on children's art.

SIDELIGHTS: Bruce Higdon belongs to that small group of unsung cartoonists and illustrators who work mainly for service newspapers. His drawings show him to be a solid and competent craftsman, whose simple line makes its point with a minimum of fuss. In his field Higdon displays perhaps more thoughtfulness and curiosity than the average army cartoonist. As he himself wrote to *CGA:* "I consider myself equally proficient in fine art, commercial art, and cartooning. I regard them as overlapping each other. Each one makes important contributions to the others, and by their very nature they demand co-existence. The dominating point that each must take, in order to succeed, is in making the viewer think. It is not necessary for a cartoon or a painting to make the viewer happy. The end result must be, *does it make the reader think and conclude a yes or no answer on his or her own?*"

With his definite opinions and strongly held point of view, it is no wonder that Higdon looks upon himself as "sort of a curiosity." But this has served him well in his artistic and editorial endeavors. The fact that he speaks fluent German and Korean has also enhanced an already open-minded outlook.

BIOGRAPHICAL/CRITICAL SOURCES: *The Patriot*, March, 1980; *The Morning Press*, April 16, 1983, September 9, 1983; *Nashville Tennessean*, May 22, 1983; *Stars and Stripes*, June, 1983; *The Courier*, June, 1983; *Nashville Banner*, July, 1983; Homer Pittard, *A History of Rutherford County*, Rutherford County Historical Society Register, 1985.

Self-portrait of Bruce Higdon. (Printed with permission.)

* * *

HOFF, Syd(ney) 1912-

PERSONAL: Born September 12, 1912, in New York, N.Y.; son of Benjamin and Mary (Barnow) Hoff; married Dora Berman, 1937; children: Susan, Bonnie Joy. *Education:* Studied fine art at National Academy of Design, New York City. *Home:* Miami Beach, Fla. *Agent:* Scott Meredith Literary Agency, 845 Third Ave., New York, N.Y. 10022.

CAREER: Cartoonist, 1928—; creator, daily cartoon panel, *Laugh It Off*, King Features Syndicate, 1958-77. Magazine contributor, comic strip artist, author and illustrator of children's books, lecturer, entertainer. *Member:* Authors Guild of the Authors League of America.

U.S. ARMY RESERVES
"Ever Alert"

A military cartoon by Bruce Higdon. (© 1984, Bruce Higdon. Reprinted with permission.)

WRITINGS—All self-illustrated, except as indicated: *Muscles and Brains*, Dial, 1940; *Military Secrets*, Hillair, 1943; *Feeling No Pain* (cartoon collection), Dial, 1944; *Mom, I'm Home!*, Doubleday, 1945; *Oops! Wrong Party!* (cartoon collection), Dutton, 1951; *It's Fun Learning Cartooning*, Stravon, 1952; *Oops! Wrong Stateroom!*, Ives Washburn, 1953; *Out of Gas!*, Ives Washburn, 1954; *Eight Little Artists*, Abelard, 1954; *Patty's Pet*, Abelard, 1955; *Okay—You Can Look Now!*, Duell, 1955; *Danny and the Dinosaur*, Harper, 1958; *Sammy: The Seal*, Harper, 1959; *Julius*, Harper, 1959.

Ogluk: The Eskimo, Holt, 1960; *Where's Prancer?*, Harper, 1960; *Oliver*, Harper, 1960; *Who Will Be My Friends?*, Harper, 1960; *Little Chief*, Harper, 1961; *Albert: The Albatross*, Harper, 1961; *The Better Hoff* (cartoon collection), Holt, 1961; *Chester*, Harper, 1961; *Upstream, Downstream, and Out of My Mind*, Bobbs-Merrill, 1961; *'Twixt the Cup and the Lipton*, Bobbs-Merrill, 1962; *Stanley*, Harper, 1962; *This Is Matrimony*, Pocket Books, 1962; *Hunting, Anyone?*, Bobbs-Merrill, 1963; *From Bed to Nurse, or What a Way to Die*, Dell, 1963; *Grizzwold*, Harper, 1963; *Lengthy*, Putnam, 1964; *Learning to Cartoon*, Stravon, 1966; *Mrs. Switch*, Putnam, 1967; *Irving and Me*, Harper, 1967; *Wanda's Wand*, C. R. Gibson, 1968; *The Witch, the Cat, and the Baseball Bat*, Grosset, 1968; *Little Red Riding-Hood* (illustrated by Charles Mikolaycak), C. R. Gibson, 1968;

Slithers, Putnam, 1968; *Baseball Mouse*, Putnam, 1969; *Mahatma*, Putnam, 1969; *Roberto and the Bull*, McGraw, 1969; *Herschel the Hero*, Putnam, 1969.

The Horse in Harry's Room, Harper, 1970; *Wilfred the Lion*, Putnam, 1970; *The Litter Knight*, Putnam, 1970; *Palace Bug*, Putnam, 1970; *Siegfried: Dog of the Alps*, Grosset, 1970; *When Will It Snow?* (illustrated by Mary Chalmers), Harper, 1971; *The Mule Who Struck It Rich*, Little, Brown, 1971; *Thunderhoof*, Harper, 1971; *My Aunt Rosie*, Harper, 1972; *Pedro and the Bananas*, Putnam, 1972; *Syd Hoff's Joke Book*, Putnam, 1972; *Giants and Other Plays for Kids*, Putnam, 1973; *The Art of Cartooning*, Stravon, 1973; *A Walk Past Ellen's House*, McGraw, 1973; *Amy's Dinosaur*, Windmill, 1974; *Jokes to Enjoy, Draw and Tell*, Putnam, 1974; *Kip Van Winkle*, Putnam, 1974; *Editorial and Political Cartooning* (anthology of cartoons), Stravon, 1976; *Barkley*, Harper, 1976; *Walpole*, Harper, 1977; *The Littlest Leaguer*, Windmill, 1977; *Gentleman Jim and the Great John L.*, Coward, 1977; *Boss Tweed and the Man Who Drew Him*, Coward, 1978; *Santa's Moose*, Harper, 1979.

Scarface Al and His Uncle Sam, Coward, 1980; *Henrietta's Fourth of July*, Garrard, 1981; *Syd Hoff's How to Draw Dinosaurs*, Windmill, 1981; *The Man Who Loved Animals*, Putnam, 1982; *Syd Hoff's Animal Jokes*, Harper, 1985.

SYD HOFF

Illustrator: Allan Sherman, *Hello Muddah, Hello Faddah*, Harper, 1964; Sherman, *I Can't Dance*, Harper, 1964; Jean M. Lexau, *I Should Have Stayed in Bed*, Harper, 1965; Lexau, *Homework Caper*, Harper, 1966; Lexau, *Rooftop Mystery*, Harper, 1968; Jerome Copersmith, *Chanukah Fable for Christmas*, Putnam, 1969; Mildred W. Wright, *Henri Goes to the Mardi Gras*, Putnam, 1971; Edward R. Ricciuti, *Donald and the Fish That Walked*, Harper, 1972.

Contributor to the *New Yorker, Esquire, Look, Playboy,* and other periodicals.

SIDELIGHTS: One of the most prolific of contemporary author/illustrator/graphic humorists, Syd Hoff began his career as a cartoonist in 1928. Since that first sale (to the *New Yorker*), he has turned out more than eighty books as author/illustrator, illustrated numerous books by other authors, contributed cartoons in freelance markets from the *Saturday Evening Post* to *Playboy* (and almost everything in between), and at various times done syndicated feature work, not to mention the many advertising commissions he has filled over the years. Obviously he could not have produced so voluminous a body of work if he did not take the greatest pleasure in the act of amusing and instructing people of all ages; and this, as much as the extrinsic merits of his work, has given him an uninterrupted half-century of success with the American public.

He started out as a student under the somewhat somber aegis of the National Academy of Design, but with the sale of that first comic drawing (when he was sixteen) he gave up all pretension to "fine" art and thence forward concentrated on producing graphic humor and children's books. Of the latter, he has written and illustrated well over sixty titles, including fanciful fiction (*Danny and the Dinosaur* and *Albert the Albatross*), biography (on figures like baseball player Babe Ruth and boxer "Gentleman Jim" Corbett), and even one how-to book on his own favorite pastime, *It's Fun Learning Cartooning*. His simple, colorful drawings for children supplement texts that teach as they revolve around such familiar children's themes as summer camp, moving to new neighborhoods, and juvenile rivalries, all of which he liberally seasons with dashes of fantasy and/or corniness. One critic (in *Twentieth Century Children's Writers*) sees in his children's books "a kind of deft simplicity in content as well as style, bringing children pleasure with little threat, sometimes reinforcing stereotype and also staying at the surface level of understanding." Particularly notable are his series of ten books about a chicken named Henrietta.

Very much the same thing might be said of his graphic humor for adults. That he understands the formal rules of composition is clear from his how-to books—in addition to the one for young people, he has written two others directed to an older market—but technique is not his strongest point. Working in ink line, washes, crayon, and watercolor, he populates his panels with pushy matrons, bosomy sirens, working class patriarchs, small-time merchants, loafers, ne'er-do-wells, and moochers—many of them drawn from the New York Jewish neighborhoods in which he grew up, but all responding in universally understandable and mirth-provoking ways to the situations in which they find themselves. His humor is rarely dark and more often than not dependent upon stereotype and cliche; but in the best gag-cartoonist tradition, it makes for more than its share of chuckles. The subordination of art to gag can be illustrated by the following examples: two convicts in a cell ("In a way I'm glad I did it. This place would be absolutely intolerable if I were innocent."); boy scout on couch to psychiatrist ("I think my feelings of inadequacy started when the old lady I was helping across the street got run over."); unctuous waiter to disgruntled diner ("You were right, sir. It *was* dishwater. The chef regrets the error.").

In addition to his graphic humor output, Hoff has written a number of volumes of humorous prose, including *'Twixt the Cup and the Lipton; Upstream, Downstream, and Out of My Mind;* and *The Syd Hoff Joke Book.*

If his output falls something short of Olympian in quality, Hoff still manages to project an honesty, an infectious good nature, and an assurance that laughter truly is the best medicine in an oft-suffering world that can make critical evaluations of his work seem superfluous if not caviling. A cartoonist, after all, need not be a cross between William Hogarth and Mark Twain to be funny. And, for over fifty years, that Syd Hoff has most assuredly been.

BIOGRAPHICAL/CRITICAL SOURCES: Young Readers Review, April, 1967; *Best Sellers,* September 1, 1967; *New York Times Book Review,* October 8, 1967; *The World Encyclopedia of Cartoons,* Chelsea House, 1980; *Contemporary Authors,* New Revision Series, Vol. 4, Gale, 1981; *Twentieth-Century Children's Writers,* St. Martin's, 1983; *Who's Who in America,* Marquis, 1984.

Some of Syd Hoff's most famous characters.

HOGARTH, Burne 1911-

PERSONAL: Born December 25, 1911, in Chicago, Ill.; son of Max (a carpenter) and Pauline (Lerman) Hogarth; married Rhoda Simons, February 29, 1936 (divorced); married Constance Green, June 27, 1955 (divorced); children: (first marriage) Michael Robin, (second marriage) Richard Paul, Ross David. *Education:* Attended Crane College, 1928-30; University of Chicago, 1930-31; Northwestern University, 1931-32; Columbia University, 1956-58. *Home and studio:* 6026 W. Lindenhurst Ave., Los Angeles, Calif. 90036.

CAREER: Artist and illustrator, Bonnet-Brown, Inc., 1933; editor, Leeds Features, Chicago, Ill., 1935; staff artist, McNaught Syndicate, New York City, 1935; staff artist, King Features Syndicate, New York City, 1936; illustrator and cartoonist of *Tarzan*, 1937-50, and *Miracle Jones*, 1947-48, United Feature Syndicate, New York City; founder, Academy of Newspaper Art, New York City, 1944-46; illustrator and cartoonist of *Drago*, Post-Hall Syndicate, New York City, 1945-46; co-founder and vice-president, School of Visual Arts, New York City, 1947-70; curriculum coordinator and instructor in anatomy, drawing, art history, and design analysis, School of Visual Arts, 1947-70; instructor in anatomy and interpretive and conceptual drawing, Parsons School of Design, New York City, 1976-79; instructor in anatomy and illustration, Otis Art Institute, Los Angeles, 1981—; instructor of analytical drawing, Art Center College of Design, Pasadena, Calif., 1982—.

MEMBER: U.S. Committee for the World Health Organization (Graphic Arts section), Het Stripschap (Amsterdam), National Cartoonists Society (president, 1977-79), National Art Education Association, American Society for Aesthetics, Society of Illustrators, Museum of Cartoon Art.

AWARDS, HONORS: Scarp Award from New York Comicon, 1968; plaque from Dallas Comicon, 1973; Premio Emilio Freixas from International Salon, Gijon, Spain, 1973; Silver Awards for best illustration from National Cartoonists Society, 1974, 1975, and 1976; Artist of the Year, Man and His World, Montreal, Canada, 1975; Ignatz Gold Brick Award from Orlando Comicon, 1975; Inkpot plaque from San Diego Comicon, 1978; Pulcinella Award, Mostra Internazionale del Fumetto, Naples, Italy, 1983; Lifetime Achievement Award, Salone Internazionale dei Comics, del Film d'Animazione e dell' Illustrazione, Lucca, Italy, 1984; Adamson "Silent Sam" Award, Swedish Academy of Comic Art, Helsingborg, Sweden, 1985.

WRITINGS—All published by Watson-Guptill, unless otherwise noted: *Dynamic Anatomy*, 1958; *Drawing the Human Head*, 1965; *Dynamic Figure Drawing*, 1970; (author of preface) Francis Lacassin, *Tarzan ou le chevalier crispe* (title means "Tarzan or the Intense Knight"), Union Generale d'Editions, 1971; (illustrator) Robert M. Hodes, *Tarzan of the Apes* (based on the original text by Edgar Rice Burroughs), 1972; (illustrator) Hodes, *Jungle Tales of Tarzan* (based on the original text by Burroughs), 1976; *Drawing Dynamic Hands*, 1977; (illustrator) Burroughs, *Burne Hogarth's The Golden Age of Tarzan, 1939-1942*, Chelsea House, 1977; *Dynamic Light and. Shade*, 1981; (illustrator) *Life of King Arthur*, Collector's Press, 1984.

BURNE HOGARTH

EXHIBITIONS: One-man shows at Societe Francaise de Photographie, Paris, 1966; Escola Panamericana de Arte, Sao Paulo, Brazil, 1969; Museum of Cartoon Art, Port Chester, N.Y., 1978.

Collective shows: "Bande Dessinee et Figuration Narrative," Musee des Arts Decoratifs (Louvre), Paris, 1967; "Exposition de Bandes Dessinees," Palais des Beaux-Arts, Brussels, 1968; "La Bienal Mundial de la Historieta," Instituto di Tella, Buenos Aires, 1968; "Le Monde de la Bande Dessinee," Musees Royaux d'Art et d'Histoire, Brussels, 1969; "Comic Strip," America House, Munich, 1969; "Comic Strip," Akademie der Kunst, Berlin, 1969-70; "Exposicao de Quadrinhos," Museu de Arte, Sao Paulo, 1970; "The Art of the Comic Strip," University of Maryland Art Gallery, College Park, Md., 1971; "75 Years of the Comics," New York Cultural Center, New York City, 1971; "The Comics," Kennedy Cultural Center, Washington, D.C., 1972; "Four Masters of Comic Art—Opper-McCay-Foster-Hogarth," Graham Gallery, New York City, 1977; "The Comic Art Show," Whitney Museum of Art, New York City, 1983; "Festival of Cartoon Art," Ohio State University, Columbus, Ohio, 1983.

WORK IN PROGRESS: A book studying eight mainstream figural styles in contemporary art and illustration; *Dynamic Wrinkles and Draperies*, an illustrated book; "The Savage Commando of God," a collector's edition portfolio; *Kitzel the Lackwit*, an illustrated book.

SIDELIGHTS: Burne Hogarth has enjoyed an extraordinary career as a comic strip artist, illustrator, writer, lecturer, and teacher. His work has been universally acclaimed and has earned him the title "Michelangelo of the Comics." While *Tarzan* represents in many ways the epitome of his illustrative work and the character he has been longer associated with (in newspaper strips from 1937 to 1950, and in books in the 1970s), it in no way exhausts the many facets of Hogarth's talents. His instruction books, from *Dynamic Anatomy* to *Dynamic Light and Shade*, have long been standards in art courses, while his teachings have helped form several generations of cartoonists and illustrators, first in New York, and now in California. It is this aspect of his career that Hogarth chose to emphasize in the comments he sent to *CGA:*

"I am a cartoonist/illustrator, artist, author, art educator, and teacher of art, all of which embrace activities over a fifty year period.

"As a cartoonist and illustrator I have worked for newspapers and national magazines, studio and art departments. As an artist I have exhibited in one-man shows and group shows in the United States and worldwide. As an author I produced, wrote (historical and didactic text), illustrated (detailed figural elements and forms in line and tone), created, and designed a number of art instruction books on

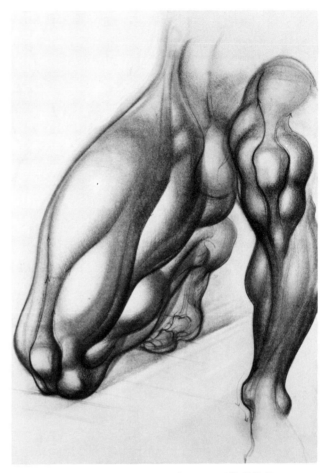

An illustration from *Dynamic Anatomy*. (© 1958, Burne Hogarth. Reprinted with permission.)

the human figure which were best-sellers and still are in print. I created several illustrated graphic novels (popular, narrative art) issued in many languages, on the life of Tarzan of the Apes, adapted from Edgar Rice Burroughs.

"As an art educator and art teacher I began teaching in the early days of the Federal WPA Arts Project, Emergency Education Program, in 1933-35 at the Erie Chapel Institute and Sholem Aleichem Institute. These were classes in drawing, cartoons, and gag humor for adolescents and young adults. From this early start I was involved in teaching, over the intervening years, a wide spectrum of art studies in studio classes, schools, and higher institutions.

"In the Academy of Newspaper Art, which I founded (1944-46), I instituted a targeted curricular program aimed at developing art for journalistic endeavors in newspapers, magazines, journals, periodicals, humor books, and comics. Students learned drawing, characterization, idea development, and finished renderings for humor, gag, caricature, satire, sports, humorous light touch, editorial/political, human interest, serious adventure, romantic-realist cartoons and illustrations. Portfolios were slanted toward newsprint media, line-cut and half-tone reproductions.

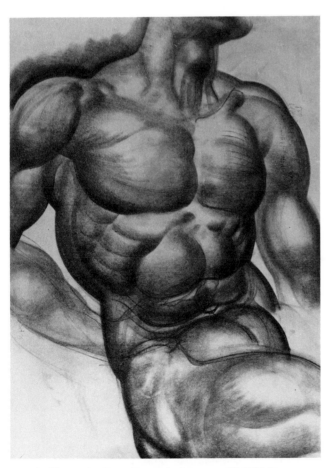

An illustration from *Dynamic Anatomy*. (© 1958, Burne Hogarth. Reprinted with permission.)

"The Cartoonists and Illustrators School, which I co-founded in 1947, developed as an outgrowth and natural

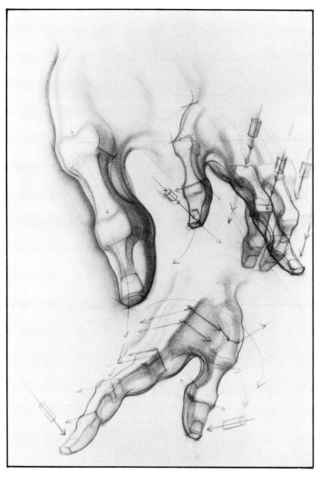

An illustration from *Dynamic Figure Drawing*. (© 1970, Burne Hogarth. Reprinted with permission.)

expansion from the successful premise of the earlier Academy. It was a more sophisticated school which advanced a broad-based curriculum, both in extent and depth, under expert professional teachers geared to the new demands of the burgeoning magazine, syndicate, and comic book industry. The school grew in enrollment and took its place as a major specialized art institution in the United States. A licensed, seasoned school, its professionalism, curriculum, and courses had a far-reaching impact; it became a first-class phenomenon, and soon drew students from all over the world.

"I count my contribution to this school as fundamental to its growth and importance. I had initiated the concept of the school, had set up its curricula and had written all its courses on every level from the Foundation Year, to the Intermediate Studies and the Advanced Workshops of completion and certification of student professionals. My position in the school was not limited to administration as a principal owner, vice president, coordinator of curriculum and art supervisor. I not only carried a full-time teaching load, but I taught courses in Journalistic Art in areas other teachers disavowed or abjured as unfamiliar.

"I taught the classic, analytical human figure in Anatomy and Drawing; developed Nine Principles of Foreshortening in human form; defined the multi-phase, sequential action

systems of figures in deep space visual viewpoints. I taught conventional measured perspective and creative non-gravitational concepts, as well as illustrational eyeball systems of direct, intuited perspective drawing. I taught the structure and schema of story creation, characterization and personification, plotting, pacing, tempo; dialogue and caption, verbal and pictorial interaction; synoptic and finished script development. Withal, I taught five categories of humor—comedy, slapstick, caricature, wit, satire—from a 'tension theory of the absurd/ridiculous polar relationship' leading to the comic and the ludicrous.

"Still, I must emphasize, I was carrying on my major career as the artist/illustrator of the internationally syndicated newspaper color page *Tarzan* for United Features. It was this factor substantially, I believe, that attracted students to the school. By 1955-56 internal and external pressures and identities demanded a name change. We were able, happily, to become the School of Visual Arts of New York. We were moving into national prominence, into higher education, qualifying soon to give a degree, and were shortly to become the largest private art school in the world in numbers of students and faculty. We were to become one of the five most prestigious art schools of quality in the country."

While the foregoing sums up Hogarth's accomplishments as a teacher and educator, it only partially explains the prominent place occupied by the artist in the movement to rehabilitate figural art and, more particularly, to reestablish the pivotal role of the human figure in art. In his own words Hogarth gives us the crux of the debate and the prominent role he played in it:

"In the mid-1950s and later, a great debate split the art world and schools where fine arts were taught. The rise of the Abstract Expressionist experiment and rebellion against figural conventions and illusionist 'subject matter' created a dichotomy and a predicament.

"The School of Visual Arts came up against a powerful contradiction: the fine arts sector and the practical and technical sector were in a collision of theory and opinion on the *concept* and *practice* of *teaching figure drawing*. The slogan that rose through every discussion, 'the figure is dead,' manifested a disagreement that was not mere academic argument. To students at center stage of learning it was a conflict of life-threatening proportions. If the figure was dead, what *was* the *basis* of art?

"The Lester Longmans letter from California in the late 1950s saying 'the figure is *not* dead' had the effect of bracketing the debate by setting up a sanctuary, to its protagonists, of salubrity, assurance and calm. But the issue was not settled, and its condemnatory, destabilizing influence is felt to this day in schools, art galleries, museums, and among the public-at-large.

"From this time forward in art teaching, as I could observe it, the figure came to be minimized, disparaged, denigrated as academic formalism, regressive philistinism, dogmatic conservatism. The human figure as a study of the most far-reaching and highest historical order was *disabled*. It became a shambles, a charnel house of obloquy, invective, and cynical vilification. It was relegated to a second-class use by an inferior caste of cartoonists, illustrators, and advertising specialists—and held in contempt by the fine arts sector. And those protagonists who upheld the prime human form became defensive, apologetic, and carried out a subservient team-play duty to a domineering, in-group adversary class.

"My part in all this was not passive. During this challenging period I was at work producing a book on figure drawing titled *Dynamic Anatomy*. It was published in 1958 at the height of the controversy by Watson-Guptill. This book was the answer to the current clamor. It was, I believe, a seminal study of the figure, which opened with an argument as to why the anatomical figure was the prior requirement of art study in an advanced, analytical, technological, scientific culture. The *anatomical, scientific figure*, I proposed, was the pivotal, anthropocentric form analogue of our culture in the modern age. This book dealt with a host of kinesthetic problems and solutions in drawing, especially a detailed examination of deep space projection in a revolutionary system of *Nine Principles of Foreshortening*.

"Through the middle 1960s, while the cross-fire in the arts continued, I published two more books with Watson-Guptill. *Dynamic Figure Drawing* advanced dozens of new perceptions and insights of the *action* figure in multiple sequence and creative inventions of forms in space. *Drawing the Human Head* was distinguished by its information and visualization of progressive aging of the head, the systematic wrinkle patterns, ethnic types and racial differentia.

"I left the School of Visual Arts [in 1970] to bend my efforts fully to painting, drawing, etching and writing books—and, in part, as it happened later, to education."

BIOGRAPHICAL/CRITICAL SOURCES—Books: Pierre Couperie and Maurice Horn, *A History of the Comic Strip*, Crown, 1968; Jerry Robinson, *The Comics: An Illustrated History of Comic Strip Art*, Putnam, 1974; Ron Goulart, *The Adventurous Decade*, Arlington House, 1975; *The World Encyclopedia of Comics*, Chelsea House, 1976; *Contemporary Authors*, Vols. 93-96, Gale, 1980; *Who's Who in American Art*, 18th edition, Bowker, 1982; *Who's Who in the*

An illustration from *Dynamic Light and Shade*. (© 1981, Burne Hogarth. Reprinted with permission.)

A plate from the "King Arthur" portfolio. (© 1983, Burne Hogarth. Reprinted with permission.)

An illustration from *Dynamic Light and Shade.* (© 1981, Burne Hogarth. Reprinted with permission.)

East, 18th edition, Marquis, 1982; *International Who's Who of Intellectuals*, International Biographical Centre (Cambridge, England), 1982.

Articles: Harry E. Habblitz, "Hogarth," *Heroes Illustrated*, spring, 1969; Paul Spencer, "Hogarth's Monsieur Tarzan," *ERBdom*, November, 1969; "Burne Hogarth and German Expressionism," *Crimmer's: The Harvard Journal of Pictorial Fiction*, winter, 1975; "Burne Hogarth," *Daybreak*, November, 1978; "Burne Hogarth, World's Greatest Comic Artist," *Comics World*, September, 1982.

* * *

HOLLAND, Brad(ford) 1943-

PERSONAL: Born October 16, 1943, in Fremont, Ohio; son of Walter Pierce (a carpenter) and Mary Ellen (Fick) Holland; married Judy Pedersen (an artist), June 7, 1980.

Education: Graduated from Ross High School, Fremont, Ohio, 1961. *Studio:* 96 Greene St., New York, N.Y. 10012.

CAREER: "Flunky" in a tattoo parlor, Chicago, Ill., 1961; freelance artist, 1961—; contributor to the *New York Times, Newsweek, Atlantic Monthly, Time, Playboy*, the *Washington Post*, and many other publications; one of the founding artists of the *New York Times'* Op-Ed page, 1971; designed stamp of Crazy Horse for U.S. Postal Service, 1982; did poster, program art, and stage art for the American Book Awards, 1982; wall drawings for the United Nations Disarmament Conference, New York City, 1983.

AWARDS, HONORS: Gold Medal from Society of Illustrators, 1973, 1976, 1978, 1984, and 1985; Gold Medal from New York Art Directors' Club, 1975, 1983, 1984, and 1985; Playboy Magazine Editorial Award, 1977, 1981; Judges' Award from Los Angeles Society of Illustrators, 1983; Gold Medal from Society of Publication Designers, 1985.

WRITINGS: Human Scandals, T. Y. Crowell, 1977.

All as illustrator: Uri Kazakov, *Arcturus the Hunting Hound and Other Stories*, Doubleday, 1967; Clair Huffaker, *The Cowboy and the Cossack*, Trident, 1973; Gregory Orr, *Gathering the Bones Together*, Harper, 1975; Craig Nova, *The Geek*, Harper, 1975; Jack London, *Tales of the Northland*, Franklin Library, 1983.

Photo by Harold Sinclair.

BRAD HOLLAND

Represented in anthologies: Harrison Salisbury and David Schneiderman, editors, *The Indignant Years*, Crown Publishers/Arno, 1973; J. C. Suares, editor, *The Art of the Times*, Darien House/Avon, 1973; *The Image of America in Caricature and Cartoon*, Amon Carter Museum of Art, 1975; Ted Hearne, editor, *The Art of Playboy*, Playboy Press, 1978; Tom Feaver, editor, *Masters of Caricature*, Knopf, 1981; Moe Foner, editor, *Images of Labor*, Pilgrim Press, 1981; Marta Thoma, editor, *Graphic Illustration*, Prentice-Hall, 1982; Robert Philippe, *Political Graphics*, Abbeville, 1982; *Great Illustrators of Our Time*, Rizzoli, 1982; Steven Heller, editor, *War Heads*, Penguin, 1983; Walt and Roger Reed, *The Illustrator in America: 1880-1980*, Madison Square Press, 1984; D. J. R. Bruckner, Seymour Chwast, and Steven Heller, editors, *Art Against War*, Abbeville, 1984; Steven Heller, *Innovators in Illustration*, Van Nostrand, 1985; *Art and the Law*, West Publishing, 1985.

EXHIBITIONS: Musee des Beaux-Arts, Bordeaux, France, 1973; Louvre Museum, Paris, 1974; Amon Carter Museum, Fort Worth, Tex., 1976; New York Historical Society, New York City, 1979; Library of Congress, Washington, D.C., 1979; (one-man show) Vontobel Gallery, Zurich, 1979. Represented in the permanent collection of the Library of Congress and the Smithsonian Institution, Washington, D.C.

SIDELIGHTS: As a boy growing up in a small Ohio community, Brad Holland cannot remember when he was not "hooked on drawing." By age five he was writing and drawing his own Hopalong Cassidy comic strips with such an intense sense of involvement that, as he once told an interviewer, "I was actually becoming all the characters." Dissatisfied with the Classic Comic Book edition of Homer's *Iliad*, the seven-year-old Holland rewrote the ending, then illustrated his version of the epic. This suggests that if his technique was not yet up to his intentions ("I must've drawn Achilles about thirty times. He never looked the same twice."), creatively he was already very much his own person. In adolescence, it was the Walt Disney universe that captured his imagination, and during his teens he sent off numerous drawings to the Disney Studio in the vain hope of getting a job there as an animator.

Naturally, these efforts were crude. With no formal training available in an environment largely devoid of higher cultural influences, Holland was thrown pretty much upon his own resources, often with results both amusing and touching. For example, having seen a drawing he liked captioned "charcoal," he attempted to reproduce the effect on a piece of shirt cardboard using starter-saturated barbecue-pit briquets purchased in a local grocery store. His first color studies were executed in hobby-shop model airplane dope. Indeed, it is fortunate that his preferred medium was pen and ink, for by posing fewer technical problems for the uninitiated user that medium allowed him to develop and nurture something of much greater value to him as an artist: a strikingly original point of view.

When he was seventeen, Holland left home for Chicago, determined to pursue his artistic career. The parting advice he reportedly received from his grandmother gives more than an inkling of the distance he was about to cover: "Now Bradford," she counseled, "when you get to the big city, you're going to see these storefronts with women sitting in

"It Could Happen," for *New York Times*, 1975. (© Brad Holland. Reprinted with permission.)

front of beaded curtains. Now you darsen't go in them places because there are Arabs behind them curtains that'll take all your money." Unfortunately, as Holland soon learned, there was little enough money to be gained, let alone lost to big city con men, in his scheme of taking his brooding, "apocalyptic" drawings around to various art directors. "Some people just politely rejected them," he recalled in 1978, "but some became downright jumpy, and some actually seemed to take offense." In desperate straits, he took a job in a tattoo parlor where he filled special requests—Mickey and Minnie Mouse *in flagrante*, for example—for sailors on liberty from the nearby Great Lakes Naval Training Center. This was followed by a job as "short-order artist" in the studio of John Dioszegi, a small-time graphic artist who worked as a subcontractor for larger studios. Despite the fact that the hard-pressed Dioszegi frequently lacked the money to pay his young assistant, he offered Holland something even more valuable at this stage of life: "John believed in me at a time when I was the only other person who did. That's no small thing in this world."

After two years with Dioszegi (during which his chief means of support was as a night stock clerk in a grocery store), he moved to Kansas City to take a job with Hallmark Cards. While neither intellectually challenging nor well-paid employment, the Hallmark experience did provide him with a grounding in the basics of illustration and graphic design as well as the satisfaction of finally seeing some of his work in print. This marked the end of his apprenticeship period; when he left Hallmark in the mid-1960s he headed straight for New York and, he hoped, an assignment on Herb Lubalin's *Fact*, a magazine he admired because of its all black-and-white format and liberal political orientation. Lubalin, as it turns out, had no work for him, as *Fact* had folded; but impressed by the originality of Holland's drawings, the editor offered him an assignment illustrating a piece in *Avant Garde*, a new magazine in the Lubalin stable. Holland responded with one of the striking chiaroscuro studies that were to become his trademark.

It was not, however, until *Playboy* art director Art Paul hired him to illustrate the magazine's monthly "Ribald

Classic" feature that he finally achieved enough financial security to pursue seriously his less commercial creative impulses. This opportunity he found in the "underground press" which had emerged during the late 1960s—deliberately outrageous tabloids with names like *Screw, Rat,* and *Ace*—and was to provide the perfect vehicle for his bizarre ink line experimentations in form and content. When one of his "underground" editors, Jean-Claude Suares of the *New York Free Press,* was hired as the first art director of *The New York Times*'s Op-Ed Page in 1972, Holland was invited to become one of the page's regular illustrators. There, with the exposure afforded by such a prestigious showcase, his work at last began to attract notice and he himself to emerge as a leading figure in a new graphic art style a 1974 exhibition in Paris would label "Beyond Illustration."

Holland has always been vague if not flatly contradictory about the sources of his inspiration. He denies, for example, that he is politically motivated and admits to no ideological bent. Yet his drawing has consistently championed the populist side of such issues as arms control, labor versus

capital, and political corruption, and he reportedly severed his association with the *Times*'s Sunday "Week in Review" rather than illustrate a piece on the allegedly "reverse discrimination" aspect of affirmative action programs. He also claims to ignore the text of the pieces he illustrates and rarely makes obvious references to their content. "A drawing," he says, "ought to stand on its own. It's really no different than someone writing an article or a book in the first place." Asked to define his works in terms like "symbol" and "metaphor," Holland balks, saying his pieces are intended to communicate in purely visual terms and using words to describe them is therefore redundant if not misleading. Their meaning, he insists, "is in the weight of the figures, the cast of the eyes, the play of light, the expression in the hands."

Not surprisingly, Holland has little use for academic theories of art. "Op, Pop, Minimal, Maximal, Terminal. . . I can't remember them all," he complains. "It's all too intellectualized." This may be in part the posturing of a self-taught, inner-directed artist, but a substantial body of work

"The Observation Deck," for *New York Times,* **1977.** (© Brad Holland. Reprinted with permission.)

"The Metaphysician," for *New York Times Magazine*, **1984.** (© Brad Holland. Reprinted with permission.)

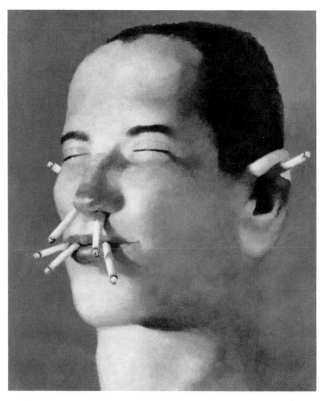

"Smoke as Much as You Can," by Brad Holland, **1978.** (© *Playboy*.)

exists to support his contention that "the way light falls on a woman's body is worth all the theories in the world." (For an uncharacteristically literal expression of this view, see his painting entitled "In a Room" which is reproduced on page 48 of the January/February 1985 issue of *Graphis*.) This same body of work has had enormous influence on a new wave of illustrators, and the very fact that he has been so widely imitated has kept Holland himself changing and evolving. Recently he has begun working more in oils and gouaches than pen-and-ink and experimenting with mood as an alternative to his early reliance on a grim kind of symbolism stressing deformity and gigantism. His ideas, nonetheless, have remained constant, and to this day he is still working on themes first developed as a teenager in rural Ohio hoping to land a job with Walt Disney. In retrospect it seems almost fortunate that Walt found his work unsuitable the first time around.

BIOGRAPHICAL/CRITICAL SOURCES: Nick Meglin, "Reading Between the Lines: An Interview with Brad Holland," *American Artist*, October, 1978; *Communication Arts*, September/October, 1977; "All the Art That's Fit to Befuddle," *New York*, March 14, 1977; *The World Encyclopedia of Cartoons*, Chelsea House, 1980; "Brad Holland," *Graphis*, January/February, 1985; "Man Bites Man: An Interview with Brad Holland," *Upper & Lower Case*, August, 1985; Judann Dagnoli, "Portraits: Master Illustrators Tell Colorful Tales of Roads to Renown," *Advertising Age*, August 8, 1985.

—*Sketch by Richard Calhoun*

*   *   *

HUBLEY, Faith Elliot   1924-

PERSONAL: Born September 16, 1924, in New York, N.Y.; daughter of Irving and Sally (Rosenblatt) Chestman; married John Hubley (a film producer and animator) June 24, 1955 (died, 1977); children: Mark, Ray, Emily, Georgia. *Education:* Attended Actor's Lab in California. *Studio:* 355 E. 50th St., New York, N.Y. 10022.

CAREER: Worked as editor, script supervisor, and music editor of motion pictures in Hollywood, Calif., and New York, N.Y., 1944-55; animated motion picture producer, 1955—; writer and director, 1975—. Founder (with husband John) of production company Storyboard (now Hubley Studio Inc.), 1955. Visiting lecturer at Yale University, 1972-85. *Member:* ASIFA, Motion Picture Editors, Art Students League of New York (life member).

AWARDS, HONORS—All with husband John Hubley: Diploma Speciale, 1956, for *Adventures of an **; honorable mention, 1957, for *Harlem Wednesday;* Grand Prize, 1958, for *Tender Game;* Special Jury Prize, 1964, for *The Hat*, all from Venice Film Festival; Academy Award from Academy of Motion Picture Arts and Sciences, 1959 for *Moonbird*, 1963 for *The Hole*, 1966 for *Tijuana Brass Double Feature;* first prize award from Venice Documentary Festival, 1960, for *Children of the Sun;* Prix Special du Jury from Annecy Film Festival, 1962, for *Of Stars and Men;* CINE Golden Eagle award, 1966 for *Urbanissimo*, 1970 for *Eggs*, 1972 for

Digs, 1978 for *A Doonesbury Special;* Blue Ribbon Award from American Film Festival, 1975, for *Everybody Rides the Carousel;* Special Jury Prize from Cannes Film Festival, 1978, for *A Doonesbury Special.*

Sole winner CINE Golden Eagle award, 1975 for *WOW* (*Women of the World*), 1976 for *Second Chance: Sea*, 1978 for *Whither Weather*, 1979 for *Step by Step*, 1980 for *Sky Dance*, 1981 for *The Big Bang and Other Creation Myths*, 1985 for *Hello* and for *Starlore;* Best Film award from Dallas USA Film Festival, 1978, for *Whither Weather;* Best Children's Film Award from Annecy Film Festival, 1979, for *Step by Step;* Outstanding Achievement Award from San Francisco Film Festival, 1979, for *Step by Step;* Diploma of Merit from Tampere Film Festival, 1982, for *Enter Life.*

Retrospectives: "A Hubley Evening," Jerusalem Cinematheque, 1982; "A Tribute to John and Faith Hubley," University of California at Los Angeles, 1983; "An Homage to the Hubleys," Second Annual Santa Cruz Film Festival, 1983.

WRITINGS—All adapted from screenplays: (With husband, John Hubley) Dig: *A Journey Under the Earth's Crust*, Harcourt, 1973; *The Hat*, Harcourt, 1974; (with John Hubley and Garry Trudeau) *A Doonesbury Special*, Sheed, Andrews & McMeel, 1977; (illustrator) Elizabeth Swados, *Lullaby*, Harper, 1980; (with Elizabeth Swados) *Sky Dance*, Harper 1981.

FILMS—With John Hubley: *The Adventures of an **, Films, Inc., 1956; *Harlem Wednesday*, Films, Inc., 1957; *Tender Game*, Films, Inc., 1958; *Moonbird*, Films, Inc., 1959; *Children of the Sun*, Films, Inc., 1960; *Of Stars and Men*, (adapted from the book by Harlow Shapley), Museum of Modern Art, 1961; *The Hole*, Films, Inc., 1962; *The Hat*, Films, Inc., in conjunction with Museum of Modern Art, 1964; *Tijuana Brass Double Feature*, A&M Records, 1965; *Urbanissimo*, Films, Inc., 1966; *The Cruise*, National Film Board of Canada, 1967; *Windy Day*, Films, Inc., 1967; *Zuckerkandl*, Films, Inc., 1968; *Of Men and Demons*, Films, Inc., 1968; *Eggs*, Films, Inc., 1970; *Dig*, Films, Inc., 1972; *Cockaboody*, Pyramid Films, in conjunction with Museum of Modern Art, 1973; *Voyage to Next*, Films, Inc., in conjunction with Museum of Modern Art, 1974; *People, People, People*, Pyramid Films, 1975; *Everybody Rides the Carousel (adapted from the works of Erik H. Erikson)*, Pyramid Films, 1976; (with Gary Trudeau) *A Doonesbury Special* (from Trudeau's strip *Doonesbury*), Pyramid Films, first produced for National Broadcasting Company, 1977.

A frame from *Hello*, 1984. (© Faith Hubley Studio. Printed with permission.)

Sole producer: *Wow (Women of the World)*, Pyramid Films, 1975; *Second Chance: Sea*, Pyramid Films, 1976; *Whither Weather*, Pyramid Films, 1977; *Step by Step*, Pyramid Films, in conjunction with Museum of Modern Art, 1978; *Sky Dance*, Pyramid Films, in conjunction with Museum of Modern Art, 1979; *The Big Bang and Other Creation Myths*, Pyramid Films, in conjunction with Museum of Modern Art, 1979; *Enter Life*, Pyramid Films, 1981; *Starlore*, Pyramid Films, 1982; *Hello*, Pyramid Films, 1984; *The Cosmic Eye*, Pyramid Films, 1985.

EXHIBITIONS: "Faith Elliot Hubley: Painter and Cineaste" (one-woman exhibit of paintings, watercolors, and films) at Theatre d'Annecy; Animator's Gallery, New York City. Many exhibitions of paintings in New York, California, and Europe.

SIDELIGHTS: Faith Hubley entered the world of animation shortly after her marriage to renowned animator John Hubley (the creative force behind the United Producers of America animated films). Here is how she recounted their meeting to John D. Ford in *The American Animated Cartoon:* "We met in Hollywood in 1946 or 47. I was editing a film called *Human Growth* on sex education (I think it was the first) produced by Eddie Albert, directed by Irving Lerner, and UPA did the animation. . . When John started to work on *Finian's Rainbow*—an animated feature that never got made—I was hired as his assistant. We were

married shortly after that and we continued working separately, some together."

The Hubleys started their own animation studio in 1955, and soon produced a number of critically praised and award-winning films, from the cheerful *Adventures of an ** to the grim *Eggs*, about an unpromising future when a couple needs a permit to have a child. Most of the Hubley films are optimistic in outlook, however, and are much admired for their poetic and lyrical mood. John Hubley died during the filming of *A Doonesbury Special* (the couple's last project together) and Faith completed the picture with Garry Trudeau, creator of the *Doonesbury* newspaper strip on which the film is based.

Since 1977 Faith Hubley has carried on alone, and her animated films have continued to enchant audiences and critics alike. Her recent production *Cosmic Eye* was her first animated feature-length film. Hubley has received many honors and awards from film societies, thus upholding with *eclat* the Hubley name and tradition.

BIOGRAPHICAL/CRITICAL SOURCES: Ralph Stephenson, *The Animated Film*, A. S. Barnes, 1973; Mike Barrier, "John and Faith Hubley Transformed," *Millimeter*, February, 1977; Leonard Maltin, *Of Mice and Magic*, McGraw-Hill, 1980; Gerald and Danny Peary, eds., *The American Animated Cartoon*, Dutton, 1980; *The World Encyclopedia of Cartoons*, Chelsea House, 1980.

I-J

IVEY, James Burnett 1925-
(Jim Ivey)

PERSONAL: Born April 19, 1925, in Chattanooga, Tenn.; son of Bernard Steele and Alise (Buford) Ivey; married Ellen Shea, August 29, 1948 (divorced, 1957); married Evelyn Rogers (a newspaper writer), January 12, 1957 (deceased); children: Susan Ellen, Donald James. *Education:* University of Louisville, 1943-44; George Washington University, Washington, D.C., A.A., 1948; National Art School, Washington, D.C., 1948-50. *Home:* 561 Obispo Ave., Orlando, Fla. 32807. *Office:* Cartoon Museum, 4300 S. Semoran Ave., Orlando, Fla. 32822.

CAREER: Political cartoonist, *Washington Star,* Washington, D.C., 1951-53; political cartoonist, *St. Petersburg Times,* St. Petersburg, Fla., 1953-59; political cartoonist, *San Francisco Examiner,* San Francisco, Calif., 1959-66; founder and curator, Cartoon Museum, Orlando, Fla., 1967—; editorial cartoonist, *Orlando Sentinel-Star,* Orlando, 1970-76; publisher and editor, *Cartoon* (a magazine), 1971-75; co-editor, *Cartoonews* (a magazine), 1975-78. Director and instructor, cartooning course, Crealde Art Center, Orlando, 1975—; adjunct professor of cartooning, University of Central Florida, Orlando, 1980-83. Member, Board of Directors, San Francisco Academy of Comic Art, 1973—; organizer and director, Orlandocon (a comic art annual convention), Orlando, 1975—. *Military service:* U.S. Navy, 1943-46. *Member:* Association of American Editorial Cartoonists (charter member), National Cartoonists Society (Florida chairman, 1970—).

AWARDS, HONORS: National Bar Award, 1957; Reid Fellowship, 1959; Silver T-Square Award from National Cartoonists Society, for outstanding service to the profession 1980; Ignatz Award, Orlandocon, Orlando, Fla., 1983.

WRITINGS: (Collections of editorial cartoons) *Jim Ivey's Cartoon Story of 1954; . . . of 1955; . . . of 1956; . . . of 1957; . . . of 1958,* St. Petersburg Times, 1954-58; (editor) *Roy Crane's Wash Tubbs: The First Adventure Strip,* Luna Press, 1974; (book of drawings) *Thoughts of Man,* Orlando Sentinel-Star, 1975; *U.S. History in Cartoons: The Civil War through WW II,* International Media Systems, 1979; *Things Boys Like to Draw,* International Media Systems, 1979; *Drawing Fun with ABCs,* International Media Systems, 1979.

Cartoons syndicated by Rothco Cartoons, 1963—.

Self-caricature of Jim Ivey, drawn specially for *Contemporary Graphic Artists.*

WORK IN PROGRESS: A book on cartoons and cartoonists; a history of the United States in editorial cartoons.

SIDELIGHTS: For more than a third of a century, Jim Ivey has contributed to every aspect of political cartooning as artist, publisher, editor, author, critic, teacher, and scholar. He states that the medium has been his "vocation and avocation since age eleven" and "the only profession [he] ever cared about or aspired to."

After a stint in the U.S. Navy from 1943-46, Ivey studied at George Washington University and the National Art School, both in Washington, D.C. In 1951 he began his professional career as an editorial cartoonist with the *Washington Star,* and during the next two decades he held the same position with the *St. Petersburg Times,* the *San Francisco Examiner* and the *Orlando Sentinel-Star.* Since 1963 he has drawn three political cartoons a week for Rothco Cartoons, and from 1970-81 the Chicago Tribune Syndicate distributed his panel "Thoughts of Man," illustrating quotations from famous figures in history. The use of scratchboard gave these portraits an impressive, often dramatic, woodcut effect.

The main body of Ivey's graphic work has been in the field of political cartooning, in which he displays a clean, economical line, a biting wit, and a gift for terse commentary. His flair for concise visual expression prompted President Harry S. Truman to write to him, "Sometimes there is more history in a single political cartoon that can be found in a whole month of newspapers."

Ivey has been a sharp critic as well as an active participant in the field of cartooning, writing extensively on the subject for magazines. In 1959 the Reid Foundation gave him a fellowship to study the work of European cartoonists, and he returned after eight months with some critical observations on our own. In general he found the political cartoonists of Europe superior to their American counterparts in humor, simplicity of line, and freedom from stereotypes and cliches. He ascribed their greater originality in part to their relative editorial freedom.

Ivey's own work makes comparatively little use of such hoary conventional symbols as Uncle Sam, John Bull, Mars, the elephant and the mule, and the Statue of Liberty, but rather relies on personal caricature. As cartoonist he has wielded considerable influence in turning American political cartooning away from trite conventions and towards freedom of imagination.

The role of educator has always been as important to Ivey as that of artists. From 1978-83 he taught cartooning at the University of Central Florida. He continues to conduct occasional courses at the Cartoon Museum and Crealde Art Center in Orlando, and he has written several introductory texts on cartooning for young artists.

Well known as an expert on the history of cartooning, Ivey holds a post on the Board of Directors of the San Francisco Academy of Comic Art. From 1971-75 he published and edited *Cartoon*, and from 1975-78 co-edited *Cartoonews*. In 1967 Ivey founded the Cartoon Museum in Madeira Beach, Florida, and has remained its curator. This museum, which moved to Orlando in 1974, is America's first gallery devoted to comic art, and has had professional and amateur visitors from all over the world.

In 1973 Ivey helped to organize the first Orlandocon, one of the nation's largest and most successful comic art conventions. These annual meetings, which he still sponsors and directs, draw both artists and collectors as well as youthful fans from many states, and have done much to galvanize and coordinate the industry.

Described in the *National Observer* in 1964 as "imaginative, always prowling for a fresh approach," Ivey reports that he draws his inspiration from "all periods, worldwide." His inquisitive, restless mind is always alert to new possibilities and new information. He is currently at work on two new projects, a volume on "cartoons and cartoonists" and a "U.S. history in editorial cartoons," for which he wryly predicts publication dates of 1995 and 2000 respectively.

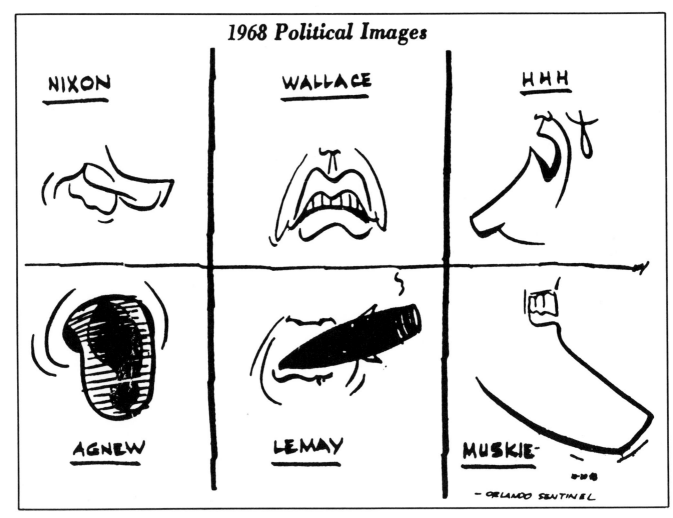

"1968 Political Images." (© Jim Ivey. Reprinted with permission.)

"20 Years of Cartoons," 1971. (© Jim Ivey. Reprinted with permission.)

BIOGRAPHICAL/CRITICAL SOURCES: Newsweek, September 14, 1959; *Editor and Publisher*, September 26, 1959; John Chase, *Today's Cartoons*, Hauser Press, 1962; *National Observer*, August 24, 1964; *Holiday*, August, 1965; *World of Comic Art*, winter, 1966; *Florida Accent*, December 31, 1967; *Carib News and Reviews*, December, 1977; *The Floridian (St. Petersburg Times)*, July 15, 1979; *The World Encyclopedia of Cartoons*, Chelsea House, 1980; *Who's Who in American Art*, Bowker, 1984; *Who's Who in America*, Marquis, 1984; *Who's Who in the World,* Marquis, 1984.

*   *   *

IVEY, Jim
  See IVEY, James Burnett

"**Thoughts of Man**" **by Jim Ivey, 1976.** (© Chicago Tribune–New York News Syndicate.)

*   *   *   *   *   *

JACQUES
    See **BOIVIN, Jacques**

JORDI
    See **BERNET (CUSSO), Jordi**

K

KEANE, Bil 1922-

PERSONAL: Born October 5, 1922, in Philadelphia, Pa.; son of Aloysius William (an iron maker) and Florence R. (Bunn) Keane; married Thelma Carne (vice-president and secretary of Bil Keane Inc.), October 23, 1948; children: Gayle, Neal, Glen, Chris, Jeff. *Education:* Attended parochial schools in Philadelphia. *Religion:* Roman Catholic. *Syndicate:* Cowles Syndicate, Inc., Des Moines, Iowa 50304.

CAREER: Staff artist, *Philadelphia Bulletin*, 1945-59; freelance cartoonist to major publications, 1946-60; creator of *Channel Chuckles*, 1954-78, and *The Family Circus*, 1960—, both for the Register and Tribune Syndicate (now the Cowles Syndicate). *Military service:* U.S. Army, 1942-45, served in First Cavalry Division; became staff sergeant. *Member:* National Cartoonists Society (president, 1982-83), Newspaper Comics Council. *Awards, honors:* Named best panel cartoonist by National Cartoonists Society, 1967, 1971, and 1974; Ohioana Book Award, 1972, for *Just Wait Till You Have Children of Your Own* (with Erma Bombeck); Elzie Segar Award, National Cartoonists Society, 1982; Reuben Award (Cartoonist of the Year), National Cartoonists Society, 1983; first annual "Billy" Award from city of Philadelphia, 1984.

WRITINGS: Channel Chuckles, Scholastic Book Services, 1964; *The Family Circus*, Register and Tribune Syndicate, Vol. 1, 1965, Vol. 2, 1966; *Sunday With the Family Circus*, Judson, 1966; *Jest in Pun*, Scholastic, 1966; *Pun-Abridged Dictionary*, Scholastic, 1968; *Through the Year With the Family Circus*, Judson, 1969; (with Erma Bombeck) *Just Wait Till You Have Children of Your Own*, Doubleday, 1971; *It's Apparent You're a Parent*, Doubleday, 1971; *More Channel Chuckles*, Scholastic, 1972; *Deuce and Don'ts of Tennis*, O'Sullivan, Woodside, 1975; *The Family Circus Treasury*, Andrews & McMeel, 1977; *That Family Circus Feeling*, Andrews & McMeel, 1982; *Love, the Family Circus*, Andrews & McMeel, 1983; *The Family Circus Parade*, Andrews & McMeel, 1984.

All *Family Circus* titles, all published by Fawcett: *The Family Circus*, 1967; *I Need a Hug*, 1968; *Peace, Mommy, Peace!*, 1969; *Wanna Be Smiled At?*, 1970; *Peekaboo! I Love You!*, 1971; *Look Who's Here*, 1972; *Hello, Grandma*, 1973; *When's Later, Daddy?*, 1974; *I Can't Untie My Shoes*, 1975; *Smile*, 1975; *Jeffry's Lookin' at Me!*, 1976; *For This I Went to College?*, 1976; *I'm Taking a Nap*, 1978; *Mine*, 1978; *Quiet! Mommy's Asleep!*, 1978; *Where's PJ?*, 1978; *Any Children?*, 1979; *Dolly Hit Me Back!*, 1979; *My Turn Next!*,

BIL KEANE

1981; *Pasghetti and Meat Bulbs!*, 1981; *Can I Have a Cookie?*, 1982; *Eggheads*, 1983; *I'm Already Tucked In*, 1983; *I Dressed Myself!*, 1984; *The Family Circus Album*, 1984; *It's My Birthday Suit*, 1984; *Unquestionably The Family Circus*, 1985; *How Do You Turn It On?*, 1985; *Kittycat's Motor Is Running*, 1985.

FILMS—All National Broadcasting Co. (NBC) animated specials: *A Special Valentine with the Family Circus*, 1978; *A Family Circus Christmas*, 1980; *A Family Circus Easter*, 1981.

"I don't like kissing Daddy on Saturdays 'cause his whiskers hurt my face."

A panel from *The Family Circus.* (© 1981, Cowles Syndicate.)

"Their mommies are gonna be mad. They're playin' in the mud."

A panel from *The Family Circus.* (© 1982, Cowles Syndicate.)

WORK IN PROGRESS: Designing "The Family Circus Collection" of porcelain figurine collectibles; "The Family Circus Calendar for 1987" for Ballantine Books; national advertising campaigns for Wyler's and Frito-Lay food products.

SIDELIGHTS: Bil Keane who signs all his work Bil (with one "l"), is best known as the creator of the daily and Sunday newspaper feature "The Family Circus," of which by 1985 there were over thirty compilations in book form; twenty years of cartooning experience, however, lay behind this overnight success. As a serviceman during and right after World War II, Keane had honed his cartooning skills in such military publications as *Yank* and *Stars and Stripes.* It was, in fact, in the pages of the latter that he had created his first panel series, *At Ease With the Japanese,* an illustrated guide for the use of the victorious GI's in Japan. Back to civilian life, as a staff artist on the *Philadelphia Bulletin,* he added two more features to this credit: *Silly Philly,* a Sunday comic which was an amused look at the more egregious goings-on in the City of Brotherly Love, and *Channel Chuckles,* a running commentary on the foibles of television and its audience. This latter series was picked up for syndication by the Register and Tribune Syndicate, and led to Keane's creation of *The Family Circus* for the same organization.

The Family Circus is a happy combination of Keane's skills as a cartoonist and his experiences as a family man. "The feature," the artist wrote, "is based on the real-life Keane family as they were growing," and with five children there was no dearth of inspiration. The panels have described the myriad incidents and funny happenings involved in bringing up a large family. Now that many of the Keane children have become adults, "four grandchildren provide the inspi-

ration," the artist says, adding that "*The Family Circus* is now syndicated to more than 1100 newspapers." While the children may keep the feature continuously fresh, it is the talent of the artist that keeps it constantly funny.

BIOGRAPHICAL/CRITICAL SOURCES: The World Encyclopedia of Cartoons, Chelsea House, 1980; Bil Keane, *The Family Circus Album* (a family history of the Keanes with photos and cartoons), Fawcett, 1984.

* * *

KENT, Jack
   See KENT, John Wellington

* * *

KENT, John Wellington 1920-
   (Jack Kent)

PERSONAL: Born March 10, 1920, in Burlington, Iowa; son of Ralph Arthur (in sales) and Marguerite (Bruhl) Kent; married June Kilstofte, June 9, 1954; children: John Wellington, Jr. *Education:* Attended high school for two years in Dallas, Tex. *Politics:* Independent. *Religion:* Episcopalian. *Home and office:* 103 W. Johnson St., San Antonio, Tex. 78204.

CAREER: Freelance commercial artist and gag cartoonist for magazines, 1935-50; author of internationally distributed comic strip *King Aroo,* syndicated by McClure Newspaper Syndicate, New York, N.Y. (later by Golden Gate Features, San Francisco, Cal.), 1950-65; freelance magazine cartoonist and humorist, 1965-68; writer and illustrator of children's books, 1968—. *Military service:* U.S. Army, 1941-45, served in artillery; became first lieutenant. *Member:* American Institute of Graphic Arts, Author's Guild, Author's League of America, National Cartoonists Society, Texas Institute of Letters.

AWARDS, HONORS: Awards from Chicago Graphics Associates, 1969, for *Just Only John,* and Chicago Book Clinic, 1971, for *Mr. Meebles, Jack Kent's Happy-Ever-After Book* was named "Outstanding Picture Book of the Year," 1976, by the *New York Times.* Awards from Texas Institute of Letters, 1983 and 1984.

WRITINGS: King Aroo (a collection of comic strips), Doubleday, 1952. All self-illustrated children's books: *Just Only John,* Parents Magazine Press, 1968; *Clotilda,* Random House, 1969, 1978; *Fly Away Home,* McKay, 1969; *The Grown-Up Day,* Parents Magazine Press, 1969; *Mr. Elephant's Birthday Party,* Houghton, 1969.

The Blah, Parents Magazine Press, 1970; *The Fat Cat: A Danish Folktale,* Parents Magazine Press, 1971, Scholastic, 1984; *The Wizard of Walloby Wallow,* Parents Magazine Press, 1971; *Jack Kent's Fables of Aesop,* Parents Magazine Press, 1972; *Dooly and the Snortsnoot,* Putnam, 1972; *Mrs. Mooley,* Golden Press, 1973; *Jack Kent's Twelve Days of Christmas,* Parents Magazine Press, 1973; *More Fables of Aesop,* Parents Magazine Press, 1974; *Jack Kent's Hop, Skip and Jump Book,* Random House, 1974; *The Egg Book,* Macmillan, 1975; *There's No Such Thing As a Dragon,* Golden Press, 1975; *The Christmas Pinata,* Parents Maga-

Self-portrait of Jack Kent. (© 1985, Jack Kent. Printed with permission.)

zine Press, 1975; *Jack Kent's Happy-Ever-After Book,* Random House, 1976; *Jack Kent's Merry Mother Goose,* Golden Press, 1977; *The Funny Book,* Golden Press, 1977; *Cindy Lou and the Witch's Dog,* Random House, 1978; *Supermarket Magic,* Random House, 1978; *Socks for Supper,* Parents Magazine Press, 1978; *Jack Kent's Hocus-Pocus Bedtime Book,* Random House, 1979; *Hoddy Doddy,* Greenwillow, 1979; *Piggy Bank Gonzales,* Parents Magazine Press, 1979; *Floyd, the Tiniest Elephant,* Doubleday, 1979.

Knee-High Nina, Doubleday, 1981; *Little Peep,* Prentice-Hall, 1981; *The Biggest Shadow in the Zoo,* Parents Magazine Press, 1981; *The Scribble Monster,* Harcourt, 1981; *The Caterpillar and the Polliwog,* Prentice-Hall, 1982; *The Once-Upon-a-Time Dragon,* Harcourt, 1982; *Round Robin,* Prentice-Hall, 1982; *Silly Goose,* Prentice-Hall, 1983; *Jim Jimmy James,* Greenwillow, 1984; *Joey,* Prentice-Hall, 1984; *Joey Runs Away,* Prentice-Hall, 1985.

Illustrator: Polly Berends, *Jack Kent's Book of Nursery Tales,* Random House, 1970; Ruth Belov Gross, *The Bremen-Town Musicians,* Scholastic, 1974; Sarah Barchas, *I Was Walking Down the Road,* Scholastic, 1975; Carla Stevens, *How to Make Possum's Honey Bread,* Scholastic, 1975; C. Stevens, *The Magic Carrot Seeds,* Scholastic, 1976; Freya Littledale, *Seven at One Blow,* Scholastic, 1976; Rita Gelman, *Why Can't I Fly?,* Scholastic, 1976; R. Gelman, *More Spaghetti, I Say,* Scholastic, 1977; R. B. Gross, *The Emperor's New Clothes,* Scholastic, 1977; S. Barchas, *Janie and the Giant,* Scholastic, 1977; Jane Yolen, *The Simple Prince,* Parents Magazine Press, 1978; Bonnie Bishop, *No One Noticed Ralph,* Doubleday, 1979; Beatrice de Regniers, *Laura's Story,* Atheneum, 1979; B. Bishop, *Ralph Rides Away,* Doubleday, 1979; Richard Margolis, *Big Bear Spare That Tree,* Greenwillow, 1980; Mary Elting and Michael Folsom, *Q Is for Duck,* Clarion, 1980; R. B. Gross, *If You Grew Up with George Washington,* Scholastic, 1982; R. B. Gross, *The Girl Who Wouldn't Get Married,* Four Winds, 1983; Charles Keller, *Grime Doesn't Pay,* Prentice-Hall, 1984; Marsha and Michael Folsom, *Easy As Pie,* Clarion, 1985; Howard Goldsmith, *The Twiddle Twins' Haunted House,* Caedmon, 1985.

FILMS: Just Only John, filmstrip by Look/Listen & Learn; *The Grown-Up Day,* filmstrip and record by Learning Corp. of America; *The Wizard of Wallaby Wallow,* animated and produced on film and cassette by Weston Woods.

EXHIBITIONS: Museum of Modern Art, Houston, Tex.; Eagle Galleries, New York, N.Y.

WORK IN PROGRESS: The Gorfu, publication by Harcourt expected in 1986; illustrations for *No Way, José* by Joe Hayes, publication by Prentice-Hall, expected in 1986.

SIDELIGHTS: Jack Kent has been writing funny stories and drawing funny pictures for a living since he dropped out of high school in 1935. "All children scribble," he wrote for the *Fifth Book of Junior Authors and Illustrators.* "Most outgrow it. I never did." For six years before he joined the army a week after Pearl Harbor, he sold advertising art at home in Chicago or wherever his roving family took him and cartoons to national magazines like *Collier's.* He spent the war in the Army Field Artillery, fighting in Alaska and

Three *King Aroo* daily strips. (© 1954, McClure; 1982, Jack Kent.)

the South Pacific and picking up Eskimo and Tagalog on the way, but he never ceased thinking of himself as an artist. Though he had no formal art education (which, he says, "explains a lot but excuses nothing"), he always drew with ease and proficiency, and from his earliest work commanded a disarming and distinctive graphic style. His expressive, flowing line and clear, sure sense of composition earned him an increasing reputation, and in November, 1950, he sold his first and only comic strip, *King Aroo*, to the McClure Syndicate.

King Aroo was a daily and Sunday strip which immediately struck a responsive chord in a small but ardent audience. (Kent reports that it made him "world famous for blocks around.") Although, according to the artist, it never ran in more than one hundred papers, it was greatly admired by those who knew it. Richard Marschall wrote in the *World Encyclopedia of Comics* that it "most certainly belongs in the uncrowded class of such creations as *Little Nemo*, *Krazy

Kat, *Barnaby*, and *Pogo:* an 'intellectual' strip not aimed at any particular age or readership group, but cherished by cults in various categories." It was much quoted for its verbal wit and loved for its narrative absurdity and visual charm.

The strip's dumpy, diminutive, eponymous hero ruled the improbable kingdom of Myopia, but his sovereignty was as benign as his land was peaceful. He wore a tiny crown and an ermine robe but bore no other signs of royalty; indeed, the plots often revolved around his endearing problems and his childlike hopes and dreams. Aroo is a fairy-tale monarch, in a fairy-tale land, but Myopia was rather a mad mirror-image of Faëry. All the conventions of fantasy are lovingly inverted in *King Aroo*, and no cliche of language or plot is left unturned. As a child, Kent loved George Herriman's *Krazy Kat* and vowed to enter the master's field. At thirty he created a kingdom as viable and self-contained as Herriman's Coconino County and a cast of characters as vital as Krazy, Offissa Pup, and Ignatz. But *King Aroo* had none of the pain and stress of Herriman's strip. Kent's pen never drew blood, and the gentle nonsense of *King Aroo* never drew issue. There is no real satire in this merry strip, and no hostility, physical or psychological. Kent holds nothing and no one up to scorn; the only conflict in *King Aroo* is the artist's playful war with sense.

The wry whimsy and literate word-play of *King Aroo* were perhaps caviar to the general public; in any event, when McClure merged with the Bell Syndicate, the strip was discontinued. As a testimony to the devotion *King Aroo* inspired in its fans, one paper, the *San Francisco Chronicle*, kept it running alone, and its editor Stanleigh Arnold went so far as to establish a new syndicate, Golden Gate Features, to distribute it. But it was not enough, and in the middle of 1960 *King Aroo* passed into history. A volume drawn from its first three years was published by Doubleday in 1952 and has become a prized collector's item.

For eight years, Kent treaded water as a freelance artist, once again selling cartoons, illustrations, and advertising art. He sold greeting cards to Hallmark, cartoons to the *Saturday Evening Post*, and whatever he could, as he reports, "to all the magazines from *Humpty Dumpty's* to *Playboy*" until 1968, when he first turned his hand to writing and illustrating children's books.

In the preschool-to-grade-three market, Kent has found his widest audience. "I discovered," he says, "I have a natural empathy with my mental peers in the sandbox set." If he has

Cover for *Jack Kent's Twelve Days of Christmas.* (© 1973, Jack Kent. Reprinted with permission.)

sacrificed some of the sophisticated nonsense of *King Aroo*, he has lost none of the sweet spirit of his kindly humor or the droll angle of vision that informed the comic strip. "In doing a comic strip," he wrote for the *Fifth Book of Junior Authors and Illustrators*, "I was writing funny little stories and scribbling funny little pictures to illustrate them. I'm still doing that." Indeed, *King Aroo* lives on in Kent's children's books—in the small, squashy characters and in the lively pleasure of the language. After fifteen years in Myopia, Kent found his way into the sunny fields of popular success.

As fertile in imagination as ever, he produces up to six books a year. He has written and illustrated over forty since his first in 1968 and illustrated more than a score of other authors'. His first book for children, *Just Only John*, won an award from Chicago Graphics Associates and sold over 400,000 copies, and the volumes which have come tumbling from his pen since have been uniformly successful. Most have gone into one or more book clubs, several as Book of the Month Club or Junior Literary Guild selections. *Dooly and the Snortsnoot* was recorded by Ginn and Co. as a read-along, *The Blah* was recorded by Learning Corporation of America, and *The Wizard of Wallaby Wallow* by Reader's Digest and by Disneyland Records. Captain Kangaroo read several of his books on television, and titles by Kent have appeared in fifteen languages. They have been widely reprinted and have been published with great success in England.

Kent's books are of course routinely reviewed by such journals as *Junior Bookshelf*, *Reading Teacher*, *School Library Journal*, and the *Center for Children's Books Bulletin*; but reviews of his work have also appeared in such wide-ranging periodicals as the *New York Times Book Review*, *Christian Science Monitor*, *Times Literary Supplement*, *New Statesman*, and the *Economist*.

Kent's stories sometimes draw from tradition. He called upon Danish folktales to supply the plot of *The Fat Cat* and the one for *Hoddy Doddy*, but even when he retells the familiar fables of Aesop or the story of the well-known song "The Twelve Days of Christmas," he illuminates them with his jolly, cartoony illustrations, and often he adds a modern

Cover for *Jack Kent's Fables of Aesop.* (© 1972, Jack Kent. Reprinted with permission.)

"There's a bug on this one!" said Tommy.
    "I'm not a bug!" said Clotilda.
"I'm a fairy godmother!"

Tommy and Betty were picking flowers.

An illustration for *Clotilda.* (© 1969, 1978, Jack Kent.)

twist: his version of Aesop's country mouse is disgusted to find artificially flavored soft drinks and TV dinners. The art in Kent's books never fails to complement and enhance the text, and often redeems what might otherwise be painful or sentimental. The fat cat of the tale of that name, for instance, eats people as heartlessly as Little Red Riding Hood's wolf, but, as the *Christian Science Monitor* observed in its review, though the folk tale has "a singularly gruesome ring . . . [Kent] with his cheerful comic drawings keeps [the story] firmly in the realm of delightfully absurd fantasy." *Clotilda* might be charged with sententiousness if it were not for the cheerfully dumpy little fairy godmother (mistaken at first for an insect) who plays the title role.

Perhaps the most striking feature of the entire Kent corpus is the harmony of text and illustration. Clearly the same harmonious and joyous spirit informs both, and the pleasure the artist/author takes in his work communicates itself to his audience. Jack Kent and his wife June call themselves bibliomaniacs—"We only buy books on the subjects in which we're interested," he explains, "but we're interested in virtually everything"—and the love of language and the play of ideas shines as brilliantly through his work for children as it does through his comic strip.

It is obvious that Jack Kent writes with pleasure, but no less so that he takes his calling seriously. The cheerful, warm pen-and-ink drawings—with "wash and tint put on top as needed," as the artist describes his work—brighten and enliven his stories and draw the young reader or listener into the text. "I like to think," Kent has written, "that my little souffles might instill an appetite for books in the wee folk and encourage them to sample weightier fare. Maybe they will learn to love books as I do." Surely the captivating

books of Jack Kent have awakened a taste for the creative imagination—and the creatively imaginative use of language—in many young readers and pre-readers over the last two decades.

BIOGRAPHICAL/CRITICAL SOURCES: Gilbert Seldes, "Introduction," Jack Kent, *King Aroo*, Doubleday, 1952; W. J. Burke and Will D. Howe, *American Authors and Books: 1640 to the Present Day*, Crown, 1972; *The World Encyclopedia of Comics*, Chelsea House, 1976; Daniel Kirkpatrick, ed., *Twentieth Century Children's Writers*, St. Martin's Press, 1978, 1983; *Contemporary Authors*, Vol. 85-88, Gale, 1980; *Something About the Author*, Vol. 24, Gale, 1981; *Fifth Book of Junior Authors and Illustrators*, Wilson, 1983; *Who's Who in America*, Marquis, 1984.

—*Sketch by Dennis Wepman*

* * *

KEY, Ted
    See KEY, Theodore

* * *

KEY, Theodore 1912-
    (Ted Key)

PERSONAL: Born August 25, 1912, in Fresno, Calif.; son of Simon Leon (in business) and Fanny (Kahn) Key; married Anne Elizabeth Wilkinson, September 30, 1937 (died July 5, 1984); children: Stephen Lewis, David Edward, Peter Lawrence. *Education:* University of California, Berkeley, B.A.,

1933. *Religion:* Jewish. *Home and office:* 1694 Glenhardie Rd., Wayne, Pa. 19087.

CAREER: Cartoonist and writer, 1933—; creator of *Hazel* gag series, *Saturday Evening Post*, 1943-69; distributed by King Features Syndicate, 1969—; author of many screenplays, teleplays, and radio scripts for National Broadcasting Co. (NBC), Columbia Broadcasting System (CBS), Walt Disney; staff radio writer, J. Walter Thompson Advertising Agency; contributor to *New Yorker, Look, Collier's, This Week,* and other publications; creator of *Diz and Liz,* monthly cartoon feature for *Jack and Jill,* 1960-70; creator of "Positive Attitude Posters," and "Sales Bullets" for Economic Press, Inc. *Military service:* U.S. Army, 1943-46, served in Signal Corps; became master sergeant. *Member:* National Cartoonists Society, Writers Guild of America West, Players Club. *Awards, honors:* Named best syndicated cartoonist, National Cartoonists Society, 1977.

WRITINGS— All *Hazel* cartoon books: *Hazel,* Dutton, 1946; *Here's Hazel,* Dutton, 1949; *If You Like Hazel,* Dutton, 1952; *Hazel Rides Again,* Dutton, 1955; *All Hazel,* Dutton, 1958; *The Hazel Jubilee,* Dutton, 1959; *Hazel Time,* Dutton, 1962; *Life With Hazel,* Dutton, 1965; *Hazel's Household Hints,* Dutton, 1965; *Hazel Power,* Curtis, 1971; *Right On, Hazel,* Curtis, 1972; *Ms. Hazel,* Curtis, 1972; *Hazel's Feline Follies,* Ace, 1982.

HAZEL

"Coming! Coming!"

A *Hazel* weekly panel, 1945. (© 1985, Ted Key. World rights reserved. Reprinted with permission.)

Also author and illustrator of books (cartoon and non-cartoon): *Many Happy Returns,* Dutton, 1951; *So'm I,* Dutton, 1954; *Fasten Your Seat Belts,* Dutton, 1956; *Phyllis,* Dutton, 1957; *The Biggest Dog in the World,* Dutton, 1960; *Diz and Liz,* Wonder Books, 1966; *Squirrels in the Feeding Station: Ted Key's Suburban Survival Kit,* Dutton, 1967; *The Cat from Outer Space,* Archway, 1978.

Also author of radio play, "The Clinic," anthologized in *Best Broadcasts of 1939-40,* McGraw-Hill. Creator of *Hazel* television series.

Screenplays: *Million Dollar Duck,* Walt Disney, 1972; *The Biggest Dog in the World,* Walter Shenson Productions, 1974; *Gus,* Walt Disney, 1976; *The Cat From Outer Space,* Walt Disney, 1978.

SIDELIGHTS: Ted Key started on his cartooning career while an undergraduate at Berkeley: he was art editor of the *Daily Californian* and associate editor of *The Pelican,* the campus humor magazine. Moving to New York after graduation from college, he contributed cartoons to *Judge,* the *New Yorker, Collier's* and many others. One of his recurrent cartoon characters, a feisty maid named Hazel, proved a hit with readers, and the *Saturday Evening Post* in 1943 signed him to an exclusive contract for a series of weekly *Hazel* cartoons.

Not even service in World War II interrupted Hazel's long and successful career in the *Post:* Key simply sent in his weekly cartoons from his post in the Army. Hazel, the domineering maid in the Baxter household, fought her winning battle with her putative bosses George and Doro-

TED KEY

thy, and their offspring Harold and Katie, for more than thirty-five years in the *Post*. The panel's popularity was helped in no small measure by a highly successful television comedy program, also called *Hazel*, with Shirley Booth in the title role: created by Ted Key, it was shown on NBC in 1961-65 and on CBS in 1965-66. When the *Post* folded in 1969, the feature was quickly picked up by King Features Syndicate for daily publication. As Stephen Becker stated in *Comic Art in America*, "Ted Key took another working girl, slightly more mature and infinitely more domineering, named her Hazel and raised her to the level of a national symbol. . . "

BIOGRAPHICAL/CRITICAL SOURCES: Stephen Becker, *Comic Art in America*, Simon & Schuster, 1959; *The World Encyclopedia of Cartoons*, Chelsea House, 1980; *Who's Who in America*, 1984; *Who's Who in the World*, 1984; *Who's Who in American Art*, 16th edition, 1984.

* * *

KLEIN, I(sidore) 1897-

PERSONAL: Born October 12, 1897, in Newark, N.J.; son of Jeremiah (a translator) and Minerva Klein; married Ann Rosenberg (deceased); children: Doris, Barbara. *Education:* Attended the National Academy of Design and the Art Students' League in New York City. *Home:* New York, N.Y.

CAREER: Freelance cartoonist, 1904-74; animator, 1914-25; 1934-70.

MEMBER: National Cartoonists Society (former vice-president); Screen Cartoonists Guild (life member). *Awards, honors:* Special citation, Montreal Exposition, 1967.

SIDELIGHTS: I. Klein started cartooning at age fifteen. In 1918 he became a full-fledged animator with Hearst's International Film Service, and later worked with such pioneers as Raoul Barré and Amédée Van Beuren. He also worked for Charles Mintz (*Scrappy* and *Barney Google*), Walt Disney (as writer and animator of short subjects) and Terrytoons (where he conceived and created *Farmer Al Falfa* and *Mighty Mouse*). After further work on the *Casper* and *Little Lulu* animation series for Famous Studios/Paramount, Klein resumed his freelance activities in the 1960s, doing animation for television, producing commercials, and directing animated shorts.

Klein is also a noted magazine cartoonist who has contributed to all major American magazines, including the *New Yorker* from the first year of its publication (1925).

BIOGRAPHICAL/CRITICAL SOURCES: Cartoonist Profiles, June 1980; *The World Encyclopedia of Cartoons*, Chelsea House, 1980.

* * *

KUBERT, Joe
See KUBERT, Joseph

KUBERT, Joseph 1926-
(Joe Kubert)

PERSONAL: Born September 18, 1926, in Yzerin, Poland; son of Jacob (a kosher butcher) and Etta (Reisenberg) Kubert; married Muriel Fogelson, July 8, 1951; children: David, Daniel, Lisa, Adam, Andrew. *Education:* Attended High School of Music and Art, New York City. *Office:* Joe Kubert School of Cartoon and Graphic Art, 37 Myrtle Ave., Dover, N.J. 07801.

CAREER: Freelance comic book artist, 1942—; president, Joe Kubert School of Cartoon and Graphic Art, 1976—.

WRITINGS: (With Robert Kanigher) *El baron rojo* (title means "The Red Baron"; version in Spanish of several *Enemy Ace* episodes), Toutain (Barcelona), 1984. Contributor to many comic book titles, including *The Hawkman, Dr. Fate, Sgt. Rock, Enemy Ace, Flash, Firehair, Newsboy Legion*, and *Tarzan*. Illustrator of the newspaper feature *Tales of the Green Beret*, 1966-68.

WORK IN PROGRESS: The Redeemer, a comic book series.

SIDELIGHTS: At age thirteen Joe Kubert started working after school and on weekends at Harry Chesler's comic book shop (a factory-like establishment turning out comic book features for different publishers on a page-rate basis), while studying at the High School of Music and Art at the same

Caricature of Joe Kubert by Stan Kay.

time. He began his professional art career in earnest in 1942, with the Holyoke comic book publishing group, drawing adventure stories such as *Volton* and *Flag-man*. Also in the 1940s he drew *Johnny Quick, Zatara, Hawkman, The Flash, Dr. Fate*, as well as *Phantom Lady* and *Espionage* for various comic book publishers. Of these and other youthful efforts *The World Encyclopedia of Comics* said: "Artistically, Kubert's early work was crude but promising. Influenced mainly by Hal Foster and Alex Raymond, and later [by] comic book artist Mort Meskin, Kubert began to develop into a highly stylized craftsman, his work always utilizing stark blacks, heavy shading and dynamic design and composition. His figures were not always anatomically correct, but they were fine studies of figures in action."

Kubert's talents came into full flower in the 1950s. After a stint at the St. John Publishing Company, drawing, publishing, and editing *Tor* (a prehistoric adventure series), he freelanced mostly for National (now DC) Comics, creating there two outstanding war features in collaboration with writer Robert Kanigher, *Sgt. Rock* and *Enemy Ace*. These are much praised to this day for their stark realism, their grittiness, and their superlative artwork. "Kubert is the DC war comics master," Michael Uslan flatly stated in *American at War*. "His highly stylized, gritty, piercing illustrations embody all the horrors of war and the intricacy of detailed war machines. When Kubert's soldiers crawl across Italy on their bellies, you see the pain, the weariness, the insanity of war in the faces of soldiers. When two World War I planes engage in a dog fight, you can identify specific types of planes . . . It is Kubert's hard-hitting interpretation of war that the readers have been viewing since the early days of *Our Army at War* [where Sgt. Rock of Easy Company first appeared before being given a comic book of his own], and it is his style that acts as the model for nearly every artist who has followed him."

In addition to drawing these war stories Kubert was also active in the period from the middle 1950s to the late 1960s in other genres of comic book adventure, such as superheroes (*Hawkman*) and sword-and-sorcery (*Viking Prince*). In 1966-68 Kubert left comic books to draw the syndicated strip *Tales of the Green Beret*, based on Robin Moore's war novel, and on texts by Moore. Though Kubert's art was generally praised, the feature came out at a time of mounting anti-Vietnam war sentiment, and did last only two years.

Returning to DC, Kubert tried his hand at a number of new comic titles, the most notable being *Tarzan*. Following in the footsteps of Harold Foster (who had created the *Tarzan* newspaper strip) and Burne Hogarth (who had brilliantly continued it), Kubert produced an outstanding piece of work which received much critical acclaim. "Joe Kubert, one of the all-time great names in comic-book illustration, was named editor, writer, and chief artist for DC's *Tarzan of the Apes*," wrote Camille Cazedessus in *The Comic-Book Book*, "and he was the best choice one could have hoped for. His first issues, starting in April of 1972, showed a strong Foster influence dating as far back as some 1929 sequences. But quickly Kubert's own strongly vigorous style asserted itself. The first four issues comprised a masterful retelling of the classic *Tarzan of the Apes*. This was followed by adaptations of other Burroughs texts and earlier classic comic-strip sequences. Kubert's *Tarzan* stands out not only

A panel from *The Redeemer*. (© 1983, DC Comics, Inc.)

A page from *Tor.* (© 1977, White Cliffs Publishing Co.)

on grounds of general excellence, but on the basis of Kubert's own distinctively innovative approach."

Since 1976 Kubert has devoted most of his time to the School of Cartoon and Graphic Art which he founded in Dover, N.J. It has a three-year curriculum leading to a diploma in either cartoon-graphics or cinematic animation. "It is the aim and purpose of this institution," Kubert stated, "to add to the ranks of our profession those people whose work and attitude reflect the highest level of the art." To this end he has assembled a faculty of outstanding cartoonists, illustrators, and animators, including Tex Blaisdell, Irwin Hasen, Jose Delbo, and Hy Eisman. In less than ten years of existence, the school has produced a great number of up-and-coming illustrators and comic book artists, chief among them Rick Veitch, Steve Bissette, Jan Dursema, Tom Yeates, and Timothy Truman.

The success of the school ultimately rests on the reputation and professional standing of its founder and president. Well aware of the fact, Kubert has kept his hand in comics and illustration, and has contributed many thousands of covers and occasional illustrations for comic books. In addition he has published the short-lived comic magazine *Sojourn*, in which he revived *Tor*, and where many of his school's alumni saw their work professionally published for the first time.

Kubert did the bulk of his work at a time when comic books received scant critical attention (if any at all), and when

most of the artists' and writers' work appeared unsigned. A reevaluation is now taking place, and Kubert's fame as a pioneer in composition, characterization, and realistic action has steadily grown beyond the confines of the profession. It has now reached foreign shores, especially Spain's, where his work is much admired and imitated.

Writing in *Historia de los Comics*, Javier Coma said: "A consummate stylist, master of expressionism and page layout, Kubert knows how to use space with a high degree of efficiency and imagination, from dramatic close-ups to long shots with suggestively deep backgrounds, without forgetting his classic and brilliant panel sequences zooming in on the action."

Brought back into active comic creation by popular demand, Kubert is currently at work on a six-part comic book series of his own, *The Redeemer*.

BIOGRAPHICAL/CRITICAL SOURCES: Cartoonist Profiles, March, 1973; September, 1978; December, 1983; Don Thompson and Dick Lupoff, editors, *The Comic-Book Book*, Arlington House, 1973; *The World Encyclopedia of Comics*, Chelsea House, 1976; Michael Uslan, editor, *America at War*, Simon & Schuster, 1979; Javier Coma, editor, *Historia de los Comics*, Toutain (Barcelona), 1983.

—*Sketch by Maurice Horn*

L

LaPALME, Robert   1908-

PERSONAL: Born April 14, 1908, in Montreal, Quebec, Canada; son of Tancrede (a carpenter) and Elodie (Beauchamp) LaPalme; married Annette Demers, January 14, 1935 (died 1978); children: Pierre. *Education:* "Autodidact." *Religion:* Roman Catholic. *Home:* 1081 St. Urbain St., Montreal, Que., H2Z 1K8 Canada. *Office:* Man and His World, Ste.-Helene Island, Montreal, Que. H3C 1A0.

CAREER: Freelance cartoonist, 1929-64; editorial cartoonist, *L'Ordre,* (a Montreal daily newspaper), 1934-37; editorial cartoonist, *Le Droit* (an Ottawa daily newspaper), 1937; editorial cartoonist, *Le Journal* (a Quebec daily), 1937-43; editorial cartoonist for Montreal daily newspapers *Le Canada,* 1943-50, *Le Devoir,* 1950-59, and *La Presse,* 1959-62. Founder and director, International Salon of Cartoons, 1964—; curator, International Pavilion of Humor, 1968—. Painter, muralist, lecturer. Television producer. Set designer. *Member:* Montreal Press Club (honorary life member), National Cartoonists Society. *Awards, honors*: Order of Canada, member of Royal Canadian Academy. Gold Medal from International Poster Exhibition, Tokyo, 1967; many cartooning awards.

EXHIBITIONS: Many exhibitions in Montreal, New York City, Toronto, Tokyo, Rio de Janeiro, Sao Paulo, Rome, and Paris.

SIDELIGHTS: In 1925 Robert LaPalme applied for admittance to the Ecole des Beaux-Arts of Montreal, and was turned down. Instead of being discouraged by this rebuff, he endeavored to teach himself art, and as early as 1929 he sold cartoons to Canadian publications. In the early 1930s he experimented with cubist elements in his cartoons, and soon established himself as one of the more promising cartooning lights in French Canada. This is evidenced by the long string of editorial cartoonist positions he held on various newspapers, starting in 1934. At the same time he continued to freelance cartoons to Canadian and U.S. publications, including the *Philadelphia Ledger,* the *Nation,* and the show magazine *Stage,* for which he did caricatures.

LaPalme is also known for his murals done for Expo '67 (they now can be seen in the Montreal Metro), as well as for his tapestries and set designs. But his crowning achievement is without a doubt the founding of the International Salon of Cartoons in 1964, an outgrowth of the Montreal National Cartoon Festival, which he had organized in 1949. Each summer the Salon hosts several exhibitions of caricatures

ROBERT LaPALME

Photo by Bernard Bohn.

and cartoons from all over the world, and awards prizes in the categories of editorial cartoons, gag cartoons, and comic strips. It also names a "Cartoonist of the Year," upon recommendations from all the participants to the Salon; this honor, international in scope, has over the years been awarded to such luminaries as the Americans Charles Schulz and Burne Hogarth, the Argentinian Guillermo Mordillo, the Czech Adolf Born, and the Frenchman Tomi Ungerer.

In LaPalme the art of cartooning has found one of its most articulate and respected champions and spokesmen. "The caricaturist looks at an object and reveals another aspect of it," he told his *Cartoonist Profiles* interviewer. "He goes as far away as he can, through exaggeration of form. He makes impressions through emphasis, but in the end he lets you know what it is."

"The Origins of Pharmacy," 1947. (© Robert LaPalme. Reprinted with permission.)

BIOGRAPHICAL/CRITICAL SOURCES: Bill Dunn, "Le 10e Salon International de la Caricature," *Cartoonist Profiles,* June, 1973; *The World Encyclopedia of Cartoons,* Chelsea House, 1980; *L'Analyste,* autumn, 1984; *Who's Who,* Marquis, 1984; *Target,* spring, 1985; *L'Actualite,* July, 1985.

* * *

LEACH, David   1946-

PERSONAL: Born April 25, 1946, in Evanston, Ill.; son of Ralph (a banker) and Harriet (Scheuerman) Leach; married Laurie Hughes in 1971; children: Megan, Katherine. *Education:* Bucknell University, B.A., 1968; Ohio University,

M.F.A., 1973. *Religion:* Protestant. *Home:* 201 Lookout Dr., Dayton, Ohio. *Studio:* 1121 E. First St., Dayton, Ohio.

CAREER: Assistant professor, 1973-78, associate professor, 1978—, chairman, department of art and art history, Wright State University, Dayton, Ohio, 1985—. *Awards:* Regional fellowship grant from National Endowment for the Arts, 1978.

WRITINGS: (Editor) *Generative Literature and Generative Art,* York Press, 1983; (illustrator) Gary Pacernik, *Wanderers and Other Poems* Prasada Press, 1985.

EXHIBITIONS: University of the South, Sewannee, Tenn., 1974; New England College, Henniker, N.H., 1976; Parke

Contemporary Graphics, Monticello, Ill., 1977; Fell's Point Gallery, Baltimore, Md., 1978; Toni Birckhead Gallery, Cincinnati, Ohio, 1981; Dayton Art Institute, 1984; Janice Forberg Gallery, Cincinnati, 1985.

WORK IN PROGRESS: Large-scale drawings of generalized interior spaces, using line to create tone.

SIDELIGHTS: David Leach, both a printmaker and a graphic artist, has until recently been working in the more traditional subject matters, such as portraits and landscapes. By their predilection for the silent, intimate essence of things, Leach's etchings and lithographs show the double influence of Paul Cézanne and Giorgio Morandi. Particularly appealing are the still lifes, which convey an immediate visual sensation, full of lyrical poetry and charm.

In addition, because he is interested in the natural links between the printed word and printmaking (he very much admires the symbiotic collaboration between novelist Alain Robbe-Grillet and artist Robert Rauschenberg), Leach has also created "images" to accompany several poems by Gary Pacernik. Collected under the title *Wanderers and Other Poems*, these seven stone lithographs, plus title page and colophon, are not illustrations in the typical sense, but rather pictorial reflections of poetic metaphors. For his purpose Leach preferred the abstract purity of geometric lines and the playing with different sizes to the representational style he usually favors. He has thus succeeded in evoking graphically the pensive moods and nuances of the soul, as well as the multiple relationships existing between the visible and language.

Considered one of the fine young artists of the 1980s, David Leach today has works in private collections and museums, among which are the Cincinnati Museum of Art, the Dayton Art Institute, and the Museum of Modern Art of New York.

Lithographic self-portrait of David Leach, 1984. (Printed with permission.)

BIOGRAPHICAL/CRITICAL SOURCES: Art in America, July-August, 1979; *Aspects of Perception* (exhibition catalogue), 1982; *Ink Under Pressure* (exhibition catalogue), 1984.

* * *

LEE, Bill
See LEE, William Saul

* * *

LEE, William Saul 1938-
(Bill Lee)

PERSONAL: Born November 15, 1938, in Brooklyn, N.Y.; married Dona Johnson (a psychotherapist), April 14, 1979; children: Jennifer Catherine. *Education:* Attended School of Visual Arts, New York, N.Y., 1960-64. *Home:* Sharon, Conn. *Office:* Penthouse International, Ltd., 1965 Broadway, New York, N.Y. 10023.

CAREER: Freelance cartoonist, 1963—; humor editor, *Penthouse* and *Omni*, New York, N.Y., 1976—. *Military service:* U.S. Army, 1957-59, served as photographer. *Member:* American Institute of Graphic Arts, Television Academy, Society of Illustrators, Writers Guild, National Cartoonists Society, Cartoonists Association. *Awards, honors:* International Humor Award from Man and His World, Montreal, Canada, 1971 and 1972.

WRITINGS—All under name Bill Lee: *Insecurity Is Better Than No Security at All*, Dell, 1970; *Hanky Panky*, Dell, 1971; (editor) *No U.S. Personnel Beyond This Point* (collection of anti-war drawings), Delta, 1973; *Oops*, Dell, 1974; *The American Princess*, Dell, 1976; *Have a Good Day at the Office, Dear*, Franklin Watts, 1983; *Every Day Is Father's Day*, Watts, 1984.

Creator of "Town and Country" (comedy series) for CBS-TV, 1978. Has had drawings collected in more than fifty anthologies; and has published six portfolios of his own drawings. Contributor to *Penthouse, Playboy, Omni, Esquire, Cosmopolitan, New Yorker, National Lampoon*, and other periodicals.

Cartoon series, *Fogarty, Alexander the Great, Americarnal, Crucifixations*, have been variously syndicated by the Chicago Tribune-New York News Syndicate, *Penthouse*, and in the underground press.

EXHIBITIONS: Leo Castelli Gallery, New York City, 1972; Hansen Gallery, New York City, 1975; Van Gogh Museum, Netherlands, 1975; Kew Gardens, London, 1975; one-man show at Visual Arts Gallery, New York City, 1973.

WORK IN PROGRESS: A series of satirical writings and drawings called *Investigative Cartooning;* preparing a show of satirical art and sculpture.

SIDELIGHTS: Bill Lee is a versatile cartoonist whose work has appeared widely in magazines, books, and anthologies.

Self-portrait of Bill Lee. (Printed with permission.)

In one of these anthologies of cartoons, *Man Bites Man: Two Decades of Satiric Art*, Steven Heller wrote: "Lee is constantly drawing. His spaghettilike lines fill countless sketchbooks with scenes, people, and still lifes. His continuing development as a humorist rests on two important priorities: his concerns for the problems of society and the desire to expand his own artistic limits. His mastery, for instance, of an expressionist color sense has recently surfaced. This is, in part, thanks to the fluidity of the studio marker, which he wields like a paintbrush. Also, as humor editor of *Penthouse* magazine, he is afforded the means to express himself in vibrant process colors and hues—color being at a premium in most American cartoon outlets. The combination of intense personal loves and hates, both aesthetic and wordly, make Lee a compelling satirist and a funny man."

A funny man Lee certainly is, and his witticisms often are quoted in newspaper columns. Here are two that can be considered representative. Soon after Ronald Reagan's election to the presidency in 1980, he sent the president-elect this note: "As a professional cartoonist, I'd like to offer my congratulations on your election and also thank you for providing me with a fresh set of features. I was so darn tired or drawing Jimmy Carter." From a trip to the Soviet Union he sarcastically described this scene: "Under the watchful eyes of Russia's not-so-secret police, these prostitutes in American jeans, Scandinavian sweaters and Italian shoes

Cartoon from *Every Day Is Father's Day*. (© 1984, Bill Lee. Reprinted with permission.)

A panel from *Bottoms*. (© 1985, Tribune Media Services.)

have become a prime source of much-needed foreign exchange currency for the Communist government. I'd say the Soviet Union's KGB (secret police) might very well be the world's most successful procurer."

In one of the installments in his current series, *Investigative Cartooning* (which he describes as "a self-created style of satiric journalism involving worldwide travel assignment, featuring drawings to illustrate the written articles"), Bill Lee humorously recounts how he was once mistaken for a secret policeman while taking photographs at the funeral of a Solidarity leader in a Warsaw cemetery, and was nearly lynched, wrily concluding: "I was saved by the Polish women's knowledge of Western clothing, and my own (unusual) personal style—designer tacky!"

Bill Lee wrote *CGA:* "Satire is the humorous alternative to the physical act of screaming! I love it! I love to draw, paint, sculpt, and live it! *Investigative Cartooning* has taken me to two Presidential conventions, to China, Russia, Poland, and to Plains, Georgia, etc."

BIOGRAPHICAL/CRITICAL SOURCES: Steven Heller (editor), *Man Bites Man*, A & W, 1981; *Contemporary Authors*, Vol. 104, Gale, 1982; *Men of Achievement*, International Biographical Centre, 1982.

*　　*　　*

LETTICK, Birney 1919-

PERSONAL: Born March 22, 1919, in New Haven, Conn.; son of Meyer and Hannah (Alexander) Lettick; married Gail

Rosenfield (an artist), December 29, 1975; children: David, Sharon, Ann, Ben. *Education:* Yale University, B.F.A., 1941. *Home and studio:* 121 E. 35th St., New York, N.Y. 10016.

CAREER: Illustrator, painter, movie poster and advertising artist, 1946—; director, New Haven Art Workshop, 1946-72. *Military service:* U.S. Army, 1942-45; became staff sergeant; recipient of eight Battle Stars. *Member:* Society of Illustrators. *Awards, honors:* Gold Medal from Society of Illustrators, 1963; First Prize, Bicentennial Coin Design for Connecticut, 1975.

EXHIBITIONS: Graham Gallery, New York City, 1970; FAR Gallery, New York City, 1974; New Britain Museum of American Art, 1975; traveling one-man poster exhibition, Japan, 1982; Museum of American Illustration, New York City, 1983.

WORK IN PROGRESS: A series of twelve still-life paintings, mostly of food, with painted *trompe l'oeil* frames; a

Self-portrait of Birney Lettick. (Printed with permission.)

series of advertising illustrations for Amaretto liqueur; covers for *Time.*

SIDELIGHTS: In discussing what he considers the fad of non-objectivism on the contemporary fine art scene, Birney Lettick recalls the caption of a cartoon from the *New Yorker:* "Why must you be a non-conformist like everyone else?" Lettick goes on to stress that non-conformity is of greater value to the representational artist than to the avant-gardist. To the abstract artist, he suggests, the desire to stand apart is of itself sufficient incentive to do so; but among realists non-conformity is the soul of originality, in

"The Fatal Gift." (© 1983, Birney Lettick. Printed with permission.)

the absence of which they become merely a set of conservative academicists. By taking the realist route, however, an artist denies himself many of the varieties of rebellion against form routinely employed by the non-objectivists. Forced to find his individuality within a far more restricted range of stylistic and substantive choices, Lettick argues, the realistic painter "must have a background of much study and practice, with great knowledge of distortion and exaggeration of form, color and perspective" superior to that required of his "modernist" colleagues. Unlike the latter, who "dedicate themselves to the abstract, to the division of a flat space with interlocking geometric forms," he contends, the realists must "in a more masterful and complex way dedicate themselves to the same problems rooted in the real world."

Without opening this debate to partisans of the other side—who might reasonably assert the elaborate mathematical underpinnings espoused by post-Mondrian geometricians—it is obvious from even a cursory review of his work that Lettick is a practitioner of that which he preaches. His mastery of form, texture, composition, and color is that of one who has studied nature and knows how to use or eliminate the possibilities it presents in order to achieve the desired effect on canvas; one who recognizes that the essence of realism is an approximation, not an imitation of nature, and that it is the emotional *re-*creation of a subject that separates a realistic painting from a photograph. Because of this understanding, he possesses the ability to invest commonplace objects with interest through a combination of painterly sophistication, *trompe l'oeil* detail, and surreal juxtaposition.

Poster art for the film *Heaven Can Wait.* (© 1975, Paramount Pictures.)

Having gained success in both the fine and commercial art worlds, he moves quite easily between the two, both philosophically and esthetically. He likens the stimulus given art by commercial encouragement to the Renaissance patronage of art by the church, but is himself equally capable of producing work for the gallery setting and for film or advertising promotion. The winner of a Society of Illustrators Gold Medal for his work in 1963, Lettick has also been featured in numerous exhibitions, including one-man shows at the Graham Gallery (1970) and the FAR Gallery (1974) in New York City. He has also contributed a number of covers for *Time*.

BIOGRAPHICAL/CRITICAL SOURCES: Art News, September, 1970, September, 1973; *Arts Magazine*, September, 1970; "Birney Lettick," *Magic and Other Realism*, Hastings House, 1979; *Outstanding American Illustrators*, Graphic Sha (Tokyo) 1984, 1985.

*   *   *

LONG, (Winfield) Scott (Jr.)   1917-

PERSONAL: Born February 24, 1917, in Evanston, Ill.; son of Winfield Scott (a sales executive) and Alice (Mousseau Des Islets) Long; married Elizabeth Ann Mitchell, September 9, 1939; children: Mitchell White, Winfield Scott III, Barbaralynn Friedlander. *Education:* Harvard University, B.A., 1939. *Politics:* "Independent (but somewhat active)." *Religion:* Presbyterian. *Home:* 4501 Dupont Ave. S., Minneapolis, Minn. 55409.

SCOTT LONG

THE GREATEST SEAL OF THE PRESIDENCY   (Drawn privately in retirement)

MORE & MORE BOMBS

Editorial cartoon. (© 1982, Scott Long. Printed with permission.)

CAREER: Cartoonist and reporter, *Zanesville News*, Zanesville, Ohio, 1939-40; political cartoonist, *St. Paul Pioneer-Press*, St. Paul, Minn., 1940-41; executive trainee, L. S. Donaldson Co. (a department store), Minneapolis, Minn., 1941-42; political cartoonist and occasional writer, *Minneapolis Tribune* and *Minneapolis Star-Journal*, 1943-80. Contributor to *Boston Globe, Harvard Guardian, Harvard Lampoon, Quill*, and other publications. Richfield Citizens League, Minnesota (president, 1954-55); American Civil Liberties Union, Minneapolis-St. Paul Committee of Foreign Relations. *Military service:* U.S. Naval Reserve, 1944-46, served in new Guinea, Philippines, China, Okinawa, Japan; became lieutenant. *Member:* Association of American Editorial Cartoonists (co-founder, 1957; president, 1962); Minnesota Press Club; Minnesota Harvard Club; The Skylight Club, Minneapolis; Lake Harriet Yacht Club; Inland Lake Yachting Association.

AWARDS, HONORS: Freedoms Foundation Award, 1949; Page One Award for journalistic achievement from Minneapolis Newspaper Guild, 1950, 1951, 1952, 1953, and 1956; Christopher Award, 1953; National Headliners Club Award, 1954; National Sigma Delta Chi Award for editorial cartooning, 1957.

Editorial cartoon. (© 1982, Scott Long. Printed with permission.)

WRITINGS: "Please Turn to Page Six" (three-act play), unproduced, 1967; *Hey! Hey! LBJ!* (cartoons and text), Ken Sorenson, 1969; (foreword) Charles Brooks, ed., *Best Editorial Cartoons of the Year*, Pelican, 1973.

EXHIBITIONS: Minneapolis Art Institute, Minneapolis, Minn., 1953.

SIDELIGHTS: Scott Long figures that he has drawn between eleven and twelve thousand editorial cartoons in the course of his long career. His cartoons, done in a sharp, uncluttered line, make their point quickly and economically, which has made them likely candidates for reprinting. While liberal in bent (not unnaturally for a cartoonist working for a liberal newspaper in a liberal state), Long has always maintained great fairness and lucidity in his comments, and the fact is reflected in the numerous professional awards he has received over the years. His articles and comments on his craft have shown him to be conscious of the power and the attending responsibility that come with wielding political comment in the pages of a large and respected publication.

"Political cartoons of mine have been reprinted in every major U.S. news publication and in several foreign newspa-

pers (China, Germany, France, Italy, etc.)," Long commented. "For some twenty-five years Scott Long of the *Minneapolis Tribune* and Roy Justus of the *Minneapolis Star* were syndicated together all over the U.S. in some 40-45 other newspapers. Over the years I wrote many articles, editorials and book reviews for the *Tribune*. I have also written many articles from overseas. The earliest article was written from Manus Island in the Admiralty Islands in 1944. It appeared in the *Minneapolis Star* under the title "Gibraltar of the Pacific." My most ambitious and (I think) best articles were written about Africa in 1956 (with *Tribune* reporter Carl Rowan) under the title "African Deadline." The African articles were syndicated all over the country."

Scott Long is now officially retired, but he has not altogether abandoned the practice of his craft. He still contributes editorial cartoons, drawn with his usual clear line and pungent point, to many publications.

BIOGRAPHICAL/CRITICAL SOURCES: John Chase, *Today's Cartoon*, Hauser Press, 1962; *Who's Who in America*, 1984.

M

MANDEL, Saul   1926-

PERSONAL: Born January 1, 1926, in New York, N.Y.; son of Jack (an independent contractor in the building trades) and Ethel Mandel. *Education:* Graduated from High School of Industrial Design, New York City; attended Pratt Institute, New York City, 1946—. *Home and studio:* 163 Maytime Dr., Jericho, N.Y. 11753.

CAREER: Freelance illustrator, cartoonist, designer, and painter, 1946—. Associate professor of concept illustration, Syracuse University, 1982—; associate professor of concept communications, South Hampton College, South Hampton, N.Y., 1982—; guest lecturer at numerous universities. *Military service:* U.S. Army, 1944-46, served in art unit of Army Intelligence. *Member:* Society of Illustrators, New York Art Directors Club, American Institute of Graphic Arts.

AWARDS, HONORS: Award of Excellence from Society of Illustrators, 1963; Gold Medal in Thirty-Fifth National Outdoor Advertising Competition from Institute of Outdoor Advertising, 1971; Gold Medal for best illustration from Connecticut Art Directors Club, 1978.

EXHIBITIONS: U.S. Information Service American Designers Traveling Exhibition to Eastern Europe, 1963-65; "Children from Around the World," Allied Chemical Building, New York City, 1964; Sichereit Lernen-Unfalle Vermeiden, Internazional Plakatwettbewerb, Essen, West Germany, 1981; Japan Design Foundation, Semba Center, Osaka, Japan, 1982; (one-man show) Museum of American Illustration, New York City, 1983.

SIDELIGHTS: Born in New York City, Saul Mandel studied art at the High School of Industrial Design and upon graduation went into the military. During World War II he served as head of a Hawaii-based art unit attached to U.S. Army Intelligence and charged with the task of disseminating important information to a broad, variegated audience scattered throughout the Pacific theatre. As a result of his wartime experiences, he developed a profound belief in the power of non-verbal, visual communications and returned to civilian life determined to devote himself to understanding and employing that power. As Stanley Roberts wrote in *Graphis*, Mandel "deliberately set out to achieve a style that was universal in language and appeal. To this deliberation he added out of his own nature a habit of humor allied to a love of children and the things of childhood. From this there has resulted a style that is simple, smiling and naive, at once and

Self-portrait of Saul Mandel. (© 1984, Saul Mandel. Printed with permission.)

widely understood by young and old, by the ingenuous and the sophisticated."

The portfolio accompanying this appraisal offers strong support for it: a series of rude, lively, and colorful works evoking, at first glimpse, the watercolors or fingerpaintings adorning the walls of a second or third grade classroom. But closer application—which the paintings invite through their cheerful naivete—reveals a subtle intelligence at work, one whose aim is not merely to charm the casual eye, but to catch, hold, and inform almost subliminally. The bright colors attract, the unsophisticated draftsmanship does not patronize, and the basic message is transmitted without resort to any written text. Roberts suggests that the briefest exposure is sufficient to convey the essence of a Mandel

An illustration. (© 1980, Saul Mandel. Printed with permission.)

graphic and reports that studies of ad effectiveness carried out during the 1950s consistently rated his work among Madison Avenue's best.

His method has been described as "thought and dream, trial and rejection," and his results produce images that are economical in visual presentation and unmistakable in meaning. He depends for immediate attention, as Roberts points out, on "the compelling power of color—offered with an uninhibited, even primitive generosity," but it is the almost ideographical simplicity of his message that finally puts it so effectively across. For example, an ingenuous rendering of a man's head turns the gaping mouth into an open furnace door, wherein orange and blue flame leaps, and the exaggerated nose into a fingerpost-like protuberance pointing to the package of Kool cigarettes he holds: without a word of text, Mandel has come up with an image the client could not have projected more convincingly by employing a legion of singing, dancing penguins. Roberts observes in his analysis of this facet of Mandel's talent as a communicator, "Words assail us on all sides, they implore and insist. Mandel is meanwhile dedicated to the proposition that 'One picture is worth a thousand words.' Not *is*, he cautions, but *can be*, when the picture is inseparable from its message."

Mandel's work has worn well in the faddish world of American graphic art. He recreated the famous Green Giant character in the 1960s, was chosen to design six postage stamps for the U.S. Postal Service in 1979 and 1981, and has won a number of awards from prestigious professional societies.

Writing in *Upper & Lower Case*, the international journal of typographics, Marion Muller summed up Mandel's career this way: "The only way to describe all his activities is to call

An illustration. (© 1980, Saul Mandel. Printed with permission.)

176

him a total creative force. He has done it all: concepts, design, illustration, photography, newspaper ads, posters, cartoons, training films, TV commercials, brochures . . . His list of clients stretches from Bank of America to *Woman's Day Magazine*, with dozens of equally prestigious names in between. But whoever calls him on a project knows that his solution will surely be unique, cheery, brightly colored and unfailingly optimistic."

Mandel's work remains within the traditions of classic graphic art, and is worthy of note for its individuality, success in communicating, and informed intelligence. It has garnered praise in many quarters, and the fact that it has been so widely exhibited testifies to the artist's international reputation.

BIOGRAPHICAL/CRITICAL SOURCES: Stanley Roberts, "Saul Mandel," *Graphis*, August, 1958; *20 Years of Award Winners*, Hastings House, 1981; Marion Muller, "Saul Mandel," *Upper & Lower Case*, August, 1984; *Who's Who in American Art*, 16th edition, Bowker, 1984.

—*Sketch by Richard Calhoun and Maurice Horn*

* * *

MARCUS, Jerry 1924-

PERSONAL: Born June 27, 1924, in Brooklyn, N.Y.; son of Julius (in women's wear business) and Clara (a housewife; maiden name Maybloom) Marcus; married Edith Keller, December 22, 1951 (divorced June 26, 1963); married Dalphine N. Costello, November 30, 1963 (divorced); children: (first marriage) Gary, Julie; (second marriage) Jeremia, Julius. *Education:* Attended Cartoonists and Illustrators School (now School of Visual Arts). *Politics:* Democrat. *Religion:* Hebrew. *Residence and studio:* Ridgefield, Conn. *Agent:* Janice Horton (casting agent), Newtown, Conn. and New York, N.Y.

CAREER: Freelance cartoonist, 1947—; actor in motion pictures, including "Exodus," Loving," and "Hail!," as well as in national television commercials. Cartoonist of syndicated panel *Trudy*, King Features Syndicate, 1963—; has contributed cartoons to most major publications, including the *Saturday Evening Post, Collier's, American, Sports Illustrated, Good Housekeeping, Ladies' Home Journal, Look*, the *New York Times, Paris-Match*, the *New Yorker, Esquire, Playboy*, and *Cosmopolitan*. *Military service*: Served in U.S. Navy and Merchant Marine in the Pacific during World War II; received Victory Medal. *Member:* National Cartoonists Society, Screen Actors Guild.

WRITINGS—All books of cartoons: *Just Married*, Dell, 1956; *Trudy*, Mac Fadden-Bartell, 1965; *Hang in There, Trudy*, Fawcett, 1974; *We Love You, Trudy*, Grosset, 1979; *Fatkat*, Thor, 1981, *Fatkat's Diary*, Thor, 1982.

SIDELIGHTS: A prolific cartoonist, Jerry Marcus has graced the pages of many magazines and publications with his work. His humor is pointed but gentle. As Bill Crouch stated in *The World Encyclopedia of Cartoons:* "Marcus draws everything from kids to pets to suburbia to the classic

JERRY MARCUS

TRUDY

"Of course mother still loves you, mother may be a little annoyed at her little boy, but mother still loves him."

A *Trudy* daily panel. (© 1964, King Features Syndicate.)

"Isn't anyone going to tell me what I've got?" Magazine cartoon by Jerry Marcus. (© 1980, *National Enquirer*.)

man-stranded-on-a-desert-island. His drawing style is loose but not sketchy. Sometimes the editors would decide they liked his roughs and publish them instead of requesting that more finished drawings be done. Numerous Jerry Marcus cartoons have been published in cartoon anthologies, and Presidents Eisenhower and Kennedy both asked for, and received, original Marcus cartoons."

Marcus is best known for his humor panel *Trudy,* which he draws weekdays and Sunday for King Features Syndicate. The joys, sorrows and tribulations of the winsome suburban housewife Trudy and her slightly bewildered husband Ted form the thread of this unfolding domestic saga. Ted is more often than not upstaged and outwitted by his wife (in the tradition of American cartooning), but both are hoodwinked in their turn by their pre-teenaged son Crawford. The feature has won a dedicated following and has been anthologized in a number of paperback volumes.

Jerry Marcus wrote *CGA:* "My main interest is my panel *Trudy.* I turn out six dailies and a Sunday *Trudy* every week. I try to keep it fresh with the hope that people will recognize

themselves and identify with my characters. Occasionally I do a national commercial, a very nice change that gets me away from the loneliness of the drawing board to the excitement and busy activity of a film studio."

BIOGRAPHICAL/CRITICAL SOURCES: Roy Paul Nelson, *Cartooning,* Contemporary Books, 1975; Mort Walker, *Backstage at the Strips,* A & W Publishers, 1977; Nelson, *Comic Art and Caricature,* Contemporary Books, 1978; *The World Encyclopedia of Cartoons,* Chelsea House, 1980; *Contemporary Authors,* Vol. 97-100, Gale, 1981; Nelson, *Humorous Illustrations,* Contemporary Books, 1984.

*   *   *

MAROTO (TORRES), Esteban 1942-

PERSONAL: Born March 3, 1942, in Madrid, Spain; son of Jacinto (a farmer) and Aurora (Torres) Maroto; married Carmen Mas Hernandez (a secretary); children: Gemma, Laura. *Education:* Secondary school. *Home:* Calle Joan Blancas, 22-24, 08012 Barcelona, Spain. *Agent:* Josep Tou-

An extract from *Dax el Guerrero*, **1971.** (© Esteban Maroto. Reprinted with permission.)

tain, Selecciones Illustradas, Diagonal, 325, 08009 Barcelona; Bernd Metz, 43 East 19th St., New York, N.Y. 10003.

CAREER: Designer and draftsman, 1955-58; industrial master craftsman, 1958-60; comic strip artist and illustrator, 1961—. *Awards, honors:* Foreign Comic Award, Academy of Comic Book Arts, New York City, 1971; named best comic artist, Warren Publishing Company, 1974.

WRITINGS—All books of comics published by Toutain, Barcelona: *Cuando el comic es arte-Esteban Maroto* (title means "When the Comics Are Art"), 1976; *Dax el guerrero* (title means "Dax the Warrior"), 1979.

EXHIBITIONS: Paintings exhibited in Madrid, Valencia, Zaragoza and Barcelona in the 1980s.

WORK IN PROGRESS: Paintings and illustrations for books.

SIDELIGHTS: Esteban Maroto has in recent years separated himself from the world of comics, where he had won international prestige, especially in the United States, in the 1970s. He emphasized his decision in these words: "After many years of struggle in the commercial field, I am more and more discouraged with the world of comics. I believe that the time of *reconversion* has now come. New fields are opening to creators, in movies, in television, in video, in computers. Traditional comics, printed on paper, are breathing their last, choked by mounting costs, by speculators, and by the lack of readers. There exists without a doubt an enormous potential within the ranks of graphic artists, and I believe we should all pull together to save our world from the destruction that, I fear, is close at hand." Following his convictions, Maroto has in recent times devoted himself to painting and to works of illustration.

In reality the painter's spirit has always animated Maroto, along with his fondness for the themes of science fiction, fantasy, horror, and, above all, "sword-and-sorcery." When, in the late 1960s, Maroto stopped churning out works on command and turned to more personal creations, what surprised readers was his ability to express new ideas in terms of page composition and design, all of them approached from a unique point of view. At the same time his instinct for plastic beauty led him to all kinds of inspirational sources (painting, sculpture, illustration, comics, etc.) which he absorbed into his own neo-romantic and baroque style.

His graphic skills were brilliantly displayed in the series *Cinco por Infinito* (title means "Five for Infinity"), on a science-fiction theme, initially produced as a team effort, and taken exclusively over by Maroto after the fifth episode. The series started publication in 1967 and was given a color version in the pages of the magazine *Dracula* in 1971. It obtained the Academy of Comic Book Artists Award for its Mexican version, retitled *Legionarios del Espacio.* Also in 1971 *Dracula* published in full color Maroto's sword-and-sorcery series *Wolff.* In the meantime the artist had produced *La tumba de los dioses* (title means "The Tomb of the Gods") in 1969, a series of fantastic variations on mythical or legendary themes, and *Dax el guerrero* (1971), which finalized his identification with the sword-and-sorcery

genre. His prestige in this field led him to work for Marvel Comics Group in the United States on some of their fantasy comic-book titles.

The publishing company that contributed most to the appreciation of Maroto's work in the United States, however, was Warren through its comic magazines *Eerie, Creepy, Vampirella* and *1984* (later changed to *1994*), to which the artist contributed numerous short stories. Among Maroto's works of the 1980s special mention should be made of *Prison Ship/Diana Jacklighter, Manhuntress,* a science-fiction series on scripts by Bruce Jones, published in *1994.*

As for *Dax the Warrior,* it appeared in the pages of *Eerie:* the different episodes were later collected in a special issue of the magazine (No. 59). Other collections of Maroto's work appeared in *Creepy* No. 82, *Vampirella* No. 107, and *Eerie* No. 112. In 1984 the comic book *The Zero Patrol,* published by Continuity Comics, started publication of the American version of *Cinco por Infinito.*

BIOGRAPHICAL/CRITICAL SOURCES: The World Encyclopedia of Comics, Chelsea House, 1976; *Historia de los Comics,* Toutain, Barcelona, 1983.

— *Sketch by Javier Coma*

* * *

MATTINGLY, David B. 1956-

PERSONAL: Born June 29, 1956, in Fort Collins, Colo.; son of John W. (an inventor) and Phyllis (a homemaker; maiden name Greene) Mattingly; married Barbara Shainen (a wholesaler), May 26, 1978. *Education:* Art Center College of Design, B.A., 1978. *Home:* 1112 Bloomfield St., Hoboken, N.J. 07030.

CAREER: Production designer for Howard Ziehm, 1978; matte artist, 1978-81, head of matte department, 1981, Walt Disney Studios, Burbank, Calif.; freelance cover artist and illustrator, 1981—. *Awards, honors:* Nominated for Academy Award for special effects from the Academy of Motion Picture Arts and Sciences for the *Black Hole.*

FILMS: Production design on sequel to *Flesh Gordon,* never produced; matte work on *The Cat from Outer Space, Return of the Apple Dumpling Gang,* and *The Black Hole* (all for Walt Disney); supervised matte work on *The Devil and Max Devlin, The Watcher in the Woods,* and *Condorman* (all for Walt Disney).

SIDELIGHTS: David B. Mattingly's first interest in the fantastic started with looking at comic books as a small child. His boyhood reading included the works of Arthur C. Clarke, Isaac Asimov, and Robert Heinlein, and he became totally entranced with science-fiction and fantasy. He started to draw and paint at the age of eight, and developed a serious interest in becoming an illustrator in his early teens.

Upon graduation from high school he attended the Colorado Institute of Art in Denver, but then transferred to the Art Center College of Design in Pasadena, California. After graduation he went to work for Howard Ziehm, producer of the infamous X-rated science-fiction parody *Flesh Gordon*, and did production work on the never-made sequel.

From there, he went to Walt Disney Studios in Burbank, where he worked as a matte artist. During his three years there he assisted Harrison Ellenshaw, working on several Disney films, and was part of the special effects crew nominated for an Academy Award for *The Black Hole*.

At the age of twenty-two he was the youngest full union member matte artist in the history of the motion picture industry, and at twenty-four he became the youngest department head in the history of the Walt Disney Studios when he was promoted to head of the matte department. He supervised work on several Disney films, and also started doing freelance jobs. His first professionally-published work outside movies was the cover of the record album, *The Commodores' Greatest Hits*, for Motown Records. His first book cover, his main area of work at present, was on *A Wizard in Bedlam*, by Christoper Stasheff, published by DAW Books. At Disney Studies he began pre-production work on *TRON*, but found himself more interested in his freelance activities, and resigned from Disney Studios.

Mattingly has painted covers for virtually every major paperback publisher in the United States, including Ace, Berkley, Ballantine, DAW, Del Rey, Playboy Press, Tor, and Signet. His work has appeared in *Amazing Science Fiction, Cinefantastique, Cycle News, Isaac Asimov's Science Fiction Magazine*, the *Magazine of Fantasy & Science Fiction, Mediascene Preview*, and *Omni*. Other past clients include Lucasfilm Ltd., New World Pictures, Paramount Pictures, 20th Century Fox, Universal Pictures, Walt Disney Studios, Totco Oil Co., Galoob Toy Co., and Motown Records.

Mattingly is best known for his vivid illustrations of science-fictional concepts, and holds the unique distinction of being the only person known to have sold the movie rights to a poster, a piece entitled "Flying High" depicting skycycles over the American West. He has never lost his youthful enthusiasm for the genre, and makes a point to read every book he illustrates and to do his best to keep the story's feel and details accurate in his art.

* * *

McCAY, Winsor Zenic   1869(?)-1934
(Silas)

PERSONAL: Born September 26, 1869 (some sources say 1871), Spring Lake, Mich: son of Zenic (a lumberman) and Ann McCay; married Maude Dufour in 1891; children: Robert Winsor, Marian. Died July 26, 1934 in New York City. *Education:* Did not finish grade school.

CAREER: Sign painter and set designer, 1886-97; newspaper cartoonist, 1897-1934; animated filmmaker, 1909-20.

WRITINGS—All reprints of his comic strip work: *Little Nemo*, Nostalgia Press, 1972; *The Dreams of the Rarebit Fiend*, Dover, 1973; *Dream Days*, Hyperion Press, 1977.

Editorial cartoon by Winsor McCay, ca. 1910.

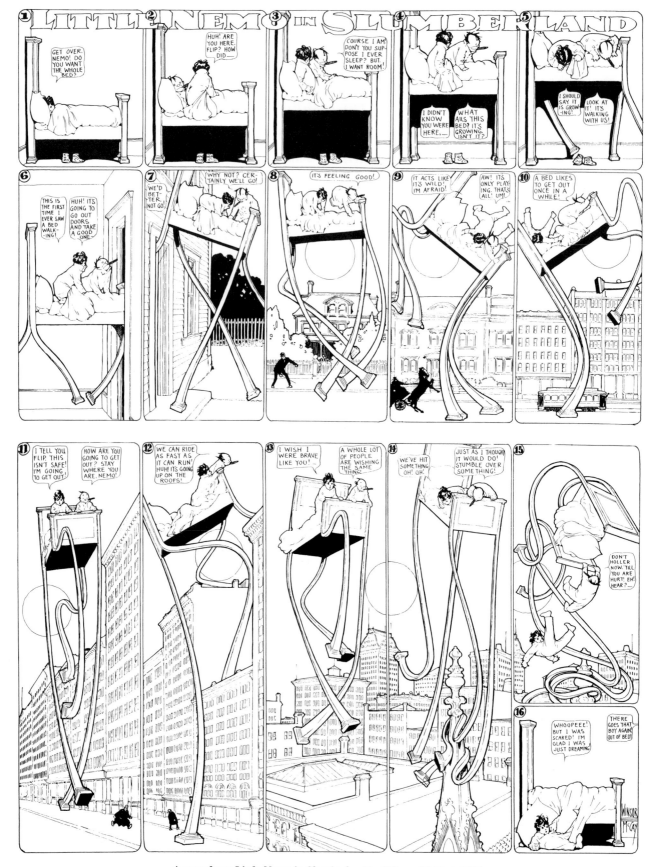

A page from *Little Nemo in Slumberland* by Winsor McCay, 1908.

FILMS—All animated cartoons: *Little Nemo*, 1909-11; *How a Mosquito Operates*, 1912; *Gertie, the Trained Dinosaur*, 1914; *The Centaurs*, 1916; *Gertie On Tour*, 1916; *Flip's Circus*, 1917; *The Pet*, 1918; *The Sinking of the Lusitania*, 1918; *The Flying House*, 1920.

SIDELIGHTS: Winsor McCay never completed grade school, but he received some rudimentary art instruction from a teacher named Godeson. His first professional job was painting signs for local stores. He then went to Chicago at age seventeen, drawing posters and taking more art lessons. In 1891 he moved to Cincinnati where he designed the murals for the Vine Street Museum. McCay started his long newspaper career first with the *Cincinnati Times-Star*, then with the *Commercial Tribune*. He eventually moved to the *Enquirer*; it was there, in 1903, that he created a weekly page filled with jungle denizens and wild animals cavorting amid a luxuriant scenery and a humorous text. *The Tales of the Jungle Imps* (as these pages were later to be called) was not yet a genuine comic strip, but already more than simple illustration.

At the invitation of James Gordon Bennett, head of the New York Herald Co., McCay came to New York toward the end of 1903 to work on the *Evening Telegram*. It is in the pages of the *Telegram* the following year that McCay's first comic strip creations made their appearance. The artist was well past thirty when he entered the medium. *Dull Care, Mr. Goodenough, Poor Jake* are early examples of McCay's comic series. They don't yet reveal the artist's full-blown talent, but in their detailed renditions, their skillful depictions of minute events they stylistically stand high above most of the comic features of the period.

It was later that year, with *Dream(s) of a Rarebit Fiend*, that McCay discovered at once his theme and his method. Signed "Silas" (as were all his *Telegram* efforts) it is an earnest attempt at exploring the depths of the unconscious and the substance of dreams. In their naked, spontaneous immediacy these dreams, or rather nightmares—caused by the inordinate ingestion of Welsh rarebits—exposed the roots of some of man's most universal fears. . . of death, of impotence, of madness, of social shame. *The Rarebit Fiend* originally appeared in black and white, as did its later permutations (*A Midsummer Night's Dream, It was Only a Dream*, etc.), but a color version later ran in the *New York Herald*.

The *Herald* was the *Telegram's* parent publication, and it was in its pages that McCay's striking color work was published as early as 1904. *Hungry Henrietta* was about a ravenous young girl who devoured everything in sight, while *Little Sammy Sneeze* concerned the cataclysmic sternutations of a little boy and the disasters they caused. In these early strips McCay displayed, along with an impressive sense of color and composition, a fine visual wit and the larger-than-life vision that remained his trademark all through his career.

One year later these early series were followed by *Little Nemo in Slumberland*, the artist's best known creation, and the one in which the dream theme was further explored and redefined. In his night wanderings Nemo is transported to the dream kingdom of Slumberland, where he meets King Morpheus and his daughter, the Princess. In her company and that of his further acolytes, the green-skinned Flip and Impy the cannibal (a leftover from the *Jungle Tales* days) he not only discovers the strange by-ways of Slumberland, but goes as far afield as the moon and the planet Mars.

In 1911 McCay left the Herald Co. and went over to William Randolph Hearst for whom he was to continue Little Nemo's adventures under the title *In the Land of Wonderful Dreams* until 1914, the same year that he also abandoned all his other strip series. For all practical purposes, and aside from a brief period in the 1920s when he revived *Little Nemo* again for the *Herald*, this marked the end of McCay's career in the comics. It had lasted almost exactly ten years.

In 1909, meanwhile, McCay had started a parallel career in animation, producing that same year *Little Nemo* (based on his strip), and later *How a Mosquito Operates*. *Gertie, the Trained Dinosaur* created a sensation when it was released in 1914. In 1918 McCay produced the first feature-length film cartoon, *The Sinking of the Lusitania*, and in 1920 his last work in the animation field, *The Flying House*, was released. In addition to his comic strips and his animated cartoons, he also did editorial cartoons of a conservative bent for the Hearst newspapers. They are much admired today for their draftsmanship and composition, but as means of persuasion they are rather flat and unmoving; while they would have been a credit to a lesser artist, they are dwarfed by McCay's achievements in animation and, above all, the comics.

It is for his comics that McCay is most admired; he is, by universal consent, the foremost master of the art. It has been said that he left no disciple, founded no school—but this is true only in the more literal sense. Certainly the sweep of his vision, the magnitude of his accomplishments awed his fellow cartoonists and discouraged imitation. McCay's genius lies in another direction: by liberating the comic strip from outmoded conventions of style and limited choices of inspiration he blazed new trails and paved the way for bold and unceasing experimentation. His example and his influence have ranged far and wide, in all periods and on every continent.

BIOGRAPHICAL/CRITICAL SOURCES: Coulton Waugh, *The Comics*, Macmillan, 1947; Stephen Becker, *Comic Art in America*, Simon & Schuster, 1959; *Redbook*, December, 1965; *New York Times*, February 13, 1966; *Arts*, April, 1966; *The World Encyclopedia of Comics*, Chelsea House, 1976; *The World Encyclopedia of Cartoons*, Chelsea House, 1980.

OBITUARY SOURCE: New York Times, July 27, 1934.

—*Sketch by Maurice Horn*

* * *

McMULLAN, James (Burroughs) 1934-

PERSONAL: Born June 14, 1934, in Tsingtao, China; son of James Cornwall (an army officer) and Rose (a bookkeeper; maiden name Fenwick) McMullan; married Karhtryn Hall

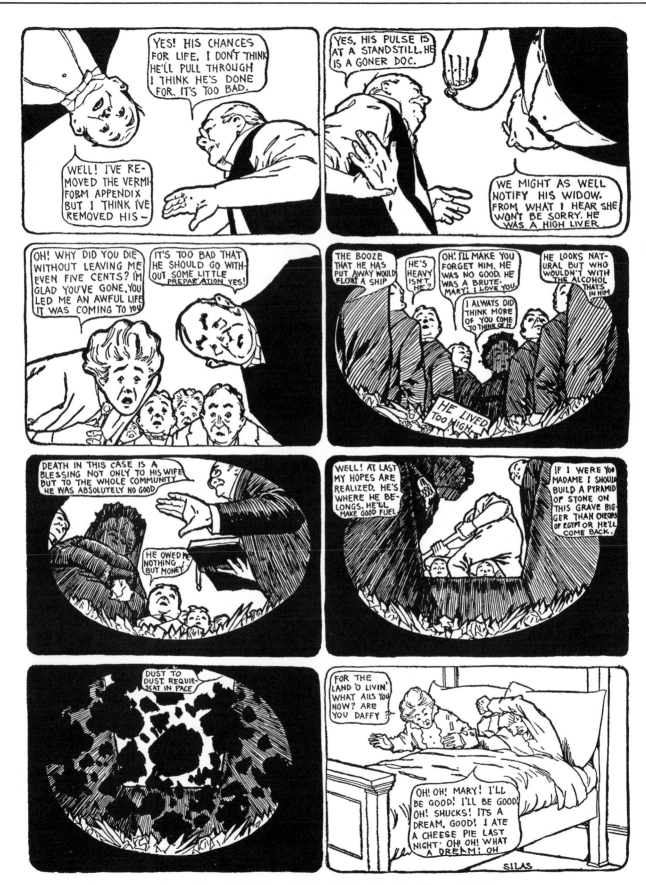

A page from *The Dream of the Rarebit Fiend* by Silas (Winsor McCay).

JAMES McMULLAN

(a writer), June 10, 1979; children: Leigh Fenwick. *Education:* Pratt Institute, B.F.A., 1958. *Politics:* Democrat. *Religion:* Episcopalian. *Studio:* Visible Studio Inc., 99 Lexington Ave., New York, N.Y. 10016.

CAREER: Freelance illustrator, 1958-65; designer and illustrator, Push Pin Studio, New York City, 1965-67; owner, designer, and illustrator, Visible Studio, New York City, 1967—; instructor, School of Visual Arts, 1971—. *Member:* Society of Illustrators; American Institute of Graphic Arts (director, 1974-76; vice-president, 1976-77; president's advisory committee, 1985); American Illustration (on advisory committee); Graphic Artists Guild. *Awards, honors:* Silver and Gold Medals, Society of Illustrators, 1981; many other awards.

WRITINGS: Revealing Illustrations, Watson-Guptill, 1981. Contributor to *New York, New West, Sports Illustrated, Rolling Stone,* and other publications.

FILMS: "Christmas 1914" segment of *Simple Gifts* (an animated film produced for Public Broadcasting System), R.O. Blechman, 1978.

EXHIBITIONS—One-man shows: Parsons Institute of Design, New York City, 1975; American Institute of Graphic Arts, New York City, 1977; Visual Arts Museum, New York City, 1978; John Jermain Library, Sag Harbor, N.Y., 1978; "Revealing Illustrations," Rizzoli Gallery, New York City, 1981; Society of Illustrators, New York City, 1982; Art Center of Design, Los Angeles, 1982; Giraffics Gallery, Sag Harbor, 1982 and 1983.

Group shows: "Push Pin Retrospective," Mead Library of Ideas, New York City, 1969, and Musee des Arts Decoratifs, Paris, France, 1970; "Zeichner Illustration Graphik," Kunstsalon Wolfberg, Zurich, Switzerland, 1970; "A Century of American Illustration," Brooklyn Museum, Brooklyn, N.Y., 1972; Pratt Alumni Show, Society of Illustrators, New York City, 1974; Maps Show, Museum of Natural History, New York City, 1977; "The Artist as Journalist," Society of Illustrators, New York City, 1977; "Design and Illustration—USA," Iran American Society, Tehran, Iran, 1978;

"Twenty Years of Award Winners," Society of Illustrators, New York City, 1978; "A Sports Illustrated Retrospective," Spectrum Gallery, New York City, 1979.

"Best of Illustrators," American Institute of Graphic Arts, New York City, 1980; "The American Illustrator," Ellis Gallery, New York City, 1980; "Great Illustrators of Our Time," Rizzoli Gallery, New York City, 1981; "Images of Labor" (a national traveling show), 1981; "Directions in Graphic Design," William Paterson College, Wayne, N.J., 1982; "Persuasive Persuasion," Mercer County Community College, Trenton, N.J., 1982; "Contemporary American Graphic Design and Illustration," Butler Institute of American Art, Youngstown, Ohio, 1982; Inaugural Exhibition, South Hampton Community College, South Hampton, N.Y., 1983.

WORK IN PROGRESS: Drawing from Life, a book on drawing, scheduled for 1986; a series of greeting cards on New York subjects to be published by Visible Press, a subdivision of Visible Studio.

SIDELIGHTS: His assignment was to interview and photograph the habituees of a Brooklyn disco with the reporter Nik Cohn for the magazine *New York.* James McMullan prepared for it with the meticulous care that had already gained him a reputation as one of the best editorial illustrators in the business. During the course of four weekend visits to various discos, he shot twenty rolls of 35mm film, recording the environment and its denizens in order to build up a working stock of information upon which to base his paintings. But as he edited the contact sheets, he began to see his snapshots as "not merely visual notes, but a kind of emotional souvenir as well." The sense of isolation and suspended anticipation that hung so heavily over the disinvolved dancers, indefinable to him at the time of observation, now became apparent, triggered by the groupings, actions, and expressions he perceived frozen on his film exposures. This discovery, he recalled later, filled him with a new kind of creative emotion.

Poster for the Hampton Classic, 1982. (© James McMullan. Reprinted with permission.)

The energy that this emotion liberated inspired not only a rethinking of his style and technique, but his ultimate departure from the fluid "lyrical surrealism" for which his work had been celebrated. The result was a series of highly realistic direct quotations in watercolor from eight selected photographs to accompany Cohn's now-famous piece, "Tribal Rites of the New Saturday Night" (which served as the basis for the movie *Saturday Night Fever*) and, more importantly, the introduction of a counterpart in illustration to the "new journalism" found in publications such as *New York, New West* and *Rolling Stone*; a movement a subsequent American Institute of Graphic Artists show would call "Socio-Journalism" and describe as "incisive social commentary on various aspects of American life."

Oddly enough, this incisive commentator on American life is the grandson of an Anglican missionary and son of a peripatetic Anglo-Colonial businessman, who was born in China, and spent his formative years there, as well as in India and Canada. He came to the United States in 1951 at the age of seventeen, and became a citizen eight years later. He attended Brooklyn's Pratt Institute, from which he received his B.F.A. in 1958. McMullan quickly established a name for himself in his adopted country. By the mid-1960s, an article in *Print* proclaimed the then thirty one-year-old artist's work "intensely personal, serious, and often brooding" in its attempt "to combine realistically detailed objects with fragmentary, disconnected images in order to achieve a feeling of tension . . . a highly original fusion of photograph and illustration." The product, perhaps, of a man making the transition from one world to another, but still suspended between east and west.

His Americanization as an artist might be said to have taken place between 1965 and 1968, during a tenure with the Push Pin Studio group. Although he was already a successful freelancer, he accepted the invitation of his friend, studio director Seymour Chwast, to sign on with Push Pin because, as he explained: "They were the most influential group of American artists, and being there then was a much better way of deriving from them whatever was meaningful to me than being on the outside." In practical terms his stint with Push Pin taught him that he could turn out more work under pressure than he had imagined he could, and that advertising work could be stimulating if approached in the proper spirit. As an artist he profited from the opportunity to absorb the senses of design, organization, and clarity that were hallmarks of Push Pin's work. At the end of his valuable apprenticeship, he established his own graphic design house (Visible Studio), and embarked on an influential career both as designer and teacher.

One of the principles he has espoused in his own work and as a teacher is what he calls "freedom through constriction." The "stretching esthetic" in art serves the student only up to a point, he argues; beyond that point the aspiring artist should begin to focus on what he or she does best and concentrate on refining the skills needed within those limits. As he explains this refining process, "It's like taking a stick and scraping a big square on the ground. It means you have to stay within the limits of the square, but you can dig deep as hell." In his own case, adherence to this principle has had a demonstrably profound effect on his work, both in style and in technique. Thus his spontaneously surreal juxtaposi-

tions fluidly portrayed in watercolors and based on impulse sketches gave way by the mid 1970s to a much more controlled realism. McMullan's efforts toward refining his own talents led him to abandon his early spontaneity in favor of a compositional technique he has likened to cartography: "I see the surface as an elaborate, geographic landmass to be plotted. There are islands of color. Everything is thought out with discrete precision."

A crucial methodological element in this radical alteration was McMullan's increasing, almost cybernetic reliance on the 35mm camera. "When I shoot photos," he stated in a 1981 issue of *Graphis*, "the camera becomes my research assistant, recording much more than I could if I drew from real life. Later, when I look at the contact sheets, I find details that I didn't see at the time, and invariably, certain exposures rekindle certain feelings of mood and atmosphere that caused me to take the shot. These nuances always seem to find their way into the finished picture." The process by which they do so is no less important than their inspiration. As McMullan explains if there is now an emotional synergy in the very act of painting: "Each stroke has an abstract vitality that has to do with the actual movement of the paint, and of the brush, and of my physical movements in the act of painting . . . It's the coming together of these abstract

Poster for the School of Visual Arts, ca. 1980. (© James McMullan. Reprinted with permission.)

A sketch of African life, ca. 1979. (© James McMullan. Printed with permission.)

things that amounts to either the effect of some realism or the effect of some emotion." Although he borrows various compositional features from photography—close cropping, freeze framing, aerial perspective, selective depth of focus, and strobe-flash lighting—he also used obvious brush strokes and deliberate violations of the borders of his image area to give the resulting work a peculiar quality, caught between photographic realism and painterly caprice.

His "socio-journalistic" pieces lack, perhaps, the superficial extemporaneity of his early work; but if there is a form of spontaneity that proceeds from deeper considerations, it comes clearly to the fore. An example is the cover he did for the July/August, 1981 issue of *Graphis*, a wonderfully evocative still life of a child's transparent plastic water pistol against the concentric circles of a raspberry and wash-blue target sheet. He chose the subject because he liked the shape of the toy and its yellow-green color, and because it used the same "ammunition" as the watercolorist. "Originally," he explained, "I had meant to cover the target with watermarks and streaks as though it had been hit by jets from the pistol; but as the painting progressed I became much more interested in the levels of transparency and refraction in the plastic gun and the water it contained. Finally, the glow of light from the pistol became the central drama of the image for me." And indeed, he did catch the shimmery, iridescent quality of the object, as the editor observed in his note on the cover art: "Much of McMullan's art consists in this ability to evoke, out of what is at a glance an unpretentious surface realism, the deeper strata of significance that turn a mere picture into a mental image."

BIOGRAPHICAL/CRITICAL SOURCES: Print, March-April, 1965; *Communication Arts*, May-June, 1974; Carol Stevens, "True to Life," *Print*, July-August, 1977; Michael Patrick Hearn, *The Art of the Broadway Poster*, Ballantine, 1980; Philip B. Meggs, *A History of Graphic Design*, Van

Nostrand, 1981; Lanny Sommese, "James McMullan," *Graphis*, July-August, 1981; Rose de Neve, "The Art of James McMullan: A Psychological Imperative," *American Artist*, July, 1982; *Who's Who in Graphic Art*, Vol. 2, De Clivo Press, 1983; Seymour Chwast and Steve Heller, editors, *The Art of New York*, Abrams, 1984.

—*Sketch by Richard Calhoun*

*　*　*

MEYER, Gary 1934-

PERSONAL: Surname is pronounced as in "wire"; born May 13, 1934, in Boonville, Mo.; son of Milton Simon (a service station owner, now retired) and Anna (a housewife; maiden name Davis) Meyer; married Hiroko Julie Ii, February 26, 1960; children: Allan. *Education:* Art Center College of Design, Bachelor of Professional Arts (with honors), 1959. *Home and studio:* 227 W. Channel Rd., Santa Monica, Calif. 90402.

CAREER: President, Graphics West Inc., El Segundo, Calif., 1964-65; motion picture production illustrator, Universal Studios, Universal City, Calif., 1965-68; designer-illustrator, Macco (amusement park design firm), Newport Beach, Calif., 1968-70; vice-president, Recretects Inc. (amusement park design firm), Costa Mesa, Calif., 1970-71; freelance illustrator, 1971—. Documentary artist for the U.S. Air Force. *Military service:* U.S. Marine Corps, 1952-55, served in Korea; held rank of sergeant; received Presidential Unit Citation and American Defense Service Ribbon. *Member:* Society of Illustrators, Society of Illustrators of Los Angeles, Society of Art Center Alumni (secretary).

AWARDS, HONORS: Awards for color illustration from the Technical Illustration Management Association (TIMA), 1962, for Saturn missile illustration and for painting of the moon; 1963, for painting of the vertical assembly building for the Saturn/Apollo project. Certificates of merit from *Industrial Photography*, 1963, for title art for *The Fastest Draw in the West;* from Industrial Film Producers of America, 1964, for *The Apollo Mission;* from Illustration West, 1965, for illustration of Honda race car; from Society of Art Center Alumni (SACA) annual shows, 1975, for period painting for film *At Long Last Love*, 1978, for movie poster for *The Deep* and for bronze sculpture "Roaring Head," 1979, for poster illustrations for "Star Squadron" and for "Dracula."

Certificates of merit from SACA annual show, 1980, for "Chicago" album cover illustration; from Communication Arts Society of Los Angeles (CASLA), 1980, for "Chicago." Also for "Chicago," 1980: Best of Category Award from Society of Illustrators of Los Angeles; award of excellence from *Communication Arts;* certificate of distinction from *Art Direction.* Certificates from Illustrators 22, 1980, for "Dracula" poster; from *Art Direction*, 1980, for "Deep Trouble" cover art for *New West;* from Illustrators 22, 1981, for "Chicago"; from SACA annual show, 1981, for Polygram movie poster and for two illustrations in Levi's calendar; from *Art Direction*, 1982, for illustration for Ray Bradbury

"Fathead," a sculpture. (© 1981, Gary Meyer. Printed with permission.)

poem "Ode to the Quick Computer"; from Illustration West, 1982, for album cover "Vendetta," for movie posters for *The Thing* and *The Boat*, and for Bradbury illustration; from Illustrators 23, 1982, for "Olde English 800" illustration. Three awards from Society of Illustrators of Los Angeles, 1983, for the painting "Visicity"; Key Arts Award from *Hollywood Reporter*, 1983, for *The Boat;* Beyond Bronze Award from North American Sculpture Exhibition, 1983, for bronze sculpture "Fathead." Certificates from *Art Direction*, 1983, for movie poster for *Night Crossing;* from Illustration West, 1983, for "Visicity," for movie poster and ad for *Endangered Species,* for "Beautiful Performers" illustration for Hughes Helicopters, and for MGM movie illustration; from *Art Direction*, 1984, for movie poster for *Mutant;* from Society of Illustrators, 1984, for "Visicity"; from Illustration West, 1984, for *Mutant* poster, for unpublished painting for "Blue Thunder Helicopter Chase" board game, for illustration of Apache helicopter, for movie poster for *The Lonely Guy*, for *Saturn 3* movie ad, for drawing "Long Head Study" for Apache illustration, for ad illustration for "Western Microtechnology," and for art direction of "Long Head Study." Silver medal in advertising category from Illustration West, 1985, for "Local Presence, National Clout" ad for Merrill Lynch Realty.

FILMS: The Apollo Mission, North American Aviation (Rockwell), 1963, a film made up totally of illustrations.

EXHIBITIONS: One-man show, Burbank Board of Education, 1952; J. Walter Thompson, Chicago, 1974. Participated in collective shows: "Illustration West," Society of Illustrators of Los Angeles, 1964, 1982, 1983, and 1984; "Illustrators," Society of Illustrators, New York, 1980-84; North American Sculpture Exhibition, 1981 and 1983.

WORK IN PROGRESS: Sculpture series of five *Life Masks,* completion expected in 1986; a series of paintings for the U.S. Air Force resulting from a trip to Viet Nam in 1968.

SIDELIGHTS: Gary Meyer wrote to *CGA:* "I am motivated by the work itself. Circumstances important to my career were parental encouragement, my training at Art Center College of Design, and the support of family and friends. My general views on things I consider vital such as peace, poverty, prosperity, crime, and the future are that things are working the way they are supposed to work. The universe is self-balancing."

GARY MEYER

Gary Meyer's award-winning album cover for "Chicago." (© 1979, CBS Records.)

The artist has had a long and varied career, as well as a highly successful one. The biography prepared for "Illustration West" perhaps sums it up best: "Gary Meyer has been involved in technical and commercial illustration, graphic arts and sculpture since 1960. During this time he has produced paintings for a diverse group of clients, including major motion picture and record companies, Levi's, Apple Computers, Hughes Helicopters, Garrett Corp., *New West* magazine, and others. He has served as design consultant on a number of motion pictures, including continuity art for *Star Wars;* produced sculptures of 15 entertainment personalities for wax museums; and designed the train for the *Supertrain* TV series."

BIOGRAPHICAL/CRITICAL SOURCES: Who's Who in California, 13th edition, 1981-82, *Who's Who Historical Society; Outstanding American Illustrators Today*, 1984; *Outstanding American illustrators Today Book II*, 1985; *Japan Creators' Association Annual 5*, Illustration Showcase, 1985.

MOORE, Ray(mond S.) 1905-1984

OBITUARY NOTICE: Born 1905, in Montgomery City, Mo.; died January 13, 1984, in Kirkwood, Mo.; cremated. Cartoonist and illustrator, Moore was the first illustrator of the famous adventure strip *The Phantom*, on scripts by Lee Falk. The Phantom is a mysterious, hooded figure of justice who maintains peace in the jungle with the help of his tame wolf, Devil, and his private army, the Jungle Patrol. The strip is still running today, still written by Falk, and drawn by Seymour (Sy) Barry; but Moore, who drew the feature from its inception in 1936 till 1942, and then again in 1945-47, is generally considered the definitive artist of *The Phantom*. He stopped drawing the feature following a grave injury (some sources say a stroke), and from 1947 till the day of his death he lived in obscurity. "The first artist to draw the strip," Maurice Horn wrote in his introduction to *The Prisoner of the Himalayas*, "was Ray Moore who brought to this feature fine draftsmanship and an imaginative yet unobtrusive use of camera techniques. Moore undoubtedly was the best artist to draw *The Phantom*, and the initial success of the strip owes much to his talent." The outpouring of nostalgic reminiscences and the number of obituary notices that marked Moore's passing are evidence that the artist might have been gone for the last thirty-seven years of his life, but that he had not been forgotten.

BIOGRAPHICAL/CRITICAL SOURCES: Famous Artists and Writers, King Features Syndicate, 1946; Maurice Horn, "The History of the Phantom," introduction to *The Prisoner of the Himalayas*, Nostalgia Press, 1969; *The World Encyclopedia of Comics*, Chelsea House, 1976.

OBITUARY SOURCES: Washington Post, January 16, 1984; *New York Times*, January 17, 1984; *Chicago Tribune*, January 17, 1984; *Newsweek*, January 30, 1984.

*   *   *

MORGAN, Jacqui 1939-

PERSONAL: First name is pronounced Jackie; born February 22, 1939, in New York, N.Y.; daughter of Henry (a musician and salesman) and Emily (a bookkeeper, maiden name Cook) Morganstern; married Onnig Kalfayan, April 23, 1967 (divorced, 1972); no children. *Education:* Pratt Institute, B.F.A., 1960; Hunter College, M.A., 1977. *Home and studio:* 315 E. 58th St., New York, N.Y. 10022.

CAREER: Textile designer, M. Lowenstein & Sons, New York, N.Y., 1960-61; textile designer, Fruit of the Loom, New York, N.Y., 1962; stylist and studio director, Au Courant, Inc., New York, N.Y., 1964-65; freelance illustrator and designer, 1966—. Adjunct associate professor, Pratt Institute, Brooklyn, N.Y., 1977—. *Member:* Graphic Artists Guild (board of directors, 1975-80); Society of Illustrators.

AWARDS, HONORS: Recipient of over a hundred awards from such organizations as the Society of Illustrators, Federal Design Council, VI Warsaw International Poster Bienniale, ASIFA East (animation design) Levi Design Competition, Communication Arts Magazine, American Institute of Graphic Arts, New York Art Directors Club. Held a scholarship Pratt Graphic Center; named to the Hunter Alumni Association Hall of Fame.

JACQUI MORGAN

EXHIBITIONS—One-woman shows: Society of Illustrators, New York City, 1977; Art Directors Club, New York City, 1978; Gallerie Nowe Miasto, Warsaw, Poland, 1978; Gallerie Baumeister, Munich, West Germany, 1978; Hansen-Feurman Gallery, New York City, 1980; Gallery 99, Florida, 1981; Linden Gallery, New York City, 1981; Arras Gallery, New York City, 1982.

Group shows: Museum of Contemporary Crafts, New York City, 1975; "The American Image," Smithsonian Institution, Washington, D.C., 1976; Museum of Warsaw, Poland, 1976 and 1978; Museum of Tokyo, Japan, 1979. Represented in the permanent poster collection of the Smithsonian Institution.

WORK IN PROGRESS: A workshop book on reflective surfaces and high-tech in watercolor, presenting a unique methodology; *Watercolor for Illustration*, scheduled for publication by Prentice-Hall in 1986.

SIDELIGHTS: Jacqui Morgan began her post-collegiate career in the field of textile design because she reportedly considered it a "purer" discipline than most other commercial applications of art. After working for two years in that milieu and learning the craft aspects of design, she embarked on an extended period of travel, visiting Africa, the Middle

East, and Europe, to absorb artistic and cultural influences. Returning to New York City, she was present when the Beatles/Carnaby Street-inspired "British Invasion" established its earliest beach-head on the Lower East Side of Manhattan in the mid-1960s and released the energies responsible for the psychedelic culture, the "Age of Aquarius," and the Op, Pop, and Conceptual Art movements (represented most notably in the work of Peter Max and Andy Warhol). It was an environment that she found extremely congenial.

By training a serious watercolorist (her teacher at Pratt has been Richard Lindner), by temperament a fantasist, and by experience well grounded in both the exotic and the surreal, Morgan soon found a way to combine her artistic seriousness with a highly commercial style, thanks to the new currents in popular culture. One of her first successes, in fact, was a 1967 poster celebrating the popular East Village night spot, the Electric Circus. In short order, however, her "look" attracted commercial accounts of a far more mainstream sort and she was soon established as one of the top young illustrators of the period. In addition to her burgeoning career as an advertising and editorial artist, Morgan with her friend Maggie Skipper created a line of clothing, featuring her handpainted, silkscreened, or airbrushed designs. (This project ultimately fell victim to Morgan's own gift for capturing contemporary notice; as she complained in 1975, mass marketers could knock off her designs faster than she could produce her own limited editions.)

"Miss America" exhibition poster, figure made of cast paper. (© 1980, Jacqui Morgan. Reprinted with permission.)

The elements that contributed to her relatively rapid emergence as a top commercial illustrator were her color sensibility (vibrantly translucent aquarelles), a predilection for "love and peace" images like flowers and birds, and a shrewd understanding of the commercial marketplace. During this period her oeuvre was notable more for its consistent appeal to the then current cult of nature and shunning of industrialism than for its variety. Although Morgan flatly rejected the label "feminine" often attached to her work, that was not an inappropriate way to describe the flowing, sensual, romantic imagery that dominated her output into the 1970s. She herself implicitly admitted a limited iconography in a 19764 profile in *American Artist* by observing that in putting her particular "look" through various commercial and fine-art permutations, "it evolves more. . . and by the time it comes back to me through illustration, it's somewhere ahead of where it started." And whatever the critical reservations, there was no denying her commercial success. Indeed by the early 1970s she was able to dispense with the services of a representative and began negotiating her own accounts with some of the biggest names—AT&T, IBM, Procter & Gamble—in the advertising universe.

If a combination of technical proficiency and a unique focus—the double image—was in no small part responsible for Morgan's initial fashion-ability, the innate intelligence which fueled her commercial design sense was bound, ultimately, to result in some distinctive work. This seems to have occurred in the late 1970s, when her ideas began to take precedence over the mechanical aspects of their execution—" a perfect computer" one critic once called her—and she began consciously to work more as a "pure" than as an "applied" artist. As she told her *American Artist* profiler, the

The famous Electric Circus poster. (© 1967, Electric Circus of New York.)

problems posed by pure art were a lot more diffuse and hard to pin down than those associated with working for a commercial account; therefore they stretched her imagination more. At that same time Morgan started exhibiting widely, here and abroad. Of her one-woman show in Warsaw, the noted Polish critic Szymon Bojko wrote: "At the precise and delicate base of Allusion and Illusion, satire and humor, the exhibition of Jacqui Morgan reveals deep pure tones of authentic expression."

This success was celebrated by *Graphis* (September/October, 1978), when it featured her work on its cover and included within a profile and portfolio of her latest pieces. Noting her reputation as a back-to-nature nostalgist, the critic G.G. Snyder found in her recent work a "satirical vein, a revealing eye and a flair for fashion" that had not heretofore been apparent. Having in the past been preoccupied with the use of the double image in her two-dimensional illustration (i.e., bird plumage as hair, flowers as lips, etc.) in order to create a third dimension for the eye, she now decided to go spatially into the round and find new uses and looks for objects of commonplace origin. The most striking of these efforts was her alteration of model heads for the display of wigs—a plastic egg on a stalk-like neck—into exotic fashion statements, inspired by cultures from North Africa to Paris to the Bronx. Adorning these items with various colors of eye shadow, sequins, spangles and accessories collected in the

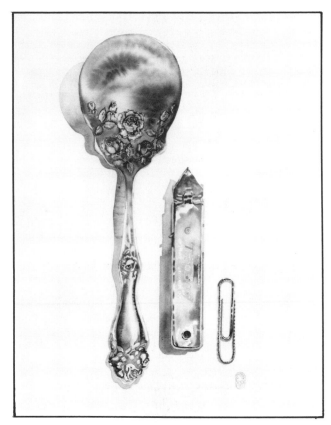

Various metal implements, design. (© 1985, Jacqui Morgan. Printed with permission.)

course of her extended travels, she made of each "a cult image. . . something rich and strange," in an attempt to show how far fashion had subverted the traditional notions of beauty.

Beside these assemblages, the accompanying *Graphis* portfolio included her paintings of women on the inner soles of various vintage openwork sandals and pumps, representing with a sly humor her fantasy of its former wearer—from nineteenth century ingenues to 1960 Hollywood starlets. In two dimensions, this new humor was evident in her spoofing of the image of women conveyed by such magazines as *Cosmopolitan* and *Officiel* by replacing the heads of cover models with reproductions of china doll heads, complete with eyes of cerulean blue and pursed rosebud mouths (documented in a portfolio in *Novum Gebrauchsgraphik,* September, 1978)—certainly representing an antidote to some of her own highly romanticized evocations of the female form during the 1960s. Morgan has also designed a fifty-feet square floor mosaic for a church and inter-faith center in Denver, Colorado.

Most recently, she has been concentrating on the painterly aspects of watercolors (she has just finished a book on the subject and is at work on another), working for a select number of high visibility commercial accounts, and teaching at Pratt Institute and in various workshops here and abroad. In her own work, Morgan continues to strive "toward lessening the distance between fine and commercial art" in her belief (first stated in *Graphis* in 1978) that "society cannot be so stratified that an artist cannot be a designer."

Poster for *The Tap Dance Kid*. (© 1983, Jacqui Morgan. Reprinted with permission.)

BIOGRAPHICAL/CRITICAL SOURCES: Print, November-December, 1970; *American Artist,* May, 1974; *Print,* September/October, 1975; *Novum Gebrauchsgraphik,* September, 1978; *Graphis,* No. 196, September/October, 1978; *Who's Who in Graphic Art,* De Clivo Press, 1980; *Today's Art and Graphics,* Vol. 29, No. 12, 1981.

—*Sketch by Richard Calhoun*

* * *

MORIN, James 1953-
(Jim Morin)

PERSONAL: Born January 30, 1953, in Washington, D.C.; son of Charles H. (a lawyer) and Elizabeth (Donnelly) Morin; married Danielle Flood (a writer), September 5, 1981; children: "None (yet)." *Education:* Suffield Academy, 1969-71; John Cass School of Art, London Polytech, London, England, 1974; Syracuse University, B.F.A. 1976. *Home:* Coral Gables, Fla. *Office: Miami Herald,* 1 Herald Plaza, Miami, Fla. 33101. *Agent:* Betty Marks, 176 E. 77th St., New York, N.Y. 10021.

CAREER: Editorial cartoonist and staff artist, *Beaumont Enterprise Journal,* Beaumont, Tex., 1976-77; editorial cartoonist, *Richmond Times-Dispatch,* Richmond, Va., 1977-78; editorial cartoonist, *Miami Herald,* Miami, Fla., 1978—. Syndicated by King Features, 1985—. *Member:* Association of American Editorial Cartoonists; Phi Kappa Psi fraternity. *Awards, honors:* Overseas Press Club Award, 1979, for Best Foreign Affairs Cartoon during 1978; Overseas Press Club Citation for Excellence, 1981.

WRITINGS: (Contributor) *Best Editorial Cartoons of the Year,* Pelican, 1978-1979; *Famous Cats,* Morrow, 1982; *Jim Morin's Guide to Birds,* Morrow, 1985.

EXHIBITIONS: "Morin Political Cartoons," Portobello Arts Gallery, Coral Gables, Fla., 1982.

SIDELIGHTS: Born into a substantial middle-class professional family, Jim Morin approached his career in art with the calm deliberation of a professional. He started drawing cartoons at the age of seven, tracing comic books a first, but soon developing his own ideas in gag cartoons and strips. His first inspirations were animated cartoons he saw on television, especially those of Warner Brothers and Hanna-Barbera. An early favorite artist was Bob Clampett, whose *Beany and Cecil* show inspired Morin to dream of animation as a career. He still thinks longingly of working as an animator, and hopes the genre may someday be effectively adapted to political cartooning.

Morin has been roundly educated in art. He transferred to the College of Arts at Syracuse University, where he majored in painting—a background he regards as invaluable to his present work. While at Syracuse, he went to London to study art, and when he returned began doing cartoons for the university newspaper at a rate of three or four a week. Gradually, cartooning became his main love, and he decided to make a career of it.

For a year after graduating in 1976, Morin freelanced and sought a position as a staff cartoonist. A brief stint with the *Beaumont Enterprise and Journal* doing editorial cartoons, spot caricatures, illustrations, maps, and some page layouts, ended when his editor proved too independent for the publisher, and Morin moved on to the *Richmond Times-Dispatch.* In 1978 he joined the *Miami Herald* as editorial cartoonist; he also draws occasional spot illustrations for the op-ed page. He values his editorial freedom there, and has built a solid following in Miami as a vigorous champion of causes and a free spirit.

Morin is motivated primarily by what he considers the main prerequisite for good editorial cartoon ideas—outrage. His tightly drawn, detailed style reveals considerable intensity of feeling, and while he has outraged his share of readers in the Miami area, he has also won the applause of many. His cartoons, syndicated nationally since February, 1985, by King Features, have been widely reprinted by such diverse publications as *Time, Newsweek, U.S. News and World Report,* the *San Francisco Examiner,* the *Washington Post,* the *Los Angeles Times,* and about sixty other papers. The range of political stances reflected in this list of periodicals is no accident: Morin's own views range as widely, and he cannot be pinned down with any convenient political label. He describes himself as "conservative-liberal, liberal-conservative."

Working in an office in the *Herald* newsroom cluttered with books, Morin has covered his walls with clippings, prints, and posters. Works by cartoonists Oliphant and Feiffer hang there alongside those of such artists as George Grosz, Ronald Searle, Van Gogh, Klee, Rembrandt, Vermeer, Jasper Johns, Soutine, and Audubon. Morin claims that everyone in this eclectic gallery has had an influence on him. His first model and inspiration as a cartoonist, though, was Honore Daumier, and it was Thomas Nast whom he first admired as a political cartoonist. He cites also the influence of cartoonists George Booth, Duncan MacPherson, Saul Steinberg, and Sempe and the graphics of Toulouse-Lautrec.

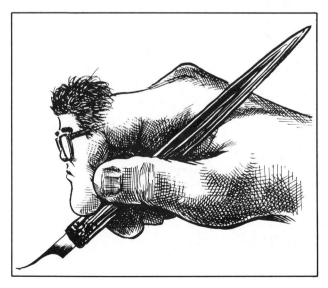

Self-portrait of Jim Morin. (© 1985, *Miami Herald.* Reprinted with permission.)

The pen-and-ink draughtsmen who most impress him have been the American illustrator A. B. Frost, and the Germans Adolf Oberlander, Heinrich Kley, and Ludwig Meidner, whose caricatures he terms "absolutely amazing."

Morin works very methodically, and his cartoons show the care he puts into them. He uses a Windsor-Newton brush, series 7, #4, and only Esterbrook pentips. For lettering he uses Speedball C-2, 3, and 4 pens, following the lead of another of his heroes, Walt Kelly, because they give him both range and control.

His first book, *Famous Cats*, was a collection of caricatures of celebrities done as cats, conflating their names and faces into feline modes. Well received even by some of the subjects it caricatured, it was widely reviewed by such newspapers as *USA Today* and the *Washington Post*, though it has not been a great financial success.

Morin's love of birds revealed by the Audubon print on his office wall led him to do a collection of watercolors, *Jim Morin's Guide to Birds*, for the same publisher in 1985. The nine months he spent on the sixty paintings it contains (while doing five political cartoons a week for the *Herald*) were "a revelation" to him, and he hopes to do more work in this medium in the future. The pictures are done in a whimsical style which incorporates sometimes racy visual puns on the birds' names. To the artist's surprise, the book was selected even before publication for distribution by the North-American Book Club.

Described by *Cartoonist Profiles* as "one of America's brightest young cartoonists," Jim Morin sees and sets no limits on his horizon. His active and versatile mind ranges through all areas of his field, and new projects are always bubbling to its surface.

BIOGRAPHICAL/CRITICAL SOURCES: Cartoonist Profiles, September, 1979.

—*Sketch by Dennis Wepman*

* * *

MORIN, Jim
See MORIN, James

* * *

MOSS, Donald 1920-

PERSONAL: Born January 20, 1920, in Somerville, Mass.; son of Frank and Eva (Davis) Moss; married Virginia ("Sally") Hardesty, June 25, 1949; children: Donald H., Elisabeth Read, Margaret DeGraff. *Education*: Attended Vesper George School of Art, Boston; Pratt Institute, Brooklyn, N.Y.; Art Students League of New York. *Home and studio*: 232 Peaceable St., Ridgefield, Conn. 06877.

DONALD MOSS

CAREER: Freelance illustrator and designer, 1946—; president, Design for Sports, Inc. Served as chairman of the annual exhibition of the Society of Illustrators, 1964; chairman of the U.S. Air Force Art Program, 1965-67; chairman of the Professional Lecture Series; and chairman of the *Sports Illustrated* Art Collections. Trustee of the National Art Museum of Sport. *Military service*: U.S. Marine Corps, 1942-46, served in the Pacific on Guadalcanal, New Guinea, New Britain, and Guam. *Member*: Society of Illustrators (Senior Vice President, 1964-68, Life Member), National Art Museum of Sport, Silver Springs Country Club.

AWARDS, HONORS: 100 Best Posters of the Year Award, 1960; Award of Excellence from the American Institute of Graphic Artists, 1974; citations by Chicago Art Directors Show and miscellaneous awards for sports art. Three of his paintings were selected for the "Champions of American Sport" exhibition at the Smithsonian Institute.

WRITINGS: (Illustrator) *Question and Answer Book of Nature*, Random House; (author and illustrator) *The Art of Water Color*, Grumbacher. Sports art represented in: *200 Years of American Illustration*; *200 Years of American Sport*; *Champions of American Sport*, Abrams, 1983; *The Best of Sports Illustrated*, Time-Life; *Magic and Other Realism*, Society of Illustrators; and *The North Light Collection*.

EXHIBITIONS: In permanent collections of the Baseball, Basketball, and Tennis Halls of Fame, U.S. Golf Association

(USGA) Golf House, the Society of Illustrators, the National Art Museum of Sport, the U.S. Air Force Art Collection, and the Portfolio, Stamford, Conn.

WORK IN PROGRESS: Aerial paintings of great golf courses of America, including Pebble Beach, Augusta, and National for the USGA and Professional Golfer's Association of America (PGA), paintings for the magazines *Golf Digest* and *Tennis*.

SIDELIGHTS: Donald Moss is a painter and designer who has specialized in sports art in both an editorial and commercial capacity. His work has become known over the past twenty-five years through his freelance illustrations for *Sports Illustrated* (including over a dozen covers). His main commercial accounts also reflect this athletic bias: Olin (ski equipment), AMF/Head (ski and tennis lines), numerous ski resorts and golf courses, and Mercedes-Benz of North America. High visibility graphic design projects have included commemorative stamps for the U.S. Postal Service (historical preservation stamps, "Physical Fitness," "The 100th Anniversary of Tennis," and the four-set 1976 Olympics issue); the official poster and program art for Super Bowl XII, and most notably the raccoon logo for the 1980 Lake Placid Winter Olympics.

Growing up in the Boston area, Moss was an avid amateur hockey player, and sometime golfer and skier, and he remains to this day a regular tennis player and an inveterate skier. It was only natural that his artistic bent should find its fullest expression in the celebration of athletic pursuits.

Super Bowl poster, 1978. (© National Football League.)

After two years at the Vesper George School of Art in Boston, service as a marine in World War II, and another year of study at Pratt Institute in Brooklyn, he began his career as a freelance illustrator, later joining a Madison Avenue advertising agency. It was while there, he claims, that he came up with the basic logo for the American Broadcasting Companies (ABC) network. "I never did get credit for it," he explained to a *New York Times* interviewer in 1979, "but it got me started in the right direction." That direction was leaving the agency and going back into the risky world of freelancing. His sports specialty, however, seems to have given him an advantage in the market, and he soon found editorial work, doing hunting and fishing illustrations for *True* magazine. His highly visible association with *Sports Illustrated* dates after this period. Today he heads Design for Sports, Inc., and considers himself very fortunate in being able not merely to combine business and pleasure, but to do so in some of the most beautiful venues (ski trails, golf courses, tennis clubs) in the world.

In this era of photojournalism—particularly in the action-oriented area of sport—Moss's work helps to sustain an important role for the graphic artist. Making the case for his aerial paintings of various famous golf courses and ski slopes, Moss argues, "Photographic aerials cannot precisely define fairways and traps or ski trails hidden by terrain and foliage. They do not bring out the values, color, depth, length, or height that an illustration can. And they do not glamorize the majestic mountain or the dramatic pitch of a downhill trail."

Similarly, art has a power to caricature and symbolize that photographs only occasionally capture. Consider Moss's pop-art, super-hero caricature of Carl Yastrzemski taking one of his classic swings, as reproduced in *The Best of Sports Illustrated*. Done in flat, bright acrylics, this visual representation of stroboscopic time-lapse photography achieves the larger-than-life quality one associates with legendary sports superstars without elevating what is, in the words of the late Red Smith, "a game little boys play" to a level of importance or solemnity. In fact, Moss generally manages to infuse all his sports art—from a *Sports Illustrated* cover portraying the heads of heavyweight boxers Muhammad Ali and George

Ski trails on Okemo Mountain. (© Okemo Mountain Corp.)

Foreman as Marvel Comics-style titans to a witty borrowing of Rene Magritte's canvas-in-context technique to recreate a golf scene—with healthy doses of fantasy, as if he were unable to believe his own good fortune in finding so congenial an occupation. He delights in each new assignment that combines painting and travel.

As a technician, Moss works with airbrush, tempera, acrylics, and oils, and is sufficiently conversant with watercolors to have written a monograph on the medium. Among those he cites as having influenced his development are the designer Paul Rand, with whom he studied at Pratt Institute; the American artist of muscular themes, John Atherton; and the French Impressionist School. (For an example of this latter debt, see his dreamy rendering of the old Forest Hills Tennis Club during a late afternoon Open match at Center Court reproduced in *200 Years of American Sport*.) His approach to the execution of his work is very much the "hands on" sort, involving photography, personal observation, and, where feasible, direct participation for the purpose of being able to "capture the flavor" of a downhill run, "the short but difficult" par-three seventh hole at Pebble Beach, Center Court at the U.S. Open, or the deck of an America's Cup yacht.

In a 1979 interview with the *New York Times* Moss stated that he liked to adapt his style to specific assignments instead of becoming known for a single style. "It's stimulating," he said, "to work on sports graphics for a month, then get an assignment to do a surrealist group of paintings." Sometimes Moss works twelve hours a day; but he notes, "For thirty years I've been doing the kind of thing I like most."

BIOGRAPHICAL/CRITICAL SOURCES: Something About the Author, Vol. 11, Gale, 1977; *New York Times*, July 15, 1979.

"Yaz" (Carl Yazstremski), ca. 1974. (© *Sports Illustrated*.)

—*Sketch by Richard Calhoun*

N

NAST, Thomas   1840-1902

PERSONAL: Born September 27, 1840, in Landau, Germany; son of Thomas, Sr. (a musician) Nast; mother's name unknown; came to the United States in 1846; married Sarah Edwards, September 26, 1861; children: Julia, Thomas, Jr., Edith, Mabel; died December 7, 1902, in Guayaquil, Ecuador, of malaria or yellow fever. *Education:* Attended Academy of Design, New York City.

CAREER: Staff artist, *Frank Leslie's Illustrated,* 1855-59; freelance illustrator, 1859-62; staff artist, *Harper's Weekly,* 1862-84; freelance cartoonist and illustrator, 1884-1902; publisher, *Nast's Weekly,* 1892-93; U.S. consul general in Ecuador, 1902. Received many honors during his lifetime.

WRITINGS—All self-illustrated: *Cartoons and Illustrations of Thomas Nast,* Dover, 1974; *Thomas Nast's Christmas Drawings,* Dover, 1978; *Thomas Nast's Christmas Drawings,* Peter Smith, n.d.

(With George P. Webster) *Santa Claus and His Works,* Evergreen, 1972.

SIDELIGHTS: Born in Landau, Germany, in 1840, Thomas Nast was the son of a German Army musician who, because of liberal political views, decided to emigrate to the United States. In 1846 he sent his wife and young Thomas on ahead to settle in New York City, where he joined them four years later. By all accounts the family made a comfortable home in their adopted land, the elder Nast easily finding work as a musician with the city's Philharmonic Society and the younger growing up much like any other city-bred boy. The only reported source of discord in the home was Nast's disinterest in school work. Despite a parental wish that he study music or learn some practical trade, young Tom's consuming passion was drawing, a passion to which he held with such firmness that he was at length permitted to take private lessons with Theodore Kaufmann, another German emigre whose specialty was historical painting. Later Nast enrolled at the Academy of Design, where he studied under Alfred Frederickson. Beside these formal studies, Nast also spent much of his spare time studying and copying such classic works as were available in the city's museums and private galleries.

His original aspiration was to become an orthodox academic painter of symbolic historical scenes (in the manner of Eugene Delacroix, for example), but he also apparently felt some pressure to demonstrate to his skeptical parents that

THOMAS NAST

his studies did have some practical value. Thus, at age fifteen he walked into the office of the recently launched *Frank Leslie's Illustrated Newspaper* and asked the proprietor for a job as an illustrator. The latter, a transplanted Englishman whose real name was Henry Carter, thought to discourage the importunate lad by sending him out to sketch a crowd scene; but so impressive was the result of this commission that he ended by hiring the boy at a salary of four dollars per week and Nast began his apprenticeship with *Leslie's.* He later worked for the rival *New York Illustrated News,* covering John Brown's funeral, traveling to Europe to sketch scenes from Garibaldi's revolt against the Sicilian monarchy, and gaining a reputation as a fine young penman.

An editorial cartoon attacking President Andrew Jackson, 1866.

It was as an artist covering the Civil War for *Harper's Weekly* beginning in 1862, however, that Nast enjoyed his first great popular successes. When Fletcher Harper hired the twenty-two-year-old Nast, it was plain the magazine was getting a highly competent technical artist with the proven ability to produce quality work under the pressure of weekly deadlines; but the astute publisher also discerned in the young man's work a singular ability to convey ideas and emotions, a degree of visual eloquence lacking in the work of more conventional illustrators. A partisan of great energy and force himself, Harper had not mistaken his man. With the publisher's encouragement and America's most widely read periodical for a forum, Nast lost little time in proving himself as ardent and effective a partisan as his employer. During the darkest years of the conflict he roused an increasingly war-weary Northern population again and again by his unprecedented ability to infuse the abstract ideal of Unionism with emotional urgency. His use of allegorical figures and images—the weeping widow at the North, the cat o' nine tails for the South—and melodramatic tableaux, created as much from his own intense convictions as from reality, moved President Lincoln to refer to him as "our best recruiting sergeant"; and there is little disagreement among historians that his savage assaults on the Democratic Party's "Peace" campaign of 1864 so effectively dyed General McClellan's candidacy with stains of coward-

ice and appeasement as to play an important role in turning the election narrowly in Lincoln's favor.

By the war's end, Nast had honed the instincts of the editorial cartoonist to razor sharpness—a sharpness he continued to employ to good effect between 1866-68 against Lincoln's successor Andrew Johnson, whom he regarded as unconscionably "soft" on the defeated South—but he was still refining his stylistic technique. His fame as a wartime illustrator opened up new commercial opportunities in painting and book illustration. These genres helped him to perfect his incisive linear style, gave him invaluable training in portraiture, and taught him how to condense complex ideas into single dramatic pictures. Then, in 1870, at the absolute peak of his creative powers, Nast embarked on the crusade that has been called arguably the greatest sustained outpouring of effective, high quality political caricature in the history of editorial cartooning, a campaign that literally defined the genre in America and supplied the benchmark for all subsequent efforts: his assault on the four principals of New York City's infamous "Tweed Ring."

While undeniably giants in the annals of municipal thievery, it is doubtful that this quartet would stand out so markedly in the Reconstruction Era's crowded gallery of scoundrels

KING DEATH'S DISTRIBUTION OF PRIZES.
BACCHUS TAKES THE FIRST PREMIUM.

An anti-alcoholism cartoon, 1871.

The Tammany Tiger Loose. —"What Are You Going To Do About It?"

One of the famous Tammany cartoons, 1871.

were it not for Nast's savagely memorable caricatures of Mayor A. Oakey Hall (or as Nast often spelled it, "Haul"), Comptroller Richard ("Slippery Dick") Connolly, Peter B. ("Brains") Sweeny, and above all William Marcy ("Boss") Tweed. Fusing genuine personal outrage with a slashing, vigorous style, the artist turned Tweed, with his vast paunch and broad, bearded face dominated by a pair of small, avaricious eyes, into an almost universal personification of the bloated, grasping politician, while portraying the fashionable, bespectacled Mayor Hall as the ideal front man, busily plying a broom in a burlesque of cleanliness while his Ring cohorts plotted some new atrocity against the City treasury.

Allegedly offered a bribe of a half million dollars (which he indignantly spurned), then threatened with bodily harm (whereupon he moved his family to New Jersey), Nast responded by escalating his attacks, particularly after the *New York Times* began publishing detailed accounts of the various frauds perpetrated by Tweed and company. Such classic drawings as "Who Stole the People's Money?—T'was Him" (an outward facing circle of grafters, the four Ringsters front and center, each affecting an innocent look and pointing to the figure immediately to his right), "It Will All Blow Over—Let Us Prey" (the four, with the bodies of vultures, cowering against a mountainside as a storm breaks overhead), and "The Tammany Tiger Loose—What Are

You Going To Do About It?" (Tweed as Caesar watching with his retinue as the ferocious cat mangles the figure of New York on the Coliseum floor) supplemented the *Times*'s exposé. The Boss, relatively untroubled by the printed evidence (since, as he put it, "my constituents can't read"), was of a very different mind about "them damned pictures." By reducing Tweed and his cronies to figures of ridicule, Nast's cartoons robbed them of the dignity of their offices, and once it became possible to laugh, their power, based on an aura of arrogant invincibility, could be broken. The 1871 municipal elections, contested by a committee of reformers, turned the Tammany machine out of office and later Tweed was successfully prosecuted on fraud charges; two accomplishments in which Nast could justifiably take personal pride. Oddly enough Nast was also to prove instrumental in keeping the Boss in jail—Tweed's escape to Spain in 1876 was thwarted when the authorities there identified him from a Nast caricature (supplied by the U.S. Consulate for lack of a photo) as he attempted to enter the country.

As brilliantly vitriolic as his anti-Ring drawings were, Nast eclipsed even that standard in his 1872 crusade against the "Liberal Republican" candidacy of *New York Tribune* publisher Horace Greeley, whom he regarded as too lenient in his attitude toward the defeated South and very much an opportunistic latecomer to the anti-Ring crusade. Whether these opinions were justified or not, they certainly supplied

Nast with incentive to go for the jugular; and poor Greeley, with his floppy hat, round spectacles, long coattails, ceaseless activity, and voluminous opinions, was a target tailormade for a parodist's pen. Boss Tweed seems an almost heroic figure compared to Nast's caricatures of the wheedling, sweating, desperate Greeley clasping hands with Tweed, the Ku Klux Klan, the Roman Catholic church (a lifelong bete noire of Nast's), John Wilkes Booth, and, in a parody of the temptation of Christ, Satan himself in his efforts to win votes.

Literally every detail in these drawings told against their hapless victim, but perhaps the cleverest stroke of all was Nast's treatment of Greeley's running mate, the aptly-named B. Gratz Brown of Missouri. Unable to find a photograph of Brown to caricature, he hit upon the brilliant expedient of turning the Vice Presidential candidate into a name tag, "& Gratz Brown," and fastening it to Greeley's coattails as a kind of afterthought. Often the tag was partially obscured, sometimes the "z" in Gratz was childishly reversed, and on one occasion when "H.G." was presented as a small, bespectacled mouse, the tiny rodent's tail was inscribed "& Gratz Brown." As Nast's grandson remarked

A political cartoon, 1877.

of this inspired bit of ridicule: "One can almost hear people asking 'Gratz who?'" It was later suggested that the savagery of Nast's attacks contributed to Greeley's death shortly after the election, and regardless of the implausibility of this suggestion, that it could even surface shows how devastating they were felt to be, even by people attuned to the ferocious politics of the time.

As the Greeley and Tweed drawings show, one of the most obvious qualities of Nast's work was its sophistication and literacy. The allusions to themes from classical literature and Shakespearean drama were suggested by his wife, whose formal education was far superior to his; but his acquaintance with the existing visual vocabulary was very much his own and a testament to the largely graphic terms in which his mind worked. "His cartoons are informed by a wealth of pictorial sources," art historian Albert Boime points out in an article on Nast's debt to contemporary French art, "and reveal a dependence on a stock of famous images to amplify his ideas." Quoting, at times directly, from works by Hadol, Gerome, Meissonier, and Millet, Nast tried to reinforce his own points by relying on the familiarity of at least a large part of his audience with these works; a rather sophisticated concept in a pre-mass media era, to say the least.

One of the famous Tammany cartoons, 1871.

The years between 1869 and 1872 found Nast at his most effective—his inventiveness, his mastery of the woodblock

"'TWAS THE NIGHT BEFORE CHRISTMAS,

and all through the house
Not a creature was stirring, *not even a mouse.*"

Illustration for "Twas the Night Before Christmas," 1886.

A political cartoon, 1878.

technique, and his partisan passions were all at their zenith. From such exalted heights he could only descend. This is not to suggest his decline was precipitous; he had yet to add to the catalogue of enduring political symbols the Democratic Donkey, the Republican Elephant, and Uncle Sam, and well into the 1880s he retained an unmatched gift for reducing complex political issues like inflation and the defense budget into striking, if partisan images. But he would never again approach the sustained quality of this period, and the reasons for this are not far to seek.

Above all, Nast's forte was the broad sarcasm of prosecution, not the subtle irony of defense. Thus, when he had to take up his pen in behalf of something—i.e., defending his hero President Grant—the result was all too often shrill and unconvincing. Moreover, the paucity of targets equally acceptable to the satirist and his audience is probably the genre's chief occupational hazard, and hardly makes for lengthy careers. The death of Fletcher Harper in 1877 also had an effect on Nast by robbing him of his staunchest supporter at the magazine and placing him under tighter editorial control, against which he naturally chafed. Nor were changes in working conditions restricted to personalities; in 1880 *Harper's* went from the woodblock engravure

reproduction technique (of which Nast was an acknowledged master) to a photochemical process which required him to execute his originals in pen and ink. This had a noticeably adverse impact on his work; the bold line and elaborate chiaroscuro-effect crosshatching gave way to the comparatively weak and faded productions of a man no longer in command of his craft. He had never been an especially gifted draftsman, and the new technique made the fact glaringly apparent.

In 1886 he severed his connection with *Harper's*. Although he continued to contribute to other magazines and for a brief time in 1892-93 edited his own weekly organ, Nast had outlived his times even more decisively than he had his abilities. In 1902, a long-time admirer of his work, President Theodore Roosevelt, learning of his financial difficulties, appointed him Consul to Ecuador, where he died of malaria (some sources say yellow fever) within six months of his arrival.

Thomas Nast towers over the history of American cartooning as no other artist does. In *The World Encyclopedia of Cartoons* Richard Marschall succinctly put his achievements in perspective: "It is a rare and fascinating thing in any of the arts when a pioneer not only defines a form but also, in the estimation of succeeding generations, remains its foremost exponent. In the field of political cartoons, many have occasionally matched the brilliance of Thomas Nast, but none have surpassed him."

BIOGRAPHICAL/CRITICAL SOURCES: Albert B. Paine, *Thomas Nast: His Period and His Pictures*, Macmillan, 1906, reprinted by Chelsea House, 1981; William A. Murrell, *A History of American Graphic Humor*, Macmillan for the Whitney Museum of Art, Vol. 1, 1933; Vol. 2, 1938; *Dictionary of American Biography*, Vol. 7, Scribner; J. C. Vinson, *Thomas Nast, Political Cartoonist*, University of Georgia Press, 1967; Albert Boime, "Thomas Nast and French Art," *American Art Journal*, spring, 1972; Thomas Nast St. Hill, editor, *Thomas Nast: Cartoons and Illustrations*, Dover, 1974; Syd Hoff, *Boss Tweed and the Man Who Drew Him* (juvenile), Coward, 1978; *The World Encyclopedia of Cartoons*, Chelsea House, 1980.

—*Sketch by Richard Calhoun*

* * *

NESSIM, Barbara 1939-

PERSONAL: Born March 30, 1939, in New York, N.Y.; daughter of Garret (a U.S. Postal Service employee and importer) and Claire (a fashion designer) Nessim; married Jules Demchick (a real estate developer), March, 1980. *Education:* Pratt Institute, B.F.A., 1960. *Studio:* 80 Varick St., New York, N.Y. 10013.

CAREER: Designer, Lady Van Heusen (a women's clothes manufacturer), New York City, 1961-66; artist, illustrator, and computer graphic artist, 1966—. Contributor to *Esquire, New York, Playboy, Viva, Seventeen, Redbook*, the *New York Times*, and many other publications. Instructor in drawing, painting, graphic design, and media concepts, School of Visual Arts, 1967—; instructor in drawing and design, Fashion Institute of Technology, 1976—; instructor in visual concepts, Pratt Institute, 1977-84. Lecturer at many colleges and institutions. *Member:* Society of Illustrators, Graphic Artists Guild, Foundation for the Community of Artists (board member, 1979-80), American Institute of Graphic Arts. *Awards, honors:* Special Mention from the Society of Illustrators, 1961; more than one hundred other awards, from Society of Illustrators, Art Directors Club, Illustrator West, and others.

WRITINGS—All as illustrator: Gloria Steinem, *The Beach Book*, Viking, 1963; Phyllis and Eberhard Kronhausen, *Erotic Art*, 1968; P. and E. Kronhausen, *Erotic Art II*, 1969; Ti-Grace Atkinson, *Amazon Odyssey*, Links Books, 1974.

Sketchbook (a compilation of her drawings), privately printed, 1975.

EXHIBITIONS—Group shows: "Panopticon," Bettman Archives, New York City, 1963; "Erotica," Van Bovenkamp Gallery, New York City, 1964; "Self Portraits," Visual Arts Gallery, New York City, 1965; "50 Years of Graphic Art by 50 Leading Graphic Artists," American Institute of Graphic Arts, New York City, 1965; "Landscape Show," Visual Arts

A drawing for *Art Worker News.* (© 1982, Barbara Nessim. Reprinted with permission.)

Gallery, 1966; "The First International Exhibition of Erotic Art," Lunds Konsthall, Lund, Sweden, 1968; "Black and White: 40 Statements on A Single Theme," Mead Gallery, New York City, 1969.

"The Push Pin Graphic Exhibit," Musee des Arts Decoratifs, Paris, France, 1970; "Posters U.S.A. 1960-1970: Best American Posters of the Past Decade," Mead Gallery, 1970; "Artists for McGovern," Feigen Gallery, New York City, 1972; "Erotic Art by Women," Erotic Art Gallery, New York City, 1973; "The Mental Picture," American Institute of Graphic Arts, 1973; "Color," Whitney Museum, New York City, 1974; "Encounter Show," Paula Cooper Gallery, 1974; "Interpretations of Sexuality," Albin-Zeglen Gallery, New York City, 1974; "200 Years of American Illustration," New York Historical Society, 1977; "Printmaking in Modern American Illustration," Pratt Graphics Center Gallery, New York City, 1979; "Women and Computers," Roanoke College, Va., 1983; Video Festival, Contemporary Arts Center, New Orleans, 1985.

One-woman shows: Rhode Island School of Design, 1966; Triangle Gallery, New York City, 1971; Corridor Gallery, New York City, 1973; Benson Gallery, Bridgehampton, N.Y., 1974; Hampshire College Gallery, Amherst, Mass., 1977.

WORK IN PROGRESS: The Electronic Art of Barbara Nessim, publication by Crown expected in 1986.

Photo by Seiji Kakizaki.

BARBARA NESSIM

SIDELIGHTS: Coyly erotic, slyly amusing, timeless, and "hip"; all are descriptions equally applicable to the work of Barbara Nessim, a successful freelance illustrator. Her preoccupation as an artist is femininity and its appurtenances, and her approach imaginative, sophisticated, and thought-provoking. Consider for example her title page illustration for an Anais Nin story "of memory and desire," set in Mallorca and entitled "Sirocco" (published in *Self*, 1979): it is a study in soft pastels of a Moorish-style foreground interior with surfaces finished in various mammary-inspired shapes, while deeper in the painting the notion of half-remembered desire is symbolized by the back side of a nude woman standing, partly obscured by the frame, just beyond an open set of double doors, her long Botticellean locks of hair blowing in a wind that the blue-white sky and sand-covered surface beyond her suggest is both hot and dry. In a later comment Barbara Nessim added: "There are two shadows, hers and the one of the anonymous person, suggesting she is not alone and her 'friend' could be either male or female." It is an illustration that is not only effective in setting the mystical and poetic tone of an Anais Nin story, but one which stands on its own as a typically evocative Nessim creation—at once literal and suggestive, illusive and very much "up front."

Born in New York City, Nessim was educated in the public schools, the High School of Industrial Art, and at Brooklyn's Pratt Institute, where she studied watercolors under Richard Lindner and graduated in 1960 with a degree in

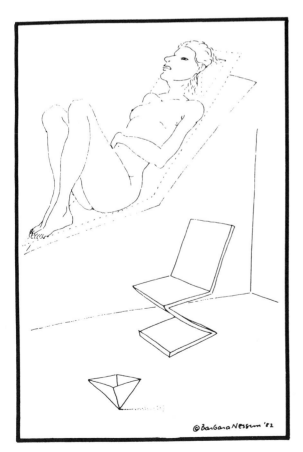

A drawing for *Art Worker News.* (© 1982, Barbara Nessim. Reprinted with permission.)

graphic design and illustration. After attending an evening class in draping at the Traphagen School of Fashion in 1965, she went to work as a designer of fabrics and clothing for the Lady Van Heusen line. Although quite successful at the creative end, she soon became disenchanted with the business aspects of the garment trade, and in the mid-1960s she dropped out to devote herself full-time to a career in freelance illustration. Again, notwithstanding the fiercely competitive nature of the commercial art market, she quickly established herself as a successful and sought-after illustrator, with a style that was equally suitable to both advertising and editorial commissions. Perhaps her greatest advantage in forging a reputation was her dependence upon imagination rather than life or other artists' work for inspiration. Straightforward representational art offered her little scope for the development of a distinctive style; nor was the mimicking of Belgian painter Rene Magritte or any other of Madison Avenue's favorite modern artists likely to result in anything very original; so she determined early on to work, as she put it, "directly from my head." The upshot was not only an identifiable style, but a concentration on the subject of femininity in its various guises—psycho-sexual, biological, emotional, even political (see her cover portrait for *Time's* E.R.A. issue of July 12, 1982)—that does not, incidentally, depend for its impact on presenting masculine stereotypes negatively.

"I like to juxtapose colors in ways that aren't usual—color makes me happy," she explains; and indeed one can expect to find much color as well as a general absence of bathos in the Nessim catalogue. Her sensibilities, says critic Erika Billeter, writing in *Graphis* (in 1981), are quintessentially New York, as "seen from its more cheerful side, with its stimulating influence in the field of advertising and applied art, swinging New York with its disco sound and a slight touch of Art Nouveau and Art Deco." For all the clutter of the urban environment which inspires her, however, Nessim's work is sparse rather than busy. She typically reduces her theme material to its essentials (as in the illustration for the Nin short story), the more elementally to present it (the story's tagline—written after the art was created—reads "the hot, dry wind that awakes memory and desire").

A compositional idiosyncrasy is her frequent resort to frames, borders, and intricate background patterns in order to create what one critic has called "a kind of surface tension" designed to unite the symbols she integrates into her paintings. In a painting illustrating an article on getting over a love affair, for example, she sets one of her stylized, mannequin-like female figures against a gridwork of ribbons (a favorite image) with hearts set in the latticework, the lower part of which is being consumed, and reduced to charred ribbon fragments and broken heart shapes. It is a peculiarly effective evocation of the situation, as seen from an affective, empathetic, and very feminine point of view. Nessim has never tried to deny the feminine bias of her work; indeed, she actually seems to regard such an identity as a strength rather than a limitation.

Recently, Nessim has become involved in the field of computer graphics. Having first investigated its potential at the Massachusetts Institute of Technology in the early 1980s, she continued to read widely on the subject and keep in touch with the newest innovations on her own. Ultimately achieving proficiency in the uses of this new technique, she

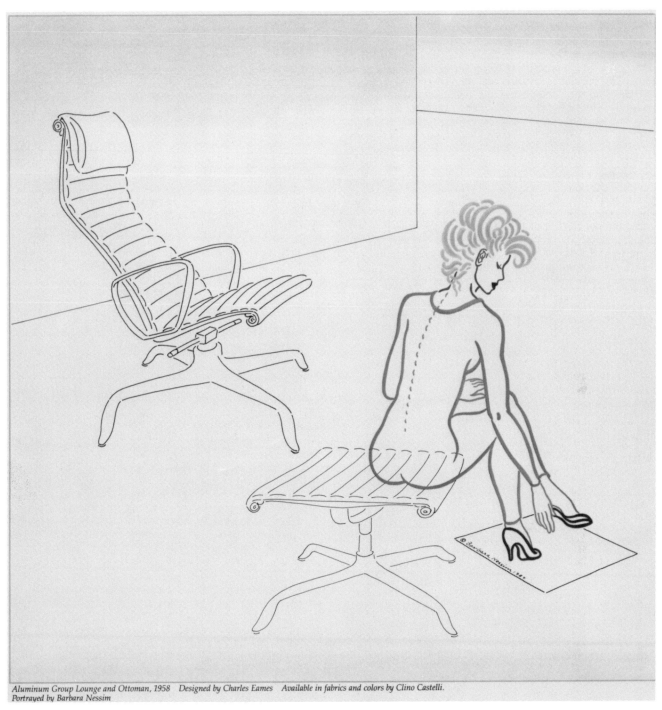

Aluminum Group Lounge and Ottoman, 1958   Designed by Charles Eames   Available in fabrics and colors by Clino Castelli.
Portrayed by Barbara Nessim

A grouping of Charles Eames furniture, as depicted by Barbara Nessim. (© 1984, Barbara Nessim. Reprinted with permission.)

helped to work up new graphic imagery for Time-Life Inc., using the Teletext-Telidon program. She has also helped in the development of a computer-related curriculum for New York's High School of Art and Design. Such endeavors as these ought not, perhaps, to surprise the student of her work; yet there remains a reflexive reluctance to associate the creator of such soft, sensual, amusing, and provocative images as hers with anything as coldly unromantic as high-

tech computer graphic software. But then, why should the artist be any easier to categorize than her work?

"Why do I find using the computer so intriguing?," Barbara Nessim states. "There is something fascinating about using a paint medium that moves as you are working with it. That you can use a finished image, take it into many different directions, finish it again, and still have the capability of keeping the original finished image intact is one of the many positive aspects the computer represents. This aspect, among others, can broaden the artist's capacity to be more flexible than ever, therefore moving the work quickly into other directions. The luminosity of color, the easily mixed palette to develop the choice of colors and the variety of tools, all in one place, all this is very attractive. Unlike any past medium or tool, this artistic communication device, using the pictorial medium, can send immediate visual messages through wire or air. The computer, which is still in its formative stage, has many uses still to be discovered and invented by the artist. The computer is now used in a variety of ways, as a tool for planning and development as well as an end product."

BIOGRAPHICAL/CRITICAL SOURCES: "Barbara Nessim: A Portfolio," *Print*, November 1968; "Cover Artist," *Art Direction*, October 1973; Erika Billeter, "Barbara Nessim," *Graphis*, January/February 1981; *American Artist*, November 1983.

—Sketch by Richard Calhoun

A computer image. (© 1984, Barbara Nessim. Printed with permission.)

O

OPPENBERG, Sheldon 1935-

PERSONAL: Born August 30, 1935, in the Bronx, N.Y.; son of Aaron (in business) and Jean (a housewife; maiden name Goldstein) Oppenberg; married Carmelita Apostol (a teacher), August 18, 1980. *Education:* School of Visual Arts, 1955-58, obtained certificate of completion; New School for Social Research, 1971; Parsons School of Design, 1975. *Home and studio:* 2076 Wallace Ave. Bronx, N.Y. 10462.

CAREER: Sales representative, Crystal Spring Water Co., Bronx, N.Y., 1960-61; sales promotion manager, Posner Papers, Brooklyn, N.Y., 1961-1964; sales representative, L. Sichel Co., New York, N.Y., 1965-69; employment counselor, Snelling & Snelling, Bronx, N.Y., 1970; art director greeting card company, and sales promotion manager, paper company, 1970-85. Legislative advisor to local assemblyman, 1981-85. *Member:* Franklin Furnace Museum, New York City.

EXHIBITIONS: (Collective) Stratford Art Gallery, Stratford, Conn., 1962; Lynn Kottler Galleries, New York, 1966; Hansen Gallery, New York, 1975; (one-man show) Simi Valley Library, Simi Valley, Calif., 1983; represented in permanent collection of the Franklin Furnace Museum.

WORK IN PROGRESS: Oaky Doak. . . Oaky Doaks!, a book on the comic strip *Oaky Doaks* created by late R. B. Fuller; completion expected in 1986.

SIDELIGHTS: Sheldon Oppenberg wrote to *CGA:* "I enjoy doing what I do (art) more than anything else. Love to create art that gives me joy and joy to others was well. Art isn't work . . . it's fun. Love to work in black and white and color. Art should attract . . . my work does! It's bold, dramatic, exciting! Love to experiment with new pens, brushes, papers, etc. Art should create interest.

"I believe the artist should sketch as much as possible . . . from life . . . from photographs, from memory . . . even from television. In this way he can improve his work, be more observant . . . and hopefully pick up more assignments. I use many pens for sketching . . . the Pentel, the Flair, Sanford's Expresso, and a host of others. Find one that is comfortable for you. In many instances I use my sketches as finished art. I use ledger bond mostly, because the paper is good for sketching and it is quite reasonable. Every artist has his favorite."

For years Oppenberg doggedly pursued an art career while

Self-portrait of Sheldon Oppenberg. (© 1985, Sheldon Oppenberg. Printed with permission.)

holding down various full-time outside positions. His illustrations, cartoons, and strips have appeared mostly in little magazines, in fanzines, and on posters for local companies. He also drew caricatures of celebrities and friends for a host of small publications, and his illustrated envelopes have become collectors' items. Appreciation of Oppenberg's work has grown steadily in the past years, and with personal appearances on local and national television shows and at comic conventions the artist has gained a wider audience, to the point that he is now devoting most of his time to drawing, illustration, and occasional lecturing and writing.

BIOGRAPHICAL/CRITICAL SOURCES: Cartoonews, No. 21, 1979; *Near Mint,* No. 9, April 1981; *Bronx Times Reporter,* April 5-18, 1984.

Drawing of the late actor Freddie Prinze. (© 1985, Sheldon Oppenberg. Printed with permission.)

* * *

OREHEK, Don(ald August) 1928-

PERSONAL: Born August 9, 1928, in Brooklyn, N.Y.; son of Valentine (a secretary) and Mary (Cizej) Orehek; married Suzanne Ruth Whitney, March 26, 1966; children: Errol MacDonald, Holly Whitney. *Education:* Cartoonists and Illustrators School (now School of Visual Arts), 1950-52. *Home and studio:* 35 Revere Rd., Port Washington, N.Y. 11050.

CAREER: Paste-up and mechanicals, Crestwood Publishing Co., 1952-56; freelance magazine cartoonist, 1956—. *Military service:* U.S. Navy, 1945-49. *Member:* National Cartoonists Society.

AWARDS, HONORS: Best Magazine Gag Cartoonist award, National Cartoonists Society, 1973, 1983, and 1985; two prizes from the Pavilion of Humor, Man and His World Exhibition, Montreal, Canada, 1971, 1972.

WRITINGS: 101 Pickle Jokes, Pyramid, 1974; *Yankee Doodle Dandies: A Star-Spangled Satire*, New American Library, 1975; *Classic Corny Joke Book*, Pyramid, 1975; *The Garage Sale Handbook*, Tempo, 1977 and 1979; *Santa Claus: Jokes and Riddles*, Tempo, 1978; *101 Hamburger Jokes*, Scholastic Book Services, 1978; *Chicken Jokes*, Tempo, 1979; *Tales of the Spooky-Natural and Vampire Jokes*, Tempo, 1980; *Gag Galaxy: Outer Space Jokes and Riddles*, Tempo, 1980; *Who's Zoo*, Tempo, 1981; *The Official Name Callers' Handbook*, Ace, 1981; *101 Fast Funny Food Jokes*, Scholastic, 1983; *101 Bug Jokes*, Scholastic, 1984.

SIDELIGHTS: A successful gag cartoonist for almost thirty years, Don Orehek dates his interest in art from childhood. His father was an avid amateur penman and liked to draw pictures to amuse young Don and his siblings. Later young Orehek turned his own hand to copying the artwork in various syndicated newspaper strips, *Smilin' Jack*, the aviator adventurer, being a particular favorite of his. (Oddly, since Maurice Horn, writing in *The World Encyclopedia of Comics*, has pronounced that strip's artwork "uniformly terrible.") While attending high school, he recalls being encouraged to draw by one of his teachers and doing very well on a drawing aptitude test, but it was not until he was serving in the Navy (1945-49) that he began to make serious use of this predilection. His first original cartoons were drawn for the Public Information Officer of a ship on which he was stationed, and later he developed a regular strip entitled *Cyphers* which appeared in various military papers. Upon discharge, he enrolled in the School of Visual Arts (then known as the Cartoonists and Illustrators School), and while still a student there sold his first gag cartoon.

After graduating in 1952, he spent four years working for a gag magazine publisher and building up a market for his freelance efforts. In 1956, he was at last able to become a full time freelancer, and since then his cartoons have appeared in virtually every major magazine showcase, including *Saturday Evening Post*, *Cosmopolitan*, *Playboy*, and *Saturday Review*. He has also been a regular contributor to the teenage humor magazine, *Cracked*, and has thirteen books to his credit as an illustrator.

Orehek acknowledges the influence in his work of the *New Yorker's* Claude Smith ("Claude") but feels his drawing is more illustration-oriented than that of most other gag

Self-portrait of Don Orehek, drawn specially for *Contemporary Graphic Artists*.

"Now if you used a Wilkinson Blade, you wouldn't find that necessary!"

A *Saturday Evening Post* **cartoon, ca. 1970.** (© Don Orehek. Reprinted with permission.)

cartoonists. It is certainly in violation of the minimalist ideal in visual humor, yet this transgression does not detract: "I like to draw all the wrinkles in the pants and detail," he explained to interviewer Bob Crouch in 1974; "However, I'm a very fast worker which helps this detail from appearing overworked in my cartoons." He also likes to portray physical action on strictly esthetic grounds: "The use of action makes the cartoon more fluid and adds a tonal quality to the gag." He works mainly in ink and wash, with an occasional finish in watercolor. "Like most cartoonists," he declares, "my materials are pretty basic." Yet, in his opinion, drawing is the most important element in a gag cartoonist's success or failure, and he attributes the failure of many young cartoonists to sell in the top markets to an inability to measure up artistically to the standards of the current day.

As to his own humor, Orehek enjoys working in a wide range of categories—from family-type material in *Ladies Home Journal* to the broad sexual humor of *Playboy*—and finds that such an approach keeps him from becoming stale or predictable. While he writes much of his own material, using personal observation and a personally assembled morgue of clippings and cartoons, he also buys gags from writers with whom he has developed working relationships over the years. If there is any unevenness in the quality of his work, it lies in the gag aspect, for the art work in an Orehek drawing is as uniformly good. Nor is this occasional weakness in the humor department surprising; given the grueling nature of the business of having to come up with the sheer volume of gags demanded of the freelancer, the surprise is that he hits as often as he does. And he has hit often enough to have been named Best Magazine Gag Cartoonist of the Year by the National Society of Cartoonists on three separate occasions (1973, 1983, and 1985). The secret of his success? "I'd really rather be drawing cartoons than almost anything else. . . . Except for the fact that I like to collect all types of naval hats and military pointed helmets, you could say cartooning is my hobby as well as my business."

BIOGRAPHICAL/CRITICAL SOURCES: Cartoonist Profiles, March, 1973; *The World Encyclopedia of Cartoons*, Chelsea House, 1980.

—Sketch by Richard Calhoun

OUTCAULT, R(ichard) F(elton) 1863-1928

PERSONAL: Born January 14, 1863, in Lancaster, Ohio; died September 25, 1928, in Flushing, N.Y.; son of J. P. and Catherine (Davis) Outcault; married Mary Jane Martin, December 25, 1890; children: Richard F., Jr. *Education:* McMicken College (later part of University of Cincinnati), graduated, 1885; studied art in Paris.

CAREER: Freelance illustrator, 1890-94; drew *Hogan's Alley* for the *New York World*, 1895-96; drew *The Yellow Kid* for the *New York Journal*, 1896-98; drew *Poor Li'l Mose* for the *New York Herald*, 1901-02; drew *Buster Brown* for the *New York Herald*, 1902-05; drew *Buster Brown* for the *New York American*, 1905-20; founder and president, Outcault Advertising Co., Chicago, Ill., 1910-20; painter and lecturer, 1920-26.

WRITINGS: (Self-illustrated) *The Yellow Kid in MacFadden's Flats*, Hearst Co., 1897.

All collections of *Buster Brown* comic pages, all published by Frederick A. Stokes: *Buster Brown and His Resolutions*, 1904, reprinted by Dover, 1974; *Buster Brown, His Dog Tige and Their Troubles*, 1905; *Buster Brown's Pranks*, 1906; *Buster Brown, His Dog Tige and Their Jolly Times*, 1907.

All collections of *Buster Brown* comic pages, all published by Cupples & Leon Co.: *Buster, Mary Jane and Tige*, 1908; *Buster's Amusing Capers*, 1908; *Buster the Busy Body*, 1909; *The Real Buster and the Only Mary Jane*, 1909; *Buster's Happy Days*, 1911; *Buster in Foreign Lands*, 1912; *Buster, the Fun Maker*, 1912; *Buster and His Pets*, 1913; *Buster and the Cat*, 1917.

Contributor of articles on comics and cartoons to various periodicals.

SIDELIGHTS: Born into a well-to-do family of German descent (whose name was originally Outcauldt), young Richard, after graduation from college, went to Paris to study. He returned to the United States in 1890, married, and settled in Flushing, N.Y. He started his career as an illustrator, working for publications such as *The Electrical World* (where his talent for drawing ingenious devices first came to light), but later decided to become a cartoonist, contributing to many major humor periodicals, including *Judge* and *Life*. Starting in 1894 he also submitted a number of cartoons to Joseph Pulitzer's *New York World*, and it was in the pages of the *World* that for the first time appeared an ugly-looking little slum kid with a bald head and big ears, who increasingly drew the interest of both the newspaper's editors and its readers.

In 1895 the feature began appearing weekly in the Sunday supplement of the *World*. The unnamed main character kept commenting on the rather unsavory goings-on with clever sayings emblazoned on the only garment he wore—a nightshirt. This nightshirt was of varying colors at first, but in 1896 it definitively was colored yellow, and its anonymous wearer was promptly dubbed "the yellow kid." The feature itself eventually became known as *Hogan's Alley*, from the slum district where most of the action took place. In it Outcault used text and dialogue enclosed within one huge panel that took up half, and sometimes the whole, of a page.

R. F. OUTCAULT

In Outcault's chaotic and teeming drawings could already be discerned all the harbingers of a new and exciting artistic form.

The feature became a prize in the struggle between Joseph Pulitzer and William Randolph Hearst for mastery over the New York market, with Hearst winning the contest and bringing Outcault over to his *New York Journal* in 1896. Promptly the now-famous kid in the yellow nightshirt became the main attraction of the *Journal*'s Sunday supplement, while the *World* hired the painter George Luks to continue *Hogan's Alley* for a time. Under Hearst's prodding Outcault made increasing use of sequential narratives and of speech balloons in a series of comical misadventures named in honor of the hero, *The Yellow Kid*: thus were the terms "comics" (applied to the Sunday features for obvious reasons) and "yellow journalism" (used to describe the practices of the sensational press) born at the same time. Because of its avowed vulgarity *The Yellow Kid* soon aroused the ire of the censors, and Outcault abandoned it in 1898. Going over to the *New York Herald*, he first created there *Poor Li'l Mose*, about a little black boy, in 1901. Then came his masterpiece, *Buster Brown*, the following year.

This full Sunday page starred a carefully dressed blonde little boy, always flanked by his faithful bulldog Tige, and often abetted in his pranks by his companion-in-mischief, a dark-tressed hellion with an angelic face affectionately named Mary Jane (as was Outcault's wife). Buster was always allowed a show of contrition in the form of a hand-lettered sign piously called "Resolution" at the end of each Sunday episode. Buster's facial expressions (and his renewed pranks) left no doubt about the insincerity of his resolutions. Moving in middle-class surroundings, unlike the Yellow Kid, he had learned the virtue of hypocrisy (and so had his creator).

One of these "resolutions" runs so strikingly counter to the spirit of all resolutions, and so much in the spirit of the strip, that it deserves special mention: "Resolved! That I will quit making resolutions. If we don't make them, we can't break them. It's the fellow who does wrong who resolves to do right." The Voltairian tone of mockery (which Outcault may have learned in Paris, along with studying art) is unmistakeable. Buster plays a cat-and-mouse game with the grownups, just as Outcault plays a cat-and-mouse game with the critics.

In 1905 Hearst, noticing the strip's immense popularity, hired Outcault for the second time; Buster and his cohorts started appearing in his *New York American* early the following year, while the *Herald* had the feature continued by various hands, including that of William Lawler. Outcault's creation (which, by court order, he was prohibited from calling *Buster Brown*) soared to even greater heights of success; Buster and Tige appeared on a multitude of commercial products, from soap to cigars and whiskey. In 1910 Outcault founded the Outcault Advertising Company, in order to further promote and exploit his characters.

Now a wealthy man, Outcault decided in 1920 to devote his time to painting and lecturing on his creations; he stopped drawing *Buster Brown* (which went into reprints until 1926) and turned the presidency of his advertising company to his son, Richard F., Jr. In 1928 he was taken suddenly ill and died in his home in Flushing in September of that year.

Outcault's pivotal contribution to the birth of the comics in their modern form has been universally noted. Despite much quibbling, the consensus among historians places the date of this birth in 1896, when *The Yellow Kid* was established in its definitive version (thus the retrospective exhibition held at the New York Cultural Center in 1971 was appropriately called "75 Years of the Comics"). "It would be possible to dig through history for thousands of years and find many examples of popular funny pictures," Coulton Waugh wrote in *The Comics*, "yet they would not be 'funnies' in the modern sense, for they would not be included in the eruption of the sensational, modern newspaper. The Yellow Kid stood right on the spot when the volcano shot off." To which Stephen Becker perceptively added, "With the Yellow Kid the words began to reflect the humor of the drawing, and vice versa, to the point—and an important point it was—where *neither was satisfactory without the other.*"

Buster Brown's contributions were of another kind. As August Derleth noted in his introduction to the Dover edition of *Buster Brown*, Outcault's hero, along with the Katzenjammer Kids, "inspired many imitations and brought into being many strips and pages reflecting the mischief-making and incorrigible boy themes. Among them, in the earlier years, were Swinnerton's *Little Jimmy*, Billy Marriner's boy panels, Frink's *Slim Jim*, Winsor McCay's graphically beautiful *Little Nemo in Slumberland*, Carl

Schultze's *Foxy Grandpa*, . . . Fera's *Just Boy*, Ross's *Mama's Angel Child*." In addition, Buster Brown's fame has lasted to this day in many forms. His name gave rise to a number of popular expressions still in currency today, as in "Wait a minute, Buster!" and "Who do you think you are, Buster?" (and the child-actor Joseph Francis Keaton was bestowed the stage name "Buster" by his vaudevillian parents from the same source). There still exists a line of Buster Brown shoes, and all kinds of garments are still merchandised by Buster Brown Apparel Inc. in New York City, which also runs the Buster Brown Museum.

BIOGRAPHICAL/CRITICAL SOURCES: Martin Sheridan, *Comics and Their Creators*, Hale, Cushman & Flint, 1942, reissued in paperback by Luna Press, 1971; Coulton Waugh, *The Comics*, Macmillan, 1947; *A Dictionary of North American Authors Deceased before 1950*, Ryerson Press, 1951, reprinted by Gale, 1968; Stephen Becker, *Comic Art in America*, Simon & Schuster, 1959; Frank Luther Mott, *American Journalism: A History, 1690-1960*, 3rd edition, Macmillan, 1962; Max J. Herzberg, *The Reader's Encyclopedia of American Literature*, Crowell, 1962; Pierre Couperie and Maurice Horn, *A History of the Comic Strip*, Crown, 1968; Horn, *75 Years of the Comics*, Boston Book & Art, 1971; *Webster's Biographical Dictionary*, Merriam, 1974; Jerry Robinson, *The Comics: An Illustrated History of Comic Strip Art*, Putnam, 1974; August Derleth, introduction, *Buster Brown*, Dover, 1974; *The World Encyclopedia of Comics*, Chelsea House, 1976; Denis Gifford, *The International Book of Comics*, Crescent, 1984.

—Sketch by Maurice Horn

WHAT THEY DID TO THE DOG-CATCHER IN HOGAN'S ALLEY.

A famous *Yellow Kid* page, 1896.

A title-less *Buster Brown* page by R. F. Outcault, 1907.

P

PARTCH, Virgil Franklin II   1916-1984
(Vip)

OBITUARY NOTICE: Born October 17, 1916, on St. Paul Island, Alaska; died August 10, 1984, in a car crash near Los Angeles, along with his wife Helen. Cartoonist, animator, illustrator, and author under the pseudonym "Vip." Partch started his career as an animator with the Walt Disney studio in 1937, and later became a prolific cartoonist, contributing to such publications as the *New Yorker, Saturday Evening Post, This Week, True,* and *Liberty*; his cartoons have been reprinted in numerous collections and anthologies. He is perhaps best known, however, for his two comic-strip creations: *Big George*, which he developed in 1960, and *The Captain's Gig*, started in 1977. *The World Encyclopedia of Cartoons* said of Partch: "While not especially original either in style or in range, Partch's work is immediately identifiable and avoids the anonymity that befalls so many cartoonists." In *Comic Art in America* Stephen Becker observed that Partch was a "proponent of logical insanity; his subjects defy all known laws of physics, chemistry and physiology, always stretching the particular situation far beyond its initial boundaries."

BIOGRAPHICAL/CRITICAL SOURCES: Stephen Becker, *Comic Art in America*, Simon & Schuster, 1959; *The World Encyclopedia of Cartoons*, Chelsea House, 1980; *Current Biography*, Wilson, 1985.

OBITUARY SOURCE: New York Times, August 12, 1984.

*   *   *

PEAK, Bob
See PEAK, Robert

*   *   *

PEAK, Robert   1929-
(Bob Peak)

PERSONAL: Born May 30, 1929, in Denver, Colo.; married; four children. *Education:* Wichita State University, 1944-45, 1946-49; Art Center College of Design, Los Angeles, 1950-52, Bachelor of Professional Arts. *Agents:* (Commercial art) Harvey Kahn & Associates, 50 E. 50th St., New York, N.Y.; (fine art) McCulley Fine Arts Gallery, 256 Two Lincoln Center, 5420 LBJ Fwy., Dallas, Tex. 75240.

CAREER: Illustrator and artist, 1953—. Major client accounts have included Old Hickory, *Life, Look, Esquire, Cosmopolitan, Playboy, Sports Illustrated, TV Guide,* TWA, Coca Cola, Paramount Pictures, Walt Disney, 20th Century Fox, United Artists, MGM, Western Bell, New York Racing Association, Philip Morris, and the U.S. Postal Service. Taught at Art Center College of Design, Los Angeles; the Art Students League, New York City; Famous Artists Schools; and the Illustrator's Workshop. *Military service:* U.S. Navy, 1945-46. *Member:* Society of Illustrators.

AWARDS, HONORS: Over one hundred awards from the New York Society of Illustrators, including the Hamilton King Award, 1968; Hall of Fame, 1977; Gold Medals, 1971, 1972, 1975, 1977, 1981, 1982; Silver Medals, 1962, 1964, 1966, 1969, 1971, 1972, 1974 through 1979; named Artist of the Year, 1961, by the Artists Guild of New York; over one hundred fifty awards from various organizations, including Art Directors Clubs of New York, Chicago, Philadelphia, Boston, Denver, and New Jersey; Mead Library of Design; Advertising Club of New York; Artists Guild of Chicago.

ROBERT PEAK

EXHIBITIONS: Participated in shows at Utah State University, Wichita State University, New-York Historical Society, Brooklyn Museum, Greenwich Workshop Gallery, National Art Museum of Sport, Westport Artists, Society of Illustrators, New York Auto Show 1969, AWIA Show, Carson Gallery of Denver, O'Grady Galleries of Chicago in 1976, 1977, and 1979, O'Grady Galleries of Scottsdale, Arizona in 1983, Smithsonian Institution, McCulley Fine Arts Gallery of Dallas, 1974 and 1983, and Rizzoli Gallery of New York.

One-man shows at Art Center College of Design in Los Angeles, Art Students League of New York, Famous Artists Schools, Society of Illustrators, New York, Oklahoma Christian College of Oklahoma City, Wichita State University 1972 and 1982, Ringling Museum of Art of Sarasota, Florida, O'Grady Galleries of Chicago, 1978, Academy of Art and Design in Denver, 1983, and the Academy of Art College of San Francisco. Represented in the permanent collections of American Express, Special Olympics, *Playboy,* Philip Morris, 20th Century Fox, Oklahoma Christian College, National Portrait Gallery of Smithsonian Institution, American Museum of Sport, Society of Illustrators, Lafayette College, Academy of Motion Picture Arts and Sciences, South Street Seaport Museum, Wichita State University, *Sports Illustrated*, Time-Life, Inc., Casa Bonita (Dallas), Jack Levy and Associates (Chicago), TWA, Clint Eastwood, Audrey Hepburn, Sidney Poitier, Tony Bennett, Lucille Ball, and Hugh O'Brien.

SIDELIGHTS: Born in Denver and raised in Kansas, Robert Peak dates his serious interest in art to a Christmas gift of paints and brushes received when he was six years old. By the age of nine he claims to have been producing likenesses that his mother (at least) could recognize. Still, when it came time to enroll in college, he did not consider the possibility of a career in art and instead entered Wichita State University as a geology major, with a minor in art. While in school, he got a part-time job in a local printing firm's art department, and it was there that the idea of art as a viable professional option first emerged. Exposed to its commercial aspects, from layout to design to lettering, he saw an occupational side to his favorite avocation; as a result he changed his major to art. At the time, Wichita State was primarily a teachers college and had no commercial art curriculum. Peak thus had to create his own, which he did by taking a potpourri of courses in the art department. Given such preparation it is not surprising that he left the university for a stint in the Navy with a rather individual vision of the commercial illustrator's craft; a vision apparently strengthened during subsequent studies (1950-52) at the Art Center College of Design in Los Angeles.

When he moved to New York City in 1953 to begin his assault on the highly competitive commercial art market, he immediately confronted two formidable obstacles. First there was his largely self-developed style. It was too flamboyant, too removed from what he recalled as the [projector-like] "carefully controlled balopticon machine" style then prevalent among the top commercial and editorial illustrators. Secondly, the heyday of magazine illustration was coming to an end with the contraction of the mass-circulation periodical market, making competition all the more arduous. Facing such a situation, Peak strove for several years to adapt his style to the needs of a market

dominated by the likes of Rene Bouche, whom Peak himself regarded as king of the hill; but this was a miserable period for him, in which lack of success was compounded by a lack of pleasure in what he was doing. Taking counsel with his wife, he decided to go back to his original flamboyant style and give it one last try. Either he would be successful or they would return to California "and live on the beach."

Renting some studio space, he spent several months simply producing work he liked, never mind the dictates of the market. He was determined, as he put it, to stop trying to "out-Bouche Bouche" and rather to "do my best Bob Peak and stand or fall on that." The upshot was that an artist's representative, called in to look over his work, submitted some of his drawings to the ad agency which represented the Old Hickory Whiskey account (whiskey was in those days a staple ad-feature on the back covers of glossy national magazines) and, competing against none other than Rene Bouche, he won the account and his work soon appeared on the back cover of *Life, Look,* and other major magazines. Overnight he became a financial and professional success, and quickly followed up his initial coup by winning the very lucrative and highly visible accounts of Puritan Sportswear and Coca Cola. "Real quick," Peak says without overstatement, "I had a name."

In the more than thirty years since making that name, Peak has steadily added to his reputation as the consummate illustrator's illustrator. "I'm a commercial illustrator," he declares proudly. "That's what I always wanted to be, even as a little kid, and I'm well suited for it." The particular abilities that gave him his edge in the commercial art field, as he sees them, are professionalism, an analytical approach, and adaptability. Professionalism is what enables him to meet the deadlines that are a constant feature of the illustrator's metier, keeps him working up to but not beyond his considerable capacities, motivates him to produce when "it's three o'clock in the morning [and] you've got yourself into a corner" and results in finished work an art director can show to a client knowing "he's not going to look like a jackass." His analytical mind supports this professionalism by reducing all assignments to problems and figuring out how best to solve them within the time-frame and restraints imposed by the client. Finally, there is the adaptability that has kept his work relevant in a changeable, not to say fickle, marketplace. "As times change, needs change," he says. "You have to be able to change very rapidly."

To remain at the top of his profession for as long as he has, Peak has had to be extremely flexible, not only as an artist but as a student of the market. Since breaking in as an advertising artist, he has also enjoyed wide acceptance as an editorial illustrator (particularly for his *Time, TV Guide,* and *Sports Illustrated* covers), and more recently, as the commercial and editorial fields became less interesting (and in the case of the latter, less lucrative), moving into the area of movie poster art. Since his first poster in 1960 (for *West Side Story*), his has been the name affixed to the posters for more than seventy-five films, among them *My Fair Lady, Camelot, Apocalypse Now, Superman, Missouri Breaks, Rollerball, Excalibur,* and *Pennies from Heaven.* It is in no small part due to Peak's work that movie-poster art has risen from a kind of "poor cousin" status in commercial art to the very well-paid, much sought-after work that it has today become. His poster art for *Camelot* won a Society of Illustrators Gold

Poster art for *Star Trek III—The Search for Spock*, 1984. (© Paramount Pictures.)

Medal, the first such recognition ever given to promotional art for a film release. His mastery of this particular genre provides an example not only of his technique as an artist but of his ability to analyze the film he is asked to work on in such a way as to anticipate the studio's ultimate marketing strategy. "A 'star' film is like a Barbra Streisand or a Marlon Brando film," Peak explains; "If it's a James Bond movie, it's more than a 'star' film—it's all the accouterments. I have a way of finding the guts of a film." And anyone who has seen that series of striking visual images—the river, the bridge, the helicopters, the brooding red sun, the incendiary flashes, the head of Brando that he incorporated into the poster art for *Apocalypse Now* will scarcely disagree with his claim on this score.

In keeping with his range of subject materials, Peak employs many different techniques and media. He prefers working commercially with watercolor and gouache because he likes the combination of fast-drying and transparency. He is equally adept in the use of charcoal, pastels, and airbrush to create feathering and flare effects. He develops glazes by separating layers of paint with an acrylic matte medium, and when working in oils he likes them diluted early on, building up heavier textures as the later touches are laid on (a technique generally applied in those paintings he can, at this stage of his career, do purely for his own satisfaction as an artist). Most of his work is preceded by extensive preliminary sketching "to get an idea just right." When he feels he has a drawing that fits, he projects it on to canvas or paper, via an opaque projector, and blocks in the various areas.

In 1983-84, recognition of his preeminent status among commercial illustrators by the U.S. Postal Service resulted in the largest single commission ever tendered to an American artist by that agency: to design thirty stamps for the 1984 Los Angeles Olympics. And in a follow-up assignment, the same agency has commissioned him to paint thirty-one watercolors depicting various Olympic sports for a book entitled *Golden Moments.*

Peak, who has thrived on a hectic, peripatetic schedule for more than three decades, counts himself among the most fortunate of mortals: working at something he loves and being amply compensated for his time, both in money and personal experience. "If I had a hobby," he told an interviewer for *American Artist* in February, 1982, "it would be painting."

BIOGRAPHICAL/CRITICAL SOURCES—Walter Reed, *The Illustrator in America*, Reinhold, 1966; *Communication Arts*, September-October, 1973, September-October, 1979; "Bob Peak: Images That Work," *American Artist*, February 1982.

—Sketch by Richard Calhoun

* * *

PENALVA, Jordi
See BOSCH PENALVA, Jordi

* * *

PEREZ, Daniel Torres
See TORRES (PEREZ), Daniel

PINI, Wendy 1951-

PERSONAL: Born June 4, 1951, in San Francisco, Calif.; daughter of Stuart and Elizabeth (Talcott) Fletcher; married Richard Alan Pini (a writer, editor, and publisher), June 17, 1972. *Education:* Pitzer College, 1970-72. *Studio:* WaRP Graphics, 5 Reno Rd., Poughkeepsie, N.Y. 12603.

CAREER: Freelance illustrator, 1974—; vice-president and art director, WaRP Graphics, 1979—. *Member:* Cartoonists Guild, Association of Science Fiction Artists. *Awards, honors:* Ed Aprill Award from the New York Comics Convention, 1979; Alley Award (a polling by mail), 1979, 1980; Ink Pot Award, San Diego Comics Convention, 1980; award for best artist, best comic from the Small Press and Writers Association, 1983, for *Elfquest*; New Yorkers Distinguished Service Award from the New York State Jaycees, 1984; Balrog Award for best artist from the Sword and Shield Corp. (Denver, Colo.), 1985, for *Elfquest.*

WRITINGS—With Richard Pini; all books of comics: *Elfquest* (twenty-volume comic series), WaRP Graphics, 1978-85; *Elfquest* (collections of comics), Donning/Starblaze, Vol. 1, 1981; Vol. 2, 1982; Vol. 3, 1983; Vol. 4, 1984; *Elfquest: Journey to Sorrow's End*, Berkley, 1983.

EXHIBITIONS: "Women in Comics," Museum of Cartoon Art, Port Chester, N.Y., 1984.

WORK IN PROGRESS: Screenplay for *Elfquest: The Animated Film,* release expected in 1988; developing new comic titles for WaRP Graphics; work on Epic Comics reprint of *Elfquest* for Marvel Comics.

RICHARD and WENDY PINI

A page from *Elfquest No. 16.* (© 1983, WaRP Graphics Inc. Reprinted with permission.)

SIDELIGHTS: Wendy Pini always had a fascination for drawing and for fairy tales; later she joined the ranks of organized comic fandom, one of the few female fans in an otherwise male-dominated field. (Indeed she met her future husband, Richard Pini, through their common love of comics.)

All the elements of fairy tale fantasy and comic book imagery coalesced into *Elfquest* (originally spelled *ElfQuest*), a project that the Pinis tried unsuccessfully to sell to every major and minor comic book company. After encountering only rejection and disappointment from all quarters, they decided to found their own publishing company which they defiantly called WaRP—a name with a definite science-fictional tinge that also stands for *W*endy *a*nd *R*ichard *P*ini.

Outwardly *Elfquest* is a story about a clan of elves, the Wolfriders, in their suspenseful search for a new home, after their ancestral grounds had been invaded by human barbarians; but it also stands both as a symbolic projection of Pini's inner life and personal turmoil and as a metaphor for the subsequent triumph of spirit over brute force. This interpretation comes from a close reading of the story and from Pini's many comments on her creation.

"*Elfquest* is almost a symbolic autobiography of mine," Pini told her *Comics Journal* interviewer. "Many of the incidents that happen in *Elfquest* are symbolic representations of things that have happened to me or to me and Richard. Quite literally some of the dialogue has been spoken by either Richard or me at certain times. We draw from our life experience and translate it into this beautiful fantasy. And I think that is one of the reasons *Elfquest* rings so true and has proved to most of our readers to be so refreshing in its originality—because it comes from us and our life experiences rather than tipping its hat to pre-existing fantasies."

With the Wolfriders now solidly established in their new home came the end of the Quest—both literally and figuratively. When the last of the twenty-episode saga came out in 1984, it culminated a success story that had resulted in numerous reprintings, four paperback collections, and a host of merchandising products. The year after *Elfquest* ended, Marvel Comics started reprinting in color for newsstand distribution the stories that had originally appeared in black-and-white for a limited audience.

The success of *Elfquest* has firmly anchored WaRP's position as an independent comic book publisher. Among the titles the company now releases are *A Distant Soil* by Richard Pini and Colleen Doran, a tale of science-fiction, and Robert Asprin and Phil Foglio's *Mythadventures*, an affectionate parody of the genre; as well as *Thunderbunny* by Martin Greim and Brian Buniak, an off-beat superhero title.

BIOGRAPHICAL/CRITICAL SOURCES: Dwight R. Decker, "A Touch of Stardust," *Comics Journal*, October, 1978; "From Poughkeepsie to Elfland: An Interview with Wendy and Richard Pini," *Comics Journal*, spring, 1981; "*ElfQuest* Wins Fantasy Award," *Comics Buyer's Guide*, May 31, 1985.

PORGES, Paul Peter 1927-

PERSONAL: Born February 7, 1927, in Vienna, Austria; son of Gustav and Jeanette Porges; married Lucie Eisenstab, 1951; children: Claudia M. Holland, Vivette C. Shorr. *Education:* Ecole d'Humanite, Lac Noir, Switzerland; Ecole des Beaux Arts, Geneva, Switzerland, B.F.A., 1947. *Office:* 41 Union Sq., New York, N.Y. 10003.

PAUL PETER PORGES

CAREER: Freelance cartoonist and graphic humorist, 1952—. *Military Service:* U.S. Army, 1950-52. *Member:* Cartoonists Association.

WRITINGS: Mad Around the World, Warner, 1978; *Mad How Not To Do It Book*, Warner, 1981; *Mad Cheap Shots*, Warner, 1984.

SIDELIGHTS: As quoted in *The World Encyclopedia of Cartoons*, Paul Peter Porges has explained his durability by saying "I was always very adaptable to the needs of the magazines with my style." Adaptability, indeed, has been the keynote in a thirty-plus year cartooning career that has seen his work featured in the pages of magazines from *Successful Farming* to *Playboy*. Sensitivity to the potentials and the requirements of a given forum is hardly a rare gift among commercially successful cartoonists, but in Porges it seems to have been developed to a very high degree. This trait may have been sharpened by his experiences as one of one hundred-eighty children whose escape from Austria to France during World War II was sponsored by Baron de Rothschild in 1939. He spent the time between the occupation of France in 1941 and his escape over the border to neutral Switzerland in 1944 evading the Nazis and their Vichy allies. This general capacity for adjustment and survival would ultimately stand him in excellent professional stead.

Between 1944 and 1947, Porges studied fine arts at the Ecole des Beaux Arts at Geneva, and upon receiving his baccalaureate from that institution in 1947 he emigrated to the United States where he was reunited in New York City with his parents, themselves survivors of a Nazi concentration camp. For the next several years his artistic career languished as he sought to acclimatize himself to yet another new environment. Then in 1950 he was drafted into the Army. While serving a two year hitch, he became interested in cartooning and his work began appearing regularly in *Stars and Stripes* and *Army Times*, and he even made some commercial sales to the American Legion magazine.

Discharged in 1952, he saw the prospect of a career before him for which the Ecole des Beaux Arts had not provided perhaps the best grounding, so using his G.I. Bill, he enrolled at New York's School of Visual Arts, then known as the Cartoonist's and Illustrator's School, where between the years 1952-54, he worked on his graphic technique and made contacts in what was at the time a very extensive network of commercial cartoon outlets. In 1954 he scored his first notable success by selling his work to the *Saturday Evening Post*, where he eventually became a contract artist

with a regular market for his cartoons. Meanwhile his drawings were also finding their place in *Playboy*, starting in 1956, and during the 1960s in the *New Yorker*.

With the collapse of the mass circulation periodical market during the middle to late 1960s thanks to the ubiquity of the new visual medium, television, Porges's income, like that of so many freelancers, suffered dramatically and once again he found it necessary to draw upon his talent for adaptation. This he did by becoming a frequent contributor to William M. Gaines's magazine of zany, sophomoric satire, *Mad*. At first, it appears that he was more of an idea man and writer than illustrator, collaborating with such outstanding staff artists as George Woodbridge, Paul Coker, Bob Clarke, and Jack Davis on such spreads as "Recruiting Posters Through History" (including one for the Hundred Years War that urges recruits "Reenlist and reenlist and reenlist and reenlist!"). Ultimately, however, he mastered the transformation from the bland, characterless ink line drawings of his early *Post* and *Playboy* work to the denser, more sophisticated comic strip medium favored by *Mad* artists and by 1972 he was a regular writer-illustrator for such recurrent features as "A Mad Look At . . . ," and "Scenes We'd Like

"But I digress."

Magazine cartoon, 1973. (© *The New Yorker*.)

Illustration for *New York Times* Op-Ed Page, 1980. (© Porges-*New York Times*. Reprinted with permission.)

to See," as well as for certain of his own departments, like "Footnotes To . . . ," which featured below-the-knee looks at the famous and infamous, and "Wait Till You Get Home and Find Out . . ." (for example, that the "narcs" are waiting to arrest you because "the weeds in your herb garden can be smoked in skinny cigarettes").

While it has provided flexibility and unusual longevity in a shrinking marketpace, Porges's ability to adapt himself to changing conditions appears to have kept him from evolving a too idiosyncratic style. From his earliest work for the *Post*, which he has himself described as a product of the "Cedar

Rapids School" in which "everybody's cartoons looked the same," through his most elaborately crafted panels for *Playboy* and *Mad*, which suggest the influences of artists as different as Charles Saxon, Barney Tobey, Warren Miller, even at times Virgil Partch, he has constantly improved his humor and technique. A review of his contributions to *Playboy* from 1960 on, for example, shows the steady evolution of a sure comic style in combination with the emergence of a confidently realized sense of composition and draftsmanship.

"You have to store up a fantastic amount of mental fuel in order to be able to turn out successful cartoons today," Porges told an interviewer from *Cartoonist Profiles*. "Idea creation should be based on a very deep kind of personal sense of humor—and it shouldn't be imitative." These principles have indeed stood Porges in good stead in his magazine cartoons, as well as in his written and illustrated travel pieces for the *New York Times* and *Signature*, the magazine of the Diner's Club. In addition to his work as a cartoonist, Porges has also taught a course in graphic humor at the School of Visual Arts.

BIOGRAPHICAL/CRITICAL SOURCES: Cartoonist Profiles, March, 1974; *The World Encyclopedia of Cartoons*, Chelsea House, 1980.

—Sketch by Richard Calhoun and Maurice Horn

Illustration for the magazine *The Movies*, 1983. (© Paul Peter Porges. Reprinted with permission.)

R

RENSIE, Willis
See EISNER, Will(iam Erwin)

* * *

ROBBINS, Trina 1938-

PERSONAL: Born August 17, 1938, in Brooklyn, N.Y.; daughter of Max Bear (a tailor and writer) and Elizabeth (a teacher; maiden name Rosenman) Perlson; children: Casey (daughter). *Education:* Attended Cooper Union, New York City ("expelled after one year"). *Politics:* Radical left, feminist. *Religion:* "Pagan." *Home:* 1982 15th St., San Francisco, Calif. 94114.

CAREER: Comic book artist, writer, and editor, 1966—. Writer and lecturer. *Member:* Women's Cartoonist Collective. *Awards, honors:* Inkpot Award from San Diego Comics Convention, 1977.

WRITINGS: Flashback Fashions, Price, Stern, Sloan, 1983; *Betty Boop Paperdolls,* Betty's Store, 1984; (with Cat Yronwode) *Women and the Comics,* Eclipse, 1985; *The Silver Metal Lover* ("a graphic novel"), Crown, 1985.

Contributor to *Playboy, National Lampoon, High Times, Heavy Metal,* and other periodicals.

EXHIBITIONS: Museum of Modern Art, San Francisco, late 1970s; Museum of Cartoon Art, Port Chester, N.Y., 1984.

WORK IN PROGRESS: Misty, a six-part comic book mini-series, for Marvel Comics; a four-part *Wonder Woman* mini-series, for DC Comics.

SIDELIGHTS: Trina Robbins wrote *CGA:* "I have been drawing all my life, and reading comics for almost that long. That has been my motivation for entering the comic field. My lack of acceptance in the early seventies, for purely sexist reasons, was certainly the most important circumstance that spurred me on to succeed as best I could—if for no other reason than spite. This also served to reinforce my already strong feelings of feminism."

After marrying in 1960, and despite a married lifestyle that left her free to design clothes for such rock stars as David Crosby, Donovan, Mama Cass, and Jim Morrison, she decided to go back to her first love—comics. "Trina in 1966," wrote Ronald Levitt Lanyi in the *Journal of Popular Culture,* "gave up six years of marriage and Los Angeles to return to New York to do an underground strip for *The East Village Other.* This work was followed by strips for the comics tabloids *Gothic Blimp Works* (New York) and *Yellow Dog* (San Francisco)." In the late 1960s and early 1970s she established herself as the preeminent woman cartoonist on the underground scene.

Though she claims lack of acceptance on the part of male underground cartoonists, she did find a growing number of outlets for her work. *The Official Underground and Newave Comix Price Guide* lists no fewer than sixty publications to which Robbins contributed, ranging alphabetically from *After Shock* to *Girl Fight Comics* to *San Francisco Comic Book* to *Yellow Dog Comics.* In 1970 she edited *It Ain't Me Babe,* which Jay Kennedy in the *Underground Price Guide* characterizes as "the first underground comix drawn and written entirely by women, [that] deals with women's liberation." She later established, along with other women cartoonists, Lee Marrs and Aline Kominsky notable among them, the longer-lasting *Wimmen's Comix,* which was still being published in 1985.

Photo by: Mark Leialoha.

TRINA ROBBINS

A page from "Meet Misty." (© Marvel Comics Group.)

comic book editor and writer Cat Yronwode. It documents in text and illustrations the lives and careers of close to three hundred women comic book and comic strips artists and writers. While it may be over-generous in its assessment of the contribution made by women to the medium, it is a valuable work of scholarship.

BIOGRAPHICAL/CRITICAL SOURCES: Ronald Levitt Lanyi, "Trina, Queen of the Underground Cartoonists: An Interview," *Journal of Popular Culture*, spring, 1979; Bill Sherman, "An Interview with Trina Robbins, the First Lady of Underground Comix," *Comics Journal*, winter, 1980; *Contemporary Literary Criticism*, Vol. 21, Gale, 1981; Jay Kennedy, ed., *The Official Underground and Newave Comix Price Guide*, Boatner Norton, 1982.

* * *

ROSEN, Hy(man J.) 1923-

PERSONAL: Born February 10, 1923, in Albany, N.Y.; son of Myer (in business) and Ray (Bellin) Rosen; married Elaine S. Lippman (a medical training coordinator), September 11, 1949; children: Edward, Eve, Benjamin. *Education:* Attended Chicago Art Institute, 1940-41; Art Students League, 1941-42; Stanford University, 1966; State University of New York at Albany, 1968-70. *Politics:* Registered Democrat. *Religion:* Hebrew. *Home:* 163 East Hague Blvd., Glenmont, N.Y. 12077. *Office:* Capital Newspapers, Times-Union, Albany, N.Y. 12122. *Agent:* Hearst Newspapers, 959 Eighth Ave., New York, N.Y. 10019.

In these and other comic books, as well as in her stories for the magazines, Robbins has often presented strong but sensitive women locked in combat with a cruel man's world. Her stated interest in "Ireland and the Celts, the Goddess, Ancient Egypt, cats" has led her to treat mythological and fairytale themes, such as in the "Exercise in Gold" story she did for *Heavy Metal* (1979). Yet she never loses sight of her twentieth-century feminist concerns, as evidenced, for example, in *Scarlett Pilgrim*, a comic book inspired by the real-life prostitute activist Margo St. James (1977).

Contrasting with these models of strength, paper dolls, usually regarded as symbols of fragility, also hold a strong fascination for Robbins. "I've always been into paper dolls," she told the interviewer for the *Comics Journal*. "I used to make my own when I was a kid. They don't do it any more, but if you look at a lot of old comics where the protagonist is a woman you'll see very very often they have paper dolls. And I think it's really a delightful tradition." She often draws paper dolls to complement her comic book stories, and has had two paper-doll books published.

Finally there is *Women and the Comics*, a book about women cartoonists Robbins wrote in collaboration with

HY ROSEN

CAREER: Political cartoonist, *Times-Union*, Albany, N.Y., 1945—; instructor in cartooning, State University of New York, Albany; lecturer on cartooning at Empire State College, Albany, N.Y.; sculptor in bronze and ceramic. Member of boards of North East Association of Sports Medicine and Capital District Ski Foundation. *Military service:* U.S. Army, 1942-45; served in 604th Engineers Camouflage Battalion. *Member:* Association of American Editorial Cartoonists (president, 1970). *Awards, honors:* National Award, Freedoms Foundation 1950, 1955, and 1960; Media Award, National Conference of Christians and Jews, 1962; Professional Journalism Fellowship, Stanford University, 1966; National Media Award, American Legion, 1980.

WRITINGS: As Hy Rosen Sees It, Capital Newspapers, 1970; *Do They Tell You What to Draw?*, Capital Newspapers, 1980.

EXHIBITIONS: One-man cartoon show, Center Gallery, Albany, N.Y., 1977.

WORK IN PROGRESS: Sculpture commissions; book of cartoons about New York State government from the late 1950s to the 1980s.

SIDELIGHTS: With his forty years as editorial cartoonist on the *Times-Union*, Hy Rosen is a long-standing public

Editorial cartoon, 1985. (© Rosen-*Albany Times-Union*. Reprinted with permission.)

Editorial cartoon, 1985. (© Rosen-*Albany Times-Union*. Reprinted with permission.)

institution in his native Albany; and he is now playing on a bigger stage as well, with his daily cartoons, titled "As Hy Rosen Sees It," enjoying national syndication and frequent reprintings in national magazines. His drawings are uncluttered and feature strong likenesses of the public figures he lampoons, be they Lyndon Johnson, Ronald Reagan, or the current governor of New York, Mario Cuomo. Rosen considers his human subjects to be important and central to his cartoons, thus helping him to make his point clearly and economically. To build the gag further, he often draws, in a corner of his cartoon, a small caricature of himself commenting on the goings-on.

Although a registered Democrat, Rosen (who likes to call his cartoons "extreme middle road") has administered the sting of sarcasm and ridicule to right and left alike; and the three awards he has received from the Freedoms Foundation bear testimony to his unbiased wielding of the satirical pen. He is a "strong advocate of freedom of expression for political cartoonists who sign their name to their work"; on the other hand, he believes in the responsibility of cartoonists to express their own opinions, and stands opposed to their illustrating other people's editorial comments.

BIOGRAPHICAL/CRITICAL SOURCES: The World Encyclopedia of Cartoons, Chelsea House, 1980; *Who's Who in American Art*, 16th edition, Bowker, 1984; *Cartoonist Profiles*, March, 1985.

S

SALMON, Donna (Elaine) 1935-

PERSONAL: Born February 23, 1935, in Los Angeles, Calif.; daughter of Thomas F. (a cabinetmaker) and Edith E. (Walters) Hartness; married Raymond M. Salmon (a cartoonist) July 19, 1956. *Education:* University of Denver School of Art, 1955-56. *Studio:* P.O. Box 712, Vallejo, Calif. 94590.

CAREER: Artist for educational television, Denver, Colo., 1955-56; freelance illustrator, 1960—; private instructor in painting, 1970-74.

WRITINGS—All as illustrator, all published by W. H. Freeman: I. Michael Lerner and William J. Libby, *Heredity, Evolution and Society*, 1976; Robert Ornstein, *Psychology of Consciousness*, 1977; Peter Abramoff and Robert G. Thomson, *Laboratory Outlines in Zoology*, 1978; Edmund Fantino and Cheryl A. Logan, *The Experimental Analysis of Behavior: A Biological Perspective*, 1979; Richard Kessel and Randy Kardon, *Tissues and Organs*, 1979; D. R. Bienz, *The Why and How of Home Horticulture*, 1980; Alfred A. Blaker, *Handbook for Scientific Photography*, 1980; Blaker, *Photography: Art and Technique*, 1980; Lubert Stryer, *Biochemistry*, 1981; Jules Janick, *Horticulture Science*, 1981; David M. Freifelder, *Physical Biochemistry*, 1982; Peter Abramoff and Robert G. Thomson, *Laboratory Outlines in Biology*, 1982; George W. Ware, *Pesticides: Theory and Application*, 1982.

EXHIBITIONS: University of Denver Museum of Art, 1955; University of Northern Colorado, 1965.

SIDELIGHTS: Donna Salmon has been a professional illustrator since 1960, working mainly, but not exclusively, on science books and manuals. While her specialization has led her to work with such publishers as McGraw-Hill, W. H. Freeman, Scientific American, University Research Association, and Stanford University Press, she has also done work for children and general illustration. She works usually in fine line and stipple, and with scratchboard and air brush techniques as well, in various styles of rendering.

"I have worked on many large projects as the principal artist," Donna Salmon commented, "doing the pencil layouts and co-ordinating art with assisting artists, as well as rendering finished art. In every case, where I have had the opportunity to work closely with the author, I have found it to be positive and beneficial to the art program. I believe in

DONNA SALMON

doing only high quality work, whether it be a complex biological illustration or a simple graph."

Donna Salmon's work as a scientific illustrator has earned her high praise in a field recognized for its technical pitfalls. Nobel Prize-winner Andre Lwoff of the Institut Pasteur in Paris, for instance, said of Stryer's *Biochemistry* book illustrated by Salmon, that it was "remarkable by the quality of both the text and the illustrations," while Scott C. Mohr of Boston University added that "the superb illustration job needs no comment." Such endorsements have contributed to make Donna Salmon one of the most sought-after artists currently working in the textbook field, and she has illustrated almost every conceivable manual, from horticulture to histology, and from photography to economics.

BIOGRAPHICAL/CRITICAL SOURCES: Who's Who in American Art, 16th edition, Bowker, 1984.

"Representative Mammals," a zoological drawing by Donna Salmon. (© W. H. Freeman & Co.)

* * *

SALMON, Raymond M.   1931-

PERSONAL: Born September 6, 1931, in Akron, Colo.; son of Ray and Marjorie (Barber) Berger; married Donna E. Hartness (an artist and illustrator) July 19, 1956. *Education:* University of Northern Colorado, B.A., 1956; M.A., 1965; attended Mesa College, University of Colorado, Chicago Academy of Fine Arts, California College of Arts and Crafts, San Francisco State University, and Colorado Springs Fine Arts Center. *Studio:* P.O. Box 712, Vallejo, Calif. 94590.

CAREER: Trumpet instrumentalist, 1947-55; cartoonist, 1952—; instructor in elementary schools in Colorado and Washington, 1957-61; art instructor in secondary schools in Washington, 1962-65; art instructor, 1965-66; professor of art, chairman of art department, 1966-74; dean, College of Creative Arts, 1966-74, John F. Kennedy University, Martinez, Calif.; Solano College, Suisun, Calif., instructor in commercial arts, 1970—. Arts in Action programs, Vallejo, Calif. (president, 1970-72); Greater Vallejo Recreational Arts Programs, 1969-72. *Military service:* U.S. Air Force, 1950-52, played in U.S.A.F. Band. *Member:* National

Cartoonists Society; Society of Professional Journalists. *Awards, honors:* First prize in First International Cartoon Competition, San Mateo, Calif., 1979.

EXHIBITIONS: University of Denver Art Museum, 1955; Colorado Springs Fine Arts Center, 1961; Tacoma Art Museum, 1964; State University of Missouri, 1965; Master Cartoonists Exhibition, Parke-Bernet, New York City, 1971; First International Cartoon Competition, San Mateo, Calif., 1979.

SIDELIGHTS: Raymond Salmon has had a long and distinguished career, both as a cartoonist and an educator. As an educator and art teacher he has been instrumental in furthering the cause of art (especially the graphic arts) in the Bay Area of California. As a cartoonist he has enjoyed a fruitful career, with contributions to many magazines, comic books, and illustrated books. He has worked as an assistant on Morrie Turner's pioneering newspaper strip about. a group of black and white kids working and playing together, *Wee Pals.* (It is of interest to note that the terms "rainbow power" and "rainbow coalition" were first coined in this strip.)

Salmon is currently writing and drawing *The Little Man*, which the author describes as "a special commentary humor panel." Using a short, baldheaded middle-aged man as his protagonist, he pokes gentle fun at the social scene. As can be expected, he often comments on his favorite subject, art, with references to abstract expressionism (he is opposed to it), television cartoons (he likes them), and the art market (he wishes it could be healthier). All this is interspersed with jokes about overpriced lawyers, crash diets, and Everyman's civic responsibilities. It is an engaging and funny feature, infused with a discreet and subtle charm.

RAYMOND M. SALMON

THE little MAN ®   by Salmon

Two daily panels of *The Little Man.* (© R. M. Salmon. Reprinted with permission.)

Salmon is also an historian of the cartoon form, and he has written a number of articles on cartoonists and their creations, notably in *Cartoonist Profiles.*

BIOGRAPHICAL/CRITICAL SOURCES: Who's Who in American Art, 16th edition, Bowker, 1984.

SAYLOR, Steven   1948-

PERSONAL: Born January 11, 1948, in Munich, West Germany; son of David W. (a colonel with the U.S. Air Force) and Jane (Heckaman) Saylor; married Aulikki Nittuyen, 1974 (divorced, 1977); married Jeanne Mahler (a design center manager), February 14, 1977; children: Stacey, Jessica. *Education:* Kent State University, B.F.A., 1970, M.A., 1971. *Office:* Evergreen Studio, P.O. Box 204, Dayton, Nev. 89403.

CAREER: Assistant television director, Norman Malone & Associates, Akron, Ohio, 1968-70; senior art director, May Advertising, Reno, Nev., 1972-74; instructor in painting and drawing, University of Nevada, 1974-76; senior art director, Evergreen Studio, 1976—. Member of Dayton Town Council, 1979-80. *Member:* Society of Illustrators, Sierra Nevada Museum of Art, American Portrait Society. *Awards, honors:* Excellence Award in the Communication Arts Competition, 1978, for Christmas card illustration; Certificate of Merit from Society of Illustrators, 1979, for "The Welcome Stranger" illustration; Certificate of Merit in the Communication Arts Competition, 1984.

EXHIBITIONS: Stremmel Galleries, Reno, Nev., 1978; Society of Illustrators, New York City, 1979; Who's Who in Art, Carmel, Calif., 1979; C. M. Russell Show, Great Falls, Mont., 1981-85; Eagle Gallery, Sun Valley, Id., 1981-83; Trailside Gallery, Jackson Hole, Wyo., 1982; Husberg Gallery, Sedona, Ariz., 1983; Rosequist Gallery, Tucson, Ariz., 1983; Hummingbird Gallery, Tucson, Ariz., 1984.

STEVEN SAYLOR

"**Crossin' the Carson.**" (© 1980, Steven Saylor/Evergreen Studio. Reprinted with permission.)

WORK IN PROGRESS: "The Birth of Mark Twain," a limited-edition print for 3-M Corporation's Contemporary Collection of Western Art.

SIDELIGHTS: "Steven Saylor didn't start out to be a western artist," Joe Galliani wrote in *Profile.* "After graduating from Kent State University in the late 60s, he took his fine arts degree and went to work as an art director for an advertising firm. He began experimenting with western themes in his artwork . . . Within a year, he had quit his art director job and had become a full-fledged cowboy working the cattle ranches of Nevada. He spent the next five years riding and roping while sketching everything he saw."

Saylor's technique consists in a painstaking mixing of watercolors and glaze, which he calls "glazed watercolors." In this method he was inspired by the great illustrator Maxfield Parrish, who glazed oils, but he also carefully studied the oil glazing methods of the painters Jan Van Eyck and Leonardo da Vinci. The finished pieces contain up to six hundred coats of watercolor and glaze, and project a photorealistic effect by the reflection of light from the white panel below. His subjects are inspired from the life and people around him, as well as from his sketches of the cowboy life on the range.

"**Landrums.**" (© 1980, Steven Saylor/Evergreen Studio. Reprinted with permission.)

Saylor never uses professional models for his paintings, but chooses instead people who look "real" for a scene. He then utilizes both his sketch pad and his camera to create the composition he will later paint. "A painting may be the result of as many as six, or more separate photo images and pencil studies," he told an interviewer. His paintings are mostly popular in the West, as may be expected, but Saylor's reputation has in recent years spread to the jaded East as well.

BIOGRAPHICAL/CRITICAL SOURCES: Peggy and Harold Samuels, *Contemporary Western Artists*, Southwest Art, 1982; Carol Eades Engstrom, "Steven Saylor's Paintings from the American West," *Art West*, May-June, 1983; Joe Galliani, "Steven Saylor's Western Art," *Profile*, fall, 1984.

"**Bar Talk.**" (© 1980, Steven Saylor/Evergreen Studio. Reprinted with permission.)

* * *

SCHWAB, Fred 1920-

PERSONAL: Born August 25, 1920, in New York, N.Y.; son of John (a painter) and Josephine (Baldasty) Schwab; married Barbara Frick (a secretary), April 1, 1956. *Education:* Attended Art Students League, New York City, 1946-47. *Home:* 411 E. 53rd St., New York, N.Y. 10022.

CAREER: Staff artist, Chesler Publishing Co., New York City, 1936-38; freelance comic book artist, New York City, 1938-42; freelance comic book artist, cartoonist, and advertising illustrator, 1946-1960; staff artist, *New York Times*, 1960-80; freelance cartoonist and advertising artist, 1980—. *Military service:* U.S. Air Force, 1942-45; drew cartoons for *Yank* (a service newspaper) and posters for the Air Force. *Member:* National Cartoonists Society, Cartoonists Guild, Graphic Artists Guild, Art Students League.

WRITINGS—All cartoon books; all published by Citadel Press: *Congratulations, You're Getting Married*, 1960; *Congratulations, You're a Grandparent*, 1960; *Congratulations, It's Your Birthday*, 1960; *The Last Damn Cat Book*, 1983.

WORK IN PROGRESS: A fifth cartoon book.

Self-portrait of Fred Schwab, drawn specially for *Contemporary Graphic Artists*.

SIDELIGHTS: One Sunday in the midst of the Depression, a teenaged boy with artistic inclinations was wandering the streets of midtown Manhattan when a "cartoonists wanted" sign tacked to a building door attracted his attention. Intrigued, the boy went up to the place, where he found a middle-aged man alone in a huge room cluttered with drawing desks. Upon averring that he was indeed a cartoonist, the boy was asked what he liked to draw. "Cowboys," he answered unhesitatingly. He was hired on the spot, handed a Western script from a thick pile, and set to work at once. That's how young Fred Schwab, aged sixteen, broke into the comic book business.

The man he had chanced upon was the legendary Harry "A" Chesler, one of the pioneer comic-book publishers and entrepreneurs. Writing of these people in *All in Color for a Dime*, Ted White said that their "first rule was, *Do it cheap.* Find cheap labor, pay cheap prices . . . Put in simple terms, most of the work being done for comic books by 1940 was being done by teenage boys." Schwab was one of these teenagers, and for the next two years he turned out Western stories upon humor strips in endless succession for Chesler's *Star Comics* and *Star Ranger*.

Some of his titles are still remembered with fond nostalgia. Calling him "a zany stylist much influenced by E. C. Segar," Denis Gifford in *The International Book of Comics* ticks off the names of some of the strips Schwab did for Chesler: "Riggin' Bill, that Lying Sailor Man," "Krazy Koot," "Killer McGee"; adding that they were "hilariously drawn comic fillers."

Leaving Chesler in 1938, Schwab then freelanced for practically all of the comic book publishers. He did "Butch the Pup" and "Salty Sam" for DC, "The Great Boodini" and "Dash in the 100th Century" for Centaur, "Lanky Lou"

for Globe, "Hemlock Shomes and Dr. Potsam" for Fox, "Slugnutty Sam" for Fiction House, "Mortimer the Monk" for Columbia, and others too numerous to mention; while also drawing covers for Dell. Only the coming of World War II could put a stop to this frenzied activity.

After three years in the Air Force, Schwab came back to comics in 1946. For about one year (1946-47) he illustrated the "Lady Luck" strip running in Will Eisner's *Spirit* newspaper comic section; then freelanced cartoons to various magazines and illustrations for a number of advertising companies. Finally, marriage and approaching middle-age prompted Schwab to leave the precarious life of the freelancer, and he joined the art department of the *New York Times* in 1960, to leave only twenty years later. He is now busy once again at what he loves most—drawing cartoons and humorous illustrations for publishing and advertising companies.

Fred Schwab wrote *CGA:* "The New York Art Students League taught me basic subjects, such as anatomy, perspective, color, etc. As for cartooning I am self-taught. I rely upon my sense of humor for ideas. I've never taken life seriously; I see humor in everything, in life's errors, absurdities, pretensions, discomforts, embarrassments, as well as in its inherent unpredictability. All these may appear tragic to some, they seem comical to me.

A page from *The Last Damn Cat Book*. (© 1982, Fred Schwab. Reprinted with permission.)

Gag cartoon. (© 1985, Fred Schwab. Printed with permission.)

"I am Manhattan-based. New York City is an art capital, and has many museums and art galleries which I like to visit regularly. This keeps me up on new art trends, and provides me with both inspiration and education.

"My cartoons have appeared in ads, newspapers, magazines, comic books, and books. Besides working in my studio, I enjoy sketching in public. In the course of my vacations, I have sketched scenes, people, and incidents in Europe, Africa, and South America. I'm rarely noticed because I act as if I were taking notes. An artist attracts attention, whereas a writer is ignored."

BIOGRAPHICAL/CRITICAL SOURCES: Richard Lupoff and Donald Thompson, editors, *All in Color for a Dime,* Arlington House, 1970; Denis Gifford, *The International Book of Comics,* Crescent, 1984.

* * *

SEA, Harvey
See CORBEN, Richard V(ance)

* * *

SEAVER, Jeff 1952-

PERSONAL: Born November 25, 1952, in Omaha, Neb.; son of James T. (a U.S. Air Force officer) and June F. (a business counselor) Seaver. *Education:* Goddard College, B.A., 1974. *Studio:* 130 W. 24th St., New York, N.Y. 10011.

CAREER: Freelance illustrator, 1974—. *Member:* Society of Illustrators, Graphic Artists Guild (president, 1982-85). *Awards, honors:* Numerous awards from Society of Illustrators, Art Directors Club, and other professional groups.

WRITINGS: Pricing and Ethical Guidelines (an industry sourcebook for pricing and business practices in the graphic arts).

Contributor to *New York, National Lampoon,* the *New York Times, Business Week,* and other publications. Editor-in-chief, *The Occasional* (a newsmagazine for professional artists).

EXHIBITIONS: Works exhibited in several Society of Illustrators annual shows; New York Art Directors Club; American Humorous Illustration Exhibit, Tokyo, Japan, 1983; Museum of Art and Science, Chicago, 1983.

SIDELIGHTS: A prolific and much sought-after illustrator, Jeff Seaver is probably best known for his humorous illustrations, which blend the treatment of sometimes serious subjects with a tongue-in-cheek approach. This deft touch is apparent even in his advertising design. "Round Up a Herd of Buffalo," done for Calgary Beer, a Canadian brewery whose logo is a buffalo head, simply and effectively shows a case of beer being roped in by an invisible hand on a bucolic background of rolling prairies. An ad for a computer company would show one Harry Glitsch, candidate for Congress, coolly tabulating the election returns on his personal computer, while his aides are frantically manning the phones.

This talent has carried Seaver's illustrations into the pages of the *New York Times, Fortune, Science Digest, Sports Afield, Mother Jones, National Lampoon,* and many other periodicals. On the advertising side his client list includes such corporations as Air Canada, American Express, Hertz, IBM, Pan American Airlines, Ralston Purina, and Texaco. Seaver is also project illustrator for the Cathedral of St. John the Divine in New York City, and he has illustrated a

Illustration for *New York Times* "Living Section," ca. **1982.** (© Jeff Seaver. Reprinted with permission.)

landmark plan that calls for a tower of solid light fifty-feet wide to be projected down from a satellite in stationary orbit over Melbourne, Australia.

Finally, Seaver has created *The Art of Negotiation*, a workshop lecture series on business management, communication skills, and sales for artists and other creative professionals; and he lectures extensively on subjects of concern to artists, such as copyright, negotiation, artists' rights, and business practices.

* * *

SHUT, Bill
　　See ALDER, Jamie

* * *

SILAS
　　See McCAY, Winsor Zenic

* * *

SMILKSTEIN, Harry　1911-
　　(Hal Stone)

PERSONAL: Born November 11, 1911, in Stamford, Conn.; son of Jacob (in clothing department store business) and Jeanette (a dress designer; maiden name, Shnitke) Smilkstein; married Jean C. Wittner (an attorney), June 30, 1960; children: Jay. *Education:* Cooper Union, B.F.A., 1938; attended Grand Central Art School, 1939-41; Art Students League, 1942-44; Mercy College, 1980. *Home and studio:* 105 Manchester Dr., Mt. Kisco, N.Y. 10549.

CAREER: Freelance illustrator, 1940—; art teacher, Adult Education, Karafin School, Mt. Kisco, N.Y., 1940—; director, American Art School, New York City, 1967—; instructor in art, Karafin School, 1972—. Art director, Mt. Kisco Centennial, 1975. President, Max Pavey Chess Club, Mt. Kisco. *Member:* Graphic Artists Guild, Art Students League (life member). *Awards, honors:* Award from Woman's Club of Pocantico Hills Show, 1979.

EXHIBITIONS: Hudson Valley Art Association; Woman's Club of Pocantico Hills, N.Y., 1979; Wichinich Community Hall, Mt. Kisco, N.Y., 1984.

WORK IN PROGRESS: Pictorial Conception, an art book.

SIDELIGHTS: After studies at the Cooper Union with Harvey Dunn and at Art Students League with Howard Trafton, Hal Stone (as he is professionally known) embarked on a long and prolific career as a freelance illustrator. He has illustrated fiction and special features in the *New York Daily News*, and done commercial art as well as cartoons and illustration work for the Lawrence, I. Steinberg's York, and Harry Kane studios in New York City.

Stone has specialized over the years in scenes of action. He has done Western and other adventure-oriented illustrations, as well as depictions of war and individual combat. His series of historical battle scenes have appeared in the pages

HARRY SMILKSTEIN (Hal Stone)

of *Esquire*, and in the motion picture *Tora! Tora!;* they are now in the permanent collection of the U.S. Army War College in Washington, D.C. At the same time he had enjoyed a parallel career in art instruction, both in New York City and in his home county of Westchester, N.Y.

"Art for communication or expression of an idea must touch base at all human disciplines," Hal Stone wrote *CGA*. "As far as I am concerned, truth in any artistic endeavor resides in the individual artist's spirit and character. Mere technique, experiments in form or media for the sake of experimentation, lacking a visual relationship to the basic pictorial idea remain a personal indulgence."

A battle scene illustration, ca. 1980. (© Hal Stone. Reprinted with permission.)

SOREL, Edward 1929-

PERSONAL: Born March 26, 1929, in New York, N.Y.; son of Morris (a salesman) and Rebecca (a factory worker; maiden name Kleinberg) Schwartz; name legally changed; married Elaine Rothenberg, July 1, 1956 (divorced, 1965); married Nancy Caldwell (a writer), May 29, 1965; children: Madeline, Leo, Jenny, Katherine. *Education:* Cooper Union College, diploma, 1951. *Home and studio:* 156 Franklin St., New York, N.Y. 10013.

CAREER: Co-founder, Push Pin Studios, New York City, 1953-55; art director, Columbia Broadcasting System (CBS-TV) promotion department, 1955-57; freelance artist, 1957—. *Awards, honors:* First prize for illustration in children's books from *New York Herald Tribune,* 1961, for *Gwendolyn, the Miracle Hen;* Augustus St. Gaudens Medal from Cooper Union, 1973; George Polk Award, 1979; many awards for illustration from Society of Illustrators, American Institute of Graphic Arts, and Art Directors Club of New York.

WRITINGS—All self-illustrated: *How to be President,* Grove, 1960; *Moon Missing,* Simon & Schuster, 1962; *Sorel's World's Fair, New York, 1964,* McGraw, 1964; *Making the World Safe for Hypocrisy,* Swallow, 1972; *Superpen,* Random House, 1978.

Illustrator: Warren Miller, *King Carlo of Capri,* Harcourt, 1958; Miller, *The Goings-On at Little Wishful,* Little, Brown, 1959; Miller, *Pablo Paints a Picture,* Little, Brown, 1959; Nancy Sherman, *Gwendolyn, the Miracle Hen,* Golden Press, 1961; Sherman, *Gwendolyn and the Weather Cock,*

Pass the Lord and
PRAISE THE AMMUNITION

A painting in the collection of Mrs. Nettie Lobsenz.

Golden Press, 1963; William Cole, *What's Good for a Five-Year Old?,* Holt, 1969; Joy Cowley, *The Duck in the Gun,* Doubleday, 1969; Jay Williams, *Magical Storybook,* American Heritage Press, 1970; Nancy Caldwell Sorel, *World People,* American Heritage Press, 1970.

Contributing editor, *New York* (a weekly magazine), 1968-76, *Esquire,* 1979-83; *Gentleman's Quarterly,* 1984—; contributor of weekly cartoon for *Village Voice,* 1974-77; contributor to *Time, Forbes, Fortune, Horizon, Atlantic, Sports Illustrated, Penthouse,* and many other periodicals.

EXHIBITIONS: Graham Gallery, New York City, 1973 and 1978; Capricorn Gallery, Washington, D.C., 1978.

WORK IN PROGRESS: Illustrations for "First Encounter," a bi-monthly column in *Atlantic.*

SIDELIGHTS: "I would rather make one hundred drawings and run the risk of none of them being worthwhile," Edward Sorel has declared, "than trace one carefully developed drawing." But risk-taking is not merely a peculiarity of his technical approach. He is also on record as saying that an illustration should reveal not only what an artist is technically capable of, but what he is thinking as well. So closely has he adhered to this conviction over the past twenty-five years that, in fact, one might rephrase the famous Cartesian dictum in his honor: "I think, therefore I draw." In such revelation there is always risk.

EDWARD SOREL

"Apres Moi, le Deluge." (© 1970, *Gentleman's Quarterly*.)

Born in 1929 in New York City, Sorel attended the High School of Music and Art and then went on to Cooper Union, graduating in 1951 with a fine arts diploma. After several years as a layout artist at *Esquire*, he joined his Cooper Union classmates Milton Glaser and Seymour Chwast to found Push Pin Studios, the innovative American design house. In 1956 he moved to CBS, working for the network's promotional ad department, and after three years there left to begin his freelance career. As he tells it, the 1950s were for him a period of learning, or more accurately unlearning, as he struggled to free himself from the technical biases of his formal art education. Art pedagogy emphasized design rather than illustration, which comes after all from the Latin word for "enlightenment." Thus an artist who sought, as he did, to illustrate in the classic sense of the verb had to forget about style and start to think narratively. His initial development of narrative skills came as an illustrator of children's books, where details of expression, costume, and action were crucial to catching and holding the young reader's attention. "This need to describe rather than to decorate was one turning point in my development," he said of his first effort, a collaboration with Warren Miller entitled *King Carlo of Capri* (1958). This was followed in 1959 by a second collaboration with Miller, *Pablo Paints a Picture*, which won an award from the American Institute of Graphic Artists, and in 1962 by *Gwendolyn the Miracle Hen* (text by Nancy Sherman), which received a *New York Herald-Tribune* award as the year's best children's book.

Having polished his ability to tell a story in pictures, Sorel now confronted the restrictive realities of the commercial and editorial art world and the consequent urge to express his own feelings in some personal fashion. Many successful graphic artists feel this same urgency and most of them turn to fine art as their chosen medium. But instead of painting derivative canvases for display in minor galleries, Sorel turned to political and social commentary as the best way of

venting his lively creative temperament. His earliest efforts in this line appeared in *Sorel's Affiche* (1959-60), a monthly promotional broadside featuring text by Warren Miller and Sorel's ink line and wash illustrations. It was mailed out free of charge to about seven hundred fifty art directors around the country, first to promote Sorel's work as an illustrator, and second "to ridicule the sacred cows of our society."

To be sacred, of course, a cow needs a devoted constituency unable to see the humor in iconoclasm, so it is not surprising that *Sorel's Affiche* raised a hackle or two among its recipients; on the whole, however, the response was favorable. The *Herald Tribune's* Sunday Magazine commissioned a droll, allegorical send-up of the American way entitled "Peace and Prosperity" for the cover of its Thanksgiving, 1959, issue. In 1960, he produced *How To Be President*, an acerbic look at the quadrennial parade of White House hopefuls, and followed it two years later with more political satire entitled *Moon Missing*. As commentary, these collections were funny and perceptive without being especially remarkable either in style or tone; but as the decade deepened and the issues of civil rights and the Vietnam War became the great national preoccupations, Sorel sharpened his pen as well as his partisanship.

It was in the pages of *Ramparts*, the house organ of the so-called "New Left," that he began consistently to meet his self-imposed objective of "getting my ideas across as bitingly as possible." Notable was his "Bestiary" series, which hearkened back to the eighteenth and nineteenth century traditions of presenting public figures as animal species, and

Editorial cartoon. (© 1976, *Village Voice*.)

Editorial cartoon. (© 1977, *Village Voice.*)

offered as fierce a skewering of its target as one is likely to find this side of a slander trial: Max Lerner as "The Common Boar" (who "would rather be fed than Red") or Robert F. Kennedy as "The Varying Hare" (whose "breeding habits are nothing short of astounding"). But perhaps his most audacious attacks were made via the unlikely medium of a syndicated feature, "Sorel's News Service," handled by King Features during 1969-70.

Jessica Mitford has called it "one of the sharpest, funniest contemporary political commentaries ever produced," and given the usual editorial preference for avoiding controversy, it is a measure of the passions aroused during the Nixon era that King Features Syndicate could place the "News Service" in forty-four papers at its distribution peak. The feature's format was simple: quotes from news service items were accompanied by a Sorel illustration. Tricia Nixon, for example, is quoted on the salutary effects of the fear inspired by Vice President Spiro Agnew's assaults on the liberal news media, and the accompanying caricature shows "Little Miss Nix-It" sitting beside a guillotine and knitting the surnames of prominent "enemies" (Cronkite, Brinkley, Mudd, Rather, et al.) into a scarf. (The allusion, of course, is to Charles Dickens's *A Tale of Two Cities*, but the spleen is pure Sorel.) "Every time I got a bit vicious," Sorel later recalled, "some paper would drop me." The end came when a caricature of Nixon gleefully juggling skulls above two news items, one reporting the week's death toll in Vietnam and the other quoting the President on how much fun it was to live in the White House, resulted in half the remaining subscribers cancelling the Service. "At that point," he observed (with, one suspects, a degree of pride), "it seemed futile to continue."

To the discomfiture of his subjects, however, he carried on his effrontery in other forums: *Ramparts, Rolling Stone, Playboy, Esquire, Atlantic* and *The Village Voice*. Beside members of the Nixon administration (especially Agnew and Martha Mitchell), he flayed with equal-opportunity vigor Democratic Party figures such as Hubert Humphrey, Arthur Goldberg, Adam Clayton Powell, Jr., and AFL-CIO President George Meany; religious leaders Billy Graham, Cardinal Spellman, and Norman Vincent Peale; and pop icons like Frank Sinatra, Sammy Davis, Jr., Jane Fonda, and John Wayne. With the Watergate Affair, Sorel achieved a kind of splenetic apotheosis—much of it collected in a 1978 collection entitled *Superpen*—after which the acid content of his work seemed to diminish. Nonetheless, on the basis of his output during the late 1960s and through the 1970s, his reputation as one of this century's truly memorable satirical artists is secure, and deserving of comparison with the best of his historical antecedents: Thomas Rowlandson, Honore Daumier, Thomas Nast, and particularly James Gillray.

Most recently, he has been turning his hand to commercial and editorial illustration, and enjoying the same success and visibility his work has always commanded thanks to its individuality and literacy. In the advertising world, he ranks with Charles Saxon and R. O. Blechman as a creative force (his Manufacturers Hanover Trust ads are perennial ad industry award winners), while his watercolor illustrations mark him as one of the most evocative graphic artists of this (or any) time. To test this assertion, one need only examine his 1982 illustration of an article in the *Atlantic* about Frederic Chopin's first meeting with George Sand: as the

elegant, sensitive composer sits playing for a drawing room audience, he is literally lassoed by smoke rings blown in his direction by the mannishly-dressed, cigar-smoking *femme terrible* of French letters. It is the portrait of a man bemused by an attraction that overwhelms a parallel repulsion. Here Sorel has caught the essence of this grand, fateful passion and made it evident even to those who might not know its particulars. It is a wonderful piece of work, both visually and intellectually, and demonstrates as strongly as ever Sorel's adherence to his guiding credo as a true "enlightener"—that an illustration should tell as much about the artist as it does about the subjects of his art.

BIOGRAPHICAL/CRITICAL SOURCES: Frederic Whitaker, "Edward Sorel," *American Artist*, May 1960; Carlos C. Drake, "Edward Sorel," *Graphis*, May 1963; *Time*, October 18, 1968; Jessica Mitford, foreword, *Making the World Safe for Hypocrisy* (edited by Liddia Ferrara), Swallow Press, 1972; *Contemporary Authors*, Vol. 9-10, Rev., Gale, 1973; *The World Encyclopedia of Cartoons*, Chelsea House, 1980; William Feaver, *Masters of Caricature*, Knopf, 1981; Steven Heller, "Edward Sorel," *Graphis*, July-August, 1983.

—*Sketch by Richard Calhoun*

*   *   *

STONE, Hal
    See SMILKSTEIN, Harry

*   *   *

SUMICHRAST, Jozef 1948-

PERSONAL: Surname is pronounced "Sum-mer-krast"; born July 26, 1948, in Hobart, Ind.; son of Joseph Steven and Stella (Ozug) Sumichrast; married Susan Snyder (a book designer and fabric illustrator), May 22, 1971; children: Kristin, Lindsey. *Education:* Attended American Academy of Art, Chicago, Ill., 1968-70. *Home:* P.O. Box 433, Deerfield, Ill. 60015.

CAREER: Freelance illustrator, 1970—; lecturer at art director clubs and colleges throughout the United States. *Member:* Society of Illustrators, Chicago Artist Guild. *Awards, honors:* Award for Excellence from Society of Illustrators, 1978; Gold Medal from Chicago Artist Guild, 1980, 1981, and 1985; Award for Excellence from New York Type Directors Club, annually 1980-84; Gold Medal from International Exhibition of Graphic Arts, Brazil, 1981; many other awards.

WRITINGS—Illustrator: Mildred W. Willard, *The Ice Cream Cone*, Follett, 1973; May Garelick, *Runaway Plane*, O'Hara, 1973; Marci Carafoli, *The Strange Hotel: Five Ghost Stories*, Follett, 1975; Ed Leander, *Q Is for Crazy*, Harlin Quist, 1977; Margaret Hillert, *The Funny Ride*, Follett, 1981; Jean Zelasney, *Do Pigs Sit in Trees?*, Follett, 1981.

EXHIBITIONS: Chicago Historical Society, 1976; Los Angeles County Museum of Art, 1976; New York Historical Society, 1981; Society of Illustrators, New York City, 1981; Centre Contemporain d'Art et de Culture, Paris, France,

JOZEF SUMICHRAST

1985. Represented in permanent collections of Society of Illustrators, Chicago Historical Society, Columbia College, University of Texas.

SIDELIGHTS: Chicago-based illustrator Jozef Sumichrast is perhaps best known for his highly stylized alphabets. Ingeniously combining the skills of the draftsman, calligrapher, and fine artist, he has reproduced the familiar characters of the English, Cyrillic, and Hebrew alphabets by manipulating the most unexpected forms—a hacksaw, a sword and plow combination, a turtle, Adam and Eve—into an intriguingly novel march of letters. The whimsy and good humor so evident in these creations, however, mask the amount of thought and planning that have gone into them. These alphabets, Sumichrast explains, are based first on color. "The Cyrillic alphabet, for example, is based on red, the Russian color; and the opposite of red would be green, so that was my second color, and then I used black and brown as neutral tones to pull everything together." His Hebrew alphabet, on the other hand, uses silver, gold, and blue as primaries, with earth tones as neutrals. Nor is the selection of images for manipulation arbitrary or impulsive: "I could like an idea for one letter, an animal say, but that would affect the letter next to it. I wouldn't want to have two animals together . . . I see something inside something else, one thing evolves into another and I constantly refine it."

The original poster prints of the English and Cyrillic alphabets have received design awards both in the United States and Europe, but the idea was actually first conceived as a commercial promotion for K and S Photolabs. "It was going to be 'K and S presents the rest of the alphabet.' They weren't interested so I did it for myself." The resulting artistic success of the concept has made it, after all, commercially viable, and since that time his fanciful letters (and numbers) have shown up in ads for Levi's (clothing and accessories as letters) and Remington cutting tools (numerals shaped out of various substances to be cut). He has also illustrated a children's book, *Q Is For Crazy*, with a winsome reworking of his English alphabet theme.

Not surprisingly, Sumichrast's style and sensibilities have made him quite successful as an illustrator of juvenile literature; his way with color and his often amusing choice of imagery are admirably suited to delight the eye of the younger reader. Yet to type him as simply a purveyor of unsophisticated graphic art is to fail to perceive the thought and intelligence he brings to the creative act. To begin with, he employs a singular technique. Each work is carefully planned out in advance and sketched out fully on watercolor paper which he then stretches on a frame as an oil painter would a canvas surface. Next he coats the paper with a gesso-like layer of sepia ink, after which he begins his painting, using transparent inks and dyes in layers. The color scheme particularly must be well planned because the disintegrative nature of the paper as well as the transparency of the media will not allow for alterations. This process may seem complex and lacking in spontaneity, but it results in pieces that glow with humor, warmth, and life.

A page from "The Chinese Lunar Calendar," ca. 1980.
(© Josef Sumichrast. Reprinted with permission.)

A page from "The Russian Alphabet." (© 1979, Jozef Sumichrast. Reprinted with permission.)

Commenting on current fashions in illustration, Sumichrast mentions a work by Henri Rousseau. It is not surprising that he should do so, for in his own work there is an identically deceptive naivete, a similarly rich vibrancy of color. Like Rousseau he has a fondness for the bestiary, returning to it again and again for subject material which he renders with the same senses of whimsy and wonder associated with the French master. A good example of this is his Chinese lunar calendar poster, which provides him with the opportunity not only to portray each of the twelve animals comprising it, but to do so in such a way as to bring out their specific Buddha-given characteristics. Thus the monkey (in this case a colorfully-masked mandrill) impresses us with its inventive, improvisational shrewdness; while the pig is palpably simple, durable, and brave. Another work in this vein is his poster "Genesis 9:17," a visual parable in grays and earth tones of a Noah figure from the depths of whose flowing beard peek pairs of anxious looking animals: the message— man as custodian, in God's name, of the place he has been given to dwell in.

"The new illustrations," Sumichrast argues, at least from his own experience, "seem to be looking back to the past, to primitive art." Thanks to this trend, he sees a growing degree of license being given the graphic artist. "In the past only in children's books, certain editorial work, and a few good studios, such as Chicago's Graphique, was an illustrator called upon to interpret the work. The illustrator has been treated as a decorator or graphic designer rather than a free individual. Today's art is freer. It's dreamy and magical. The illustration not only has to convey the message, but given a more demanding audience, it has to entertain."

BIOGRAPHICAL/CRITICAL SOURCES: Something About the Author, Vol. 29, Gale, 1981; "Jozef Sumichrast," *Communication Arts,* January/February, 1981; *Who's Who in America,* Marquis, 1985.

—*Sketch by Richard Calhoun*

* * *

SWORDS, Betty 1917-

PERSONAL: Born August 17, 1917, in Gilroy, Calif.; daughter of John (an Oakland public school administrator) and Gertrude (Gahr) Edgemond; married Henry Leonard Swords (a geologist and geophysicist for an oil company); children: Richard, Stephen. *Education:* University of California at Berkeley, B.A., 1938; attended Academy of Advertising Art, San Francisco, 1938-40. *Home:* 2490 S. Holly St., Denver, Colo. 80222.

CAREER: Freelance fashion illustrator, 1943, 1948-55; freelance cartoonist, 1955-70, 1972-74; magazine writer, lecturer, and college instructor, 1970—. *Member:* National Organization for Women, Colorado Authors' League, Denver Woman's Press Club.

WORK IN PROGRESS: Writing a book on humor power.

SIDELIGHTS: A latecomer to cartooning, Betty Swords switched from fashion illustration to a commercial art

BETTY SWORDS

field—cartooning—that could be conducted by mail from the small towns where her husband's explorations took them. "Marriage, mothering and moving made it difficult to pursue any kind of career, especially in those marriage-*or*-career days," said Swords. "Still, my cartooning gave me an invaluable lifeline to the world outside my home. And my home—the domestic doings—supplied my material."

Swords's first cartoon sales were to King Features Syndicate and the *Saturday Evening Post* in 1955. Over the following years she contributed numerous cartoons, as well as many self-illustrated humor essays, to such publications as the *Post, Look, Redbook,* the *Ladies' Home Journal, Good Housekeeping* and *Modern Maturity.* In 1970 an injury to her right arm forced her to temporarily abandon cartooning (her last major projects were a two-page spread on the new woman candidate for *Changing Times* in 1972 and the Male Chauvinist Pig Calendar in 1974). She turned to writing, and had articles published in *Reader's Digest, McCall's* and the *Christian Science Monitor.* She also became a lecturer and college instructor on humor and cartooning at the University of Denver and other places. Currently she teaches a course on humor power at the University of Colorado.

Betty Swords wrote *CGA:* "I was always puzzled by the scarcity of women cartoonists. In 1967 I discovered the main reason while reviewing a book of one-liners. I suddenly realized that women were always the butt of the jokes. They were the 'dumb dames' trying to trap a man into marriage, whereupon they became vicious, avaricious battleaxes (and always dumb). Cartoons were the same. It wouldn't come naturally or easily to women to draw themselves in such a degrading way, but unless they did, they just weren't funny! Syndicated cartoonist Dorothy Bond presented a feature about bright secretaries and not-so-smart bosses. Male syndicate editors howled, "That's not funny!" So she published the cartoons in a book, which sold well (presum-

ably to secretaries). I concluded: *women don't make the jokes because they are the joke.* In 1974, when more women were entering the 'man only' professions, like medicine and law, the number of women cartoonists declined even further. Jack Markow wrote in his column in *Writer's Digest,* that of the handful 'only Betty Swords is still active.'

"I saw that this contemptuous view of women in humor stretched back through our history, to turn venomous when women demanded their rights in the nineteenth century. Both the venom, and the cartoons, were to be duplicated in men's humor attack against the second wave of the women's movement. I saw how humor was used as a secret weapon in what James Thurber called 'the war against women': 'bloomer girls' and 'bra-burners' were ways to trivialize and ridicule the women, and to ignore the serious issues involved. Women were only first on the Humor Hit List. Everyone who differs from some status quo is a victim of caricature assassination.

"It was painful to give up my Pollyanna perception of humor as a good, though frivolous, 'fun-thing.' I was shocked by humor's destructive powers—but I discovered more constructive uses as well, especially in the humor of minorities. Native Americans, and blacks like Dick Gregory used humor to unite, rather than to polarize. I see humor now as a great natural resource, like nuclear energy, that can be used to benefit or to destroy."

BIOGRAPHICAL/CRITICAL SOURCES: Cartoonist Profiles, September, 1973; *The World Encyclopedia of Cartoons,* Chelsea House, 1980.

"**Back to Nature**" cartoon. (© 1971, *Redbook.*)

A page from ''The Male Chauvinist Pig Calendar'' by Betty Swords, 1974. (© R/M Hurley.)

T

TERRY, Hilda
See D'ALESSIO, Hilda

* * *

TEZUKA, Osamu 1926-

PERSONAL: Born November 3, 1926, in Toyonaka City, Osaka, Japan; son of Yutaka and Fumiko Tezuka; married Etsuko Okada, 1959; children: Makoto, Rumiko, Chiiko. *Education:* Graduated from Osaka University College of Medicine, 1951; Nara Medical College, M.D., 1960. *Home:* Tokyo, Japan.

CAREER: Comic artist, 1946—; licensed medical doctor, 1960—; animator and director, 1961—; director and owner, Tezuka Productions. *Member:* Japan Cartoonists Association (director); Japan Animation Association (chairman); Japan Science Fiction Writers Club.

AWARDS, HONORS: Numerous awards for comics, including Kodansha Publishing Cultural Awards, 1969 and 1977; Shogakkan Comics Awards, 1957 and 1983; Bungei Shunju Comic Award, 1975. Awards for animation include Silver (Ragazzi) Lion Award from the Venice International Film Festival and Special Division Award from the Asia Film Festival, both 1967; Grand Prix from the Zagreb Animation Festival, 1984.

WRITINGS: Best-known comics include *Jungle Taitei* (title means "Jungle Emperor"), 1950; *Tetsuwan Atomu* (title means "Mighty Atom"), 1952; *Hinotori* (title means "The Phoenix"), 1954—; *Buddha*, 1972-83; *Black Jack*, 1973-78. Also author of *Boku wa Mangaka* (title means "I am a Cartoonist"), 1978, and *Tezuka Osamu Rando* (title means "Osamu Tezukaland"), 1979.

FILMS: Numerous theatrical features, television series, and experimental animation efforts, including *Tetsuwan Atomu* (title means "Mighty Atom"; broadcast in the United States as "Astroboy"), 1961; *Jungle Taitei* (title means "Jungle Emperor"), 1965; *Tenrankai no E* (title means "Pictures at an Exhibition"), 1966; *Hinotori 2772* (title means "Phoenix 2772"), 1980; *Jumping*, 1984; *Broken Down Film*, 1985.

EXHIBITIONS: Display marking Tezuka's fortieth anniversary as an artist toured Japan in 1985.

SIDELIGHTS: Osamu Tezuka began doodling as a tiny boy, and by junior high school his artistic talents were already in full bloom. Viewed today, illustrations made of his childhood passion—his collection of butterflies and beetles—rival those of the best professional in their realism and attention to detail. His professional debut as a cartoonist came in 1946, when he published a four-panel strip titled *Ama-chan no Nikkicho* (title means "Little Ama's Diary"). Reflecting his childhood hobby, he began signing the last character of his first name with the ideograph for "insect."

Tezuka grew up under the influence of Japanese artists such as Suiho Tagawa, Ryuichi Yokoyama, and Noboru Oshiro, but his real love was animation, especially that of Max Fleischer and Walt Disney. His father, moreover, was an avid amateur photographer, well known at the time under the name Hokufu.

With Japan (and its animation industry) devastated at the end of World War II, Tezuka threw himself into comics, eventually revolutionizing the medium in Japan by incorporating a fast-paced, cinematic style of drawing to tell complex, humanistic stories.

Where other artists used ten or twenty pages to tell a story, Tezuka began using hundreds, sometimes thousands, in the process turning children's comics into long, saga-like visual novels. This was accomplished through superhuman productivity and an above average intellect which allowed him to synthesize a broad variety of influences. In the last forty years Tezuka has drawn over one hundred and fifty thousand pages, and nearly one hundred million copies of his stories in paperback form have been published. At his peak, using assistants, he has created over three hundred pages per month. Stories range from *Tsumi to Batsu*, an adaptation of Dostoevsky's *Crime and Punishment*, to romances for girls such as *Ribon no Kishi* ("Princess Knight"), to a recent semi-historical account of his ancestors titled *Hidamari no Ki* ("Tezuka's Ancestor Dr. Ryoan"). The target readership of these comics ranges from the very young to those in their forties and fifties, and reflects both the diversity of their themes and the sheer size of comics culture in Japan.

What is the secret of Tezuka's success? Undoubtedly part of it is attributable to his sheer productivity, but his long term popularity has been made possible by his own innate curiosity about the world. At the end of World War II, when Tezuka entered the Osaka University to pursue a career in medicine, the "cartoonist" was not a practical occupation, either economically or socially. One result, however, was that he devoted much of his time to doodling and drawing rather than to his studies. While a medical student, and later

An excerpt from *Tetsuwan Atomu*, known in the United States as *Astroboy*, 1957. (© Osamu Tezuka. Reprinted with permission.)

a resident, he began publishing some of his work, and actually achieved considerable success. The struggle between comics and medicine was not fully resolved until he became a licensed physician in 1960, with a thesis on the sperm of pond snails. At that point Tezuka was already a nationally famous cartoonist, with considerable income.

Tezuka thereafter dedicated himself to comics and animation, but never lost his scientific interest in the world. In comic stories such as *Black Jack, Hi no Tori,* and the recent *Hidamari no Ki,* he has consistently woven in medical and philosophical themes. In science fiction, moreover, he has found a forum for his interest in the sciences and the future. All of Tezuka's stories, however, are characterized by their humanism and rejection of war.

Success with comics eventually made it possible for Tezuka to pursue his original dream of creating animation. As he himself often confesses, the former is his "wife", while the latter is his "mistress." Over the past thirty years the money amassed from sales of his comics has frequently been lavished, even dissipated, on animation. Unlike Walt Disney, Tezuka is more artist than manager, and his productions usually lose money. It is the animation, however, which has earned Tezuka an international reputation, beginning with *Tetsuwan Atom,* which was broadcast in the United States by the National Broadcasting Company (NBC) in 1965 as *Astroboy.* Other Tezuka animation which has received international exposure includes *Jungle Taitei* (shown as "Kimba the White Lion") and, more recently, the theatrical feature, *Phoenix 2772.*

Because of Tezuka's stature and his art style, he is often referred to overseas as "Japan's Walt Disney." In Japan, however, he is a national hero, in the media called the *manga no kamisama,* or "God of Comics." All his other talents aside, perhaps Tezuka's most remarkable achievement has been to maintain his popularity over the last forty years, in what is surely one of the world's most fad and fashion-conscious nations.

Still, even Tezuka has not been without his critics. As fashions in clothes change, so do those in art work; the trend in Japan in recent years has been towards a more realistic style, distinctly different from Tezuka's rounded, Disneyesque lines. Although Tezuka has catered to this new fashion by inserting more detail and realism, he is clearly most relaxed with his old style. Another problem is that over the years Tezuka has developed a type of dialogue with his huge readership, which now spans several generations. Jokes and gags comprehensible only to the initiated appear frequently in both his comics and animation. While the fans have come to expect, and even demand this, it at times confuses outsiders.

The degree to which Tezuka has influenced the comics and animation world in Japan is apparent not only from his popularity, but also from the artists working today who credit him as either mentor or former employer. Most of the popular artists in Japan today grew up reading Tezuka comics and watching Tezuka animation; many of them worked as his assistants, either filling in details in comics or as animators on his films. Comic artists affiliated with Tezuka at some point during their career include Fujio Akatsuka, Shotaro Ishimori, Fujiko Fujio, Hideko Mizuno,

Keiko Takemiya, and Reiji Matsumoto. In animation the list includes Shinnichi Suzuki, Renzo Kinoshita, Yoshiyuki Tomino, and on and on. Recently, he is also being credited as an influence by a younger generation of American artists, including the artist for the *Elfquest* series, Wendy Pini, and Scott McCloud, creator of the *ZOT* series.

BIOGRAPHICAL/CRITICAL SOURCES: The World Encyclopedia of Comics, Chelsea House, 1976; *The World Encyclopedia of Cartoons,* Chelsea House, 1980; Frederik Schodt, *Manga! Manga! The World of Japanese Comics,* Kodansha International, 1983.

—*Sketch by Frederik Schodt*

* * *

THORNE, Frank   1930-

PERSONAL: Born June 16, 1930, in Rahway, N.J.; son of George Washington (an elevator operator) and Edna (Rahway city treasurer; maiden name Johnson) Thorne; married Marilyn E. Schneider (a musician), April 14, 1951; children: Frank Jr., Wende, Amy Hreiz, Becky. *Education:* Attended Art Career School, New York City, three years. *Politics:* Independent. *Religion:* "Free thinker." *Residence and studio:* 1967 Grenville Rd., Scotch Plains, N.J. 07076.

FRANK THORNE

A page from *Ghita of Alizarr*. (© 1985, Frank Thorne. Reprinted with permission.)

CAREER: Trumpet-player with big bands and jazz groups and stage magician, 1946-52; freelance illustrator and comics artist and writer, 1948—. *Military service:* U.S. Army Reserves, served with special service unit, New York City ("designed scenery, played in pit band"). *Member:* Authors Guild of the Authors League of America. *Awards, honors:* National Cartoonists Society Award for Best Comic Book, 1963; New Jersey Art Directors' Award for Excellence, 1975; San Diego Comics Convention "Inkpot" Award, 1978; *Playboy's* Best Comic Strip Award, 1981.

WRITINGS—All books of comics: *Ghita of Alizarr,* Blue Dolphin Enterprises, 1983, Catalan Communications, 1985; *Ghita of Alizarr: The Thousand Wizards of Urd,* Catalan Communications, 1985; *Lann,* Ken Pierce, 1986.

WORK IN PROGRESS: Continuing *Moonshine McJugs,* a full-page color comic for *Playboy.*

SIDELIGHTS: As the foregoing suggests, Frank Thorne has led an eventful and varied life. It is perhaps best to sum it up in the artist's own words: "New Jersey is Thorne's home state. In his teen years he developed his musical skills. Through the late forties he played trumpet with several big bands and jazz groups in and around the Garden State. His musical activity was lucrative enough to help pay for his tuition in the Art Career School atop the Flatiron Building in New York City.

"Along with his interest in music, Thorne became involved with performing stage magic and producing original magic tricks that were packaged in his Rahway home and distributed by several large Manhattan magic shops. The role as magician was to play a key role in later life as he assumed the character of Thenef the Wizard in the *Wizard and Red Sonja* shows.

"Thorne entered art school in 1947. Frank picked up his first professional art assignments in his freshman year. Standard Comics gave him several stories to pencil in their romance books. He also was assigned to produce illustrations for publishers of pulp magazines in New York City.

"Even before graduation in 1950 Frank had approached a local newspaper with the idea of writing and drawing a history of the county. Thus in 1950 began *The Illustrated History of Union County.* The series ran for almost a year in the *Elizabeth Daily Journal.* A lucky break in 1951 landed him the assignment to draw *Perry Mason* for King Features Syndicate. After a year carrying the crushing load of a daily and Sunday newspaper strip, Thorne went to Dell Comics to turn out many well-known features. In the 1950s Frank produced *Flash Gordon, Jungle Jim, Tom Corbett Space Cadet, Green Hornet, Twenty Thousand Leagues Under the Sea,* and *Moby Dick* to name a few. In the early sixties, when Dell became Gold Key, Thorne returned to draw *Mighty Samson.* It was his first opportunity to design a character. Samson is looked back upon by comics historians as a forerunner of the sword-and-sorcery genre in comics.

"In 1957 Thorne was chosen to draw the syndicated newspaper series *Dr. Guy Bennett.* For seven years Thorne toiled at the good doctor's adventures. . . The 1960s brought many commercial assignments to the Thorne studio

in Scotch Plains. Book jackets, illustrations for many of the stories in *The Golden Magazine,* telephone book covers, children's book illustrations gave him wide experience in the commercial field.

"The early seventies found him freelancing at DC Comics doing *Tomahawk, Enemy Ace, Tarzan,* and *Korak Son of Tarzan.* A brief stint at the short-lived Atlas Seaboard doing covers and *Son of Dracula* and *Lawrence of Arabia* led to the turning point in Thorne's career. In the year 1975 Marvel Comics decided to try Red Sonja, a secondary character in the *Conan* series, in her own magazine. Frank was chosen to draw the books. . . *Red Sonja* became the first successful comic book featuring a heroine to be published by Marvel.

"Early in Sonja's rise to stardom Thorne developed the wizard role and originated the *Wizard and Red Sonja Show.* The performances were seen coast to coast and on network television. In a hectic year of celebration by the media Sonja landed in *Newsweek, Esquire, Rolling Stone* and *Playboy.* In 1978, at the height of *Sonja's* popularity, Frank left and originated *Ghita of Alizarr.*

"Soon after Ghita's premier in Warren Publishing's magazine *1994,* she was credited with boosting the sales of the magazine to the leader in the Warren line. As both writer and artist of the adventures of the blonde warrior woman,

A page from *Lann.* (© 1985, Frank Thorne. Reprinted with permission.)

Frank found total freedom of expression. With *Ghita* firmly established, Thorne went to *Playboy* with *Danger Rangerette* in hopes of placing an adult comic in the new comic section. *Moonshine McJugs* was soon a regular feature of the magazine. Much of the material for *Moonshine* was spun from skits written by Frank for the *Danger Rangerette and Barf Beltless Show* that he developed after the success of the *Wizard and Red Sonja* shows.

"Among the earliest influences on Thorne's drawing style were Alex Raymond, Hal Foster, and Neil O'Keefe. He has many favorite writers, from Rabelais through Samuel Beckett and Vladimir Nabokov. Movies fascinate Frank; he especially admires the films of Federico Fellini.

"In the summer of 1984, Thorne developed live action video sequences of *Ghita* and *Moonshine McJugs*. These segments, adapted from his graphic novel and the *Playboy* comic, were shown on the Playboy Channel in February, 1985. The antic world of *Moonshine McJugs* is in stark contrast to *Ghita's* antediluvian age, and junk-strewn Neon 6, scene of *Lann's* adventures. The obsessive self-indulgence of the *Ghita* books is indicative of Thorne's individuality. He has always worked totally alone, without use of assistants, models or photographs. *Ghita of Alizarr* is his ultimate inner theater. Ghita's world is the total outpouring of the dark, perfumed dreams of her creator. In giving her life, her craftsman follows her into the books as Thenef the Wizard. Together with Dahib, the faithful halftroll, they rollick through nightmare orgies, ogre-filled forests, and realms of black magic beyond the imagination of demon troubadours."

In his work Thorne considers himself a storyteller more than a cartoonist, and the fact is clearly evidenced by his membership in the Authors Guild, while at the same time he has refrained from associating himself with any of the numerous cartoonists' associations in existence. In the afterword to *Ghita of Alizarr* he gives us a clue to his artistic credo: "How I envy the creator of Gargantua and Pantagruel," he wrote. "His characters are so luxuriantly fleshed out in the straight narrative form. In designing and writing a comic page the integration of picture and text is so demanding that too little space is left to properly develop character in the limited speech areas and captions. Ghita struggles proudly to be more than a two-dimensional comic book heroine. Hopefully, in the final judgment, I fancy that she will be traced back to Rabelais and Sterne rather than to Popeye and the Katzenjammers."

BIOGRAPHICAL/CRITICAL SOURCES: The Art of Frank Thorne, Cartoonews, 1978; Afterword, *Ghita of Alizarr*, Blue Dolphin, 1983.

* * *

TIERNEY, Tom 1928-

PERSONAL: Born October 8, 1928, in Beaumont, Tex.; son of John T. (an accountant) and Mary Lou (a florist; maiden name Gripon) Tierney. *Education:* University of Texas, B.F.A., 1949. *Home:* Drawer D, Hopewell Junction, N.Y. 12533. *Studio:* Tom Tierney Studio, Inc., 151 W. 74th St., New York, N.Y. 10023.

Photo by: Sandy's Photos.

TOM TIERNEY

CAREER: Freelance fashion illustrator, 1949—. *Military service:* U.S. Army, 1951-53, served as a recruiting illustrator. *Awards, honors:* Texas Fellowship Painting Award, 1948; Texas General Exhibition, Purchase Award for watercolor, 1952; Beaumont Art Museum, First Prize, oil painting, 1953.

WRITINGS—All Dover unless otherwise noted: *Thirty from the 30s*, Prentice-Hall, 1976; *Glamorous Movie Stars of the Thirties Paper Dolls*, 1978; *Rudolph Valentino Paper Dolls*, 1979; *Marilyn Monroe Paper Dolls*, 1979; *Attitude*, St. Martin's, 1979; *John Wayne Paper Dolls*, 1980; *Pavlova and Nijinsky Paper Dolls*, 1981; *Vivien Leigh Paper Dolls*, 1981; *Cut and Assemble a Toy Theater: The Nutcracker Ballet*, 1981; *Carmen Miranda Paper Dolls*, 1982; *Judy Garland Paper Dolls*, 1982; *Great Fashion Designers of the Belle Epoque Paper Dolls*, 1982; *Great Empresses and Queens Paper Dolls*, 1982; *Isadora Duncan, Martha Graham and Other Stars of the Modern Dance Paper Dolls*, 1983; *Great Fashion Designers of the Twenties Paper Dolls*, 1983; *Nancy Reagan Fashion Paper Dolls*, 1983; *A Colonial Family Paper Dolls*, 1983; *Cat Snips*, Tribeca Publishing, 1983.

Santa Claus Paper Dolls, 1984; *(More) Erte Paper Dolls*, 1984; *Joan Crawford Paper Dolls*, 1984; *Cut and Assemble a Toy Theater: Peter Pan*, 1984; *Cupie Paper Dolls*, 1984; *Great Fashion Designers of the 1930's Paper Dolls*, 1984; *Ronald*

Reagan Paper Dolls, 1984; *Pope John Paul II Paper Dolls*, 1984; *Great Opera Stars of the Golden Era Paper Dolls*, 1984; *Famous Black Entertainers Paper Dolls*, 1984; *Supergirl*, Putnam, 1984; *Greta Garbo Paper Dolls*, 1985; *Ziegfeld Follies*, 1985.

EXHIBITIONS: Texas General Exhibition, Witte Museum, San Antonio, 1952; Beaumont (Texas) Museum, 1952.

SIDELIGHTS: Best known for his paper dolls of movie stars and celebrities, Tierney began his long and successful freelance illustration career while in high school, doing illustrations for local department stores in his home town, which he continued in Austin, while attending the University of Texas. Upon graduation he became a fashion illustrator for Scarborough's department store and Goodfriend's speciality shop in Austin, and later with Foley's department store.

While stationed with the U.S. Army from 1951 to 1953 in Dallas and San Antonio, he continued his illustration career with local stores and a local TV station. Coming to New York in 1954 Tierney started an association with J.C. Penney's that lasted for fourteen years. At the same time his clients have included Gimbel's, Lane Bryant, Macy's, Korvette's, Ohrbach's and many more prestigious department stores; while he also contributed illustrations to such publications as *Harper's Bazaar*, *Sports Illustrated* and *Show Magazine*. He has also done a great number of portrait paintings. In 1965 Tierney incorporated as Tom Tierney Studios, Inc., and all of his work is now produced under this name.

The paper dolls came into being in 1975 when Tierney was casting about for a unique Christmas present for his mother. Remembering that she had saved the paper dolls of her childhood, he decided to make her some paper dolls of the

A page of Marlene Deitrich paper dolls. (© 1976, Tom Tierney. Reprinted with permission.)

A page of Mae West paper dolls. (© 1976, Tom Tierney. Reprinted with permission.)

1930s movie stars who had been her favorites. She then showed them to a number of friends, one of whom was a literary agent who persuaded Tierney to do a book on the subject. As a result *Thirty from the 30s* was born. In 1978 Dover contacted him and proposed that he do some paper doll books for them. A happy relationship followed which resulted in the publication of more than two dozen books by 1985.

In addition to the books that he did for Dover, Tierney also worked for other publishers. *Attitude* is characterized by its author as "a jaundiced look at the cocktail party set, slightly naughty but proper," while *Cat Snips* is "a cat paper doll book, done tongue in cheek with, for example, the Persian cat wearing veils and a tambourine." *Supergirl* was based on the movie of the same title.

About his work Tierney declared to *CGA:* "I feel that the most important thing about my work is that I am using the medium of the paper doll as an art form. To me paper dolls can be more than just some 'cutesie' bit of fluff to be thrown at the children to perpetuate boredom. They can be artistic, vital, and alive and can tell us much about people, the

clothes they wore, the way they lived and something of the times in which they lived. I also feel that the animation of the dolls and the costumes can indicate much about the personality of the subject. In conjunction with drawing the dolls I also write my own text, which I feel is an important adjunct to my books, explaining my "raison d'etre" for treating the subject."

*   *   *

TOLES, Thomas G. 1951-
(Tom Toles)

PERSONAL: Born October 10, 1951, in Buffalo, N.Y.; son of George E. (a freelance writer) and Rose (Riehle) Toles; married Gretchen Saarnijoki (a seamstress), May 26, 1973. *Education:* State University of New York at Buffalo, B.A., 1973. *Office: Buffalo News*, One News Plaza, Buffalo, N.Y. 14240. *Agent:* Universal Press Syndicate, 4400 Johnson Dr. Fairway, Kan. 66205.

CAREER: Staff artist, 1973-80, graphics director, 1980, editorial cartoonist, 1980-82, *Buffalo Courier-Express*, Buffalo, N.Y.; editorial cartoonist, *Buffalo News*, Buffalo, 1982—. *Awards, honors:* Twenty Page One Awards from the Buffalo Newspaper Guild, 1973-82; George W. Thorn Award from University of Buffalo Alumni Association, 1983; Honorable Mention, John Fischetti Editorial Cartoonist Competition, Columbia College, Chicago, Ill., 1983; First Place, John Fischetti Editorial Cartoonist Competition, 1984; Golden Apple Award for Excellence in Educational Journalism, New York State United Teachers, 1984; New York State Historic Preservation Award, 1985; finalist in Pulitzer Prize competition, 1985.

WRITINGS: The Taxpayer's New Clothes (collection of editorial cartoons), Andrews, McMeel & Parker, 1985.

SIDELIGHTS: Tom Toles was not drawn into editorial cartooning by his admiration for an earlier, established figure in the field; in fact, the work of such cartoonists as Patrick Oliphant scared him off and delayed his entry into it. It was not until an editor at the *Buffalo Courier-Express*, where Toles was working as an artist, pressured him into it that he consented to try his hand. "I didn't think I could come up with something new and original," he reports. Only now, after several awards and one published collection, is he beginning to think he can do it.

Toles's work first appeared in the University of Buffalo campus paper *Spectrum*, where he was graphics director while getting a degree in English. Still with no aspirations to become a political cartoonist, he joined the art department of the *Buffalo Courier-Express* when he graduated in 1973 and remained with them until they went out of business nine years later. He worked his way up to the graphics director's post by 1980, and later that year he went from part-time to full-time editorial cartooning. In the next two years Toles's reputation grew rapidly, and when that newspaper closed its doors in 1982 he had many offers of work around the country. He chose to remain in Buffalo, and accepted the offer of the *News*. According to *News* editor Murray B. Light, "Since the closing of the *Courier*, the one talent from that newspaper most readers urged us to bring to the *News*

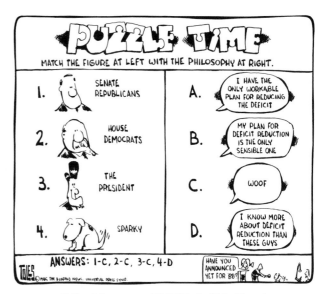

Editorial cartoon. (© 1985, *Buffalo News*.)

was Toles. Even those who . . . disagreed with his views felt that his talent was too great a community asset to lose to another city."

Toles's post with the *News* began auspiciously. Twelve days after accepting it on October 19, 1982, his syndication, which had been contracted for in August with Universal Press Syndicate began. By February, 1985, his cartoons were carried by one hundred and ten papers in the United States. Universal Press reported in 1983 that Toles was "the fastest growing syndicated editorial cartoonist in the country today."

Since reluctantly consenting to try his hand at the job, Toles has evolved a highly personal and distinctive style. His cartoons often resemble comic strips, taking the form of four- or six-panel sequences. They develop their points like a stand-up comic, building toward a punchline in the last panel. A coda, a final stinging comment made in the lower right-hand corner of the cartoon, is often delivered directly by the cartoonist himself—a tiny abstraction, simplified almost to a hieroglyph, of the bearded, somewhat Mephistophelian Toles seated at his drawing board.

Toles's ear for vernacular is acute and his mastery of jargon keen. He catches the speech of the 1980s as surely as Feiffer did that of the 1960s and Trudeau that of the 1970s. Toles renders the rhetoric of politics, advertising, and journalism with frequently devastating effect. The wit of his cartoons is often as much verbal as it is graphic.

But more distinctive than his format or language is his draftsmanship. His characters are *sui generis:* his stylized Ronald Reagan, with a pompadour almost as high as his face is long; his often eyeless or, perhaps even more significantly, mouthless average citizen; his trenchant caricatures of local politicians. The clean, economical line and bare composition of his panels, their empty backgrounds highlighting the simply drawn characters, are almost abstract; but whether he is portraying Reagan in a frock tenderly fondling a lamb or a Buffalo official as *Mad*

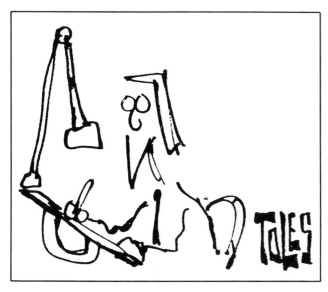

Self-caricature of Tom Toles. (Printed with permission.)

Editorial cartoon. (© 1985, *Buffalo News*.)

magazine's Alfred E. Neuman, Toles's intentions are always unmistakable. New York Governor Mario Cuomo praised Toles for his "concise drawing and stinging wit" in presenting him with a Historic Preservation Award in 1985, and *Chicago Tribune* cartoonist Jeff McNelly wrote of him that his cartoons "are done in delightfully childlike simplicity, befitting the childlike simplicity of the minds of his subjects . . . He's reduced our art form to its bare essentials."

Philosophically, Toles is his own man. From the beginning of his career with the *News*, it was clear that he spoke for himself and not for the paper. "He has been given a completely free hand to express his own point of view," a *News* editorial promised on his first day there, and the name of his feature, "Tom Toles' View," testifies to his editorial freedom. This often puts him in conflict with the position of his paper as well as with that of the government of his city

and state. His acerbic drawings of the Mayor of Buffalo and the Governor of New York have made him a controversial figure. He is, according to one of his editors, "not a favorite of the politicians." But even when his view opposes that of the editorial it faces, his paper supports him proudly. "I see a Pulitzer not far down the road for Toles," says Assistant Managing Editor Bill Malley. "It's just a matter of when the judges get around to giving him one."

Tom Toles's views are far-reaching in their subjects, ranging from general observations on the human condition to pointed comments on the local scene. He takes his material where he finds it, but his sympathies are balanced; no one on either side of an issue is safe from his pen, and he is as likely to make fun of the press as he is of the President when he sees an opening. Working swiftly from pencil sketches to finished drawings made with a Rapidograph pen, he varies his tone with his subject. Whimsical and lyrical, vitriolic and compassionate by turns, Tom Toles wields the rapier as skillfully as he does the axe.

The judges who granted Toles first place in the 1984 John Fischetti Editorial Cartoonist Competition cited him for "a balancing act of politics and real life in a whimsical and sometimes biting way that ranks him as one of the foremost cartoonists in the country." The reviews of his first published collection of cartoons, *The Taxpayer's New Clothes*, have supported this high estimate.

BIOGRAPHICAL/CRITICAL SOURCES: Jeff MacNelly, "Foreword," *The Taxpayer's New Clothes*, 1985; *Who's Who in America*, Marquis, 1985.

—Sketch by Dennis Wepman

Editorial cartoon. (© 1985, *Buffalo News*.)

* * *

TOLES, Tom
See TOLES, Thomas G.

* * *

TORRES (PEREZ), Daniel   1958-

PERSONAL: Born August 20, 1958, in Valencia, Spain; son of Francisco (a physician) and Maria (Perez) Torres. *Education:* School of Fine Arts, Valencia, Spain, B.F.A., 1980. *Home:* Santa Amalia, 2, Torre 1-34, 46009 Valencia, Spain. *Agent:* Rafael Martinez, Agencia Norma, Ali Bey, 11, 08010 Barcelona, Spain.

CAREER: Comic strip artist and writer, 1980—; illustrator, 1982—.

WRITINGS—All books of comics: *L'ange dechu* (title means "The Fallen Angel"), Futuropolis (France), 1982; *Opium*, Humanoides Associes (France), 1983; *Sabotage!*, Magic Strip (Belgium), 1983; *Triton*, Norma (Barcelona), 1984.

EXHIBITIONS: Salon de la Bande Dessinee, Angouleme, France, 1985; Convegno Internazionale del Fumetto e del Fantastico, Prato, Italy, 1985.

SIDELIGHTS: Daniel Torres started to make himself known as a promising author of comics (that is, an artist who both draws and writes his strips) at the time he was completing his art studies, at age twenty-two. Since then his young career has experienced a meteoric rise, first in Spain, from which his fame spread in short order to France, Belgium, Denmark, Italy, and lastly to the United States. A precocious professional, who manifested an interest in a wide range of esthetic endeavors, Torres traces his artistic roots to the so-called "Valencia School" of Spanish comics, and to the international movement known as "the clear line" that claims as its precursor the Belgian Herge (Georges Remi), the creator of the comic strip *Tintin*. Taking a post-modernist stance, the "clear line" practitioners prefer heavily black, hard-edged contours to the softer line, halftones, and shaded areas favored by the majority of modern graphic artists. At any rate Torres shows in his work a clear determination to assimilate a variety of concepts currently in fashion (especially with the young generation), in a vast compilation of fragments from the visual history of our century. In this he shows a highly personal and creative spirit, and he enriches his experiments with the stylistic flourishes of an artist who enjoys his own creative discoveries. His vitality, at once adventurous and ironic, and the exquisiteness of his line succeed in giving birth to a very personal world of characters, clothes, objects, places, and incidents.

Torres first made his name in the pages of the magazine *El Vibora*, in which the cult of "underground" comics was nurtured along with an interest for the most recent modes of graphic expression. There, in 1980, Torres created his comic strip character, Claudio Cueco, and, with or without him, successively published from 1980 to 1983 *Asesinato a 64 imagenes por segundo* (title means "Murder at Sixty-Four Frames per Second"), *Alas y azar* ("Wings and Chance"), *El angel caido* ("The Fallen Angel"), *Raul Cautela, Tropicana, Crimen de gravedad* ("The Crime of Seriousness"), *Heroes sin querer* ("Heroes in Spite of Themselves"), and *Carton mojado* ("Wet Cardboard"). In the meantime he had started, with the comic story *Opium*, his long collaboration with *Cairo*, a magazine whose esthetic ideology (in short, the defense of Herge's legacy) was more in accordance with his own tastes than that of *El Vibora*.

After completing an original story, *Sabotage!*, for a Belgian publisher, Torres began in 1982 the first of the adventures of his new hero, Roco Vargas: *Triton*, later followed by *El misterio de Susurro* (1984). He is currently at work on a third adventure, *Saxxon*.

The saga of Roco Vargas represents a trend currently much in fashion, a version (between parody and homage) of the "space-opera" genre, and it is replete with quotes, visual and

A page from *El mistero de Susurro*, **1985.** (© Daniel Torres. Rights controlled by Norma Agency, Barcelona. Reprinted with permission.)

textual, from works that have influenced the artist's peculiar mythos. As Armando Mistral, the protagonist is the owner of an entertainment club, and a science-fiction writer to boot; as Roco Vargas he doubles as a space hero. Humor is a fundamental element of the graphic style, the narrative context, and the dialogue; joined to a deliberate blurring of the lines between different realities, the psychological instability of the characters, and the constant shifting of the situations, it adds depth and distancing to the ostensibly escapist plot. In 1984—a propitious year!—*Heavy Metal* started serialization in the United States of the adventures of Roco Vargas.

BIOGRAPHICAL/CRITICAL SOURCES: Daniel Torres: Valencia Copyright, Ayuntamiento de Valencia, 1984.

* * *

TOWNSEND, Marvin   1915-

PERSONAL: Born July 2, 1915, in Kansas City, Mo.; son of Grover Ranson and Irene (Cottrell) Townsend; married Kathleen Bruce (an artist), September 20, 1941; children: Carolyn Kathleen Black. *Education:* Attended Kansas City College of Commerce, 1935-37; Kansas City Art Institute, 1940-41. *Religion:* Protestant. *Studio:* Snappy Cartoons, 631 W. 88th St., Kansas City, Mo. 64114.

CAREER: Freelance cartoonist, 1937—. *Awards, honors:*

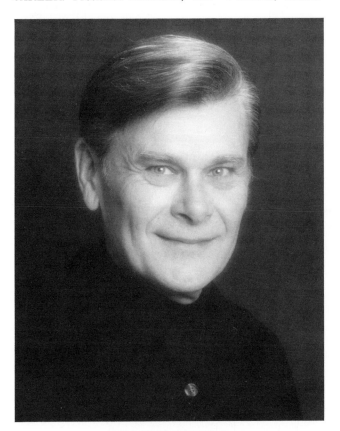

MARVIN TOWNSEND

"Local, or knocked clear out?" A gag cartoon for *Cal Magazine*, ca. 1982. (© Doe Laboratories.)

Earl Temple Award, 1973; Pewter Plaque for best cartoon from *Highlights for Children*, 1983 and 1984.

WRITINGS: Moontune Jokes and Riddles, American Education Publications, 1970; *Ghostly Ghastly Cartoons*, American Education, 1971; *Laugh It Up* (a juvenile), Pal Paperbacks, 1974.

EXHIBITIONS: Represented in permanent collection of Syracuse University, N.Y.

WORK IN PROGRESS: Supplying cartoons to publications on a monthly basis.

SIDELIGHTS: Marvin Townsend started his long cartooning career in the 1930s, at a time when publications of every sort and description were blossoming with comic strips, and when the new publications known as comic books were establishing themselves on the newsstands. Among his early creations in the field were such animal and juvenile comic features as "Poochie," "Foxy," "Cubby the Bear," "Quaker," "Jane and Joey," "Meg and Greg," "Art on the Job," "Bert, the Safety Engineer," and "Sanitary Sam." He also did specialized cartoon pages, such as "OSHCO," a strip for *National Safety News*, the house organ of the Safety and Health Administration, and "Floralaffs," a page for the magazine of the florist trade, *FTD Florist*.

Townsend has contributed cartoons literally by the thousands to national, business and trade magazines, as well as to religious periodicals and to school publications, both public and parochial. He specializes in cartoons for specific age groups and for specialized interest: one of his pantomime series, for instance, was used in the teaching of deaf children. In contrast he has also sold a number of cartoons to the *National Enquirer*.

Townsend's style is simple and uncluttered, and his captions to the point (as befits the name he has chosen for his studio, "Snappy Cartoons"). The fact that his cartoons have been seen all over the country, not only in publications, but also as promotion aids for corporations and institutions such as Eastman Kodak, the Glass Container Institute, and the Falstaff Brewing Corporation, and have been reprinted all over the world, testifies to their appeal and their durability.

BIOGRAPHICAL/CRITICAL SOURCES: Who's Who in American Art, 16th edition, Bowker, 1984.

V

VALENTINE, Francesca
See CATHERINE, Susan

* * *

VEITCH, Rick 1951-

PERSONAL: Surname is pronounced "Veech"; born May 7, 1951, in Walpole, N.H.; son of Robert (a paper company vice-president) and Margaret (MacDonald) Veitch; married Kristin Keefe, October 20, 1973 (divorced, 1978); children: Ezra. *Education:* Joe Kubert School of Cartoon and Graphic Art, diploma, 1978. *Home:* 58 Windham Hill Rd., West Townshend, Vt. 05359.

CAREER: Freelance cartoonist, comic book artist, and illustrator, 1973—.

WRITINGS: (With Stephen Bissette and Allan Asherman) *1941: The Illustrated Story*, HM Communications, 1979; *Heartburst* (a "graphic novel"), Marvel Comics Group, 1984.

Contributor to *Heavy Metal, Epic Illustrated, Marvel Comics,* and *Eclipse Comics.*

EXHIBITIONS: "Newave Comix Exhibition," Edinboro State College, Pennsylvania, 1983; "Science and Popular Culture." Miami Museum of Science, 1984; two-man show (with Stephen Bissette), Museum of Cartoon Art, Port Chester, N.Y., 1984.

WORK IN PROGRESS: The One, six-issue limited comic book series, for Marvel; cover illustrations. "Current research: dual-brain research and how it pertains to reading comics."

SIDELIGHTS: Among comic book practitioners the airbrush has come of late to replace pen and ink as the medium of choice, and none is more proficient in the use of the instrument—this side of Richard Corben—than the up-and-coming illustrator Rick Veitch.

Born in 1951, Veitch grew up during the golden age of the ten-cent comic book. Much of his early incentive to learn to read, he says, came from Little Lulu and Uncle Scrooge, while Stan Lee's *Fantastic Four* inspired his earliest attempts to draw. These efforts grew ultimately into an obsession and although his talent was obvious, both his parents and his

RICK VEITCH

Photo by Bob Ross.

teachers tried to discourage his fascination with comics. But when he came into contact with the work of the underground artists in the late 1960s, his fate, so to speak, was sealed, for in the works of eccentrics like Robert Crumb, "Spain," and Rick Griffin he found inspiration for his own eccentricities. A trip to the Mecca of the underground art movement, San Francisco, gained him a commission to produce a title for Ron Turner's "All New Underground Artists" series (result, *Two-Fisted Zombies*, 1973), but shortly thereafter the underground movement lost its fledgling distribution network in the wake of the U.S. Supreme Court's ruling on obscenity.

Veitch thus sat down and reevaluated his "introverted" style and came to the conclusion that what he needed was some formal training. This led to his enrollment in Joe Kubert's School for Cartoon and Graphic Art, where as a member of the first graduating class he not only learned drafting and layout design from such accomplished instructors as Hy Eisman, Lee Elias, Ric Estrada, and of course Kubert himself, but was able to make the sorts of professional contacts one needs to turn a personal passion into a paying profession.

A page from "Landmass." (© 1985, Rick Veitch. Reprinted with permission.)

With these newly polished skills and contacts, it was nonetheless a stroke of luck that finally put him on the road to success. When the established artist originally hired by Pocket Books to do a graphic novelization of the script for Steven Spielberg's film *1941* pulled out of the project at the last minute, Veitch and frequent collaborator Stephen Bissette were hired as replacement artists. They went to work on the basis of almost no information and against an almost impossible deadline, and produced a chaotic college of cartoon, caricature, frames from period films, 1940s ad copy, anti-Japanese wartime propaganda, and black-and-white photo inserts from *Life* magazines of the time. Their version caught, albeit much more gorily, the frantic, disjointed quality of the movie, but when *1941* proved a box office and critical bomb this must have seemed a dubious achievement.

Still, they had produced under trying circumstances, and this would not be forgotten in the industry. In fact, Archie Goodwin, editor of Marvel Comics' Epic imprint, was sufficiently impressed with Veitch to give him a year's worth of short story assignments. This enabled him, he recalls, "to explore further the possibilities of airbrush and collage in a full color format." In 1981 he got the go-ahead for his first major project, *Abraxas and the Earthman*, an eight-part science-fiction fantasy retelling of *Moby Dick* that took a year to complete. This was followed in 1984 by the "graphic novel" *Heartburst* (Marvel), and most recently by a six-part limited series for the Epic imprint entitle *The One*, as well as several book covers. His current project is another collaboration with Bissette, a two-part horror anthology for Eclipse comics to be called *Bedlam*.

Veitch is master of a style that appeals to his hard-to-shock, easy-to-bore, rock video/high tech, mostly teen-age audience. A keen scholar of past influences, from Stan Lee's superhero approach to the grisly legacy of William M. Gaines's EC horror classics of the 1950s, Veitch also incorporates a number of quick-cutting, mixed-media effects in his layouts that are more associated with video and film than static comic art. And, as the parodied Tide detergent box trompe l'oeil cover for *The One* shows, he knows how to employ the Pop Art esthetic to striking advantage.

BIOGRAPHICAL/CRITICAL SOURCES: Cartoonist Profiles, September, 1984.

*   *   *

VIP
See PARTCH, Virgil Franklin, II

WARD, Lynd (Kendall)   1905-1985

OBITUARY NOTICE: Born June 26, 1905, in Chicago, Ill.; died June 28, 1985, in his home in Reston, Va.; was afflicted with Alzheimer's disease. Illustrator, printmaker, and writer; former director of the graphic arts division of the Federal Art Project, and former president of the Society of American Graphic Artists. Ward became famous with his so-called "novels in woodcuts," starting with *God's Man* in 1929, about an artist's worldly success and ultimate spiritual disillusionment. This was followed by *Madman's Drum* (1930), *Wild Pilgrimage* (1932), *Prelude to a Million Years* (1933), *Song Without Words* (termed by its author "a poem," 1936), and *Vertigo* (1937), the last of his pictorial narratives and, with 230 blocks, the longest and the most complex in plot and characterization. Ward was also a gifted and much sought after illustrator: among the authors whose works he illustrated are Goethe, Thomas Mann, Victor Hugo, Oscar Wilde, and Ernest Hemingway. He also occasionally illustrated books written by his wife, May McNeer. In all, the number of volumes he illustrated totals well over two hundred. Ward is also the author and illustrator of a juvenile, *The Biggest Bear*, which won the 1953 Caldecott Medal. Among the other awards he garnered over his long career are the Library of Congress award for wood engraving and the National Academy of Design award. It is, however, for his woodcut novels that Ward will be best remembered: they have been reprinted over the years, and were collected into a single volume by Abrams in 1974.

BIOGRAPHICAL/CRITICAL SOURCES: Lee Bennett Hopkins, *Books Are by People*, Citation Press, 1969; *Something About the Author*, Vol. 2, Gale, 1971; *Storyteller Without Words: The Wood Engravings of Lynd Ward*, Abrams, 1974.

OBITUARY SOURCE: New York Times, July 1, 1985.

* * *

WOODMAN, Bill
See WOODMAN, William

* * *

WOODMAN, William   1936-
(Bill Woodman)

PERSONAL: Born October 30, 1936, in Bangor, Me.; son of Frederick Leland (an antique restorer) and Ada (Scanlin) Woodman; married second wife, Barbara Shelley, 1976 (separated, 1981); children: (first marriage) Jowill, (from second marriage) Anne. *Education:* Graduated from Bangor High School, 1954. *Home:* 9411 Fifth Ave., Brooklyn, N.Y. 11209.

CAREER: Freelance cartoonist and illustrator, 1959—; painter. *Military service:* U.S. Navy, 1954-1957.

WRITINGS: Fish and Moose News, Dodd, 1980; (illustrator) Carl Ewald, *The Spider and Other Stories*, translated by Eva Le Gallienne, Crowell, 1980; *Whose Birthday Is It?*, Crowell, 1980; *Buzzwords*, Simon & Schuster, 1983.

SIDELIGHTS: Maine native Bill Woodman is very much the downeaster, not merely in his economic way with words—his own contribution to this personal comments sections was the telegraphic assurance "Have always enjoyed cartooning"—but also in a spare artistic style and a preference for subject material that contrasts markedly with the urbane sophistication characteristic of so many of his contemporaries. As might be expected of one whose work and demeanor stamp him something of a loner, Woodman's formal training consists of a brief stint at the Phoenix School of Design after his discharge from the Navy, and a few courses taken subsequently at the Pratt Institute in Brooklyn and Manhattan's School of Visual Arts.

A similar individualist bent has likewise been evident in his approach to the business of cartooning. He belongs to no professional organizations and can claim the backing of no influential mentor or patron. Persistence has been the chief means of advancement in his career. The same stick-to-it strain led him to take his first buyer to small claims court in order to get paid and ultimately was responsible for the appearance of his work in the pages of men's magazines like *Cavalier* and *Gent*, beginning in the early 1960s. In the 1970s, after countless unsuccessful weekly submissions, he began placing his drawings regularly in that most prestigious of showcases, the *New Yorker*, becoming one the more prolific of that magazine's non-contract contributors. Other major periodicals in which his work has been published include *Playboy, Saturday Review, Gourmet, Esquire*, and *National Lampoon*.

Woodman's chief medium of expression is the ink-line drawing (felt-tip pens are favored), and his idiosyncratic, easily identifiable compositions range from the deliberately crude and naive to the more conventionally representational. Details, however, are always kept to a minimum and the

Magazine cartoon, 1984. (© Bill Woodman. Reprinted with permission.)

humor of his work is in the interdependence of art and gag, the latter being based on an action, a situation, or a condition.

As a humorist of action, Woodman is at his best in the absurdist vein—fish on skates skim past a frustrated ice-fisherman; an industrialist enters his office, presses a button on his desk, and the towering stacks visible through the window behind him immediately belch black smoke; a dog brings his homecoming master slippers, a paper, and a good laugh when he strolls past on his hind legs with a lampshade on his head—and he shows a Maine woodsman's fondness for the outdoor motif, with bears, moose, and fish outwitting/dumbfounding man being a recurrent theme in his work. He also seems to have a sharp eye for the foibles of the upwardly mobile, but it as a commentator on the human condition that Woodman makes his strongest collective impact.

The body of his work, in fact, is that of an outsider, or at least of one who has placed himself outside what television and the pop culture generally would describe as the mainstream of American life. There is nothing chic about Woodman's bittersweet human comedy, revolving as it does around the faceless, the unglamorous, the lost. His is a world of forlorn greasy-spoon diners where a cook can wistfully recall a cold night thirty years earlier when a diner paid his

bill and said "My compliments to you"; of gloomy blue-collar barrooms in which a patron might be reprimanded by a serious drinker for raising a window shade: "Hey buddy, if you want light go out and sit in the park"; and of a philosophical vagrant commenting upon the human condition with an admirable disdain for its vaunted complexities: "What can I tell you? You got spring, you got summer, you got fall, you got winter. What can I tell you?" On the evidence of his work—minimal, simple, uncluttered, direct—Woodman seems to have put his own distinctly downscale philosophy of life and work in the mouth of this shabby, bewhiskered pilgrim.

BIOGRAPHICAL/CRITICAL SOURCES: The World Encyclopedia of Cartoons, Chelsea House, 1980.

* * *

WRIGHT, Don 1934-

PERSONAL: Born January 23, 1934, in Los Angeles, Calif.; son of Charles (an aircraft engineer supervisor) and Evelyn (Olberg) Wright; married Rita Rose Blondin, October 1, 1960 (died June, 1968); married Carolyn Ann Jay (a newspaper writer), February 5, 1969. *Education:* Attended public schools in Florida. *Politics:* Registered Democrat but votes independent. *Office: Miami News*, 1 Herald Plaza, Miami, Fla. 33101.

CAREER: Copyboy and staff photographer, 1952-56, picture editor, 1958-60, political cartoonist, 1960-63, editorial cartoonist, *Miami News*, Miami, Fla., 1963—. Syndicated, *Washington Star*, 1970; *New York Times*, 1976; Tribune Co., New York, N.Y., 1982. Produced animated editorial cartoons for Newsweek Broadcasting Service, 1978. *Military service:* U.S. Army, 1956-58. *Member:* Overseas Press Club of America, Society of Professional Journalists (Sigma Delta Chi), National Cartoonists Society.

AWARDS, HONORS: Outstanding Young Man in Communications Media, Young Democrats of Florida, 1965; Best Cartoon Used in National Catholic Press Award, National Catholic Press Association, 1965; Citation, Freedoms Foundation, Valley Forge, Penn., 1966; Pulitzer Prize, 1966, for editorial cartoons; School Bell Award, Florida Education Association, 1968; first national Award for Best Cartoon on Foreign Affairs, Overseas Press Club of America, 1969; Greville Clark Editorial Page Cartoon Award, Stanley Foundation of Iowa, 1969, for Best Cartoon Relating to World Peace.

Edward J. Meeman Conservation Award, Scripps-Howard Foundation, 1971; Best Cartoon on Foreign Affairs, Overseas Press Club of America, 1972; First Place Award, Florida Better Newspaper Daily Contest, Florida Press Association, 1972; First Prize, Editorial Category, Population Institute Cartoon Contest, 1975; Award for Distinguished Service in Journalism for 1977, Sigma Delta Chi, 1978; Best Cartoon on Foreign Affairs, Overseas Press Club of America, 1980; National Headliner Award for Consistently Outstanding Editorial Cartoons, Press Club of Atlantic City, N.J., 1980; Pulitzer Prize, 1980, for editorial cartoons; Best Cartoon on Foreign Affairs, Overseas Press Club of America, 1982; Tom Wallace Award in Recognition of Political Cartooning on Latin America in 1982, Inter-American Press Association, Lima, Peru, 1983; first Robert F. Kennedy Memorial Journalism Award for Outstanding Coverage of the Problems of the Disadvantaged, Washington, D.C., 1983; Best Cartoon on Foreign Affairs, Overseas

Editorial cartoon by Don Wright. (© 1979, *Miami News*.)

Press Club of America, 1985; Reuben Award, editorial cartoon category, National Cartoonists Society, 1985.

WRITINGS: Wright On!, Simon & Schuster, 1971 (reprints of his cartoons); *Wright Side Up*, Simon & Schuster, 1981 (reprints of his cartoons); (contributor, cartoons and commentary) *The Gang of Eight*, Faber & Faber, 1985.

EXHIBITIONS: Lowe Art Museum, University of Miami, Coral Gables, Fla., 1968 and 1979; The Four Arts, Institute for Contemporary Arts, Florida State University, Tallahassee, Fla., 1982. Represented in permanent collection of Syracuse University.

SIDELIGHTS: Wright spent his childhood copying comic books and illustrations while other children were outside playing baseball, but he has had ample opportunity to vent his aggressions since then in his professional life. His career as a political cartoonist has advanced with extraordinary speed from the traditional humble beginnings as a copyboy to what columnist John Keasler has called "one of the very best among a handful of top commentators-by-cartoon."

Starting with the *Miami News* as a copyboy at the age of eighteen, Wright quickly moved up to a job as a photographer, and after two years in the U.S. Army (1956-58) returned as graphics editor. In 1963 editor Bill Baggs offered him the post of editorial cartoonist of that paper. He accepted and has been there ever since.

Wright's art has never ceased to grow, and the one adjective he rejects for his work is "finished." For Wright, art is never static. In both technique and subject, he hates predictability, and he feels that he is "still learning a lot about being an artist." Beginning with the "crayon style" of Herblock and Bill Mauldin, his earliest heroes in the field, he now uses Grafix board sparingly. He finds that it permits feathering and enables him to achieve subtleties of shading impossible with Zipatone or Benday, which he never uses now. Often he resorts to painstaking crosshatching to get his tonal effects, even though he knows that the effect will frequently be lost in the engraving.

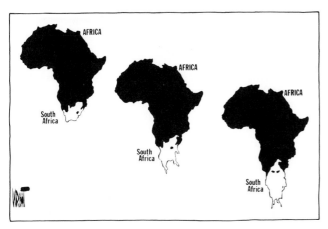

Cartoon by Don Wright that won the 1978 Sigma Delta Chi award. (© *Miami News*.)

Editorial cartoon by Don Wright. (© 1982, *Miami News.*)

His cartoons evolve through many rough pencil sketches on newsprint before he is satisfied with a composition and trusts himself with pen, brush, and india ink. The results are meticulous in detail but clean and uncluttered, usually without elaborate backgrounds. Both his style and his composition are masterful, but never facile. He needs at least five hours to do a cartoon, working over it many times until he gets what he wants. With an 8 A.M. deadline for his afternoon paper, he often toils through the night on a cartoon before sending it in to the engraver.

Wright acknowledges the influence of John Fischetti and Ronald Searle, but his work is unmistakably his own. Still, he has never permitted himself to be locked into a personal style. *Cincinnati Enquirer* editorial cartoonist Jim Borgman, who considers Wright "in some ways a mentor," says of him, "I find him to be one of the most experimental. . . He always excites me. . . He is always pushing things one step further than would occur to me."

Wright's handling of social and moral issues discloses the humane sensitivity associated with liberalism, but he is too intellectually complex to be easily classified. He is himself profoundly suspicious of labels. "Everybody thinks I am a liberal," he observes cautiously, "but I don't think I am." What he is, above all, is a passionately concerned citizen who has found in newspaper work the perfect opportunity to

express his convictions. "I feel privileged to have space," he states, "and I live in dread of wasting it."

Wright loves newspapers and considers himself a journalist who uses graphic art as his medium rather than as an artist who uses journalistic subjects as his material. For all his meticulosity of technique, he is more preoccupied with "saying something" than with the form his statements make. But it is the often stunning marriage of content and form with which his visual metaphors are instilled that has won him his many awards and his wide following. His rough treatment of Presidents Johnson and Nixon, and former Vice-President Agnew shows the force of his feelings as much as the virtuosity of his technique.

His work is born, as he feels all political cartooning should be, in indignation. It is his opportunity to "hammer away at what [he] think[s] wrong" that he values most in his position at the *Miami News*. A true *malleus malorum*, Don Wright has been a powerful force for a quarter of a century. His pictures have done more than many thousands of words to shape the thought—and perhaps the behavior—of his large national audience.

BIOGRAPHICAL/CRITICAL SOURCES: Newsday, July 24, 1971; *Time*, February 11, 1974; *Cartoonist Profiles*, September, 1974; *Newsweek*, October 13, 1980; *World Encyclopedia of Cartoons*, Chelsea House, 1980; *Contemporary Authors*, Vol. 104, Gale, 1982.

Editorial cartoon by Don Wright. (© 1983, *Miami News.*)

WRIGHT, Larry   1940-

PERSONAL: Born February 2, 1940, in Youngstown, Ohio; son of Orrin B. (a journalist) and Dorothy (Marquette) Wright; married Naoko Yogi, April 20, 1962; children: Sheryl Lynn, Robert Orrin. *Education:* Attended public high school in Allen Park, Mich.; studied Chinese at the U.S. Army Language School, Monterey, Calif. *Home:* 14965 Morris, Allen Park, Mich. 48101. *Office:* Detroit News, 615 W. Lafayette, Detroit, Mich. 48231. *Syndicates:* United Feature Syndicate (*Wright Angles*); Newspaper Enterprise Association (*Kit 'N' Carlyle*). *Agent:* United Media Enterprises, Inc., 200 Park Avenue, New York, N.Y. 10016.

CAREER: News editor and cartoonist (*Uncle Milton*), *Okinawa Morning Star*, Ginowan City, Okinawa, Japan, 1961-65; news editor and cartoonist, *Detroit Free Press*, Detroit, Mich., 1965-67; cartoonist (*Uncle Milton*), *Detroit Daily Express*, Detroit, 1967; cartoonist (*Needlescope*), *Scope*, 1968; news editor and cartoonist (*Wright Angles*), *Detroit Free Press*, Detroit, 1968-76; cartoonist, *Detroit News*, Detroit, 1976—. *Wright Angles* syndicated by United Features Syndicate, August, 1976; *Kit 'N' Carlyle* syndicated

by Newspaper Enterprises Association, December 1, 1980. *Military service:* U.S. Army 1958-61, served as Chinese-language interpreter; became sergeant. *Member:* National Cartoonists Society, Association of American Editorial Cartoonists. *Awards, honors:* Best Editorial Cartoon from National Cartoonists Society, 1980.

WRITINGS—Books of cartoons: *Kit 'N' Carlyle*, Simon & Schuster, 1983; *Celebrity Cats*, Holt 1983.

SIDELIGHTS: The son of a *Youngstown Vindicator* crime reporter, Larry Wright has been connected with newspapers all his life. While still in his teens, he did a comic strip for his high-school paper and contributed (literally; he was not paid for his work) little weather-forecast cartoons to the *Detroit Times*, where his father was then working. But it was not until he traveled to Asia that he was first paid for doing a comic strip. A Chinese interpreter with the U.S. Army in Okinawa from 1958 to 1961, Wright stayed on after his discharge for four years with the *Okinawa Morning Star*, where he did political cartoons and a strip called *Uncle Milton*.

Wright returned to Detroit with his Japanese wife in 1965 and, after three years as a copyreader with the *Detroit Free Press*, developed the strip which became *Wright Angles*. It began in the *Free Press* in August, 1968, as a six- to eight-panel weekly with no reappearing characters and assumed its present form during the next fews years. In 1974 it acquired a regular cast of characters. In July, 1976, Wright joined the *Detroit News* with the strip as a full-time editorial and strip cartoonist, and in August of that same year *Wright Angles* was syndicated by United Feature. For some years it was called *Citizen Kane* in Florida's *Miami Herald* to prevent confusion with *Miami News* editorial cartoonist Don Wright.

Wright Angles is a daily gag strip about Tom and Nancy Kane and their children, Joey and Sharon. They are a normal middle-class family with conventional problems and aspirations, but the sharply-drawn strip has something more of a bite than the usual family series on the comics page. The political cartoonist in Wright shows through in his acid portrayal of Mayor Orwell Twit, for whom Tom Kane works. The children are typical pre-adolescents, but some of their friends are rather more original: Joey's pal Toady Fester, a buck-toothed second-generation loser whose father failed to get a job with the sanitation department because he flunked out of garbage academy, for example, and Knuckles Bifoss, girl bully, who had a crush on Joey but, when he told her he didn't love her, responded, "Give me your money, creep." Other characters appearing from time to time include Dr. Nauseous, a newspaper columnist who advises "Terrified in Tulsa" to "take two aspirin and write me in the morning," and Mortimer Tort, door-to-door attorney who boasts that he finished in the top seventy percent of his class in law school.

In 1977, Wright introduced a cat, Motley, into the Kane household. According to *Detroit News* writer Tom Drake, Motley "has become the best recognized and most popular character in the strip. Ninety-five percent of Wright's mail is about Motley." There have been Motley look-alike contests and Motley T-shirts, and the character has taken his place among the major cartoon cats of the American comics. Motley's ironic, self-serving thought balloons reflect what every cat-owner suspects his cat of thinking. Motley is not hostile, but he is the ultimate cynic and sybarite whose life

revolves around napping, scratching furniture, and eating mice. His first reflection when he was taken into the household was, "It's always tough when you move to a new place to get used to where things are. I wonder where they

Larry Wright's self-portrait with cats, drawn specially for *Contemporary Graphic Artists*.

A *Wright Angles* daily strip. (© 1985, United Features Syndicate.)

Editorial cartoon by Larry Wright. (© 1985, *Detroit News*.)

keep their rats." If he worries, it is only about his own well-being. Fear of overweight prompts him to wonder if there is such a thing as low-cal mice, and his main regret about being a cat is that he can't use a telephone to send out for a pizza and a six-pack of mice.

The popularity of cats in the comics has directed Wright's career into a certain amount of specialization. Although he continues to do political cartoons for the *News*, he has become increasingly a cat-cartoonist. In 1980 he began a new feature, a panel series called *Kit 'N' Carlyle*, syndicated by Newspaper Enterprise Association. Published six days a week, *Kit 'N' Carlyle* features a single girl, Kit, and the kitten she adopts. Carlyle is very different from Motley, both graphically and psychologically. Black with white paws and tail-tip (Motley is more or less a Siamese), Carlyle is less acerbic, more dependent on conventions of inexperience. He is in every way a kitten, and a recurring theme for the humor of *Kit 'N' Carlyle* is his discovery of the laws of nature: the danger of sharpening his claws on a beanbag chair or sleeping in a bathtub or a laundry basket, the fear that his purring was a sign of a defective muffler. Where Motley sees mice as a snack, Carlyle plays poker with them and protests to his horrified owner, "You can have friends. Why can't I?" When Carlyle is taken to be fixed (December 13, 1980), he trusts that he is still under warranty; when the more informed Motley learns that he is to undergo that experience (August 13, 1977), he grimly reflects, "He'd better be talking about a bribe." Carlyle is at that awkward age—"cute enough to get away with anything but too young to do anything worth getting away with." Motley knows exactly what he wants and rules the Kane household with a steel claw.

More loosely drawn and conventional in theme than *Wright Angles*, the later series has far outstripped it in popularity. It is carried by more than four hundred papers (*Wright Angles* runs in about one hundred) and has had a collection published by Simon & Schuster. Another feline spinoff of Wright's is his book *Celebrity Cats*, published by Holt, Rinehart & Winston in 1983.

A *Kit 'n' Carlyle* daily panel. (© 1985, Newspaper Enterprise Association.)

265

Editorial cartoon by Larry Wright. (© 1985, *Detroit News*.)

With two series syndicated regularly, an additional book, and an award-winning editorial cartoon featured in the *Detroit News*, Larry Wright has established a secure place for himself in the American cartoon field.

BIOGRAPHICAL/CRITICAL SOURCES: Cartoonist Profiles, March, 1981.

—*Sketch by Dennis Wepman*

Y

YEH, Phil 1954-

PERSONAL: Born October 7, 1954, in Chicago, Ill.; son of Te Fung (an engineer) and Ruth (Williams) Yeh; married Janet Valentine, July 7, 1977 (divorced, 1983); married Philamer Tambio (a social worker and gallery manager), September 8, 1984; children: (first marriage) Robyn Alexis Valentine, Jesse Vincent Valentine; (second marriage) Gabriel David Tambio. *Education:* Attended California State University at Long Beach, 1972-77 ("no degree"). *Office:* 3908 E. 4th St., Long Beach, Calif. 90814.

CAREER: Freelance cartoonist and writer, 1970—; owner and publisher, Fragments West, Long Beach, Calif., 1970—. *Member:* Comic Arts Professional Society, Publishers Association of Southern California, The Licensing Association.

WRITINGS—All books of cartoons; all published by Fragments West: *Cazco,* 1976; (with Don DeContreras and Roberta Gregory) *Jam,* 1977; *Even Cazco Gets the Blues,* 1977; *Ajaneh,* 1978; *Godiva,* 1979; *Cazco in China,* 1980; *The Adventures of a Modern Day Unicorn,* 1981; *The Magic Gumball Machine and Company,* 1982; *Frank on the Farm,* 1982; *Mr. Frank the Unicorn Goes to Washington, D.C.,* 1984; (with Dennis Niedbala) *Frank the Unicorn and Syd Ha Sitbird on the Brooklyn Bridge,* 1985.

WORK IN PROGRESS: "Working on twenty new Frank the Unicorn books that will take Frank around the world. Upcoming: England, Paris, China, the Philippines, Australia, New Zealand, Hawaii." Also working on his first novel, *Shanghai Waltz,* to be published in 1986.

SIDELIGHTS: On a somewhat more modest scale, Phil Yeh's is a story out of an Horatio Alger novel. He started his publishing company while still in high school, turning out on an offset press a little magazine called *Cement* ("Where would you be without it?"), which first appeared in 1970. In 1973, while in college, he started a campus newspaper, mainly as a vehicle for his comic strip, *Cazco,* which had been banned by the college newspaper editor. Called *Uncle Jam,* the new publication was an instant success; it is still being published as a free newspaper that Yeh claims "is the best-read free paper in the area—if not the world." In 1976 a book division was added to the burgeoning Fragments West corporation. In addition to Yeh's cartoon books it has published paperbacks on Howard Hughes's HK-1 Hercules ("The Spruce Goose") and on science-fiction writer Philip K. Dick, as well as a series of photo-illustrated guidebooks. Fragments West also owns a flourishing art studio, a small art gallery, and a cartoonist agency.

Photo by: Judith Angel.

PHIL YEH

Along with all his business activities Yeh has found time to develop as a cartoonist. His first creation had been Cazco, a Tibetan cartoonist somewhat baffled by his encounters with the inscrutable west, who sprang into the college newspaper in 1972, and who later migrated to the pages of *Uncle Jam.* The *Cazco* strips were later collected into several comic books that were well received by the fans. Yeh, who in his own words "wanted to be the next Garry Trudeau or Charles Schulz," wasn't satisfied with this modest success and decided to come up with a more whimsical and noticeable character. That's how Frank the Unicorn was born.

Frank the Unicorn first saw print in the pages of *Uncle Jam* in 1979, with the strips later compiled into a book titled *The Adventures of a Modern Day Unicorn,* published, naturally, by Fragments West. It told of the struggles of a unicorn in a striped windbreaker and a Japanese-American actress named Gail Tokuda, in their search for acceptance and success, from California to New York City. The second volume, *Frank on the Farm,* featured an enterprising Mexican farmworker who had burned-out businessmen working the California fields as stress therapy—and paying a thousand dollars a week for the privilege. In *Mr. Frank*

A page from *Mr. Frank the Unicorn Goes to Washington, D.C.* (© 1984, Phil Yeh. Reprinted with permission.)

Goes to Washington, D.C., the unicorn is elected vice-president of the United States on a ticket headed by Aunt Patti, a black cleaning woman.

Frank the Unicorn is drawn in a simple, straightforward, unsophisticated style that owes as much to James Thurber and Crockett Johnson as to the underground cartoonists. While the concerns expressed in the strip—about the environment, the plight of minorities, the disparity between rich and poor countries—sound pretty much like distant echoes from the committed 1960s, their treatment is defi-nitely low-key, whimsical, and gentle, not shrill or despairing. It is a very winsome creation.

* * *

YOUNG, Lyman W.   1893-1984

OBITUARY NOTICE: Born October 20, 1893, in Chicago, Ill.; died February 12, 1984, in Port Angeles, Wash. A noted cartoonist, brother of Murat "Chic" Young, creator of *Blondie*, Lyman entered cartooning at the urging of his brother. He started drawing *The Kelly Kids* (a kid strip created years before by C. W. Kahles) in 1924. For King Features Syndicate he originated *The Kid Sister* in 1927. Young is best noted, however, for his next feature, *Tim Tyler's Luck*, which started in 1928 as an aviation strip, but soon turned into a jungle adventure series. In the 1950s he turned the drawing of the strip over to his son Bob, while another son, James, took over the writing. At the time of his father's death James told reporters that *Tim Tyler's Luck*, like many other adventure strips, had fallen in demand in the United States, due to competition from TV, but that many foreign papers still carried it.

BIOGRAPHICAL/CRITICAL SOURCES: Famous Artists and Writers, King Features Syndicate, 1946; *The World Encyclopedia of Comics*, Chelsea House, 1976.

OBITUARY SOURCES: Port Angeles News, Wash., February 14, 1984.

A page from *Mr. Frank the Unicorn Goes to Washington, D.C.* (© 1984, Phil Yeh. Reprinted with permission.)

Z

ZALME, Ron 1954-

PERSONAL: Surname is pronounced "Zol-me"; born July 11, 1954, in the Netherlands; son of John A. (in business) and Cora (a municipal printer; maiden name Van Straaten) Zalme; married Linda Welsh, May 28, 1977; children: Jessica Lin, Warren John. *Education:* Upsala College, East Orange, N.J., B.A., 1976; Joe Kubert School of Cartoon and Graphic Art, diploma, 1978. *Home:* 168 Sparta Ave., Newton, N.J. 07860.

CAREER: Assistant production manager, Marvel Comics Group, 1978-85; Freelance artist, 1978—. *Member:* Sussex County Agricultural Society.

Self-portrait of Ron Zalme, drawn specially for *Contemporary Graphic Artists*.

Gag cartoon. (© 1985, Ron Zalme. All rights reserved.)

WORK IN PROGRESS: "Freelance graphic art and cartoons for *Scholastic*, Marvel Comics, Computech, Educational Services, Marvel Books, and CTW."

SIDELIGHTS: Ron Zalme always liked to draw and caricature. "Having been exposed at an early age," he wrote, "to the talents of my father and older sister, I developed an ability to cartoon and entertain." This ability was strengthened later while he worked on several art projects at college; whereupon, he adds, "I decided to forego my scientific interests and further develop my artistic talents, in which I had a head start." After graduating from college, he enrolled at the Joe Kubert School of Cartoon and Graphic Art, from which he got his diploma in 1978.

Having put himself through college, and later through art school, by working as a grocery clerk in a supermarket, Zalme was gratified to find employment in the production department of Marvel Comics, where his artistic talents could be put to better use. Since that time he has been a steady contributor of cartoons and illustrations to a number of publications, has drawn a number of comic-book characters, and has illustrated the Marvel Age Calendar for 1985.

"I am somewhat of a handyman and workaholic," Zalme wrote *CGA*. "When not freelancing I occupy my time renovating my sixty-year old home, restoring antiques (clocks in particular). My hobbies include reading, video-camera work, films, toys, and my two children." Zalme is fluent in the Dutch language, as can be expected, and he has kept a lively interest in scientific subjects, particularly biology.

* * *

ZAMORA, Sanchez
See BEA (I FONT), Josep Maria

A page by artist Ron Zalme from the Marvel Age Calendar. (© 1985, Marvel Comics Group. All rights reserved.)

ZIEGLER, Jack (Denmore) 1942-

PERSONAL: Born July 13, 1942, in New York, N.Y.; son of John Denmore (a salesman) and Kathleen (a teacher, maiden name Clarke) Ziegler; married Jean Ann Rice, April 20, 1968; children: Jessica, Benjamin, Maxwell. *Education:* Fordham University, B.A., 1964. *Home and studio:* 61 Prospect Hill Rd., New Milford, Conn. 06776.

CAREER: Freelance cartoonist, 1972- ; contract cartoonist, *New Yorker*, 1974-. *Military service:* U.S. Army, 1966-67. *Member:* Cartoonists Association (treasurer, 1981-83).

WRITINGS: Hamburger Madness, Harcourt, 1978; *Filthy Little Things*, Doubleday, 1981.

EXHIBITIONS: Bethel Gallery, Bethel, Conn., 1977; International Tennis Hall of Fame, Newport, R.I., 1977; Washington Art Gallery, Washington Depot, Conn., 1978; Nancy Roth Gallery, Katonah, N.Y., 1978; Foundry Gallery, Washington, D.C., 1983; Parsons Gallery, New York, N.Y., 1984.

WORK IN PROGRESS: A book of drawings, as yet untitled, publication by Pinnacle expected in 1986.

SIDELIGHTS: "People have said," Jack Ziegler writes, "that they find many of my cartoons quirky or odd. On the contrary, I find them normal and logical; they are just visual expressions of the way I've always thought, so for me there's nothing strange at all about that." This is the sort of apologia one expects of an "original"—and that Ziegler most assuredly is.

His career as a cartoonist began in 1972 with the sale of a drawing to the *Saturday Review/World*, and two years later he made his debut in the *New Yorker*, where he is today a contract artist. In the graphic humor business, this is the sort of progress that can only be described as "meteoric," yet Ziegler has had no formal fine art training and is not a particularly gifted or distinctive draughtsman. In fact, the origins of his rapid rise to prominence can be found in what he refers to as "the way I've always thought." If one considers the relationship of idea and technique to be rather like that of pigment and vehicle, then brilliance will frequently overwhelm execution; in Ziegler's case this is precisely what has happened.

The peculiar orientation of Ziegler's work as well as its post-McLuhanesque flavor most likely derives from his academic major in communication arts, an advertising industry training discipline stressing the dissemination of information

Self-portrait of Jack Ziegler, drawn specially for *Contemporary Graphic Artists*. (© 1985, Jack Ziegler.)

Cartoon for *American Health*. (© 1983, *American Health*.)

view of some rather tired old cliches. Neither is he above pot-shotting at the very media madness that has created professions like communication arts. Thus when "Countess Mara" (represented by a Balkan-style castle silhouetted against the setting sun) receives Madison Avenue "aristo-crats" Sergio Valente, Gloria Vanderbilt, and Calvin Klein, she wonders grumpily, "Who the hell ARE these people?" Finally, in a clever melding of trend, cliche, and sloganeer-ing he imagines "Conrail's Latest Merger," in which long lines of customers in a depot-like setting are being advised of one-hour delays on hamburgers, up to ninety-minute delays on cheeseburgers, and scattered fifteen-minute delays on large and small fries.

"There is no greater joy than coming up with an idea that's funny to me," this delightful Madison Avenue turncoat declares, "and knowing that it has never occurred to anyone ever before." Such facility, it should be added, is as rare as it is gratifying.

BIOGRAPHICAL/CRITICAL SOURCES: The World En-cyclopedia of Cartoons, Chelsea House, 1980; Who's Who in America, Marquis, 1984.

Cartoon for *Update*. (© 1979, American Bar Association Press.)

in highly economic, often symbolic fashion. This has apparently supplied Ziegler with a visual and verbal vocabu-lary which he has been able to combine with an inherently sardonic world-view in order to create a personal, often innovative approach to his chosen medium of expression. While he can deal in conventional gag presentations, he is at his best when he is "selling" an idea; i.e., communicating moods, feelings, or concepts through the use of graphic humor. His drawings will not as often be greeted by belly laughs as those of fellow *New Yorker* cartoonists Sam Gross or Bill Woodman, with whom he has exchanged views and influences over the years, but Ziegler's works have the knack of staying with one, and, like the most effective of commer-cials, lobbying for their creator's point of view.

For example, in one *New Yorker* drawing, a minimally detailed urban street scene features three grim, menacing figures labeled "The Issues" watching malevolently as three similar, but cheerful figures labeled "The Answers" walk past, whistling merrily. This may not provoke laughter, nor even a smile; yet it sticks in the consciousness after the page has been turned with even more tenacity than the most hilarious cartoon because it presents a compellingly fresh

"Hey, Bobby! Bobby Swope! Remember me?
Chip Ronsdale, Yale, class of '54. They voted me least likely to succeed."

Cartoon for *Management Digest.* (© 1982, American Management Association.)

DATE DUE

	PRINTED IN U.S.A.